PENGUIN CLASSICS

THE KORAN

Born in Baghdad, N. J. Dawood came to England as an Iraq State Scholar in 1945 and graduated from London University. In 1959 he founded the Arabic Advertising & Publishing Co. Ltd, London (ARADCO), which is now one of the major producers of Arabic typesetting outside the Middle East. His translation of *Tales from the Thousand and One Nights* was first published as Penguin No. 1001 in 1954 and has since been printed in over twenty various formats and editions.

He is best known for his translation of the Koran, the first in contemporary English idiom, which was first published as a Penguin Classic in 1956 and has since sold over one million copies. An illustrated hardback edition of the Koran was published by Allen Lane in 1978. In the present revised edition the translation follows even more closely the standard Islamic commentaries and interpretations. It includes an introduction and an exhaustive index. The *sūrahs* follow the traditional sequence. This translation is also available in a parallel English–Arabic edition published in the Penguin Classics series.

As well as contributing book reviews and articles on literary subjects to the national press, N. J. Dawood has retold for children two selections from *The Arabian Nights*, published in the Puffin Classics. He has edited and abridged *The Muqaddimah of Ibn Khaldūn* (Princeton University Press), translated numerous technical works into Arabic, written and spoken radio and film commentaries and contributed to specialized English–Arabic dictionaries.

THE

KORAN

TRANSLATED WITH NOTES BY
N. J. DAWOOD

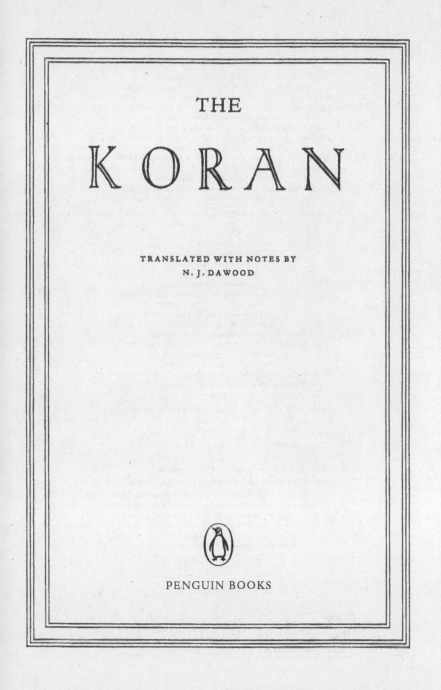

PENGUIN BOOKS

PENGUIN CLASSICS

Published by the Penguin Group
Penguin Books Ltd, 80 Strand, London WC2R ORL, England
Penguin Group (USA) Inc., 375 Hudson Street, New York, New York 10014, USA
Penguin Group (Canada), 90 Eglinton Avenue East, Suite 700, Toronto, Ontario, Canada M4P 2Y3
(a division of Pearson Penguin Canada Inc.)
Penguin Ireland, 25 St Stephen's Green, Dublin 2, Ireland (a division of Penguin Books Ltd)
Penguin Group (Australia), 707 Collins Street, Melbourne, Victoria 3008, Australia
(a division of Pearson Australia Group Pty Ltd)
Penguin Books India Pvt Ltd, 11 Community Centre, Panchsheel Park, New Delhi – 110 017, India
Penguin Group (NZ), 67 Apollo Drive, Rosedale, Auckland 0632, New Zealand
(a division of Pearson New Zealand Ltd)
Penguin Books (South Africa) (Pty) Ltd, Block D, Rosebank Office Park,
181 Jan Smuts Avenue, Parktown North, Gauteng 2193, South Africa

Penguin Books Ltd, Registered Offices: 80 Strand, London WC2R ORL, England

www.penguin.com

English translation first published in Penguin Classics 1956
First revised edition 1959
Second revised edition 1966
Third revised edition 1968
Fourth revised edition 1974
Fifth revised edition following the traditional sequence of *sūrahs*,
published in Penguin Classics 1990
Reprinted with revisions 1993
Reprinted with minor revisions 1994
Reprinted with minor revisions and additional notes 1995
Reprinted with further revisions and additional notes 1997
Reprinted with minor revisions 1999
Reprinted with minor revisions 2003
The 50th anniversary edition published with further revisions 2006
This extensively revised edition published with additional notes 2014

020

Copyright © N. J. Dawood, 1956, 1959, 1966, 1968, 1974, 1990, 1993, 1994,
1995, 1997, 1999, 2003, 2006, 2014
All rights reserved

The moral right of the translator has been asserted

Set in 10.75/11.75pt Garamond MT Std
Typeset by Jouve (UK), Milton Keynes
Printed and bound in Great Britain by Clays Ltd, Elcograf S.p.A.

ISBN: 978-0-141-39383-4

www.greenpenguin.co.uk

CONTENTS

CONTENTS

CONTENTS

vii

CONTENTS

INTRODUCTION

The Koran[1] is the earliest and by far the finest work of Classical Arabic prose. For Muslims it is the infallible Word of God, a transcript of a tablet preserved in heaven, revealed to the Prophet Muḥammad by the Angel Gabriel. Except in the opening verses and some passages in which the words are clearly those of the Prophet or the Angel, the speaker throughout is God.[2]

The posthumous son of 'Abdullāh bin 'Abd al-Muṭṭalib, of the tribe of Quraysh, Muḥammad was born in Mecca about the year 570. His mother Āminah died when he was still a child, and he was brought up by his grandfather and then by his uncle Abū Ṭālib. As a youth he travelled with the trading caravans from Mecca to Syria, and at the age of twenty-five married Khadījah, daughter of Khuwailid, a rich widow fifteen years his senior. Meanwhile he had acquired a reputation for honesty and wisdom, and had come under the influence of Jewish and Christian teachings.

Long before Muḥammad's call, Arabian paganism was showing signs of decay. At the Ka'bah the Meccans worshipped not only Allāh, the supreme Semitic God, but also a number of female deities whom they regarded as the daughters of Allāh. Among these were Al-Lāt, Al-'Uzzā, and Manāt, who represented the Sun, Venus, and Fortune respectively. Impressed by Jewish and Christian monotheism, a number of theists, or spiritual fundamentalists, known as ḥanīfs had already rejected idolatry for an ascetic religion of their own. Muḥammad appears to have been influenced by them. It was

1. The Arabic name (Qur'ān) means 'The Recital'.
2. God speaks in the first person plural, which often changes to the first person singular or the third person singular in the course of the same verse.

his habit to retire to a cave in the mountains in order to give himself up to solitary prayer and meditation. According to Muslim tradition, one night in Ramaḍān about the year 610, as he was asleep or in a trance, the Angel Gabriel came to him and said: 'Read!' He replied: 'What shall I read?' The order was repeated three times, until the Angel said:

'Read in the name of your Lord who created; created Man from clots of blood.

'Read! Your Lord is the Most Bountiful One, who by the pen taught Man what he did not know.'

When he awoke, these words, we are told, seemed to be 'inscribed upon his heart'.

Muḥammad, who disclaimed power to perform miracles, firmly believed that he was the Apostle of God, sent forth to confirm previous Scriptures. God had revealed His will to the Jews and the Christians through chosen apostles, but they disobeyed God's commandments and divided themselves into schisms. The Koran accuses the Jews of corrupting the Scriptures and the Christians of worshipping Jesus as the son of God, although He had expressly commanded them to worship none but Him. Having thus gone astray, they must be brought back to the right path, to 'the True Religion preached by Abraham'. This was Islām – absolute submission or resignation to the will of God.

The Koran preaches the oneness of God and emphasizes divine mercy and forgiveness. God is almighty and all-knowing, and though compassionate towards His creatures He is stern in retribution. He enjoins justice and fair dealing, kindness to orphans and widows, and charity to the poor. The most important duties of the Muslim are faith in God and His apostle, prayer, almsgiving, fasting, and (if possible) pilgrimage to the Sacred House at Mecca, built, according to the Koran, by Abraham for the worship of the One God.

The Koranic revelations followed each other at brief intervals and were at first committed to memory by professional remembrancers. During Muḥammad's lifetime verses were written on palm-leaves, stones, and any material that came to hand. Their collection is said to have been completed during the caliphate of 'Umar, the second Caliph, and an authorized version was established, according to Muslim scholars, during the caliphate of 'Uthmān, his successor (644–56). To this day this version is regarded by believers as the authoritative Word of God. But, owing to the fact that the kufic script in which the Koran was originally written contained no indication of vowels or diacritical points, variant readings are recognized by Muslims as of equal authority.

In preparing the contents of the Koran for book-form its editor or editors followed no chronological sequence. The *sūrahs*, or chapters, were arranged generally in order of length, the longest coming first and the shortest last. Attempts have been made by Noldeke, Grimme, Rodwell, and Bell to arrange the *sūrahs* in chronological order, but scholars are agreed that a strictly chronological arrangement is impossible without dissecting some into scattered verses, owing to the inclusion of revelations spoken in Medina in *sūrahs* begun several years earlier in Mecca.

In preparing this translation it has been my guiding principle to present the modern reader with an intelligible version of the Koran in contemporary, grammatically correct and natural English. The translation, first published in 1956, has been regularly revised in the light of a life-long study of the style and language of the Koran, and has been brought as close to the original as English idiom and usage will allow. Basic changes include 'God' instead of 'Allāh'; 'Lord of the Universe' instead of 'Lord of the Creation'; and 'alms levy' instead of 'alms tax'.

It is universally acknowledged that the Koran is one of the most influential books of prophetic literature; by Muslims it is also regarded as a literary masterpiece in its own right, flawless and inimitable. In adhering to a rigidly literal rendering of Arabic idioms, previous translations have, in my opinion, failed to convey both the meaning and the rhetorical grandeur of the original. The Koran contains many statements which, if not recognized as altogether obscure, lend themselves to more than one interpretation. I have taken pains to reproduce these ambiguities wherever they occur, and have provided explanatory footnotes in order to avoid turning the text into an interpretation rather than a translation. Throughout this rendering the standard commentaries of Al-Bayḍāwī and Al-Jalālayn have been closely followed.

Here a word should also be said about the cryptic Arabic letters which head certain chapters of the Koran. Various theories have been put forward by Muslim and Western scholars to explain their meaning, but none of them is satisfactory. The fact is that no one knows what they stand for. Traditional commentators dismiss them by saying 'God alone knows what He means by these letters.'

In the foregoing paragraphs I have endeavoured to confine myself to a bare outline of the facts regarding the genesis of the Koran and its subsequent preservation. It is the text itself that matters; and the reader should be allowed to approach it with a free and unprejudiced mind.

N. J. D.

This translation of the Koran, first published in 1956, has since undergone at least eight major revisions over the years. This 50th anniversary edition strives more tenaciously than ever before to combine accuracy with clarity and respect for the English language.

London, 2006   N. J. D.

This revision, the outcome of a further seven years' study of orthodox Koranic commentaries, attempts to reconcile the 'literal' with the 'liberal'. It may help the English-speaking general reader to get a better glimpse of the stylistic mannerisms and distinctive structural patterns characteristic of the Koranic text; it may also help the student to understand the Arabic by direct reference to the English. I have again retained the use of 'God' instead of 'Allāh', although in my view it might be more logical and appropriate to refer to God as

Allāh, as Muslims do in daily life. This extensively revised version also takes into its compass the many valid changes over the past fifty-seven years in the connotation and usage of certain English words and expressions.

London, 2013   N. J. D.

NOTE TO THE GENERAL READER

It is recognized that reading the *sūrahs* in their traditional sequence – as presented in this translation – is not essential for an adequate understanding of the Koran. Readers approaching the Koran for the first time may therefore find it helpful to begin with the shorter and more poetic chapters, such as those describing the Day of Judgement, Paradise and Hell (e.g. 'The Cessation' and 'The Merciful') and those with biblical themes (e.g. 'Mary' and 'Joseph'), before attempting the much longer and often more complex chapters in the first half (e.g. 'The Cow' and 'The Table'), which presuppose familiarity with events in the early days of Islām.

CHRONOLOGICAL TABLE OF THE MAIN EVENTS IN THE LIFE OF MUḤAMMAD

627 The Jewish tribe of Qurayẓah raided and put to the sword

628 The Treaty of Ḥudaybiyya; truce with the Quraysh, who recognize Muḥammad's right to proselytize without hindrance

629 The Jews of Khaybar crushed and expelled
Muḥammad sends letters and messengers to the kings of Persia, Yemen, and Ethiopia and the Emperor Heraclius, inviting them to accept Islām

630 Truce broken by the Quraysh. Mecca taken by Muḥammad – the entire population converted, and the Ka'bah established as the religious centre of Islām

631 'The Year of Embassies' – Islām accepted by the Arabian tribes

632 Muḥammad's Farewell Pilgrimage to Mecca

632, 8 June Death of Muḥammad, three months after his return to Medina

THE EXORDIUM[1]

IN THE NAME OF GOD
THE MERCIFUL
THE COMPASSIONATE

1:1

Praise be to God, Lord of the Universe,
The Merciful, the Compassionate,
Sovereign of the Day of Judgement!
You alone we worship, and to You alone
we turn for help.
Guide us to the straight path,
The path of those whom You have favoured,
Not of those who have provoked Your ire,
Nor of those who have lost their way.

1:7

---

1. Or: 'Opening Verses'; generally recited as a prayer for the dead, and corresponds to the Lord's Prayer in Christendom.

THE COW

In the Name of God, the Merciful, the Compassionate

2:1

ALIF *lām mīm.* This Book is not to be doubted. It is a guide for the righteous, who believe in the Unseen and are steadfast in prayer; who give[1] from what We gave them; who believe in what has been revealed to you[2] and what was revealed before you, and have absolute faith in the life to come. These are rightly guided by their Lord; these shall surely succeed.

As for the unbelievers, it is the same whether or not you forewarn them; they will not have faith. God has set a seal upon their hearts and ears; their sight is dimmed and grievous punishment awaits them.

And some there are who declare: 'We believe in God and the Last Day,' yet they are no true believers. They seek to deceive God and those who believe in Him: but they deceive none save themselves, though they may not perceive it. There 2:10 is a sickness in their hearts which God has aggravated: grievous punishment awaits them for the lies they ever told.

If they are told: 'You shall not do evil in the land,' they reply: 'Surely we are doing only what is good.' But it is they who are the evil-doers, though they may not perceive it.

And if they are told: 'Believe as the people believe,' they reply: 'Are we to believe as fools believe?' It is they who are the fools, if they but knew it.

And when they meet the faithful, they declare: 'We, too, are believers.' But when alone with their demons they say to them: 'We follow none but you: we were only mocking.' God will mock them and keep them long in sin, ever straying from the right path.

Such are those that barter guidance for error: they profit nothing, nor are they on the right path. They are like one who 2:17 kindled a fire, but as soon as it lit up all around him God put

---

1. Literally, spend.   2. Muḥammad.

2:18 it out and left him in darkness: they do not see. Deaf, dumb, and blind, they will never return to the right path.

Or like those who, beneath a dark storm-cloud charged with thunder and lightning, thrust their fingers into their ears at the sound of every thunder-clap for fear of death (God thus encompasses the unbelievers). The lightning almost snatches away their sight: whenever it flashes upon them they walk on, but as soon as it darkens they stand still. Indeed, if God pleased, He could take away their hearing and their sight: God has power over all things.

You people! Worship your Lord, who has created you and those who have gone before you, so that you may guard yourselves against evil; who has made the earth a bed for you and the sky a dome, and has sent down water from the sky to bring forth fruits for your sustenance. Do not knowingly set up other deities besides God.

2:23 And if you doubt what We have revealed to Our servant, produce one *sūrah* comparable to it. Call upon your idols to assist you, if what you say be true. But if you fail (as you are sure to fail), then guard yourselves against the Fire whose fuel is humans and stones, prepared for the unbelievers.

And proclaim joyful tidings to those that believe and do good works. They shall dwell in Gardens watered by running brooks: whenever they are given fruit to eat they will say: 'This is what we used to eat before,' for they shall be given the like. Wedded to chaste spouses, they shall abide therein for ever.

Surely God does not disdain to make comparison with a gnat or with a larger creature. The faithful know that it is the Truth from their Lord, but the unbelievers ask: 'What could God mean by this comparison?'

By such comparison God confounds many and enlightens many. But He confounds none except the ungodly, who break God's covenant after accepting it, and put asunder what God has bidden to be united, and perpetrate corruption in the land. It is these who will surely be the lost ones.

How can you deny God? Did He not give you life when you were dead, and will He not cause you to die and then
2:29 restore you to life? Will you not return to Him at last? He

2

created for you all that the earth contains; then, ascending to the sky, He fashioned it into seven heavens. And He has knowledge of all things.

And when your Lord said to the angels: 'I am placing on the earth one that shall rule as My deputy,' they replied: 'Will You put there one that will do evil and shed blood, when we have for so long sung Your praises and sanctified Your name?' 2:30

He said: 'I know what you know not.'

He taught Adam the names of all things and then set them before the angels, saying: 'Tell Me the names of these, if what you say be true.'

'Glory be to You,' they replied, 'we have no knowledge except that which You have given us. You alone are all-knowing and wise.'

Then said He: 'Adam, tell them their names.' And when Adam had named them, He said: 'Did I not tell you that I know the secrets of the heavens and the earth, and know all that you reveal and all that you conceal?'

And when We said to the angels: 'Prostrate yourselves before Adam,' they all prostrated themselves except Satan, who in his pride refused and became an unbeliever. 2:34

We said: 'Adam, dwell with your spouse in Paradise and both of you eat of its fruits to your hearts' content wherever you will. But never approach this tree or you shall both become transgressors.'

But Satan lured them thence and brought about their banishment. 'Get you down,' We said, 'and be enemies to each other. The earth will provide for you an abode and comforts for a time.'

Then Adam received commandments from his Lord, and his Lord relented towards him. He is the Relenting One, the Compassionate.

'Get you down hence, all,' We said. 'When My guidance is revealed to you, those that follow My guidance shall have nothing to fear or to regret; but those that deny and reject Our revelations shall be the inmates of the Fire, wherein shall they abide for ever.'

Children of Israel, remember the favour I have bestowed 2:40

upon you. Keep your covenant, and I will be true to Mine.
2:41 Dread My power. Have faith in My revelations, which confirm
your Scriptures, and do not be the first to deny them. Do not
sell My revelations for a paltry price; fear Me. Do not confound Truth with falsehood, nor knowingly conceal the Truth.
Attend to your prayers, render the alms levy, and kneel with
those who kneel. Would you enjoin people to be charitable
and forget yourselves? Yet you recite the Scriptures. Have you
no sense?

Fortify yourselves with patience and with prayer. This may
indeed be an exacting discipline, but not to the devout, who
know that they will meet their Lord and that to Him they will
return.

2:47 Children of Israel, remember the favour I have bestowed
upon you, and that I exalted you above the nations. Guard
yourselves against a day on which no soul shall stand for
another: when no intercession shall be accepted for it, no
ransom be taken from it, and none shall be helped.

And remember how We delivered you from Pharaoh's
people, who had oppressed you cruelly, slaying your sons and
sparing only your daughters. Surely that was a great trial by
your Lord. We parted the sea for you and, taking you to safety,
drowned Pharaoh's men before your very eyes. We made a
tryst with Moses for the fortieth night, and in his absence you
took up the calf and thus committed evil. Yet after that We
pardoned you, so that you might give thanks.

We gave Moses the Book and Salvation,[1] so that you might
2:54 be rightly guided. Moses said to his people: 'You have wronged
yourselves, my people, in worshipping the calf. Turn in penitence to your Creator and slay the culprits among you.' That
will be best for you in your Creator's sight.' And He relented
towards you. He is the Relenting One, the Compassionate.

1. *Al-Furqān*: Variously interpreted by traditional commentators as
'the difference between right and wrong', or 'between good and
evil'; the word makes its first appearance in the Koran, and is the
Arabicized form of the Aramaic *purqān*, as in the Aramaic Qad-
dish. See also A. J. Arberry's interpretation.

When you said to Moses: 'We will not believe in you until 2:55
we see God[1] with our own eyes,' the thunderbolt struck you
while you were looking on. Then We revived you from your
stupor, so that you might give thanks.

We caused the clouds to draw their shadow over you and
sent down for you manna and quails,[2] saying: 'Eat of the
wholesome things We have given you.' Indeed, they[3] did not
wrong Us, but they wronged themselves.

'Enter this city,' We said, 'and eat where you will to your
hearts' content. Make your way reverently through the gates,
saying: "We repent." We shall forgive you your sins and bestow
abundance on the righteous.' But that which they were told
the wrongdoers replaced with other words; and We let loose
on the wrongdoers a scourge from heaven as punishment for
their misdeeds.

And when Moses requested water for his people, We said 2:60
to him: 'Strike the Rock with your staff.'[4] Thereupon twelve
springs gushed from the Rock, and each tribe knew their
drinking-place. We said: 'Eat and drink of that which God has
provided and do not foul the land with evil.'

'Moses,' you said, 'we will no longer put up with this mon- 2:61
otonous diet. Call on your Lord to give us some of the varied
produce of the earth, green herbs and cucumbers, corn[5] and
lentils and onions.'

'What!' he answered. 'Would you exchange that which is
good for what is worse? Go back to Egypt.[6] There you will
find all you have asked for.'

Servility and misery were stamped upon them and they
incurred the wrath of God; because they disbelieved God's
signs and slew the prophets unjustly; because they were rebels
and transgressors.

---

1. Cf. Exodus 19:21.
2. Cf. Exodus 16.
3. The Israelites.
4. Cf. Numbers 20:8.
5. An alternative reading gives *thūm*, garlic. Cf. Numbers 11:5.
6. Or: to a 'big city', according to another reading (Al-Bayḍāwī).

2:62   Believers, those who follow the Jewish Faith,[1] Christians, and Sabaeans – whoever believes in God and the Last Day and does what is right – shall be rewarded by their Lord; they have nothing to fear or to regret.

We made a covenant with you[2] and raised the Mount above you, saying: 'Hold fast to what We have given you and bear in mind its precepts, that you may guard yourselves against evil.' Yet after that you turned away, and but for God's grace and mercy you would have surely been among the lost.

You have heard of those of you that broke the Sabbath. We said to them: 'Change into detested apes!' We made their fate an example to their own generation and to those who followed them, and a lesson to the righteous.

And when Moses said to his people: 'God commands you to sacrifice a cow,'[3] they replied: 'Are you mocking us?'

'God forbid that I should be so foolish!' he rejoined.

2:68   'Call on your Lord,' they said, 'to make known to us what kind of cow she shall be.'

He replied: 'Your Lord says: "Let her be neither an old cow nor a young heifer, but in between." Do, therefore, as you are bidden.'

'Call on your Lord,' they said, 'to make known to us what her colour shall be.'

He replied: 'Your Lord says: "Let the cow be yellow, a rich yellow, pleasing to those that see it."'

'Call on your Lord,' they said, 'to make known to us the exact type of cow she shall be; for to us cows look all alike. If God wills we shall be rightly guided.'

2:71   Moses replied: 'Your Lord says: "Let her be a healthy cow, not worn out with ploughing the earth or watering the field; a cow free from any blemish."'

---

1. *Alladhīna hādū*, as distinct from *al-Yahūd* (the Jews), would also include Arabian converts to the Jewish faith.
2. The Israelites.
3. Cf. Numbers 19, which refers merely to a sacrificial 'cow'; it contains none of the verbal exchanges related in this *sūrah*.

'Now you have told us all,' they answered. And they slaugh-
tered a cow, after they had nearly declined.

And when you slew a man and then fell out with one   2:72
another concerning him, God made known what you concealed. We said: 'Strike him with a part of it.' Thus God
restores the dead to life and shows you His signs, that you may
grow in understanding.

Yet after that your hearts became as hard as rock or even
harder; for from some rocks rivers take their course: some
break asunder and water gushes from them: and others tum-
ble down through fear of God. God is not unaware of what
you do.

Do you[1] then hope that they will believe in you, when some
of them have already heard the Word of God and knowingly
perverted it, although they understood its meaning?

And when they meet the faithful they declare: 'We, too, are
believers.' But when alone they say to each other: 'Must you
declare to them what God has revealed to you? They will only
dispute with you about it in your Lord's presence. Have you
no sense?'

Do they not know that God has knowledge of all that they   2:77
conceal and all that they reveal?

Some among them are illiterate, ignorant of the Book and
know of nothing but wishful fancies and vague conjecture.
Woe betide those that write the Book with their own hands
and then declare: 'This is from God,' in order to gain some
paltry end. Woeful shall be their fate, because of what their
hands have written, because of what they did.

They declare: 'The Fire will never touch us – except for a
few days.' Say: 'Did God make you such a promise – God will
not break His promise – or do you assert of God what you
know not?'

Truly, those that commit evil and become engrossed in sin
shall be the inmates of the Fire, wherein shall they abide for
ever. But those that have faith and do good works shall be the
tenants of Paradise, wherein shall they abide for ever.

1. The believers are here addressed.

2:83   And when We made a covenant with the Israelites, We said: 'Serve none but God. Show kindness to your parents, to your kin, to orphans, and to the destitute. Exhort people to righteousness. Attend to your prayers and render alms.' But you all

2:84   broke your covenant except a few, and paid no heed.

And when We made a covenant with you, We said: 'You shall not shed your kin's blood or turn them out of their dwellings.' To this you consented and bore witness. Yet there you were, slaying your own kin, and turning a number of you out of their dwellings, and helping each other against them with sin and aggression; though had they come to you as captives, you would have ransomed them. Surely their expulsion was unlawful. Do you believe in one part of the Book and deny another?

So what reward is there for those of you that act thus but disgrace in this world and grievous punishment on the Day of Resurrection? God is never heedless of what you do.

Such are they who buy the life of this world at the price of the life to come. Their punishment shall not be mitigated, nor shall they be helped.

2:87   To Moses We gave the Book and after him We sent other apostles. We gave Jesus son of Mary veritable signs and strengthened him with the Holy Spirit. You scorn each apostle who comes to you with whatever does not suit your fancies, charging some with imposture and slaying others.

And they say: 'Our hearts are sealed.' But God has cursed them for their unbelief. They have but little faith.

And now that a Book confirming their own has come to them from God, they deny it, although they know it to be the Truth and have long prayed for help against the unbelievers. God's curse be upon the infidels! Evil is that for which they have bartered their souls. To deny God's own revelation, grudging that He should reveal His bounty to whom He chooses from among His servants! They have incurred God's most inexorable ire. Ignominious punishment awaits the unbelievers.

2:91   And if they are told: 'Believe in what God has revealed,' they reply: 'We believe in what was revealed to *us*.' And they deny what has since been revealed, although it is the Truth, corroborating their own Scriptures.

Say: 'Why did you kill the prophets of God, if you are true
believers? Moses came to you with veritable signs, but in his   2:92
absence you worshipped the calf and committed evil.'

And when We made a covenant with you and raised the
Mount above you, saying: 'Hold fast to what We have given
you and hear Our commandments,' you[1] replied: 'We hear,
and will not obey.'

For their unbelief they were made to drink down the calf
into their hearts.[2] Say: 'Evil is that to which your faith prompts
you if you are true believers.'

Say: 'If God's Abode of the Hereafter is for yourselves
alone, to the exclusion of other people, then wish for death if
your claim be true!'

But they will never wish for death, because of what they
did; and God knows the wrongdoers. Indeed, you will find
that, of all people, they love life most: more than the pagans
do. Each of them would love to live a thousand years. And
even if his life were indeed prolonged, that will surely not save
him from the scourge. God is cognizant of what they do.

Say: 'Whoever is an enemy of Gabriel' (who has by God's   2:97
grace revealed to you[3] the Koran as a guide and joyful tidings
for the faithful, confirming previous Scriptures) 'whoever is
an enemy of God, His angels, or His apostles, or of Gabriel
or Michael, will surely find that God is the enemy of the unbelievers.'

We have sent down to you clear revelations: none will deny
them except the ungodly. What! Whenever they make a covenant, must some of them cast it aside? Most of them do not
believe.

And now that an apostle has come to them from God confirming their own Scriptures, some of those to whom the
Book was given cast off the Book of God over their backs,
as though they know nothing of it, and accept what the   2:102
demons tell of Solomon's kingdom. Not that Solomon was an

---

1. Literally, they.
2. Cf. Exodus 32:20.
3. Muḥammad.

unbeliever: it is the demons who are unbelievers. They teach the people witchcraft and that which was revealed to the angels Hārūt and Mārūt in Babylon. Yet they never instruct any without saying beforehand: 'We have been sent only to tempt you; do not blaspheme.' From these two, they learn that which creates discord between husband and wife, although they can harm none with what they learn except by God's leave. They learn what harms them and does not profit them; yet they knew full well that anyone who engaged in that traffic would have no share in the life to come. Vile is that for which they have sold their souls, if they but knew it. Had they embraced the Faith and feared God, far better for them would God's reward have been, if they but knew it.

2:103

Believers, do not say *rā'inā*, but say *unzurnā*.[1] Take heed; woeful punishment awaits the unbelievers.

The unbelievers among the People of the Book, and the pagans, resent that any blessings should have been sent down to you from your Lord. But God chooses whom He will for His mercy. God's grace is infinite.

2:106

Any verse We abrogate or cause to be forgotten, We will replace by a better one or one similar. Did you not know that God has power over all things? Did you not know that it is God who has sovereignty over the heavens and the earth, and that there is none besides God to protect or help you?

Or would you rather demand of your Apostle that which was once demanded of Moses? He that barters faith for unbelief has surely strayed from the right path.

Many among the People of the Book wish, through envy, to lead you back to unbelief, now that you have embraced the Faith and the Truth has been made plain to them. Forgive them and bear with them until God makes known His will. God has power over all things.

2:110

Attend to your prayers and render the alms levy. Whatever

---

1. The words mean 'listen to us' and 'look upon us' respectively; but in Judaeo-Arabic the sound of the first conveyed the sense, 'our evil one'.

good you do shall be recompensed by God: God is watching all your actions.

And they declare: 'None shall enter Paradise but Jews and Christians.' Such are their wishful fancies. Say: 'Let us have your proof, if what you say be true.' Indeed, those that submit to God and do good works shall be recompensed by their Lord: they shall have nothing to fear or to regret. 2:111

The Jews say the Christians are misguided, and the Christians say it is the Jews who are misguided. Yet they both recite the Book. And the ignorant say the same of both. God will on the Day of Resurrection judge what they disagreed about.

And who is more wicked than those that forbid God's name to be pronounced in the mosques of God and seek to destroy them, when they should enter them only with fear in their hearts? They shall be held up to shame in this world, and in the world to come grievous punishment awaits them.

To God belongs the East and the West. Whichever way you turn there is the Face of God. God is omnipresent and all-knowing. 2:115

And they say: 'God has begotten a son.' Glory be to Him! His is what the heavens and the earth contain; all is obedient to Him. Creator of the heavens and the earth! When He decrees a thing, He need only say 'Be,' and it is.

And the ignorant ask: 'Why does God not speak to us or give us a sign?' The same demand was made by those before them: their hearts are all alike. But to those whose faith is firm We have already revealed Our signs.

We have sent you forth to proclaim the Truth and to give warning. You shall not be questioned about the heirs of Hell.

You will please neither the Jews nor the Christians unless you follow their faith. Say: 'God's guidance is the only guidance.' And if after all the knowledge you have been given you yield to their whims, there shall be none to help or protect you from God's ire. Those to whom We have given the Book, and who recite it as it ought to be recited, truly believe in it; those that dissent from it will surely be lost. 2:121

2:122   Children of Israel, remember the favour I have bestowed upon you, and that I exalted you above the nations. Guard yourselves against a day on which no soul shall stand in for another: when no ransom shall be accepted from it, no intercession avail it, no help be given it.

When his Lord put Abraham to the proof by enjoining on him certain commandments and Abraham fulfilled them, He said: 'I have appointed you a leader of mankind.'

'And what of my descendants?' Abraham asked.

'My covenant,' said He, 'does not apply to wrongdoers.'

We made the House[1] a resort and a sanctuary for mankind, saying: 'Make the place where Abraham stood a house of worship.' We enjoined Abraham and Ishmael to cleanse My House for those who walk round and round it, who meditate in it, and who kneel and prostrate themselves.

2:126   'Lord,' said Abraham, 'make this a secure land and bestow plenty upon its people, those of them that believe in God and the Last Day.'

'As for those that do not,' He answered, 'I shall let them live awhile, and then shall drag them to the scourge of the Fire: a wretched fate!'

Abraham and Ishmael laid the foundations of the House and dedicated it, saying: 'Accept this from us, Lord. You are the One that hears all and knows all. Lord, make us submissive to You; make of our descendants a community that will submit to You. Teach us our rites of worship and turn to us with mercy; You are the Forgiving One, the Compassionate. Lord, send forth to them an apostle of their own who shall declare to them Your revelations, and shall instruct them in the Book and in wisdom, and shall purify them of sin. You are the Mighty, the Wise One.'

Who but a foolish man would renounce the faith of Abraham? We chose him in this world, and in the world to come he 2:131 shall abide among the righteous. When his Lord said to him: 'Submit,' he answered: 'I have submitted to the Lord of the Universe.'

1. The Ka'bah at Mecca.

Abraham enjoined the Faith on his children, and so did   2:132
Jacob, saying: 'My children, God has chosen the Faith for you.
Do not depart this life except as Muslims.'

Were you present when death came to Jacob? He said to
his children: 'What will you worship when I am gone?' They
replied: 'We will worship your God and the God of your forefathers Abraham and Ishmael and Isaac: One God. To Him
we will submit as Muslims.'

That community has passed away. Theirs is what they did
and yours what you have done. You shall not be questioned
about their actions.

They say: 'Follow the Jewish or the Christian Faith and you
shall be rightly guided.'

Say: 'By no means! Only the faith of Abraham, the upright
one. And he was no idolater.'

Say: 'We believe in God and that which has been revealed   2:136
to us; in what was revealed to Abraham, Ishmael, Isaac, Jacob,
and the tribes; to Moses and Jesus and the other prophets by
their Lord. We make no distinction among any of them, and
to Him we do submit as Muslims.'

If they believe as you believe, they shall be rightly guided;
if they turn away, they shall surely be in schism. Against them
God is your all-sufficient defender. And it is He that hears all
and knows all.

We take on God's own dye. And who has a better dye than
God's? Him will we worship.

Say: 'Would you dispute with us about God, who is our
Lord and your Lord? We shall both be judged by our works.
To Him alone we are devoted.

'Or do you claim that Abraham, Ishmael, Isaac, Jacob, and
the tribes, were all Jews or Christians?' Say: 'Who knows better, you or God? Who is more wicked than he that hides a
testimony he has received from God? God is never heedless
of what you do.'

That community has passed away. Theirs is what they did   2:141
and yours what you have done. You shall not be questioned
about their actions.

2:142   The foolish will ask: 'What has made them turn away from their former *qiblah*?'[1]

Say: 'The East and the West are God's. He guides whom He will to a straight path.'

Thus have We made you a just community, so that you may testify against mankind and that your own Apostle may testify against you. We decreed your former *qiblah* only in order that We might know the Apostle's true adherents and those who were to disown him. It was indeed a hard test, but not to those whom God has guided. God's aim was not to make your faith fruitless. God is benignant and compassionate to mankind.

Many a time have We seen you[2] turn your face hither and thither towards the sky. We will henceforth make you turn towards a *qiblah* that will please you. Turn your face towards the Holy Mosque; wherever you[3] be, turn your faces towards it.

Those to whom the Book was given know this to be the Truth from their Lord. God is never heedless of what they do.
2:145   But even if you gave them every proof they would not accept your *qiblah*, nor would you accept theirs; nor would any of them accept the *qiblah* of the other. If, after all the knowledge you have been given, you yield to their desires, then you will surely become a wrongdoer.

Those to whom We gave the Scriptures know him[2] as they know their own sons. But some of them deliberately conceal the Truth. This is the Truth from your Lord: therefore never doubt it.

Each one has a goal towards which he turns. But wherever you are, emulate one another in good works. God will bring you all before Him. God has power over all things.
2:149   Whichever way you depart, face towards the Holy Mosque.

---

1. The direction which the Muslim faces in prayer. At first the believers were ordered to turn towards the 'Holy Temple' (Bayt al-Maqdis) in Jerusalem (thus Al-Bayḍāwī); afterwards to Mecca.
2. Muḥammad.
3. The faithful.

This is surely the Truth from your Lord. God is never heedless of what you do.

Whichever way you depart, face towards the Holy Mosque: and wherever you are, face towards it, so that people will have no cause to reproach you, except the wrongdoers among them. Have no fear of them; fear Me, so that I may perfect My favour to you and that you may be rightly guided.   2:150

Thus have We sent forth to you an apostle of your own who will recite to you Our revelations and purify you of sin, who will instruct you in the Book and in wisdom and teach you what you knew not. Remember Me, then, and I will remember you. Give thanks to Me and never deny Me.

Believers, fortify yourselves with patience and with prayer; God is with those that are patient. Do not say that those slain in the cause of God are dead. They are alive, but you are not aware of them.

We shall test your steadfastness with fear and famine, with loss of property and life and crops. Give joyful tidings to those who endure with fortitude; who in adversity say: 'We belong to God, and to Him we shall return.' On such shall be God's blessing and mercy; such are those that are rightly guided.   2:155

Ṣafā and Marwa[1] are two of God's beacons. It shall be no offence for the pilgrim or the visitor to the Sacred House to walk around them both. He that does good of his own accord shall be recompensed by God. God has knowledge of all things.

Those that hide the clear proofs and the guidance We have revealed to mankind after We had proclaimed them in the Book shall be cursed by God and cursed by those who invoke damnation; except those that repent and mend their ways and make known the Truth. Towards them I shall relent. I am the Relenting One, the Compassionate. But the infidels who die unbelievers shall incur the curse of God, the angels, and people all. Under it they shall remain for ever; their punishment shall not be mitigated, nor shall they be reprieved.

Your God is one God. There is no god but Him. He is the Merciful, the Compassionate.   2:163

1. Two hills near Mecca, held in reverence by pagan Arabs.

2:164   Surely in the creation of the heavens and the earth; in the alternation of night and day; in the ships that sail the ocean with cargoes beneficial to mankind; in the water which God sends down from the sky and with which He revives the earth after its death, dispersing over it all manner of beasts; in the disposal of the winds, and in the clouds that are driven between sky and earth: surely in these there are signs for rational people.

And yet there are some who worship idols, bestowing on them the adoration due to God (though the love of God is stronger in the faithful). But when they face their punishment the wrongdoers will learn that might is God's alone, and God is stern in retribution. When they face their punishment those who were followed will disown their followers, and the bonds which now unite them will break asunder. Those who followed them will say: 'Could we but live again, we would disown them as they have now disowned us.'

Thus will God show them their own works. They shall sigh with remorse, but shall never emerge from the Fire.

2:168   You people! Eat of what is lawful and wholesome on the earth and do not walk in Satan's footsteps, for he is your veritable foe. He enjoins on you evil and lewdness, and bids you assert about God what you know not.

If they are told: 'Follow what God has revealed,' they say: 'We will follow what our fathers practised,' even though their fathers understood nothing and had no guidance.

The unbelievers are like those that, call out to them as one may, can hear nothing but a shout and a cry. Deaf, dumb, and blind, they do not understand.

Believers, eat of the wholesome things with which We have provided you and give thanks to God, if it is Him you worship.

2:173   He has forbidden you carrion, blood, and the flesh of swine;[1] also any flesh that is consecrated other than in the name of God. But whoever is driven by necessity, intending neither to sin nor to transgress, shall incur no guilt. God is forgiving and compassionate.

---

1. Cf. Leviticus 17:15; 17:10–12; and 11:7.

Those that suppress any part of the Book which God has 2:174 revealed in order to gain some paltry end shall swallow nothing but fire into their bellies. On the Day of Resurrection God will neither speak to them nor purify them. Woeful punishment awaits them.

Such are those that barter guidance for error and forgiveness for punishment. How steadfastly they seek the Fire! That is because God has revealed the Book with the Truth; those that disagree about it are in extreme schism.

Righteousness does not consist in whether you turn your faces to the East or to the West. The righteous are those who believe in God and the Last Day, in the angels and the Book and the prophets; who, though they love it dearly, give their wealth to kin, to orphans, to the destitute, to the traveller in need and to beggars, and for the redemption of captives; who attend to their prayers and render the alms levy; who are true to their promises and steadfast in trial and adversity and in times of war. Such are the true believers; such are the God-fearing.

Believers, retaliation is decreed for you in bloodshed: a free 2:178 man for a free man, a slave for a slave, and a female for a female. He who is pardoned by his aggrieved brother shall be prosecuted according to usage and shall pay him a liberal fine. This is a merciful dispensation from your Lord. Whoever transgresses thereafter, a woeful punishment awaits him.

In retaliation you have a safeguard for your lives – you that are of good sense possessed; perchance you will fear God.

It is decreed that when death approaches, those of you that leave property shall bequeath it equitably to parents and kin. This is a duty incumbent on the God-fearing. He that alters a will after hearing it shall be accountable for his crime: God hears all and knows all.

He that suspects an error or an injustice on the part of a testator and brings about a settlement among the parties incurs no guilt. God is forgiving and compassionate.

Believers, fasting is decreed for you as it was decreed for those before you; perchance you will fear God. Fast a cer- 2:184 tain number of days, but if any one among you is ill or on a journey, let him fast a similar number of days later; and for those that cannot[1] endure it there is a penance ordained: the feeding of a poor man. He that does good of his own accord shall be well rewarded; but to fast is better for you, if you but knew it.

2:185 It was in the month of Ramaḍān that the Koran was revealed, a guide for mankind with proofs of guidance and Salvation.[2] Therefore whoever of you is present in that month let him fast. And he who is ill or on a journey shall fast a similar number of days later.

God desires your well-being, not your discomfort. He desires you to fast the whole month so that you may magnify God for His guidance and render thanks.

If My servants question you about Me, tell them that I am near. I answer the prayer of the suppliant when he calls to Me; therefore let them answer My call and put their trust in Me, that they may be rightly guided.

2:187 It is now lawful for you to lie with your wives on the night of the fast; they are a comfort to you as you are a comfort to them. God knew that you were deceiving yourselves. He has relented towards you and pardoned you. Therefore you may now lie with them and seek what God has ordained for you. Eat and drink until you can tell a white thread from a black one in the light of the coming dawn. Then resume the fast till nightfall and do not approach them, when you should be preoccupied with your prayers in the mosques.

These are the bounds set by God: do not approach them. Thus God makes known His revelations to mankind that they may guard themselves against evil.

Do not devour one another's property by unjust means, nor bribe the judges with it in order that you may wrongfully and knowingly devour other people's possessions.

2:189 They ask you about the phases of the moon. Say: 'They are times set for the people and for the Pilgrimage.'

1. Thus Al-Jalālayn; the negative being understood. Alternatively: 'and for those well able to fast there is a penance ordained:'.
2. See p. 4, note 1.

Righteousness does not consist in entering your dwellings from the back.[1] The righteous are those that fear God. Enter dwellings by their doors and fear God, so that you may prosper.

Fight in the cause of God those that fight you, but commit no aggression. God does not love the aggressors.   2:190

Slay them wherever you find them. Drive them out of the places from which they drove you. Idolatry[2] is more grievous than bloodshed. But do not fight them within the precincts of the Holy Mosque unless they attack you there; if they attack you, slay them. Thus shall the unbelievers be requited: but if they desist, God is forgiving and compassionate.

Fight them until idolatry is no more and God's religion reigns supreme. But if they desist, attack none except the wrongdoers.

A sacred month for a sacred month: sacred things too are subject to retaliation. If anyone attacks you, attack him as he attacked you. Have fear of God, and know that God is with those that fear Him.   2:194

Give generously for the cause of God and do not with your own hands cast yourselves into destruction. Be charitable; God loves the charitable.

Make the Pilgrimage and the Visit for His sake. If you cannot, send such offerings as you can afford and do not shave your heads until the offerings have reached their destination. But if any of you is ill or suffers from an ailment of the head, he must do penance either by fasting or by almsgiving or by offering a sacrifice.   2:196

If in peacetime anyone among you combines the Visit with the Pilgrimage, he must offer such gifts as he can afford; but if he lacks the means let him fast three days during the Pilgrimage and seven when he has returned; that is, ten days in all. That is incumbent on him whose family are not present at the Holy

1. It was the custom of pagan Arabs, on returning from the Pilgrimage, to enter their homes from the back.
2. Thus Al-Jalālayn. The noun *fitnah* occurs about thirty times in the Koran and is used in several different senses, according to context. It can also mean sedition, persecution, temptation, etc.

Mosque. Have fear of God, and know that God is stern in retribution.

2:197   The Pilgrimage shall be made in the appointed months. He that intends to perform it in those months must abstain from sexual intercourse, obscene language, and acrimonious disputes while on pilgrimage. God is aware of whatever good you do. Provide well for yourselves: the best provision is fear of God. Fear Me, then, you that are of good sense possessed.

It shall be no offence for you to seek the bounty of your Lord. When you come down from 'Arafāt[1] remember God as you approach the Sacred Monument. Remember Him that gave you guidance when you were assuredly among the lost. Then go out from the place whence the pilgrims will go out and implore the forgiveness of God. God is forgiving and compassionate. And when you have fulfilled your sacred duties, remember God as you remember your forefathers or with deeper reverence.

There are some who say: 'Lord, give us a good life in this
2:201   world.' These shall have no share in the world to come. And there are some who say: 'Lord, give us what is good both in this world and in the world to come, and keep us from the torment of the Fire.' These shall have a share, according to what they did. Swift is God's reckoning.

Give glory to God on appointed days. He that departs in haste after two days incurs no sin, nor does he who stays on longer, if he truly fears God. Have fear of God, then, and know that before Him you shall all be herded.

Among people there may be one whose views on the life of this world please you: he even calls on God to vouch for that which is in his heart; whereas in fact he is the deadliest of adversaries. No sooner does he turn away than he hastens to perpetrate evil in the land, destroying crops and cattle; and God does not love evil.

And if he is told: 'Fear God,' vanity carries him off to sin. Sufficient is Hell for him; an evil resting-place.

2:207   And among people there may be one who would give away

1. Near Mecca.

his soul to find favour with God. God is compassionate to
His creatures.

Believers, submit all of you to God and do not follow in
Satan's footsteps; he is to you a veritable foe. If you lapse after
the conspicuous signs that have come to you, know that God
is mighty and wise. 2:208

Are they waiting for God to come down to them in the
shadow of a cloud, with the angels? But judgement has been
duly passed, and to God shall all return.

Ask the Israelites how many conspicuous signs We gave
them. He that tampers with the gift of God after it had been
bestowed on him shall find that God is stern in retribution.

For the unbelievers the life of this world is decked with all
manner of temptations. They scoff at the faithful, but those
that fear God shall be above them on the Day of Resurrection. God gives to whom He will without reckoning.

People were once but one community. Then God sent
forth prophets to give them joyful tidings and to warn them,
and with these He sent down the Book with the Truth, that it
might serve as arbiter in people's disputes. None disputed it
save those to whom it was given, and that was through envy
of one another, after veritable signs had been vouchsafed
them. So God guided by His will those who believed in the
Truth which had been disputed. God guides whom He will to
a straight path. 2:213

Or did you suppose that you would enter Paradise
untouched by the suffering endured by those before you?
Affliction and adversity befell them; and so shaken were they
that each apostle, and those who shared his faith, cried out:
'When will God's help come?' Surely God's help is ever near.

They will ask you about almsgiving. Say: 'Whatever you
give in charity shall go to parents and to kin, to the orphans
and to the destitute, and to the traveller in need. God is fully
aware of whatever good you do.'

Fighting is obligatory for you, much as you dislike it.
But you may hate a thing although it is good for you, and
love a thing although it is bad for you. God knows, but you
know not. 2:216

2:217 They ask you about the Sacred Month and about fighting therein. Say: 'To fight in this month is a grave offence; but to debar people from the path of God, to blaspheme against Him and against the Holy Mosque, and to expel its worshippers from it, is more grievous in God's sight. Idolatry[1] is more grievous than bloodshed.'

They will not cease to fight you until they force you to renounce your religion – if they are able. But whoever among you renounces his religion and dies an unbeliever, his works shall come to nothing in this world and in the world to come. Such shall be the tenants of the Fire, wherein shall they abide for ever.

Those that have embraced the Faith, and those that have fled their land and fought for the cause of God, may hope for God's mercy. God is forgiving and compassionate.

2:219 They ask you about drinking and gambling. Say: 'There is great harm in both, although they have some benefits for the people; but their harm is far greater than their benefit.'

They ask you what they should give in alms. Say: 'What you can spare.' Thus God makes plain to you His revelations so that you may reflect upon this world and the Hereafter.

They question you concerning orphans. Say: 'To deal justly with them is best. If you mix their affairs with yours: they are your brothers: God knows the unjust from the just. If God pleased, He could afflict you. God is mighty and wise.'

You shall not wed pagan women, unless they embrace the Faith. A believing slave-girl is better than an idolatress, although she may please you. Nor shall you wed idolaters, unless they embrace the Faith. A believing slave is better than an idolater, although he may please you. These call you to the Fire; but God calls you, by His will, to Paradise and to forgiveness. He makes plain His revelations to mankind, so that they may remember.

2:222 They ask you about menstruation. Say: 'It is an indisposition. Keep aloof from women during their menstrual periods and do not approach them until they are clean again; when

---

1. Thus Al-Jalālayn. See p. 19, note 2.

they are clean, have intercourse with them whence God
enjoined you. God loves those that turn to Him in penitence
and strive to keep themselves clean.'

Women are your fields: go, then, into your fields whence   2:223
you please. Do good works and fear God. Know that you
shall meet Him. Give joyful tidings to the believers.

And do not make God, when you swear by Him, a means to
prevent you from dealing justly, from fearing Him, and from
making peace among people. God hears all and knows all.
God will not call you to account for that which is inadvertent
in your oaths. But He will take you to task for that which is
intended in your hearts. God is forgiving and lenient.

Those that renounce their wives on oath must wait four
months. If they change their minds, God is forgiving and
compassionate; but if they decide to divorce them, know that
God hears all and knows all.

Divorced women must wait, keeping themselves from   2:228
men, three menstrual courses. It is unlawful for them, if they
believe in God and the Last Day, to hide what God has created in their wombs: in which case their husbands would do
more justly to take them back, should they desire reconcili-
ation.

Women shall with justice have rights similar to those exer-
cised against them, although men have a status above them.
God is mighty and wise.

Divorce[1] may be pronounced twice, and then a woman
shall be retained in honour or allowed to go with kindness. It
is unlawful for you to take from them anything you gave them,
unless both fear that they may not be able to keep within the
bounds set by God; in which case it shall be no offence for
either of them if the wife redeems herself.

These are the bounds set by God; do not transgress them.
Those that transgress the bounds of God are assuredly the
wrongdoers.

If a man divorces[2] his wife, he shall not remarry her until   2:230

---

1. Revocable divorce, or the renunciation of one's wife on oath.
2. By pronouncing the formula 'I divorce you' for the third time.

she has wedded another man and been divorced by him; in which case it shall be no offence for either of them to return to the other, if they think they can keep within the bounds set by God.

Such are the bounds of God. He makes them plain to those endowed with knowledge.

2:231 When you have renounced your wives and they have reached the end of their waiting period, either retain them in honour or let them go with kindness. But you shall not retain them in order to harm them or to wrong them. Whoever does this wrongs his own soul.

Do not trifle with God's revelations. Remember the favour God has bestowed upon you, and the Book and the wisdom He has revealed for your instruction. Fear God and know that God has knowledge of all things.

When you have renounced your wives and they have reached the end of their waiting period, do not prevent them from remarrying their husbands if they have come to an honourable agreement. This is enjoined on every one of you who believes in God and the Last Day; this is more honourable for you and more chaste. God knows, and you know not.

2:233 Mothers shall give suck to their children for two whole years if the father wishes the sucking to be completed. They must be maintained and clothed in a reasonable manner by the child's father. None shall be charged with more than one can bear. A mother shall not be allowed to suffer on account of her child, nor shall a father on account of his child. The same duties devolve upon the father's heir. But if, by mutual consent and consultation, they choose to wean the child, they shall incur no offence. Nor shall it be any offence for you if you prefer to have a nurse for your children, provided that you pay her what you promise, according to usage. Fear God, and know that God is cognizant of what you do.

2:234 Those of you who die and leave wives behind, their widows shall wait, keeping to themselves for four months and ten days. When they have reached the end of their waiting period, it shall be no offence for you to let them do whatever they choose for themselves, provided that it is decent. God is cognizant of what you do.

It shall be no offence for you openly to propose marriage   2:235
to such women or to cherish them in your hearts. God knows
that you will remember them. But do not arrange to meet
them in secret, and, if you do, speak to them honourably, and
you shall not consummate the marriage before the end of
their waiting period. Know that God has knowledge of all
that is in your minds. Therefore fear Him and know that God
is forgiving and lenient.

It shall be no offence for you to divorce your wives unless
the marriage has been consummated and the dowry settled.
And provide for them; the rich man according to his means
and the poor man according to his: a fair provision. This is
incumbent on men of virtue. And if you divorce them
before the marriage is consummated, but after their dowry
has been settled, give them the half of their dowry, unless
they or the husband agree to waive it. But it is more proper
and decent that the husband should waive it. Do not forget
to show kindness to each other. God is cognizant of what
you do.

Attend regularly to your prayers, including the middle   2:238
prayer, and stand up with all devotion before God. When you
are exposed to danger pray on foot or while riding; and when
you are restored to safety remember God, as He has taught
you what you did not know.

Those of you who die leaving wives behind shall bequeath
their widows a year's maintenance without causing them to
leave their homes; but if they leave of their own accord, no
blame shall be attached to you for any course they may deem
reasonable to pursue. God is mighty and wise. Reasonable
provision shall also be made for divorced women; this is
incumbent on those who fear God.

Thus God makes known to you His revelations that you
may grow in understanding.

Consider those that fled their homes in their thousands for   2:243
fear of death. God had said to them: 'You will die,' and then

He brought them back to life. Surely God is bountiful to mankind, but most do not give thanks.

2:244   Fight for the cause of God, and know that He assuredly hears all and knows all.

Who will grant God a generous loan? He will repay him many times over. God gives abundantly and in scant measure. To Him shall you be recalled.

Have you not heard of what the leaders of the Israelites demanded of a prophet of theirs after the death of Moses? 'Raise up for us a king,' they said, 'and we will fight for the cause of God.'

He replied: 'What if you refuse, when ordered so to fight?'

'Why should we refuse to fight for the cause of God,' they said, 'when we have been driven from our dwellings and our children?'

But when they were ordered to fight, they all refused, except a few of them. God knows the wrongdoers.

2:247   Their prophet said to them: 'God has appointed Saul to be your king.' They replied: 'Why should he be given the kingship, when we are more deserving of it than he? Besides, he has not been given abundant wealth.'

He said: 'God has chosen him to rule over you and made him grow in knowledge and in stature. God gives His sovereignty to whom He will. God is munificent and all-knowing.'

Their prophet also said to them: 'The portent of his reign shall be the advent of the Ark. Therein shall be a Divine Presence[1] from your Lord, and the relics which the House of Moses and the House of Aaron left behind. It will be borne by the angels. That will be a sign for you, if you are true believers.'

2:249   And when Saul marched out with his warriors, he said: 'God will put you to the test at a certain river. He that drinks from it shall be no soldier of mine, but he that does not drink

---

1. The Arabic word *sakīnah* derives from the same Semitic root as *shekhīna* = Divine Presence. See also Arberry, who renders *sakīnah* as *Shechina* (without mention of its meaning in English).

26

from it, or scoops a little in the hollow of his hand, shall fight by my side.'[1]

They all drank from it, except a few of them. And when he had crossed the river with those who shared his faith, they said: 'We have no power this day against Goliath and his warriors.'

Those of them who believed that they would meet with God said: 'Many a small band has, by God's grace, vanquished a mighty army. God is with those who endure with fortitude.'

And when they confronted Goliath and his warriors they said: 'Lord, fill our hearts with steadfastness; make us firm of foot and help us against the unbelievers.'

2:250

By God's will they routed them. David slew Goliath,[2] and God bestowed on him sovereignty and wisdom and taught him what He pleased. Had God not defeated some by the might of others, the earth would have been utterly corrupted. But God is bountiful to mankind.

Such are God's revelations: We recite them to you in all truth; and one of Our emissaries you surely are. Of these emissaries We have exalted some above others. To some God spoke; others He raised to a lofty status. We gave Jesus son of Mary conspicuous signs and strengthened him with the Holy Spirit. Had God pleased, those who succeeded them would not have fought each other after the conspicuous signs had been given them. But they disagreed among themselves; some had faith and others had none. And had God pleased they would not have fought each other; but God does what He will.

2:252

Believers, bestow in alms a part of what We have given you before that day arrives when no commerce or friendship or intercession shall avail. It is the unbelievers who are the wrongdoers.

God: there is no god but Him, the Living, the Eternal One.[3] Neither slumber nor sleep overtakes Him. His is what

2:255

1. Cf. Judges 7.
2. 1 Samuel 17.
3. Al-Ḥayyu 'l Qayyūm; cf. Ḥāy wa Qiyyām, in the Old Testament.

the heavens and the earth contain. Who can intercede with Him except by His permission? He knows what is before them and behind them. They can grasp only that part of His knowledge which He wills. His throne is as vast as the heavens and the earth, and the preservation of both does not weary Him. He is the Exalted, the Immense One.

2:256 There shall be no compulsion in religion. True guidance is now distinct from error. He that renounces idol-worship and believes in God shall grasp a firm handle that will never break. God hears all and knows all.

God is the Patron of the faithful; He leads them from darkness to the light. As for the unbelievers, their patrons are false gods, who lead them from the light to darkness. They are the inmates of the Fire, wherein shall they abide for ever.

2:258 Have you not thought of him who argued with Abraham about his Lord because He had bestowed sovereignty upon him? Abraham said: 'My Lord is He who has power over life and death.'

'I, too,' replied the other, 'have power over life and death.'

'God brings up the sun from the east,' said Abraham. 'Bring it up yourself from the west.'

The unbeliever was confounded. God does not guide the wrongdoers.

Or of him, who, when passing by a ruined and desolate city, remarked: 'How can God give life to this city, now that it is dead?' Thereupon God caused him to die, and after a hundred years brought him back to life.

'How long have you been here?' God asked.

'A day,' he replied, 'or part of a day.'

God said: 'You have been here a hundred years. Yet look at your food and drink: they have not rotted. And look at your ass. We will make of you a sign for the people: and look at the bones, how We will revive them and clothe them with flesh.'

And when it had all become manifest to him, he said: 'Now I know that God has power over all things.'

2:260 And when Abraham said: 'Show me, Lord, how You will raise the dead,' He replied: 'Have you no faith?'

'Yes,' said he, 'but just to reassure my heart.'

He said: 'Take four birds, and cut them to pieces. Scatter them over the mountain-tops, then call them back. They will come swiftly to you. Know that God is mighty and wise.'

Those that give their wealth for the cause of God can be 2:261 compared to a grain of corn which brings forth seven ears, each bearing a hundred grains. God gives more and more to whom He will; God is munificent and all-knowing.

Those that give their wealth for the cause of God and do not follow their almsgiving with taunts and insults shall be rewarded by their Lord; they shall have nothing to fear or to regret.

A kind word with forgiveness is better than charity followed by insult. God is self-sufficient and gracious.

Believers, do not nullify your almsgiving with taunts and mischief-making, like him who spends his wealth only to be seen by people, and believes neither in God nor in the Last Day. He can be compared to a rock covered with earth: a shower falls upon it and leaves it hard and bare. They shall gain nothing from their works; and God does not guide the unbelievers.

But those that give their wealth from a desire to please God 2:265 and to reassure their own souls can be compared to an orchard on a hillside: if a shower falls upon it, it yields up twice its normal produce; and if no shower falls upon it, it's watered by the dew. God is cognizant of what you do.

Would any one of you, being well advanced in age with helpless children to support, wish to have an orchard planted with palm-trees, vines, and all manner of fruits, and watered by running brooks – only to be blasted and consumed by a fiery whirlwind?

Thus God makes plain to you His revelations, so that you may give thought.

You believers! Give in alms from the wealth you have lawfully earned and from that which We have brought out of the earth for you; not worthless things which you yourselves would but reluctantly accept. Know that God is self-sufficient and worthy of praise.

Satan threatens you with poverty and enjoins lewdness on 2:268 you. But God promises you His forgiveness and His bounty: God is munificent and all-knowing.

2:269 He gives wisdom to whom He will; and he that receives the gift of wisdom is rich indeed. Yet none remembers but those that are of good sense possessed.

And whatever alms you give and whatever vows you make are known to God. The wrongdoers shall have none to help them.

To be charitable in public is good, but to give alms to the poor in private is better for you and will atone for some of your sins. God has knowledge of all your actions.

It is not for you to guide them; God gives guidance to whom He will.

Whatever alms you give shall rebound to your own advantage, provided that you give them only for the love of God. And whatever alms you give shall be repaid to you in full: you shall not be wronged.

As for the poor who are preoccupied with fighting in the cause of God, and cannot travel the land in quest of a livelihood: the ignorant take them for men of wealth on account of their modest behaviour. But you recognize them by their look – they never importune people for alms. Whatever alms you give are known to God.

2:274 Those that give of their wealth by night and by day, in private and in public, shall be rewarded by their Lord and have nothing to fear or to regret.

Those that devour usury shall rise up before God like him that Satan has demented by his touch; for they claim that trading is no different from usury. But God has permitted trading and made usury unlawful. He that has received an admonition from his Lord and mended his ways may keep his previous gains; God will be his judge. Those that turn back shall be the inmates of the Fire, wherein shall they abide for ever.

God has laid His curse on usury and blessed almsgiving with increase. God bears no love for the impious and the sinful.

Those that believe and do good works, attend to their prayers and render the alms levy, shall be rewarded by their Lord and have nothing to fear or to regret.

2:278 Believers, fear God and waive what is still due to you from

usury, if your faith be true; or war shall be declared against 2:279
you by God and His apostle. If you repent, you may retain
your principal, suffering no loss and causing loss to none.

If your debtor be in straits, grant him a delay until he can
discharge his debt; but if you waive the sum as alms it will be
better for you, if you but knew it.

Fear the day when you shall all return to God; and then
every soul shall be paid back for what it did. None shall be
wronged.

Believers, when you contract a debt for a fixed period, put 2:282
it in writing. Let a scribe write it down for you with fairness;
no scribe should refuse to write as God has taught him.
Therefore let him write; and let the debtor dictate, fearing
God his Lord and not diminishing the sum he owes. If the
debtor be an ignorant or feeble-minded person, or one who
cannot dictate, let his guardian dictate for him in fairness.
Call in two male witnesses from among you, but if two men
cannot be found, then one man and two women whom you
judge fit to act as witnesses; so that if either of them make an
error, the other will remind her. Witnesses shall not refuse
if called upon to give evidence. So do not fail to put your
debts in writing, be they small or large, together with the
date of payment. This is more just in the sight of God; it
ensures accuracy in testifying and is the best way to remove
all doubt. But if the transaction be a bargain concluded on
the spot, it shall be no offence for you if you do not put it
into writing.

See that witnesses are present when you barter with one
another, and let no harm be done to either scribe or witness.
If you harm them you will commit a transgression. Have fear
of God; God teaches you, and God has knowledge of all
things.

If you are travelling the road and cannot find a scribe, then 2:283
let pledges be given. If one of you entrusts another with a
pledge, let the trustee restore the pledge to its owner; and let
him fear God, his Lord.

You shall not withhold testimony; sinful is the heart of him
who withholds it. God has knowledge of what you do.

2:284   To God belongs all that the heavens and the earth contain. Whether you reveal your thoughts or hide them, God will bring you to account for them. He will forgive whom He will and punish whom He pleases; God has power over all things.

    The Apostle believes in what has been revealed to him by his Lord, and so do the faithful. They all believe in God and His angels, His Scriptures, and His apostles: We discriminate against none of His apostles. They say: 'We hear and obey.

2:286 Grant us Your forgiveness, Lord; to You shall all return. God does not charge a soul with more than it can bear. It shall be requited for whatever good and whatever evil it has done. Lord, do not reproach us if we forget or lapse into error. Lord, do not lay on us a burden such as You laid on those before us. Lord, do not charge us with more than we can bear. Pardon us, forgive us our sins, and have mercy upon us; You alone are our Protector. Give us victory over the unbelievers.'

THE HOUSE OF 'IMRĀN

In the Name of God, the Merciful, the Compassionate

3:1   ALIF *lām mīm*. God! There is no god but Him, the Living, the Ever-existent One.

    He has revealed to you the Book with the Truth, confirming that which preceded it; for He had already revealed the Torah and the Gospel for the guidance of mankind, and revealed Salvation.[1]

    Those that deny God's revelations shall be sternly punished; God is mighty and capable of revenge. Nothing on earth or in heaven is hidden from God. It is He who shapes your bodies in your mothers' wombs as He pleases. There is no god but Him, the Mighty, the Wise One.

3:7   It is He who has revealed to you the Book. Some of its verses are precise in meaning – they are the foundation of the Book – and others ambiguous. Those whose hearts are

1. See p. 4, note 1.

infected with disbelief observe the ambiguous part, so as to create dissension by seeking to explain it. But no one knows its meaning except God. Those who are well-grounded in knowledge say: 'We believe in it: it is all from our Lord. Yet none remembers but those that are of good sense possessed. Lord, do not cause our hearts to go astray after You have guided us. Grant us mercy through Your own grace; You are the munificent Giver. Lord, You will surely gather up all mankind upon a day of which there is no doubt. God will not fail the time appointed.' 3:8

As for the unbelievers, neither their riches nor their children will in the least save them from God's judgement. They will surely be the fuel of the Fire. Like Pharaoh's people and those before them, they denied Our revelations, and God smote them in their sins: God is stern in retribution.

Say to the unbelievers: 'You shall be overthrown and driven into Hell – an evil resting-place!'

Indeed, there was a sign for you in the two armies which 3:13
met on the battlefield.[1] One was fighting for the cause of God, the other being a host of unbelievers. The faithful saw with their very eyes that they were twice their own number. But God strengthens with His aid whom He will. Surely in that there was a lesson for the discerning.

Men are tempted by the lure of women and offspring, of hoarded treasures of gold and silver, of splendid horses, cattle, and plantations. These are the enjoyments of this life, but far better is the return to God.

Say: 'Shall I tell you of better things than these, with which the God-fearing shall be rewarded by their Lord? Gardens watered by running brooks, wherein shall they abide for ever: spouses of perfect chastity and grace from God.'

God is ever observant of His servants, those who say: 'Lord, we do believe: forgive us our sins and keep us from the torment of the Fire'; who are steadfast, sincere, obedient, and charitable; and who implore forgiveness at break of day.

God bears witness that there is no god but Him, and so do 3:18

---

1. In the Battle of Badr. See p. 116, notes 1 and 2.

the angels and the sages; the Executor of Justice, the Only God, the Almighty, the Wise One.

3:19 The only religion in God's sight is Islām. Those to whom the Book was given dissented, through insolence, only after knowledge had been vouchsafed them. He that denies God's revelations should know that swift is God's reckoning.

If they argue with you, say: 'I have submitted my face to God and so have those that follow me.'

And to those who were given the Book and to the Gentiles say: 'Will you submit to God?' If they embrace Islām, they shall be rightly guided; and if they pay no heed, then your only duty is to warn them. God is ever observant of His creatures.

Those that deny God's revelations, and slay the prophets unjustly, and kill those among the people who preach fair dealing – warn them of a woeful scourge. Their works shall come to nothing in this world and in the world to come, and there shall be none to help them.

3:23 Do but consider those who have received a portion of the Book: when they are called on to accept the judgement of God's Book, some turn their backs and pay no heed. For they declare: 'We shall endure the Fire for a few days only.' In their religion they are deceived by their own lies.

What will they do when We gather them all together upon a day of which there is no doubt, when every soul will be given what it has earned, with none treated unjustly?

Say: 'Lord, Sovereign of all sovereignty, You bestow sovereignty on whom You will and take sovereignty away from whom You please; You exalt whomever You will and abase whomever You please. In Your hand all goodness lies; You have power over all things. You cause the night to pass into the day, and the day to pass into the night; You bring forth the living from the dead and You bring forth the dead from the living. You give without reckoning to whom You will.'

Let not believers take infidels as their friends in preference to the faithful – he that does this has nothing to hope for from God – except in self-defence. God admonishes you to fear Him: for to God shall all return.

3:29 Say: 'Whether you hide what is in your hearts or reveal it, it is known to God. He knows all that the heavens and the earth contain; and God has power over all things.'

The day will surely come when each soul will be confronted with whatever good it did. As for its evil deeds, it will wish them far away. God admonishes you to fear Him. God is kindly to His servants. 3:30

Say: 'If you love God, follow me. God will love you and forgive you your sins; God is forgiving and compassionate.'

Say: 'Obey God and the Apostle.' If they pay no heed, then, surely, God does not love the unbelievers.

God exalted Adam and Noah, Abraham's descendants and the descendants of 'Imrān[1] above the nations. They were the offspring of one another. God hears all and knows all.

Remember the words of 'Imrān's[2] wife. 'Lord,' she said, 'I dedicate to You that which is in my womb. Accept it from me; You alone hear all and know all.'

And when she was delivered of the child, she said: 'Lord, I have given birth to a daughter' – God knew better of what she was delivered: the male is not like the female – 'and have named her Mary. I beseech you to protect her and all her descendants from Satan, the Accursed One.' 3:36

Her Lord graciously accepted her. He made her grow a goodly child and entrusted her to the care of Zacharias.[3]

Whenever Zacharias visited her in the Shrine he found she had food with her. 'Mary,' he said, 'where is this food from?'

'It is from God,' she answered. 'God gives without reckoning to whom He will.'

Thereupon Zacharias prayed to his Lord, saying: 'Lord, grant me of Your own grace upright descendants; You hear all prayers.'

And as he stood praying in the Shrine, the angels called out to him, saying: 'God bids you rejoice in the birth of John, who 3:39

---

1. Amram, the father of Moses and Aaron (Exodus 6:20).
2. In the Koran, 'Imrān (Amram) is also the Virgin Mary's father.
3. Or Zachariah. See Luke 1:12–22 for the accepted spelling of the name.

shall confirm the Word of God. He shall be princely and chaste, a prophet and a righteous man.'

3:40 'Lord,' he said, 'how shall I have a son when I am now overtaken by old age and my wife is barren?'

'Such is the will of God,' He said. 'He does what He pleases.'

'Lord,' said he, 'vouchsafe me a sign.'

'Your sign is that for three days and three nights,' He replied, 'you shall not speak to people except by symbols. Remember your Lord always; give glory to Him evening and morning.'

And remember the angels' words to Mary. They said:[1] 'God has chosen you. He has made you pure and exalted you above womankind. Mary, be obedient to your Lord; bow down and worship with the worshippers.'

This is an account of a divine secret: We reveal it to you.[2] You were not present when they cast lots to see which of them should have charge of Mary; nor were you present when they argued about her.

3:45 The angels said: 'Mary, God bids you rejoice in a Word from Him. His name is the Christ, Jesus son of Mary; noble in this world and in the world to come, and one of the favoured. He shall preach to people in his cradle and in the prime of manhood, and shall lead a righteous life.'

'Lord,' she said, 'how can I bear a child when no man has touched me?'

He said: 'Even thus: God creates whom He will. If He decrees a thing He need only say: "Be," and it is. He will instruct him in the Scriptures and in wisdom, in the Torah and in the Gospel, and send him forth an apostle to the Israelites. He will say: "I bring you a sign from your Lord. From clay I will create for you the likeness of a bird. I shall breathe into it and, by God's leave, it shall become a living bird. By God's leave I shall heal the blind man and the leper, and raise the dead to life. I shall tell you what to eat and what to store up in your houses. Surely that will be a sign for you, if you are true

3:50 believers. I come to confirm the Torah which preceded me

1. Cf. Luke 1:26–38.   2. Muhammad.

and to make lawful for you some of the things you are forbidden. I bring you a sign from your Lord: therefore fear God and obey me. Surely God is my Lord and your Lord: therefore worship Him. That is a straight path."' 3:52

And when Jesus observed that they had no faith, he said: 'Who will help me in the cause of God?'

The disciples replied: 'We are God's helpers. We believe in God, and bear witness that we are Muslims. Lord, we believe in Your revelations and follow the apostle. Count us among Your witnesses.'

They contrived, and God contrived; God is the supreme Contriver. God said: 'Jesus, I am about to claim you back and lift you up to Me. I shall cleanse you of the unbelievers and exalt your followers above them till the Day of Resurrection. Then to Me you shall all return and I shall judge your dissensions. To the unbelievers I shall mete out grievous punishment in this world and in the world to come: there shall be none to help them. As for those that have faith and do good works, He will give them their rewards in full. God does not love the wrongdoers.'

This revelation, and the Wise Admonition, We recite to you. Jesus can be compared to Adam in the sight of God. He created him from dust and then said to him: 'Be,' and he was. 3:58

This is the Truth from your Lord: therefore do not doubt it. To those that dispute with you concerning him after the knowledge you have received, say: 'Come, let us gather our sons and your sons, our wives and your wives, our people and your people. We will then fervently pray and call down the curse of God on the liars.'

Surely this is the true story. There is no deity but God. And surely it is God who is the Almighty, the Wise One.

If they pay no heed, God surely knows the evil-doers.

Say: 'People of the Book, let us come to a fair agreement between us: that we will worship none but God, that we will associate none with Him, and that none of us shall set up mortals as deities besides God.' 3:64

If they turn away, say: 'Bear witness, then, that we are Muslims.'

3:65   People of the Book, why do you argue about Abraham when both the Torah and the Gospel were not revealed till after him? Have you no sense?

Indeed, you have argued about things of which you have some knowledge; must you now argue about that of which you have no knowledge? God knows, but you know not.

Abraham was neither Jew nor Christian. He was a devout Muslim. And he was no idolater. Surely those who are nearest to Abraham are those who followed him, this Prophet, and the true believers. God is the guardian of the faithful. Some of the People of the Book wish to mislead you; but they mislead none but themselves, unaware though they are.

People of the Book! Why do you deny God's revelations when you can clearly see?

People of the Book! Why do you confound Truth with falsehood, and knowingly hide the Truth?

3:72   Some of the People of the Book say: 'Believe in that which is revealed to the faithful in the morning and deny it at the end of the day, so that they may recant. Believe in none except those that follow your own religion.' (Say: 'The only guidance is God's guidance!') 'Do not believe that anyone will be given the like of that which you were given, or that they will ever dispute with you in your Lord's presence.'

Say: 'Grace is in the hands of God: He bestows it on whom He will. And God is munificent and all-knowing. He is merciful only to whom He will. God is He whose grace is infinite.'

Among the People of the Book there are some who, if you trust them with a heap of gold, will return it to you intact; and some who, if you trust them with one dinar, will not hand it back unless you demand it with importunity. For they say: 'We are not bound to keep faith with Gentiles.' And they knowingly utter falsehood against God. Indeed, those that are true to their covenant and fear God know that God loves those that fear Him.

3:77   Those that sell God's covenant and their own oaths for a paltry price shall have no share in the world to come. God will neither speak to them nor look at them on the Day of Resurrection; nor will He purify them: woeful punishment awaits them.

And there are some among them who twist their tongues 3:78 when quoting the Scriptures, so that you may think it from the Scriptures, whereas it is not from the Scriptures. They say: 'This is from God,' whereas it is not from God. And they knowingly utter falsehood against God.

No mortal to whom God has given the Book and wisdom and prophethood would say to people: 'Worship me instead of God.' But rather: 'Be devoted masters, for you have taught and studied the Book.' Nor would he enjoin you to adopt the angels and the prophets as deities; for would he enjoin you to be unbelievers after you have become Muslims?

And when God made His covenant with the prophets: 'Here is the Book and the wisdom which I have given you. An apostle will then come forth to confirm them. You shall believe in him and you shall help him.' And He said: 'Will you affirm this and accept the burden I have laid on you in these terms?'

They replied: 'We do affirm.'

'Then bear witness,' He said, 'and I will bear witness with you. He that hereafter turns away is a transgressor.'

Are they seeking a religion other than God's, when every 3:83 soul in the heavens and the earth has submitted as a Muslim, willingly or with reluctance? To Him shall they be recalled.

Say: 'We believe in God and what was revealed to us; in that which was revealed to Abraham and Ishmael, to Isaac and Jacob and the tribes; and in that which was given to Moses and Jesus and the prophets by their Lord. We discriminate against none of them. To Him we submit as Muslims.'

He that follows a religion other than Islām, it will not save him[1] and in the world to come he will surely be among the lost.

How will God guide people who lapsed into unbelief after embracing the Faith and acknowledging the Apostle as true, and after receiving veritable proofs? And God does not guide the wrongdoers. Their reward will be the curse of God, the 3:87

---

1. Literally, will not be accepted from him.

3:88 angels, and mankind all; under it shall they abide for ever. Their punishment shall not be mitigated, nor shall they be reprieved; except those who afterwards repent and mend their ways; for surely God is forgiving and compassionate.

But those that recant after they had believed and grow in unbelief, their repentance shall not be accepted; these are the truly erring ones.

As for those that recant and die unbelievers, no ransom shall be accepted from any of them: be it as much gold as would fill the earth entire. Woeful punishment awaits them; and none shall help them.

You shall never attain righteousness until you give in alms what you dearly cherish. Whatever you give, it shall be known to God.

All food was lawful to the Israelites except what Israel forbade himself before the Torah was revealed. Say: 'Bring the Torah and read it, if what you say be true.'

Those that after this invent falsehood about God are the real transgressors.

3:95 Say: 'God has declared the Truth. Follow the faith of Abraham. He was an upright man, never an idolater.'

The first temple ever to be built for mankind was that at Bakkah,[1] a blessed site, a beacon for the nations. Therein are veritable signs and the spot where Abraham stood. Whoever enters it is safe. Pilgrimage to the House is a duty to God for all who can make the journey. As for the unbelievers, God can surely do without them all.

Say: 'People of the Book, why do you deny God's revelations? God is witness of what you do.'

Say: 'People of the Book, why do you debar believers from the path of God and seek to make it crooked when you have witnessed all? God is never heedless of what you do.'

Believers, if you obey a group from among those who were given the Book, they will turn you back after your faith 3:101 into unbelievers. And how can you disbelieve when God's revelations are recited to you and His own apostle is in your

1. Another name for Mecca.

midst? He that holds fast to God shall surely be guided to a straight path.

Believers, fear God as you rightly should, and die only as 3:102 Muslims. Cling one and all to the Faith[1] of God and never be divided. Remember the favour God has bestowed upon you: how, after your enmity, He united your hearts, so that you are now brothers through His grace; and how, when you were on the brink of an abyss of fire, He delivered you from it. God thus makes plain to you His revelations, that you may be rightly guided.

And of you let there become a community that shall call for righteousness, enjoin justice, and forbid the reprehensible. Such are those that will surely thrive.

Do not follow the example of those who became divided and opposed to each other after veritable proofs had been given them. Grievous punishment awaits them, on the day when some faces will be bright with joy and other faces blackened. The black-faced will be asked: 'Did you recant after embracing the true Faith? Taste then the scourge, for you were unbelievers!' As for those whose faces will be bright, in God's mercy shall they abide for ever.

Such are God's revelations; We recite them to you in Truth. 3:108 God desires no injustice to mankind. His is all that the heavens and the earth contain. To God shall all things return.

You are the noblest community ever raised up for people. You enjoin justice and forbid the reprehensible and believe in God.

Had the People of the Book accepted the Faith, it would surely have been better for them. Some are true believers, but most of them are ungodly.

If they harm you, they can cause you but little hurt; and if they fight you they will turn their backs and run away. Then there shall be none to help them. Servility shall be 3:112 stamped upon them wherever they are found, unless they make a covenant with God and a covenant with man. They have provoked God's ire, and wretchedness is stamped upon

1. Literally, rope.

them: because they disbelieved God's revelations and slew the prophets unjustly; and because they were rebels and transgressors.

3:113   Yet they are not all alike. There is among the People of the Book an upright community who all night long recite God's revelations and bow down in worship; who believe in God and the Last Day; who enjoin justice, and forbid the reprehensible, and strive to do good works. These are among the righteous; whatever good they do, its reward shall not be denied them. God well knows those that fear Him.

As for the unbelievers, neither their riches nor their children shall in the least protect them from the scourge of God. They are the inmates of the Fire, wherein shall they abide for ever. The wealth they spend in this world can be compared to a freezing wind that smites the tillage of people who have wronged themselves, laying it waste. God is not unjust to them; they are unjust to their own souls.

3:118   Believers, do not make friends with any but your own people. They will spare no pains to corrupt you; they desire nothing but your ruin; their hatred is evident from what they utter with their mouths, but greater is the hatred which their bosoms conceal.

We have made plain to you Our revelations; perchance you will understand.

Behold how you love them and they do not love you; because you believe in the Book entire.

When they meet you they say: 'We believe.' But when alone, they bite their fingertips with rage. Say: 'May you perish in your rage! God has knowledge of your innermost thoughts.'

If you are blessed with something good it grieves them: but if something bad befalls you they rejoice. If you persevere and fear God, their machinations will not a whit harm you. God has full knowledge of what they do.

3:121   Remember when you[1] left your people at an early hour to

---

1. Muḥammad.

lead the faithful to their battle-posts.[1] And God heard all and
knew all. Two of your battalions became faint-hearted, but   3:122
God was their protector. In God let the faithful put their
trust.

God had already given you victory at Badr when you were
helpless. Therefore fear God. Perchance you will give thanks.

You said to the believers: 'Is it not enough that your Lord
should send down three thousand angels to help you?'

Yes! If you have patience and fear God; and if they suddenly attack you, your Lord will send to your aid five thousand
angels splendidly accoutred.

God designed this to be but good news for you, so that
your hearts might be comforted (victory comes only from
God, the Almighty, the Wise One) and that He might cut off
the flank of the unbelievers or put them to flight, that they
might withdraw defeated.

It is no concern of yours whether He will forgive or punish   3:128
them. Wrongdoers they surely are. His is all that the heavens
and the earth contain. He pardons whom He will and punishes whom He pleases. God is forgiving and compassionate.

Believers, do not live on usury, doubling your wealth many
times over. Have fear of God, that you may prosper. Guard
yourselves against the Fire, prepared for unbelievers. Obey
God and the Apostle that you may find mercy. Vie with each
other to earn forgiveness from your Lord and a Paradise as
vast as the heavens and the earth, prepared for the righteous:
those who give, alike in prosperity and in adversity; who curb
their anger and pardon their fellow men (God loves the charitable); who, if they commit a lewd act or wrong their souls,
remember God and seek forgiveness for their sins (for who
but God can forgive sins?) and do not knowingly persist in
their misdeeds. These shall be rewarded with forgiveness   3:136
from their Lord and with Gardens watered by running brooks,
wherein shall they abide for ever. And blessed is the reward of
those who do good works.

---

1. The allusion is to the Battle of 'Uhud, in which the Muslims were
   defeated by the Quraysh of Mecca.

3:137 . Numerous were the cults that came and went before you. Roam the earth and behold what was the fate of those who disbelieved.

This is a declaration to the people: a guide and an admonition to the righteous. Do not waver and do not despair. Have faith and you shall triumph.

If once a defeat hit you, the foe was hit by a like defeat. These vicissitudes We alternate among people, that God may know the true believers and choose martyrs from among you: God does not love the wrongdoers; and that God may test the faithful and annihilate the infidels.

Did you suppose that you would enter Paradise before God knew which of you had fought and which of you endured with fortitude? You used to wish for death before you met it, and now you behold what it is like. Muḥammad is but an apostle: other apostles have passed away before him. If he should die or be slain, will you recant? He that recants will in no way harm God. And God will recompense the thankful.

3:145 And it is not for a soul to die except with God's will: upon a time decreed. He that desires the reward of this world shall have it; and he that desires the reward of the life to come shall have it also. We will recompense the thankful.

Many a large army fought by the side of its prophet. They were never daunted by whatever befell them on the path of God: they neither weakened nor cringed abjectly. God loves the steadfast. Their only words were: 'Lord, forgive us our sins and our excesses; make us firm of foot and give us victory over the unbelievers.' Therefore God gave them the reward of this life, and the glorious recompense of the life to come; God loves the righteous.

You believers! If you yield to the infidels they will drag you back to unbelief and you will return headlong to perdition. But God is your protector, and He is the best of helpers.

We will cast terror into the hearts of the unbelievers, because they serve other deities besides God for whom He has revealed no sanction. The Fire shall be their dwelling; and evil is the wrongdoers' dwelling.

3:152 Surely God fulfilled His pledge to you when, by His leave, you defeated them. But afterwards your courage failed you; discord reigned among you and you disobeyed the Apostle after he had brought you within sight of what you wished for. Some among you wanted this world; and some wanted the world to come. He allowed you to be defeated in order to test you. But now He has pardoned you, for God is gracious to the faithful.

Remember how you fled in panic while the Apostle at your rear was calling out to you. Therefore He paid you back with tribulation for every vexation, that you might not grieve for what you missed or what befell you. God is cognizant of what you do. 3:153

Then, after tribulation, He let peace fall upon you – a sleep which overtook some among you, while others lay troubled by their own fancies, thinking unjust and foolish thoughts about God. 3:154

'Have we any say in the matter?' they ask.

Say: '*All* is in the hands of God.'

They conceal in their minds what they do not reveal to you.

They complain: 'Had we had any say in the matter, we should not have been slain here.'

Say: 'Had you stayed in your homes, those of you who were destined to be slain would have died in their beds; for it was God's will to test what was in your bosoms and to scrutinize what was in your hearts. God has full knowledge of one's innermost thoughts.'

Those of you who ran away on the day the two armies met[1] must have been seduced by Satan on account of some evil they had done. But now God has pardoned them; God is forgiving and lenient.

Believers, do not follow the example of the infidels, who say of their brothers when they meet death abroad or in battle: 'Had they stayed with us they would not have died, nor would they have been killed.' God will turn that into a sigh in their hearts. God has power over life and death, and God is ever observant of what you do. 3:156

---

1. In the Battle of 'Uḥud.

3:157 If you should be slain in the cause of God or die, God's forgiveness and His mercy would surely be better than the riches they amass. And if you should die or be slain, before God shall you all be herded.

It was thanks to God's mercy that you[1] dealt so leniently with them. Had you been cruel or hard-hearted, they would have surely deserted you. Pardon them and implore God to forgive them. Take counsel with them in the conduct of affairs; and when you are resolved, put your trust in God. God loves those that are trustful.

And if God helps you, none can overcome you; if He abandons you, who then can help you after Him? Therefore in God let the faithful put their trust.

No prophet would steal; for anyone that steals shall on the Day of Resurrection bring with him that which he has stolen. Then shall every soul be paid what it has earned: none shall be wronged.

3:162 Can the man who seeks to please God be compared to him who has incurred God's anger? Hell shall be his home, evil his fate.

Varied are the rewards of God. God is cognizant of all their actions.

God has surely been gracious to the faithful in sending them an apostle of their own to recite to them His revelations, to purify them, and to instruct them in the Book and in wisdom; for before that they surely were in monstrous error.

When a disaster befell you after you had yourselves inflicted losses twice as heavy, you said: 'Whose fault was that?'

Say: 'It was your own doing. God has power over all things. And the misfortune which befell you when the two armies met was ordained by God, so that He might know the true 3:167 believers and know the hypocrites.'

And when they were told: 'Come, fight for the cause of God and defend yourselves,' they said: 'If we only knew how to fight, we would surely follow you.'

1. Muḥammad.

46

On that day they were nearer unbelief than faith. Their words belied their intentions: but God knew their secret thoughts. Such were the men who, as they sat at home, said of their brothers: 'Had they listened to us, they would not have been slain.' 3:168

Say: 'Ward off death from yourselves, then, if what you say be true!'

Never think that those who were slain in the cause of God are dead. They are alive, and well provided for by their Lord; pleased with what God of His own bounty has given them; and rejoicing that those they left behind, who have not yet joined them, shall have nothing to fear or to regret; rejoicing in God's grace and bounty. God will not deny the faithful their reward.

As for the men who after their defeat answered the call of God and the Apostle, those of them that do what is right and fear God shall be richly recompensed. They are those who, when people said to them: 'The people have mustered a great force against you: fear them,' grew more tenacious in their faith and said: 'Sufficient for us is God, the best of guardians.'

Thus did they earn God's grace and bounty, and no harm befell them. For they had striven to please God, and God's bounty is infinite. 3:174

It is Satan that causes his followers to be feared. But have no fear of them, and fear Me, if you are true believers. Do not grieve for those that rush back headlong to disbelief; in no way will they harm God. God intends to give them no share in the Hereafter. And grievous punishment awaits them.

Those that barter their faith for unbelief will in no way harm God. Woeful punishment awaits them.

Let not the unbelievers think We prolong their days for their own good; We give them respite only that they may commit more grievous sins. Shameful punishment awaits them.

It was not God's aim to leave the faithful in their present plight, but only to tell the evil from the good. Nor was God to reveal to you what is hidden. But God chooses those of His apostles whom He will. Therefore have faith in God and His 3:179

47

apostles; for if you have faith and fear God, your recompense shall be rich indeed.

3:180 Let not those who stingily hoard the wealth which God has given them out of His bounty think it good for them: rather it is an evil thing for them. They shall be shackled round with what they hoarded on the Day of Resurrection. It is God who shall inherit the heavens and the earth, and God is cognizant of what you do.

God has surely heard the words of those who said: 'God is poor, but we are rich.' Their words We will record, and their slaying of the prophets unjustly. We shall say: 'Taste now the torment of the Conflagration. This is the reward of your misdeeds. God is never unjust to His servants.'

To those that say: 'God has bidden us believe in no apostle until he bring down for us an offering to be consumed by fire,'[1] say: 'Other apostles before me have come to you with veritable signs and worked the miracle you asked for. Why did you slay them, if what you say be true?'

3:184 If they deny you, other apostles have been denied before you, although they came with veritable signs, psalms, and the light-giving Book.

Every soul shall taste death. You shall receive your rewards only on the Day of Resurrection. Whoever is spared the Fire and is admitted to Paradise will surely triumph; for the life of this world is but a frivolous show of vanity.

You shall be sorely tried in the matter of your possessions and your persons, and will hear much that is hurtful from those who were given the Book before you, and from the pagans. But if you endure with fortitude and fear God, your triumph shall be assured.

3:187 And when God made a covenant with those to whom the Book was given He said: 'Proclaim it to the people and suppress it not.' But they cast the Book over their backs and sold it for a paltry price. Evil was their bargain.

---

1. The reference is probably to the story of Elijah and the prophets of Baal (1 Kings 18:17–46).

Never think that those who rejoice in what they did 3:188
and wish to be praised for what they failed to do – never
think they will escape the torment; woeful torment awaits
them.

God has sovereignty over the heavens and the earth. And
God has power over all things.

In the creation of the heavens and the earth, and in the
alternation of night and day, surely there are signs for those
that are of good sense possessed; those that remember God
when standing, sitting, and lying down, and reflect on the
creation of the heavens and the earth, saying: 'Lord, You have
not created this in vain. Glory be to You! Save us from the
torment of the Fire. Lord, those whom You will cast into the
Fire You will disgrace: none will help the wrongdoers. Lord,
we have heard a summoner summoning to the Faith, saying:
"Believe in your Lord," and we believed. Lord, forgive us our
sins and purge us of our evil deeds and claim us back with the
righteous. Lord, grant us what You promised through Your
apostles, and do not hold us up to shame on the Day of Resurrection. You never fail the time decreed.'

Their Lord will answer them: 'I will deny none among you, 3:195
male or female, the reward of their labours. The one of you is
as the other.'

Those that fled their land and were expelled from their
homes, and suffered persecution for My sake and fought
and were slain: I shall surely acquit them of their evil deeds
and admit them into Gardens watered by running brooks, as
a recompense from God; God dispenses the richest recompense.

Never be deluded by the goings-on of the unbelievers in
the land: a little enjoyment – then Hell shall be their home: an
evil resting-place. But for those that fear God, theirs shall be
Gardens watered by running brooks, wherein shall they abide
for ever: a gracious welcome from God. And that which is in
store with God is surely better for the righteous.

Some there are among the People of the Book who truly 3:199
believe in God, and in what has been revealed to you and what
was revealed to them: they humble themselves before God

and do not sell God's revelations for a trifling price. These shall be rewarded by their Lord. Swift is God's reckoning.

3:200   Believers, be patient and forbear; stand firm in your faith and fear God, that you may succeed.

WOMEN

In the Name of God, the Merciful, the Compassionate

4:1   YOU PEOPLE! Fear your Lord, who created you from a single soul. From that soul He created its spouse and through them He bestrewed the earth with countless men and women.

Fear God, in whose name you plead with one another, and honour the mothers who bore you. God is ever watching you.

Give orphans the property which belongs to them. Do not exchange their valuables for worthless things or cheat them of their possessions; for this would surely be a grievous sin. If you fear that you cannot treat orphans[1] with fairness, then you may marry other women who seem good to you: two, three, or four. But if you fear that you cannot maintain equality among them, marry one only or any slave-girls you may own. This will make it easier for you to avoid injustice.

4:4   Give women their dowry as a free gift; but if they willingly choose to make over to you a part of it, you may enjoy it as lawfully yours.

Do not give the feeble-minded the property with which God has charged you for their support; but maintain and clothe them with its proceeds, and speak kind words to them.

4:6   Put orphans to the test until they reach a marriageable age. If you find them capable of sound judgement, hand over to them their property, and do not cheat them of it by squandering it before they come of age.

Let not the rich guardian touch the property of his orphan ward; and let him who is poor use no more than a fair portion of it for his own advantage.

1. Orphan girls.

When you hand over to them their property, call in some witnesses to be present; sufficient is God's reckoning.

Men shall have a share in what their parents and kin leave; and women shall have a share in what their parents and kin leave: whether it be little or much, they shall be entitled to a share decreed. 4:7

If relatives, orphans, or needy men are present at the division of an inheritance, give them, too, a share of it, and speak kind words to them.

Let those who are solicitous about the welfare of their young children after their own death take care not to wrong orphans. Let them fear God and speak for justice.

Those that devour the property of orphans unjustly, do swallow fire into their bellies; they shall burn in a mighty conflagration.

God has thus enjoined you concerning your children: 4:11

A male shall inherit twice as much as a female. If there be more than two girls, they shall have two-thirds of the inheritance; but if there be one only, she shall inherit the half. Parents shall inherit a sixth each, if the deceased have a child; but if he leave no child and his parents be his heirs, his mother shall have a third. If he have brothers, his mother shall have a sixth after payment of any legacy he may have bequeathed or any debt he may have owed.

You may wonder whether your parents or your children are more beneficial to you. But this is a decree from God; surely God is all-knowing and wise.

And you shall inherit the half of your wives' estate if they die childless. If they leave children, a quarter of their estate shall be yours after payment of any legacy they may have bequeathed or any debt they may have owed. 4:12

Your wives shall inherit one-quarter of your estate if you die childless. If you leave children, they shall inherit one-eighth of your estate, after payment of any legacy you may have bequeathed or any debt you may have owed.

If a man or a woman leave neither children nor parents and have a brother or a sister, they shall each inherit one-sixth. If there be more, they shall equally share the third of the estate, after payment of any legacy he may have bequeathed or any debt he may have owed, without prejudice to the rights of the heirs. That is a commandment from God. God is all-knowing, and gracious.

4:13 Such are the bounds set by God. He that obeys God and His apostle shall be admitted by Him into Gardens watered by running brooks, wherein shall they abide for ever. That is the supreme triumph. But he that defies God and His apostle and transgresses His bounds, shall be cast into a Fire wherein he shall abide for ever. Shameful punishment awaits him.

If any of your women commit a lewd act, call in four witnesses from among yourselves against them; if they testify to their guilt, confine them to their houses till death overtakes them or till God finds another way for them.

If two men among you commit a lewd act, punish them both. If they repent and mend their ways, let them be. Surely God is forgiving and compassionate.

4:17 God pardons those who commit evil in ignorance and then quickly turn to Him in penitence. These God will pardon. God is all-knowing and wise. But He will not pardon those who do evil and, when death comes to any of them, he says: 'Now I repent!' Nor those who die unbelievers: for them We have prepared a woeful scourge.

Believers, it is unlawful for you to inherit the women of your deceased kinsmen against their will, or to bar them from remarrying, in order that you may force them to give up a part of what you have given them, unless they be guilty of a proven lewd act. Live with them in modest conduct; for even if you dislike them, it may well be that you dislike a thing which God has meant for your own abundant good.

If you wish to replace one wife with another, do not take anything from the dowry you gave her even if it be a talent. That would be improper and a veritable sin; for how can you take it back when you have lain with each other and entered into a firm contract?

4:22 You shall not marry the women whom your fathers married: all previous such marriages excepted. That was an evil practice, indecent and abominable.

Forbidden to you are your mothers, your daughters, your 4:23
sisters, your paternal and maternal aunts, the daughters of
your brothers and sisters, your foster-mothers, your
foster-sisters, the mothers of your wives, your stepdaughters
who are in your charge, born of the wives with whom you
have lain (it is no offence for you to marry your stepdaughters
if you have not consummated your marriage with their mothers), and the wives of your own begotten sons.[1] You are
forbidden also to marry two sisters at one and the same time:
all previous such marriages excepted. Surely God is forgiving
and compassionate. Also married women, except those whom
you own as slaves. Such is the decree of God. All women
other than these are lawful for you, provided you court them
with your wealth in modest conduct, not in fornication. Give
them their dowry for the enjoyment you have had of them as
a duty; but it shall be no offence for you to make any other
agreement among yourselves after you have fulfilled your
duty. Surely God is all-knowing and wise.

If any one of you cannot afford to marry a believing free 4:25
woman, let him marry a slave-girl who is a believer (God best
knows your faith: you are born one of another). Marry them
with their masters' permission and give them their dowry in
all justice, provided they are honourable and chaste and have
not courted other men. If after marriage they commit a lewd
act, they shall suffer half the penalty inflicted upon free
women. Such is the provision for those of you who fear
impropriety: but if you abstain, it will be better for you. God
is forgiving and compassionate.

God desires to make this clear to you and to guide you
along the paths of those who have gone before you, and to
pardon you. God is all-knowing and wise.

And God wishes to pardon you, but those who follow their
own appetites wish to see you stray grievously into error. God
wishes to lighten your burdens, for Man was created weak.

Believers, do not consume your wealth among yourselves 4:29
in vanity, but rather trade with it by mutual consent.

---

1. Cf. Leviticus 18.

Do not kill one another.[1] Surely God is compassionate to
4:30 you, but he that does that through wickedness and injustice
We shall burn in fire. Surely that is[2] easy enough for God.

If you avoid the enormities you are forbidden, We shall
pardon your misdeeds and usher you in with all honour. Do
not covet the favours by which God has exalted some among
you above others. Men shall be rewarded according to their
deserts, and women shall be rewarded according to their deserts. Rather implore God to bestow on you His bounty. Surely
God has knowledge of all things.

To every parent and kin We have appointed heirs who will
inherit from them. As for those with whom you have entered
into agreements, let them, too, have their share. Surely God
bears witness to all things.

4:34 Men have authority over women because God has made
the one superior to the other, and because they spend their
wealth to maintain them. Good women are obedient. They
guard their unseen parts because God has guarded them. As
for those from whom you fear disobedience, admonish them,
and forsake them in beds[3] apart, and beat them. Then if they
obey you, take no further action against them. Surely God is
high, supreme.

If you fear a breach between a man and his wife, appoint
an arbiter from his people and an arbiter from her people. If
they wish to be reconciled, God will bring them together
again. Surely God is all-knowing and wise.

Serve God and associate none with Him. Show kindness
to parents and to kin, to orphans and to the destitute, to near
and distant neighbours, to those that keep company with you,
to the traveller in need, and to the slaves you own. God does
4:37 not love the arrogant and the boastful, who are themselves
niggardly and enjoin people to be niggardly; who conceal that
which God of His bounty has given them (We have prepared

1. Literally, do not kill yourselves.
2. Literally, was; in the language of the Koran, the use of *kana* is for
emphasis, not as a form of past tense.
3. Or: bedrooms.

a shameful punishment for the unbelievers); and who spend   4:38
their wealth only to be seen by people, believing neither in
God nor in the Last Day. He that chooses Satan for his friend,
an evil friend has he.

What could harm them if they believed in God and the
Last Day and gave in alms from that which God bestowed on
them? God surely knows them well.

God will wrong none by as much as the weight of an atom.
A good deed He will repay two-fold. Of His own bounty He
will bestow a rich recompense.

How will it be when We produce a witness from each community and call upon you to testify against them? On that day
those who disbelieved and disobeyed the Apostle will wish
that they were levelled with the dust; they cannot hide from
God any word that is spoken.

Believers, do not approach your prayers when you are   4:43
drunk, until you know what you are saying; nor when you
are unclean – unless you are travelling the road – until you
have washed yourselves. If you are sick or on a journey, or if,
when you have relieved yourselves or had intercourse with
women, you can find no water, take some clean sand and
rub your faces and your hands with it. God will surely pardon
and forgive.

Consider those to whom a portion of the Book was given.
They purchase error for themselves and wish to see you go
astray. And God best knows your enemies. Sufficient is God
as a protector, and sufficient is God as a helper.

Among those who follow the Jewish Faith are some who
take words out of their context and say:[1] 'We hear, but will
disobey. May you be bereft of hearing! *Rā 'inā!*' – thus distort-
ing the phrase with their tongues and reviling the Religion.
But if they said: 'We hear and obey: hear us and *unzurnā*,'[2]
it would be better and more proper for them. But God has
cursed them in their unbelief. They have no faith, except a
few.

You to whom the Book was given! Believe in that which   4:47

---

1. To Muḥammad.   2. See p. 10, note 1.

We have revealed, confirming your own, before We obliterate some faces and turn them backward, or curse them as We cursed the Sabbath-breakers. What God ordains shall be accomplished.

4:48 God will not forgive those who serve other deities besides Him; but He will forgive whom He will for other sins. He that serves other deities besides God is guilty of a heinous sin.

Do but consider those who think themselves pure. God purifies whom He will. They shall not be wronged by as much as the husk of a date-stone.

Behold how they invent falsehoods about God; this in itself is a most grievous sin.

Consider those to whom a portion of the Book was given. They believe in idols and false gods and say of the infidels: 'These are better guided than those who believe.' These are they whom God has cursed; and he who is cursed by God has none to help him.

4:53 Will they have a share in sovereignty? If so, they will not give people so much as the speck on a date-stone.

Or do they envy others what God has of His bounty given them? We gave Abraham's descendants the Book and wisdom, and an illustrious kingdom. Some among them believe in him,[1] and some reject him. Sufficient scourge is the fire of Hell.

Those that deny Our revelations We will burn in fire. No sooner will their skins be consumed than We shall give them other skins, so that they may taste the torment. Surely God is mighty and wise.

As for those that believe and do good works, We shall admit them into Gardens watered by running brooks, wherein, wedded to chaste spouses, shall they abide for ever. To a cool shade shall We admit them.

4:58 God commands you to hand back your trusts to their rightful owners, and, when you pass judgement among people, to judge with fairness. Noble is that to which God exhorts you. Surely God hears all and observes all.

1. Muhammad.

Believers, obey God and obey the Apostle and those in   4:59
authority among you. Should you disagree about anything
refer it to God and the Apostle, if you believe in God and the
Last Day. This will in the end be better and more just.

Mark those who profess to believe in what has been
revealed to you and what was revealed before you. They seek
the judgement of the devil, although they were bidden to
deny him. Satan would lead them far into error.

If they are told: 'Come to be judged by that which God has
revealed and by the Apostle,' you see the hypocrites reject you
vehemently. But how would it be if some disaster befell them
on account of what their hands committed? They would
come to you swearing by God that 'we desired nothing but
amity and conciliation.' But God knows what their hearts
conceal. Let them be. Admonish them and eloquently rebuke
them.

We have sent forth apostles only so that they are obeyed by
God's leave. If, when they wronged themselves, they had
come to you imploring God's forgiveness, and if the Apostle
had sought forgiveness for them, they would have found that
God pardons and is compassionate.

But, by your Lord, they will not believe until they seek your   4:65
arbitration in their disputes. Then they will not doubt the justice of your verdicts and will submit entirely.

And had We commanded them: 'Lay down your lives,' or
'Flee from your homes,' only a few would have complied. Yet,
had they done what they were admonished to do, it would
have been better for them and their faith would have been
strengthened. We would have bestowed on them of Our grace
a rich recompense and guided them to a straight path.

And he that obeys God and the Apostle shall dwell with
the prophets and the saints, the martyrs and the righteous
whom God has favoured. Gracious companions will be those.

Such is God's bounty; and sufficient is God's infinite knowledge.

Believers, be ever on your guard: march in detachments or
in one body. Someone among you is sure to lag behind, so that   4:72
if a disaster befell you, he would say: 'God was gracious to

4:73 me; I was not present with them.' But if, by God's grace, you were successful, he would surely say, as though there was no friendship between you and him: 'Would that I had been with them! I should have won a great victory.'

Let those who would exchange the life of this world for the Hereafter, fight for the cause of God; whoever fights for the cause of God, whether he be slain or he triumph, on him We shall bestow a rich recompense.

And how should you not fight for the cause of God, and for the helpless old men, women, and children[1] who say: 'Deliver us, Lord, from this city of wrongdoers; send forth to us a guardian from Your presence; send to us from Your presence one that will help us'?

The true believers fight for the cause of God, but the infidels fight for the devil. Fight then the friends of Satan; Satan's cunning is weak indeed.

4:77 Mark those who were told: 'Lay down your arms; recite your prayers and render the alms levy.' When they were ordered to fight, some of them feared man as much as they feared God or even more. 'Lord,' they said, 'why do You bid us fight? Could you not give us a brief respite?'

Say: 'Trifling are the pleasures of this life. Better is the life to come for those who fear God. You shall not be wronged by as much as the husk of a date-stone. Wherever you may be, death will overtake you: though you put yourselves in lofty towers.'

When they are blessed with good fortune, they say: 'This is from God.' But when evil befalls them, they say: 'It was your[2] fault.'

Say: 'All is from God!'

What has come over these people that they can hardly understand a word?

4:79 Whatever good befalls you,[3] it is from God: and whatever ill befalls you is from yourself.

We have sent you forth as an apostle to mankind. Sufficient is God as a witness.

---

1. In Mecca.   2. Muḥammad's.   3. Man.

He that obeys the Apostle has assuredly obeyed God. As 4:80
for those that pay no heed, We have not sent you to be their
keeper.

They promise obedience: but as soon as they leave your
presence a band of them plot in secret to do otherwise. God
takes note of all their plots. Therefore let them be, and put
your trust in God. Sufficient is God as a guardian.

Will they not ponder on the Koran? If it had come from
other than God, they could have surely found in it many con-
tradictions.

When they hear any news, good or bad, they at once make
it known to all; whereas if they reported it to the Apostle and
to those in authority among them, those who sought news
could learn it from them. But for God's grace and mercy, all
but a few of you would have followed Satan.

Therefore fight for the cause of God. You are accountable
for none but yourself. Rouse the faithful: perchance God will
overthrow the might of the unbelievers. Mightier is God and
more terrible is His retribution.

He that mediates in a good cause shall gain by his media- 4:85
tion; and he that mediates in a bad cause shall be held
accountable for its evil. God surely has control over all things.

If a man greets you, let your greeting be better than his – or
at least return it. God surely keeps count of all things.

God: there is no god but Him. He will surely gather you all
together on the Day of Resurrection of which there is no
doubt. And who has a truer word than God?

Why are you thus divided concerning the hypocrites, when
God has cast them off on account of their misdeeds? Would
you guide those whom God has confounded? He whom God
confounds you cannot guide.

They would have you disbelieve as they themselves have
disbelieved, so that you may be all alike. Do not befriend them
until they have fled their homes in God's cause. If they desert
you, seize them and slay them wherever you find them. Look
for neither friend nor helper among them, except those who 4:90
seek refuge with your allies or come over to you because
their hearts forbid them to fight you or to fight their own

people. Had God pleased, He would have given them power over you, so that they would have taken arms against you. Therefore, if they keep away from you and cease their hostility and offer you peace, God bids you not to harm them.

4:91 Others you will find who seek security from you as well as from their own people. Whenever they are called back to sedition they plunge into it headlong. If these do not keep their distance from you, if they neither offer you peace nor cease their hostilities against you, lay hold of them and slay them wherever you find them. Over such men We give you absolute authority.

It is unlawful for a believer to kill another believer, accidents excepted. He that accidentally kills a believer shall free one Muslim slave and pay blood-money to the family of the victim, unless they choose to give it away in alms. If the victim be a Muslim from a hostile tribe, the penalty shall be the freeing of one Muslim slave. But if the victim be a member of an allied tribe, then blood-money shall be paid to his family and a Muslim slave set free. He that lacks the means shall fast two consecutive months. Such is the penance imposed by God: God is all-knowing and wise.

4:93 He that kills a believer by design shall burn in Hell for ever. And he shall incur the ire of God, who will lay His curse on him and prepare for him a mighty scourge.

Believers, if you go to fight for the cause of God, show discernment and do not say to him that offers you peace: 'You are not a believer,' seeking the chance booty of this world; for with God there are abundant gains. Such was your custom in days gone by, but now God has bestowed on you His grace. Therefore show discernment; God is cognizant of what you do.

The believers who stay at home – apart from those that suffer from a grave disability – are not the equals of those who fight for the cause of God with their goods and their persons. God has exalted in rank those who fight with their goods and their persons above those who stay at home. God has promised all a good reward; but far richer is the recompense of 4:96 those who fight for Him: ranks of His own bestowal, forgiveness, and mercy. Surely God is forgiving and compassionate.

The angels will ask those whom they claim back while   4:97
steeped in sin: 'What were you doing?' 'We were oppressed in
the land,' they will reply. They will say: 'Was not the earth of
God spacious enough for you to fly for refuge?' Hell shall be
the abode of these: a wretched fate!

As for the helpless men, women, and children who have
neither the strength nor the means to escape, God may pardon them: surely God pardons and forgives.

He that leaves his home in God's cause shall find many a
refuge in the land and great abundance. He that leaves his
dwelling to fight for God and His apostle and is then overtaken by death shall be recompensed by God. Surely God is
forgiving and compassionate.

It is no offence for you to shorten your prayers when travelling the road if you fear that the unbelievers may attack you.
The unbelievers are your veritable foe.

When you[1] are among them, conducting the prayers, let   4:102
one party of them rise up to pray with you, armed with their
weapons. After making their prostrations, let them withdraw
to the rear and then let another party who have not prayed
come forward and pray with you; and let these also be on their
guard, armed with their weapons. It would much please the
unbelievers if you neglected your arms and your baggage, so
that they could swoop upon you with one assault. But it is no
offence for you to lay aside your arms when overtaken by
heavy rain or stricken with an illness, although you must be
always on your guard. God has prepared a shameful punishment for the unbelievers.

When your prayers are ended, remember God standing,
sitting, and lying down. When you are safe, attend to your
prayers: for prayer is a duty incumbent on the faithful, to be
conducted at appointed times.

Seek out the enemy relentlessly. If you have suffered, they   4:104
too have suffered as you have: but you at least hope to receive
from God what they cannot hope for. Surely God is all-
knowing and wise.

1. Muḥammad.

4:105   We have revealed to you the Book with the Truth, that you may arbitrate among people by that which God has shown you. You shall not plead for the treacherous. Implore God's forgiveness: God is ever forgiving and compassionate. Nor shall you plead for those who betray their own souls; God does not love the treacherous or the sinful.

They seek to hide from people, but they cannot hide from God. He is with them when they utter in secret what does not please Him: God has knowledge of all their actions.

Yes, you may plead for them in this life, but who will plead for them with God on the Day of Resurrection? Who will be their defender?

He that does evil or wrongs his own soul and then seeks God's forgiveness, will find God forgiving and compassionate.

He that commits sin commits it against his own soul. God is all-knowing and wise.

And he that commits an offence or a crime and charges an innocent man with it, shall bear the guilt of calumny and gross injustice.

4:113   But for God's grace and mercy you would have been led astray by some among them. They lead astray none but themselves, nor can they do you any harm.

God has revealed to you the Book and wisdom and taught you what you did not know before. God's goodness to you has been great indeed.

There is no virtue in much of their counsel: only in his who enjoins charity, kindness, or peace among people. He that does this seeking to please God, on him We shall bestow a rich recompense.

He that defies the Apostle after guidance has been revealed to him, and follows a path other than that of the faithful, shall be given by Us what he has chosen. We will burn him in the fire of Hell: a wretched fate!

God will not forgive the worship of other deities besides Him. But He will forgive whom He will all other sins. He that serves other deities besides God has strayed far into error.

4:117   Rather than to Him, they pray but to females: they pray but to a rebellious Satan. God laid His curse on him, for he had *4:118* said: 'I shall entice a determined share of Your servants and shall lead them astray. I shall arouse in them vain desires and order them to slit the ears of cattle. I shall order them to tamper with God's creation.' Indeed, he that chooses Satan rather than God for his protector ruins himself beyond redemption.

He makes promises and stirs up in them vain desires; Satan makes them promises only to deceive them. Hell shall be their abode, and from it shall they find no refuge.

As for those that believe and do good works, We shall admit them into Gardens watered by running brooks, wherein shall they abide for ever. Such is God's true promise: and who has a truer word than God?

It shall not be in accordance with your wishes, nor shall it be as the People of the Book desire. He that does evil shall be requited with evil: he shall find none besides God to protect or help him. But the believers who do good works, be they men or women, shall enter Paradise. They shall not suffer the least injustice.

And who has a nobler religion than he who submits to *4:125* God, does what is right, and follows the faith of saintly Abraham, God having chosen Abraham as His friend?[1]

To God belongs all that the heavens and the earth contain. God encompasses all things.

They consult you concerning women. Say: 'God has instructed you about them, and so have the verses proclaimed to you in the Book, concerning the orphan girls whom you deny their lawful rights and refuse to marry; also regarding helpless children. He has instructed you to deal justly with orphans. Of the good you do, surely God has full knowledge.'

If a woman fear ill-treatment or desertion on the part of her husband, it shall be no offence for them to seek a mutual agreement, for agreement is best. People are prone to avarice. But if you do what is right and guard yourselves against evil, know then that God is cognizant of all your actions.

Try as you may, you cannot treat all your wives impartially. *4:129*

1. Cf. Isaiah 41:8.

63

Do not set yourself altogether against any of them, leaving her, as it were, in suspense. If you do what is right and fear God, God is forgiving and compassionate. If they separate, God will compensate each out of His own abundance: God is munificent and wise.

4:130

To God belongs all that the heavens and the earth contain. We exhort you, as We have exhorted those to whom the Book was given before you, to fear God. If you deny Him, know that to God belongs all that the heavens and the earth contain. God is self-sufficient and worthy of praise.

To God belongs all that the heavens and the earth contain. Sufficient is God as a guardian. If He pleased, He could obliterate you all, you people! and replace you by other men. This God has the power to do.

Let him who seeks the reward of this life know that it is God who dispenses the reward of both this life and the life to come; God hears all and observes all.

4:135

Believers, conduct yourselves with justice and bear true witness before God, even though it be against yourselves, your parents, or your kin. Be they rich or poor, God knows better about them both. So do not be led by passion, lest you swerve from the truth. If you distort your testimony or decline to give it, know that God is cognizant of all your actions.

Believers, have faith in God and His apostle, in the Book He has revealed to His apostle, and in the Scriptures He formerly revealed. He that denies God, His angels, His Scriptures, His apostles, and the Last Day has strayed far indeed.

Those who accept the Faith and then renounce it, who again embrace it and again deny it and grow in unbelief – God will neither forgive them nor rightly guide them.

Give warning to the hypocrites that woeful punishment awaits them: those who choose the unbelievers rather than the faithful for their friends. Are they seeking glory at their hands? Surely all glory belongs to God.

4:140

He has instructed you in the Book that if you hear God's revelations being blasphemed or ridiculed you shall not sit with them until they engage in other talk; or else you shall yourselves become like them. God will surely gather in Hell the hypocrites and the unbelievers all.

They watch your fortunes closely. If God grants you victory, they say: 'Did we not stand on your side?' And if it be the unbelievers' turn, they say to them: 'Were we not mightier than you, and did we not protect you from the faithful?' 4:141

God will judge between you on the Day of Resurrection. God will not let the unbelievers triumph over the faithful.

The hypocrites seek to deceive God, but it is He who deceives them. When they rise to pray, they stand up sluggishly: they pray only to be seen by people and remember God but little, wavering between this and that and belonging neither to these nor those. You cannot guide the man whom God has confounded.

Believers, do not choose the infidels as your allies rather than the faithful. Would you give God clear evidence against yourselves?

The hypocrites shall be cast into the lowest depths of the Fire; and you shall find none to help them: except those who repent and mend their ways, who hold fast to God and are sincere in their devotion to God – they shall be numbered with the faithful, and God will richly recompense the faithful. 4:145

And why should God punish you if you render thanks and truly believe in Him? God will surely recompense your labours, for He has full knowledge of them all.

God does not love harsh words to be openly uttered, except by the truly wronged. God hears all and knows all. Whether you do good openly or in private, whether you pardon a wrong – God pardons and is omnipotent.

Those that deny God and His apostles, and those that discriminate between God and His apostles, saying: 'We believe in some, but deny others,' thus seeking a middle way – these truly are the unbelievers; and for the unbelievers We have prepared a shameful punishment.

As for those that believe in God and His apostles and discriminate against none of them, they shall be recompensed by Him. God is ever forgiving and compassionate. 4:152

4:153 The People of the Book ask you to bring down for them a book from heaven. Of Moses they demanded a harder thing than that; they said to him: 'Show us God openly.' And for their wrongdoing the thunderbolt smote them. Then they took up the calf after clear signs had been revealed to them; yet We pardoned them that, and bestowed on Moses clear authority.

We raised the Mount above them when We made a covenant with them, and said to them: 'Enter the gates bowing down.' And We said to them: 'Do not break the Sabbath.' We took from them a solemn covenant. But they broke their covenant, denied God's revelations, and killed the prophets unjustly. They said: 'Our hearts are sealed.'

It was God who sealed their hearts, on account of their unbelief. They have no faith, except a few.

They denied the Truth and uttered a monstrous falsehood
4:157 against Mary. They declared: 'We have killed the Christ, Jesus son of Mary, the apostle of God.' They did not kill him, nor did they crucify him, but they thought they did.[1]

Those that disagreed about him were in doubt concerning him; they knew nothing about him that was not sheer conjecture; they did not kill him for certain. Rather God lifted him up to Himself; God is Almighty and wise. There is none among the People of the Book but will believe in him before his death; and on the Day of Resurrection he will bear witness against them.

Because of their iniquity, We forbade those who followed the Jewish Faith wholesome things which were formerly allowed them; because time after time they have debarred many from the path of God; because they practise usury – although they had been forbidden it – and cheat people of their possessions. Woeful punishment have We prepared for
4:162 those of them that disbelieve. But those of them that are well-grounded in knowledge, and the believers who believe in what has been revealed to you and what was revealed before you; who attend to their prayers and render the alms levy and believe in God and the Last Day – on these We shall bestow a rich recompense.

1. Or: literally, he was made to resemble another for them.

We have revealed Our will to you as We revealed it to Noah   4:163
and to the prophets who came after him; as We revealed it to
Abraham, Ishmael, Isaac, Jacob, and the tribes; to Jesus, Job,
Jonah, Aaron and Solomon; to David We gave Psalms. Apostles of whom We have already told you, and apostles of whom
We have not yet told you; God spoke directly to Moses; apostles who brought joyful tidings as well as warnings, so that
people might have no plea against God after the apostles'
coming: God is Almighty and wise.

But God bears witness, by that which He has revealed to
you, that He revealed it with His knowledge; the angels bear
witness, too. And there is no better witness than God.

Those that disbelieve and debar others from the path of
God have strayed far into error. God will not forgive those
who disbelieve and act unjustly; nor will He guide them to any
path other than the path of Hell, wherein shall they abide for
ever. Surely that is easy enough for God.

You people! The Apostle has brought you the Truth from   4:170
your Lord. Have faith and it shall be well with you. If you disbelieve: to God belongs all that the heavens and the earth
contain. God is omniscient and wise.

People of the Book,[1] do not transgress the bounds of
your religion. Speak nothing but the Truth about God. The
Christ, Jesus son of Mary, was no more than God's apostle
and His Word which He cast to Mary: a spirit from Him.
So believe in God and His apostles and do not say: 'Three.'
Forbear, and it shall be better for you. Surely God is but
one God; God forbid that He should have a son! His is all that
the heavens and the earth contain. Sufficient is God as a
patron. Christ does not disdain to be a servant of God, nor
do the angels who are nearest to Him. Those who through
arrogance disdain to worship Him shall be herded, all,
before Him.

As for those that believe and do good works, God will   4:173
bestow their rewards on them and enrich them from His own
abundance. But those who are scornful and proud He will

---

1. Christians.

sternly punish, and they will find none besides God to protect or succour them.

4:174 You people! Clear evidence has come to you from your Lord. We have sent down to you a veritable light. Those that believe in God and hold fast to Him He will admit to His mercy and to His grace; He will guide them to Him along a straight path.

4:176 They seek your guidance. Say: 'Thus God instructs you regarding those that die childless and without living parents. If a man die childless and he have a sister, she shall inherit the half of his estate. If a woman die childless, her brother shall be her sole heir. If a childless man have two sisters, they shall inherit two-thirds of his estate; but if he have both brothers and sisters, the share of the male shall be that of two females.'

God enlightens you, so that you may not err. God has knowledge of all things.

THE TABLE

In the Name of God, the Merciful, the Compassionate

5:1 BELIEVERS, BE true to your obligations. It is lawful for you to eat the flesh of all beasts other than that which is hereby announced to you. Game is forbidden while you are on the Pilgrimage. God decrees what He will.

Believers, do not violate the rites of God, or the sacred month, or the offerings or their ornaments, or those that repair to the Sacred House seeking their Lord's grace and pleasure. Once your Pilgrimage is ended, you shall be free to go hunting.

Do not allow your hatred for those who would debar you from the Holy Mosque to lead you to commit aggression. Help one another in what is good and pious, and help not one another in sin and belligerence. And fear God; God is stern in retribution.

5:3 You are forbidden carrion, blood, and the flesh of swine; also any flesh dedicated to any other than God. You are forbidden the flesh of strangled animals and of those beaten or gored to death; of those killed by a fall or mangled by beasts of prey (unless you make it clean by giving the death-stroke yourselves); also of animals sacrificed to idols.

You are forbidden to settle disputes by consulting the Arrows. That is a pernicious practice.

The unbelievers have this day abandoned all hope of vanquishing your religion. Have no fear of them: fear Me.

This day I have perfected your religion for you and completed My favour to you. I have chosen Islām to be your religion.

He that is constrained by hunger to eat of what is forbidden, not intending to commit sin, will find that God is forgiving and compassionate.

They ask you what is lawful for them. Say: 'All wholesome things are lawful for you, as well as that which you have taught the birds and beasts of prey to catch, training them as God has taught you. Eat of what they catch for you, pronouncing upon it the name of God. And fear God: swift is God's reckoning.' 5:4

Wholesome things are this day made lawful for you. The food of those to whom the Book was given[1] is lawful for you, and yours for them. 5:5

Lawful for you are the believing women and the free women from among those who were given the Book before you, provided that you give them their dowries and live in honour with them, neither committing fornication nor taking them as mistresses.

He that denies the Faith shall gain nothing from his labours; and in the world to come he will surely be among the lost.

Believers, when you rise to pray wash your faces and your hands as far as the elbow, and wipe your heads and your feet to the ankle. If you are unclean, cleanse yourselves. But if you are sick or on a journey, or if, when you have just relieved yourselves or had intercourse with women, you can find no water, take some clean sand and rub your faces and your 5:6

---

1. The Jews (but not the Christians).

hands with it. God does not wish to inconvenience you; but He seeks only to purify you and to perfect His favour to you, so that you may give thanks.

5:7 Remember God's favour to you, and the covenant with which He bound you when you said: 'We hear and obey.' Fear God; God knows your innermost thoughts.

Believers, fulfil your duties to God and bear true witness. Do not allow your hatred for other people to turn you away from justice. Deal justly; that will bring you closer to true piety. Fear God; God is cognizant of what you do.

God has promised those that believe and do good works forgiveness and a rich reward. As for those who disbelieve and deny Our revelations, they are the heirs of Hell.

Believers, remember the favour God bestowed upon you when He restrained the hands of those who sought to harm you. Fear God; in God let the faithful put their trust.

5:12 God made a covenant with the Israelites and We raised among them twelve chieftains. And God said: 'I shall be with you. If you attend to your prayers and render the alms levy; if you believe in My apostles and support them and give God a generous loan, I shall forgive you your sins and admit you to Gardens watered by running brooks. But whoever of you hereafter disbelieves will surely stray from the straight path.'

But because they broke their covenant We laid on them Our curse and hardened their hearts. They have tampered with words out of their context and forgotten much of what they were enjoined. You will ever find them deceitful, except for a few of them. But pardon them and bear with them; God loves those who do good.

And with those who said they were Christians We made a covenant, but they too have forgotten much of what they were exhorted to do. Therefore We stirred among them enmity and hatred, which shall endure till the Day of Resurrection, when God will declare to them all that they have done.

5:15 People of the Book! Our apostle has come to reveal to you much of what you have hidden of the Book, and to pardon you much. A light has surely come to you from God and a veritable Book, with which God will guide to the paths of peace those that seek to please Him; He will lead them by His will from darkness to the light; He will guide them to a straight path.

They do blaspheme, who declare: 'God is Christ, the son of Mary.' Say: 'Who could prevent God, if He so willed, from destroying Christ, the son of Mary, his mother, and all the people of the earth? God has sovereignty over the heavens and the earth and all that lies between them. He creates what He will; and God has power over all things.'

The Jews and the Christians say: 'We are the children of God and His loved ones.' Say: 'Why then does He punish you for your sins? Surely you are mortals of His own creation. He forgives whom He will and punishes whom He pleases. God has sovereignty over the heavens and the earth and all that lies between them. All shall return to Him.'

People of the Book! Our apostle has come to you with revelations after an interval which saw no apostles, lest you say: 'No one has come to give us joyful tidings or to warn us.' Now someone has come to give you joyful tidings and to warn you. God has power over all things.

Bear in mind the words of Moses to his people. He had said: 'Remember, my people, the favour God bestowed upon you. He has raised up prophets among you, made you kings, and given you that which He has given to no other nation. Enter, my people, the holy land which God has assigned for you; do not turn back, and thus lose all.'

'Moses,' they said, 'a race of giants dwells in this land; we will not set foot in it till they are gone. As soon as they are gone we will enter.'

Thereupon two God-fearing men[1] whom God had favoured said: 'Go in to them through the gates, and when you have entered you shall surely be victorious. In God put your trust, if you are true believers.'

But they said: 'Moses, we will never go in as long as *they* are in it. Go, you and your Lord, and fight. Here will we stay.'

1. Cf. Numbers 14:6.

5:25 'Lord,' said Moses, 'I have none but myself and my brother. Keep us apart from the iniquitous people.'

He said: 'They shall be forbidden this land for forty years, during which time they shall wander homeless on the earth. Do not grieve for the iniquitous people.'

Recount to them in all truth the story of Adam's two sons: how they each made an offering, which was accepted from the one and was not accepted from the other. One said: 'I will surely kill you.' The other said: 'God accepts only from the righteous. If you stretch your hand to kill me, I shall not stretch my hand to kill you; for I fear God, Lord of the Universe. I would rather you should add your sin against me to your other sins and thus become an inmate of the Fire. Such is the recompense of the unjust.'

His soul prompted him to slay his brother; he slew him, and thus became one of the lost. Then God sent down a raven, which clawed the earth to show him how to bury the naked corpse of his brother. 'Alas for me!' he said. 'Have I not strength enough to do as this raven has done and so bury my brother's naked corpse?' And he repented.

5:32 That was why We laid it down for the Israelites that whoever killed a human being, except as punishment for murder or other villainy in the land, it shall be as if he has killed all mankind; and that whoever saved a life, it shall be as if he has saved all mankind.

Indeed, Our apostles brought them veritable proofs: yet many among them after that did prodigious evil in the land.

The punishment of those that make war against God and His apostle and spread disorder in the land shall be to be slain or crucified or have their hands and feet cut off on alternate sides, or be banished from the land. They shall be held up to opprobrium in this world, and in the world to come grievous punishment awaits them: except those that repent before you reduce them. For you must know that God is forgiving and compassionate.

Believers, have fear of God and seek the right path to Him. Fight valiantly for His cause, that you may triumph.

5:36 As for the unbelievers, if they offered all that the earth contains and as much besides to redeem themselves from the torment of the Day of Resurrection, it shall not be accepted from them. Woeful punishment awaits them.

They will strive to get out of the Fire, but get out of it they shall not. Lasting torment awaits them. 5:37

As for the man or woman who is guilty of theft, cut off their hands to punish them for what they did. That is the punishment enjoined by God. And God is Almighty and wise. But whoever repents after his wrongdoing, and mends his ways, shall be pardoned by God; God is forgiving and compassionate.

Did you not know that God has sovereignty over the heavens and the earth? He punishes whom He will and forgives whom He pleases. God has power over all things.

Apostle, do not grieve for those who plunge headlong into unbelief; those who say with their mouths: 'We believe,' but have no faith in their hearts, and those of the Jewish Faith who avidly listen to lies and avidly listen to others who have not come to you. They tamper with words out of their context and say: 'If such-and-such be given you, accept it; if it be not given you, beware!' 5:41

You cannot help a man if God intends to try him. Those whose hearts God does not intend to purify shall be held up to shame in this world, and in the world to come grievous punishment awaits them.

They avidly listen to lies and avidly devour the unlawful. If they come to you, give them your judgement or avoid them. If you avoid them, they can in no way harm you; but if you do act as their judge, judge them with fairness. God loves those that deal justly.

But how will they come to you for judgement when they already have the Torah which enshrines God's own judgement? Soon after, they will turn their backs: they are no believers.

We have revealed the Torah, in which there is guidance and light. By it the prophets who submitted to God were to judge those of the Jewish Faith, and so would the rabbis and the clerics, according to God's Book which had been committed to their keeping and to which they themselves were witnesses. 5:44

Have no fear of people; fear Me, and do not sell My revelations for a paltry sum. Unbelievers are those who do not judge according to God's revelations.

5:45   Therein We decreed for them a life for a life, an eye for an eye, a nose for a nose, an ear for an ear, a tooth for a tooth, and a wound for a wound. But if a man charitably forbears from retaliation, his remission shall atone for him. Wrongdoers are those that do not judge according to what God has revealed.

In their trail We sent forth Jesus son of Mary, confirming the Torah revealed before him; and We gave him the Gospel, in which there is guidance and light, corroborating what was revealed before him in the Torah: a guide and an admonition to the righteous. Let those who follow the Gospel judge by what God has revealed in it; ungodly are those that do not judge by what God has revealed.

5:48   And to you We have revealed the Book with the Truth. It confirms the Book which came before it and supersedes it. Therefore pronounce judgement among them by what God has revealed and do not follow their whims or swerve from the Truth made known to you.

For each of you We have ordained a law and assigned a path. Had God pleased, He could have made of you but one community: but it is His wish to prove you by that which He has given you. Vie with each other in good works; to God shall you all return and He will resolve your differences for you.

Pronounce judgement among them by what God has revealed and do not follow their whims. Beware of them, lest they tempt you away from a part of that which God has revealed to you. If they turn away, know that it is God's wish to scourge them for some of their sins. A great many people are ungodly.

Is it the pagan laws that they wish to be judged by? And who is a better judge than God for those whose faith is firm?

5:51   Believers, take neither the Jews nor the Christians for your friends. They are friends to each other. Whoever of you seeks their friendship shall become one of their number. God does not guide the wrongdoing people.

You see the faint-hearted hastening to woo them. They say: 5:52
'We fear lest a change of fortune should befall us.' But it may
well be that when God grants victory or makes known His
will, they will regret their secret plans. Then will the faithful
say: 'Are these the men who solemnly swore by God that they
would stand by you?' Their works will come to nothing and
they will lose all.

Believers, if any among you renounce their religion, God
will replace them by others who love Him and are loved by
Him, who are humble towards the faithful and stern towards
the unbelievers, zealous for God's cause and fearless of man's
censure. Such is the grace of God: He bestows it on whom
He will. God is munificent and all-knowing.

Your only protectors are God, His apostle, and the faithful:
those who attend to their prayers, render the alms levy, and
kneel down in worship. Those who seek the protection of
God, His apostle, and the faithful must know that God's party
is sure to triumph.

Believers, do not seek the friendship of those who have 5:57
mocked and derided your religion, among those who were
given the Book before you; nor of the infidels. And fear God,
if you are true believers. If you call them to the prayer, they
treat it as a jest and a diversion. This is because they are a
people devoid of understanding.

Say: 'People of the Book, is it not that you hate us only
because we believe in God and in what has been revealed to
us and what was formerly revealed, and because most of you
are ungodly?'

Say: 'Shall I tell you who will receive a worse reward from
God? Those whom God has cursed and with whom He has
been angry, transforming them into apes and swine, and those
who serve the devil. Worse is the plight of these, and they
have strayed farther from the right path.'

When they came to you they said: 'We are believers.'
Indeed, infidels they came and infidels they departed. God
knew best what they concealed.

You see many among them rush headlong into sin and 5:62

transgression and practise what is unlawful. Surely evil is what they do.

5:63 Why do their rabbis and clerics not forbid them to blaspheme or to practise what is unlawful? Evil indeed are their doings.

The Jews say: 'God's hand is chained.' May their own hands be chained! May they be cursed for what they say! By no means. His hands are both outstretched: He bestows as He will.

That which is revealed to you from your Lord will surely increase the wickedness and unbelief of many among them. We have stirred among them enmity and hatred, which shall endure till the Day of Resurrection. Whenever they kindle the fire of war, God puts it out. They perpetrate evil in the land, and God does not love the evil-doers.

And if the People of the Book accept the Faith and fear God, We will pardon them their misdeeds and admit them to

5:66 the Gardens of Delight. If they observed the Torah and the Gospel and what has been revealed to them from their Lord, they would enjoy all that is good, from above, and from beneath their feet.

Among them there is a righteous community; but many among them are evil-doers.

Apostle, proclaim what has been revealed to you from your Lord; if you do not, you will surely fail to convey His message. God will protect you from all people. God does not guide the unbelievers.

Say: 'People of the Book, you will attain nothing until you observe the Torah and the Gospel and that which has been revealed to you from your Lord.'

That which has been revealed to you from your Lord will surely increase the wickedness and unbelief of many among them. But do not grieve for the unbelievers.

Believers, those who follow the Jewish Faith, Sabaeans, and Christians – whoever believes in God and the Last Day and does what is right – shall have nothing to fear or to regret.

5:70 We made a covenant with the Israelites and sent forth apostles among them. But whenever an apostle came to them with a message that did not suit their inclinations, some they accused of lying and some they killed. They thought no punishment[1] would follow: they were blind and deaf. Then God turned to them in mercy, but many again were blind and deaf. God is ever observant of what they do. 5:71

They do blaspheme, that say: 'God is the Christ, the son of Mary.' For Christ himself said: 'Children of Israel, worship God, my Lord and your Lord.' He that worships other deities besides God, God will deny him Paradise, and his abode shall be the Fire. The wrongdoers shall have none to succour them.

They do blaspheme, that say: 'God is one of three.' There is but one God. If they do not desist from so saying, those of them that disbelieve shall be smitten by grievous torment.

Will they not turn to God in penitence and seek forgiveness of Him? God is forgiving and compassionate.

Christ, the son of Mary, was no more than an apostle: other apostles passed away before him. His mother was a saintly woman; they both ate earthly food. 5:75

Behold how We manifest to them Our revelations. Then behold how they ignore the Truth.

Say: 'Will you serve instead of God that which can neither harm nor help you? And God it is who hears all and knows all.'

Say: 'People of the Book! Do not transgress the bounds of Truth in your religion. Do not yield to the desires of those who have erred before; who have led many astray and have themselves strayed from the even path.'

Those of the Israelites who disbelieved were cursed by the tongue of David and of Jesus son of Mary for their rebelliousness and transgression. Nor did they reproach each other for any reprehensible act they committed. Evil indeed is what they did.

You see many among them make friends with unbelievers. Evil is that to which their souls prompt them. They have incurred the wrath of God and shall endure eternal torment. 5:80

---

1. See p. 19, note 2.

5:81 Had they believed in God and the Prophet and that which has been revealed to him, they would not have befriended them. But the greater part of them are ungodly.

You will assuredly find that the most hostile of people to the faithful are the Jews and the pagans; and you will assuredly find that the nearest in affection to the faithful are those who say: 'We are Christians.' That is because there are priests and monks among them; and because they are free from pride.

When they listen to that which was revealed to the Apostle, you see their eyes overflow with tears as they recognize its Truth. They say: 'Lord, we believe. Count us among the witnesses. Why should we not believe in God and in the Truth that has come down to us? Why should we not hope our Lord will admit us among the righteous?' And for their words God has rewarded them with Gardens watered by running brooks, wherein shall they abide for ever. Such is the recompense of the righteous. But those that disbelieve and deny Our revelations shall become the inmates of Hell.

5:87 Believers, do not forbid the wholesome things which God made lawful for you. Do not transgress; God does not love the transgressors. Eat of the lawful and wholesome things which God has given you. And fear God, in whom you do believe.

God will not take you to task for that which is inadvertent in your oaths. But He will take you to task over the oaths which you solemnly swear. The penance for a broken oath shall be the feeding of ten needy men with such food as you normally offer to your own people; or fitting them out with clothes; or the freeing of a slave. He that cannot afford any of these shall fast three days. In this way you shall atone for your broken oaths. Therefore be true to that which you have sworn. Thus God manifests to you His revelations, so that you may give thanks.

You that believe! Wine and games of chance, idols and divining arrows, are abominations devised by Satan. Avoid
5:91 them, so that you may prosper. Surely Satan seeks to stir up enmity and hatred among you by means of wine and gambling, and to keep you from the remembrance of God and from your prayers. Will you then desist?

Obey God, and obey the Apostle. Beware; if you pay no 5:92
heed, know that Our apostle's duty is but to give clear warning.

In regard to any food they may have eaten, no blame shall
be attached to those that have embraced the Faith and done
good works so long as they fear God and believe in Him and
do good works; so long as they fear God and believe in Him;
so long as they fear God and do good works. God loves the
charitable.

Believers, God will surely put you to the proof by means
of the game which you can catch with your hands or with
your spears, so that God may know those who fear Him in
their hearts. He that transgresses hereafter, woeful punishment awaits him.

Believers, you shall not kill game while on the Pilgrimage.
He that kills game by design, shall present, as an offering to
the Ka'bah, an animal equivalent to the one he killed, to be
determined by two just men among you; or he shall, in atone-
ment, either feed the destitute or fast, so that he may taste the
evil consequences of his deed. God has pardoned what is
past; but if anyone relapses God will avenge Himself on him:
God is Almighty and capable of revenge.

Lawful for you is what you catch from the sea and the sus- 5:96
tenance it provides; wholesome, for you and for the seafarers.
But you are forbidden the game of the land while on the Pilgrimage. And fear God, before whom you shall be herded.

God has made the Ka'bah, the Sacred House, a standing
shrine for people; also the sacred month, and the sacrificial
offerings with their ornaments, so that you may know God
has knowledge of all that the heavens and the earth contain;
that God has knowledge of all things.

Know that God is stern in retribution, and that God is forgiving and compassionate.

The Apostle's duty is only to give warning. God knows all
that you reveal and all that you conceal.

Say: 'Evil and good are not equal, even though the abundance of evil may tempt you. Fear God, you that are of good
sense possessed, that you may thrive.'

Believers, do not ask questions about things which, if made 5:101

known to you, would only pain you; but if you ask them when the Koran is being revealed, they shall be made plain to you. God will pardon you for this; God is forgiving and gracious. 5:102 People asked them before you, only to disbelieve them thereafter.

God demands neither a *baḥīrah*, nor a *sā'ibah*, nor a *waṣīlah*, nor a *ḥāmi*.[1] The unbelievers invent falsehoods about God; and most of them are lacking in judgement.

If they are told: 'Come to that which God has revealed, and to the Apostle,' they say: 'Sufficient for us is the faith of our fathers,' even though their fathers knew nothing and did not follow the right path.

Believers, you are accountable for none but yourselves; he that strays cannot harm you if you are on the right path. To God shall you all return, and He will declare to you what you have done.

5:106 Believers, when death approaches you, let two just men from among you act as witnesses when you make your testament; or two men from another tribe if while you are travelling the land the calamity of death overtakes you. Detain them after prayers, and if you doubt their honesty, let them swear by God: 'We will not sell our testimony for any price even to kin. We will not hide the testimony of God; for we should then be sinners.' If both prove dishonest, replace them by another pair from among those immediately concerned, and let them both swear by God, saying: 'Our testimony is truer than theirs. We have told no lies, for we should then be wrongdoers.' Thus will they be more likely to bear true witness or to fear that the oaths of others may contradict theirs. Fear God, and be attentive. God does not guide the ungodly.

On the day God gathers the apostles and says to them: 'How were you received?' they will say: 'We have no know-5:110 ledge. You alone know what is hidden.' God will say: 'Jesus son of Mary, remember the favour I bestowed on you and on your mother: how I strengthened you with the Holy Spirit, so

1. Names given by pagan Arabs to sacrificial animals offered at the Ka'bah.

that you spoke to people in the cradle and in the prime of manhood; how I instructed you in the Book and in wisdom, in the Torah and in the Gospel; how by My leave you fashioned from clay the likeness of a bird and breathed into it so that, by My leave, it became a living bird; how, by My leave, you healed the blind man and the leper, and, by My leave, restored the dead to life; how I protected you from the Israelites when you had come to them with conspicuous signs: when those of them who disbelieved said: "This is but sorcery manifest"; how, when I enjoined the disciples to believe in Me and in My apostle, they said: "We do believe; bear witness that we are Muslims."'

5:111

'Jesus son of Mary,' said the disciples, 'is your Lord able to send down to us from heaven a table spread with food?'

He said: 'Fear God, if you are true believers.'

'We wish to eat of it,' they said, 'so that we may reassure our hearts and know that what you said to us is true, and that we may be witnesses of it.'

'Lord,' said Jesus son of Mary, 'send down to us from heaven a table spread with food, that it may mark a feast for the first of us and for the last of us: a sign from You. Give us our sustenance; You are the best provider.'

5:114

God said: 'I am sending one to you. But whoever of you disbelieves hereafter shall be punished as no man will ever be punished.'

Then God will say: 'Jesus son of Mary, did you ever say to the people: "Worship me and my mother as gods besides God?"'

'Glory be to You,' he will answer, 'I could never have claimed what I have no right to. If I had ever said so, You would have surely known it. You know what is in my mind, but I know not what is in Your mind. You alone know what is hidden. I told them only what You bade me: "Worship God, my Lord and your Lord." I was a witness over them while living in their midst, and ever since You took me to Yourself, You Yourself have been watching them. Over all things You are the witness. If You punish them, they surely are Your creatures; and if You forgive them, surely You are the Almighty, the Wise One.'

5:118

81

5:119   God will say: 'This is the day when their truthfulness will benefit the truthful. They shall for ever dwell in Gardens watered by running brooks. God is pleased with them, and they are pleased with Him. That is the supreme triumph.'

5:120   God it is who has sovereignty over the heavens and the earth and all that they contain. And He has power over all things.

CATTLE

In the Name of God, the Merciful, the Compassionate

6:1   PRAISE BE to God, who created the heavens and the earth and ordained darkness and light. Yet the unbelievers set up other gods as equals with their Lord.

He it was who created you from clay. Then He decreed a term for you in this world and another specified by Him. Yet you are still in doubt.

God is He in the heavens and on earth. He knows what you conceal and what you reveal; He knows what you do.

6:5   Yet every time a revelation comes to them from their Lord, they pay no heed to it. Thus do they deny the Truth when it is declared to them: but they shall learn the consequences of their scorn.

Can they not see how many generations We have destroyed before them? We had given them more power in the land than the power We have given you,[1] We sent down for them abundant water from the sky, and We gave them rivers that rolled at their feet. Yet because they sinned We obliterated them, and raised up other generations after them.

If We sent down to you a Book inscribed on real parchment and they touched it with their own hands, the unbelievers would still assert: 'This is but sorcery manifest.'

6:8   And they ask: 'Why has no angel been sent down to him?' If We had sent down an angel, judgement would have been

---

1. The Meccans.

passed and they would have never been reprieved. And if   6:9
We had made him an angel, We would have given him the
semblance of a man, and would have thus added to their
confusion.

Other apostles have been laughed to scorn before you; but
those that scoffed at them were felled by the very scourge they
had derided.

Say: 'Roam the earth and see what was the fate of those
that disbelieved.'

Say: 'To whom belongs all that the heavens and the earth
contain?' Say: 'To God. He has decreed mercy for Himself,
and will gather you all on the Day of Resurrection: a day not
to be doubted. Those who have forfeited their souls will never
believe.'

And His is whatever takes its rest in the night or in the day.
And He it is who hears all and knows all. Say: 'Should I take   6:14
any but God for my Protector? Creator of the heavens and
the earth, He gives nourishment to all and is nourished by
none.'

Say: 'I was commanded to be the first of the Muslims. You
shall serve no other god besides Him.'

Say: 'I will never disobey my Lord, for I fear the torment of
a fateful day.'

He who is spared that day shall have received His mercy.
That is the glorious triumph.

If God afflicts you with an evil, none can remove it but
Him; and if He blesses you with good fortune, know that He
has power over all things.

He reigns supreme over His servants; and He alone is the
Wise One, the Omniscient.

Say: 'What counts most in testimony?'   6:19
Say: 'God is my witness and your witness. This Koran has
been revealed to me that I may thereby warn you and all whom
it may reach. Will you really testify there are other gods
besides God?'

Say: 'I will testify to no such thing!'

Say: 'He is but one God. I disown the gods you serve
besides Him.'

6:20 Those to whom We have given the Book[1] know him as they know their own children. But those who have forfeited their souls will never have faith.

And who is more wicked than the man who invents a falsehood about God or denies His revelations? The wrongdoers shall never succeed.

On the day We herd them all together We shall say to the pagans: 'Where are your idols now, those whom you claimed to be your gods?' They will then have no case to argue, but will only say: 'By God, our Lord, we have never worshipped idols.'

You shall see how they have deceived themselves and how the deities of their own invention will forsake them.

And some among them listen to you. But We have cast veils over their hearts and made them hard of hearing lest they understand your words. They will believe in none of Our signs, even if they see them, one and all.

When they come to argue with you the unbelievers say: 6:26 'This is nothing but fables of the ancients.' They forbid it and distance themselves from it. They ruin none but themselves, though they do not perceive it.

If you could see them when they are set before the Fire! They will say: 'Would that we could return! Then we would not deny the revelations of our Lord and would be true believers.' Indeed, that which they concealed before will manifest itself to them.

But if they were sent back, they would return to that which they had been forbidden; they are surely lying.

They say: 'It is but this, our nether life; nor shall we ever be raised to life again.'

If you could see them when they are set before their Lord! He will say: 'Is this not real?' 'Yes, by our Lord,' they will reply, and He will say: 'Taste then the torment, the reward of your unbelief!'

6:31 Lost indeed are those who deny they will ever meet God. When the Hour overtakes them unawares, they will say: 'Alas,

---

1. Christians and Jews.

we have neglected much in our lifetime!' And they shall bear their burdens on their backs; evil are the burdens they shall bear.

The life of this world is but a sport and a diversion. Surely better is the life to come for those that fear God. Will you not understand? 6:32

We know too well that what they say grieves you. It is not you that they are disbelieving; the wrongdoers deny God's own revelations. Other apostles have been denied before you; but they patiently bore with disbelief and persecution until Our help came down to them: for none can change the decrees of God. You have already heard of those apostles.

And if you find their aversion hard to bear, seek if you can a tunnel in the earth or a ladder to the sky by which you may bring them a sign. Had God pleased He would have given them guidance, one and all. Do not be foolish, then.

Those that can hear will surely answer. As for the dead, God will bring them back to life. Then to Him shall they be recalled.

They ask: 'Why was no sign sent down to him from his Lord?' 6:37

Say: 'God is well able to send down a sign.' But most of them have no knowledge.

All the beasts that roam the earth and all the birds that soar on high are but communities like your own. We have left out nothing in the Book. Then to their Lord they shall be herded all.

Deaf and dumb are those that deny Our revelations: they are in darkness. God confounds whom He will, and whom He pleases He guides on to a straight path.

Say: 'Do but consider. When God's scourge smites you and the Hour suddenly overtakes you, will you call on any but God to help you? Answer me, if you are truthful! No, on Him you will call; and He will relieve your affliction if He pleases. Then you will forget your idols.'

We sent forth apostles before you to other communities, and afflicted them with calamities and misfortunes that they might humble themselves. If only did they humble them- 6:43

selves when Our scourge overtook them! But their hearts hardened, and Satan made their deeds seem fair to them.

6:44 And when they had clean forgotten Our Admonition We opened every door for them; but just as they were rejoicing in what they were given, We suddenly smote them, and, lo, they were despondent. Thus were the wrongdoers annihilated. Praise be to God, Lord of the Universe!

Say: 'Do but consider: if God took away your hearing and your sight and set a seal upon your hearts, could any but God restore them to you?'

See how We expound the revelations; and yet they turn away.

Say: 'Do but consider: if the scourge of God overtook you suddenly or predictably, would any perish but the wrongdoers?'

We send forth apostles only to proclaim joyful tidings and to give warning. Those that believe in them and mend their ways shall have nothing to fear or to regret; and those that deny Our revelations shall be punished for their foul deeds.

6:50 Say: 'I do not tell you that I possess God's treasures or know what is hidden, nor do I say to you I am an angel; I follow only that which is revealed to me.'

Say: 'Are the blind and the seeing equal? Will you not reflect?'

Warn those who dread to be herded before their Lord that they have no guardian or intercessor besides Him, so that they may fear Him. Do not drive away those that call on their Lord morning and evening, seeking only to gain His favour. You are in no way accountable for them, nor are they in any way accountable for you. If you dismiss them, you shall yourself become a wrongdoer.

And thus have We made some among them a means for testing others, so that they should say: 'Are these the ones God has favoured among us?' But does not God best know the thankful?

6:54 If those that believe in Our revelations come to you, say: 'Peace be upon you. Your Lord has decreed mercy for Himself. If any one among you has done a bad deed through ignorance and then repented and mended his ways, he will find God forgiving and compassionate.'

Thus do We expound Our revelations, so that the path of the guilty may be laid bare. 6:55

Say: 'I am forbidden to worship the deities you invoke besides God.'

Say: 'I will not yield to your wishes, for then I would have strayed and ceased to be on the right path.'

Say: 'I have received veritable proofs from my Lord, yet you deny Him. I have no power to hasten that which you challenge; judgement is for God only. He it is who declares the Truth and is the best of arbiters.'

Say: 'Had I the power to hasten that which you challenge, judgement would have been passed between myself and you. But God best knows the wrongdoers. He has the keys to all that is hidden: none knows it but Him. He knows all that land and sea contain: every leaf that falls is known to Him. There is no grain in the darkest bowels of the earth, nor anything green or sear, but is recorded in a veritable Book.

'He it is who claims you back by night, knowing what you have done by day, and then rouses you up to fulfil your allotted span of life. Then to Him shall you return, and He will then declare to you all that you have done. 6:60

'He it is who reigns supreme over His servants. And He sends forth guardians to watch over you, so that when death overtakes any one of you, Our emissaries will claim him back; they never fail. Then are all restored to God, their true Lord. His alone is the Judgement, and most swift is His reckoning.'

Say: 'Who delivers you from the dark perils of land and sea, when you call out to Him humbly and in secret, saying: "Save us from these and we will be truly thankful!"?'

Say: 'God delivers you from them, and from all afflictions; yet you worship idols.'

Say: 'He it is who has power to let loose a scourge upon you from above your heads and from beneath your feet, and to divide you into discordant factions, causing the one to suffer at the hands of the other.' 6:65

See how We expound Our revelations, that they may understand them.

6:66   Your people have rejected this[1] although it is the very
Truth. Say: 'I am not your keeper. The time will come when
every prophecy shall be fulfilled, and you shall learn.'

If you see those that scoff at Our revelations, withdraw
from them till they engage in other talk. And should Satan
cause you to forget, take leave of the wrongdoers as soon as
you remember. Those that fear God are in no way accountable for them. Remind them only that they may fear Him.

Avoid those that treat their faith as a sport and a diversion
and are seduced by the life of this world. Admonish them
with this lest their souls be damned by their own actions, having no guardian or intercessor besides God: and though they
offer every ransom, it shall not be accepted from them. Such
are those that are damned by their own actions. Scalding water
shall they drink, and suffer woeful torment for their unbelief.

6:71   Say: 'Are we to call on idols which can neither help nor
harm us? Are we to turn upon our heels after God has guided
us, like him who, being bewitched by demons in the land, blun-
ders along perplexed, although his friends call him to the right
path, shouting: "Come this way!"?'

Say: 'God's guidance is the only guidance. We are commanded to submit to the Lord of the Universe, to pray, and to
fear Him. Before Him shall you be herded all.'

He it was who created the heavens and the earth with
Truth. On the day He says: 'Be,' it shall be. His word is Truth:
and sovereignty shall be His on the day when the Trumpet is
blown. He has knowledge of the unknown and the manifest.
He alone is the Wise One, the Omniscient.

Tell of Abraham, who said to Azar, his father: 'Will you
worship idols as your gods? I can see that you and your people
are in palpable error.'

6:75   Thus did We show Abraham the kingdom of the heavens
and the earth, so that he might become a firm believer.

---

1. The Koran.

When night drew its shadow over him, he saw a star. 'That,' 6:76
he said, 'is surely my God.'

But when it faded away, he said: 'I have no love for such
that fade.'

When he beheld the rising moon, he said: 'That is my God.'
But when it set, he said: 'If my Lord does not guide me, I shall
surely go astray.'

Then, when he beheld the sun rising, he said: 'That must
be my God: it is larger.'

But when it set, he said to his people: 'I disown your idols.
I will turn my face to Him who has created the heavens and
the earth, and will live a righteous life. I am no idolater.'

His people argued with him. He said: 'Will you argue with
me about God, who has given me guidance? I do not fear
your idols, unless my Lord so willed for a purpose. My Lord
has prodigious knowledge of all things: will you not reflect?
And how should I fear your idols when you yourselves are
not afraid of serving idols not sanctioned for you by God?
Which of us is more deserving of salvation? Tell me, if you
know. Those that have faith and do not taint their faith with
wrongdoing shall surely earn salvation, and are rightly guided.'

Such was the argument with which We furnished Abraham 6:83
against his people. We raise whom We will to an exalted rank.
Your Lord is wise and all-knowing.

We gave him Isaac and Jacob and guided both as We had
guided Noah before them. Among his descendants were
David and Solomon, Job and Joseph and Moses and Aaron
(thus do We reward the righteous); Zacharias and John, Jesus
and Elias[1] (all were upright men); and Ishmael, Elisha, Jonah,
and Lot. All these We exalted above the nations as We had
exalted some of their fathers, their children, and their brothers.
We chose them and guided them to a straight path.

Such is God's guidance; He guides those of His servants
whom He chooses. Had they served other gods besides Him,
their labours would have been vain indeed.

On those We bestowed the Book, wisdom, and prophet- 6:89

---

1. Elijah.

hood. If these are denied by them, We will entrust them to others who will not deny them.

6:90 It was those whom God had guided: follow then their guidance and say: 'I demand of you no recompense for this. It is but an admonition to mankind.'

And they have no true notion of God's glory, those that say: 'God has never revealed anything to a mortal.'

Say: 'Who, then, revealed the Scriptures which Moses brought down, a light and a guide for mankind? You have transcribed them on scraps of paper, declaring some and suppressing much, though now you have been taught what neither you nor your fathers knew before.'

Say: 'God!' Then leave them to amuse themselves with foolish chatter.

This is a blessed Book which We have revealed, confirming what came before it, that you may warn the mother city[1] and those that dwell around her. Those who believe in the life to come believe in it and are steadfast in their prayers.

6:93 Who is more wicked than he who invents a falsehood about God, or says: 'This was revealed to me,' when nothing was revealed to him? Or says: 'I can reveal the like of what God has revealed'?

Could you but see the wrongdoers when death overwhelms them! With hands outstretched, the angels will say: 'Yield up your souls this day. You shall be rewarded with the scourge of shame, for you have said of God what is untrue and scorned His revelations. And now you have returned to Us, one by one, as We created you at first, leaving behind all that We bestowed on you. Nor do We see with you your intercessors, those whom you claimed to be God's equals. Broken are the ties which bound you, and that which you claimed has failed you.'

God it is who splits the seed and the fruit-stone. He brings forth the living from the dead, and the dead from the living. Such is God: how then can you turn away?

6:96 He kindles the light of dawn; He has ordained the night for

1. Mecca.

rest and the sun and the moon for reckoning. Such is the ordinance of the Mighty One, the All-knowing.

He it was who created for you the stars, so that you may be guided by them in the darkness of land and sea. We have expounded Our revelations for those endowed with knowledge. 6:97

And He it was who created you from a single soul and furnished you with a dwelling and a resting-place. We have expounded Our revelations for those who understand.

And He it is who sends down water from the sky with which We bring forth the buds of every plant. From these We bring forth green foliage and close-growing grain, palm-trees laden with clusters of dates, vineyards and olive groves, and pomegranates alike and different. Behold their fruits when they ripen. Surely in these there are signs for those who truly believe.

And they made the jinn God's partners, though He Himself created them, and in their ignorance ascribe to Him sons and daughters. Glory be to Him! Exalted be He above their imputations!

Creator of the heavens and the earth. How should He have a son when He had no consort? He created all things, and of all things He has knowledge. 6:101

Such is God, your Lord. There is no god but Him, Creator of all things. Therefore serve Him. And of all things He is the Guardian.

No mortal eyes can see Him, though He sees all eyes. He is the Benign One, the Omniscient.

Momentous portents have come to you from your Lord. He that sees them shall himself have much to gain, and he who is blind to them shall lose much indeed, I[1] am not your keeper.

Thus do We expound Our revelations, that they may say: 'You[1] have studied deep,' and that We may make it clear for those endowed with knowledge. Therefore follow what has been revealed to you from your Lord; there is no god but 6:106

1. Muḥammad.

91

6:107 Him. Avoid the pagans; had God pleased, they would not have worshipped idols. We have not made you their keeper, nor are you their guardian.

Do not revile[1] the idols which they invoke besides God, lest in their ignorance they revile God with rancour. Thus have We made the actions of each community seem pleasing to itself. Then to their Lord shall they return, and He will declare to them what they have done.

They solemnly swear by God that if a sign be given them they would assuredly believe in it. Say: 'Signs are only vouchsafed by God.' And how can you tell? Even if a sign be given them they may still not believe.

And We will turn away their hearts and eyes from the Truth, even as they did not believe in it at first. We will let them blunder about in their wickedness.

6:111 And if We sent the angels down to them, and caused the dead to speak with them, and ranged all things in front of them, they would still not believe, unless God willed otherwise. But most of them are ignorant men.

Thus have We assigned for every prophet an adversary: the demons of people and of jinn, who inspire each other with vain and varnished falsehoods. And had your Lord pleased, they would not have done so. Therefore leave them to their own inventions, so that the hearts of those who have no faith in the life to come may be inclined to what they say and, being pleased, persist in their sinful ways.

Should I[2] seek a judge other than God when He it is who has revealed the Book for you with all its precepts? Those to whom We gave the Book know that it is revealed with Truth from your Lord. Therefore never doubt it.

Perfected are the words of your Lord in Truth and Justice. None can change His words. And He it is who hears all and knows all.

6:116 If you obeyed the greater part of those on earth, they would lead you away from God's path. They follow nothing

---

1. These words are addressed to the believers.
2. Muḥammad.

but idle fancies and preach nothing but falsehoods. Surely   6:117
your Lord is best aware of those who stray from His path, as
He best knows the rightly guided.

Eat only of that which has been consecrated in the name
of God, if you do believe in His revelations. And why should
you not eat of that which has been consecrated in God's name
when He has expounded to you what He forbade you, except
when you are constrained?

Many are those that are misled through ignorance by their
desires: surely your Lord best knows the transgressors.

Sin neither openly nor in secret. Those that commit sins
shall be punished for the sin they committed.

Therefore do not eat of that which has not been consecrated in the name of God; for that is ungodly.

The demons will teach their votaries to argue with you; if
you obey them, you shall yourselves become idolaters.

Can the dead man We have raised to life, and given a light
to walk with among people, be compared to him who is in
darkness from which he will never emerge? Thus do their
deeds seem fair to the unbelievers.

We have placed in every city arch-transgressors who   6:123
scheme within its walls. But they scheme only against themselves, though they may not perceive it. When a sign is revealed
to them they say: 'We will not believe in it unless we are given
the like of what God's apostles were given.' But God knows
best whom to entrust with His message.

God will humiliate the transgressors and mete out to them
grievous torment for their scheming.

If God intends to guide a man, He opens his bosom to
Islām; and if He pleases to confound him, He makes his
bosom small and narrow as though he were climbing up to the
sky. Thus shall God lay the abomination on the unbelievers.

Such is the path of your Lord: a straight path. We have
expounded the revelations to people who reflect. They shall
dwell in peace with their Lord. He will give them His protection as recompense for what they do.

And on the day He herds them all together, He will say: 6:128
'You clans of jinn, you have seduced mankind in great

numbers.' And their votaries among mankind will say: 'Lord, we did enjoy each other's fellowship. But now we have reached the end of the term You have decreed for us.'

He will say: 'The Fire shall be your home, therein to abide for ever: unless God ordain otherwise.' Surely your Lord is wise and all-knowing.

6:129 Thus do We give the wrongdoers sway over each other as punishment for their misdeeds.

'You clans of jinn and humankind! Did there not come to you apostles of your own who proclaimed to you My revelations and warned you of this day?'

They will say: 'We bear witness against our own souls.' The life of this world has seduced them. They will testify against their own souls that they were unbelievers.

Nor would your Lord destroy the cities without just cause, with their people unaware. For each there shall be grades, according to their deeds. Your Lord is never heedless of what they do.

6:133 Your Lord is the Self-sufficient One, the Merciful. He takes you away if He wills and replaces you with whom He pleases, just as He raised you from the offspring of other people.

That which you are promised is sure to come. Resist it you shall not.

Say: 'My people, do all that is in your power, and I will do what is in mine. You shall learn who is to gain the recompense of the Hereafter; the wrongdoers shall never succeed.'

They set aside for God a share of their produce and of their cattle, saying: 'This is for God' – so they pretend – 'and this for our idols.' Their idols' share does not reach God, but the share of God is wholly given to their idols. How ill they judge!

Thus did their idols induce many pagans to kill their children, seeking to ruin them and to confuse them in their religion. Had God pleased they would not have done so. Therefore leave them to their false devices.

6:138 They say: 'These animals and these crops are forbidden. None may eat of them save those whom we permit.' So they assert. And there are beasts which they prohibit men from riding, and others over which they do not pronounce the name of God, thus inventing lies against Him. He will punish them for the lies they invented.

They also say: 'The offspring of these animals is lawful for our males but forbidden to our females.' But if it is stillborn, they all partake of it! He will punish them for their imputations. Surely He is wise and all-knowing. 6:139

Losers are those that in their ignorance have wantonly slain their own children and made unlawful what God has given them, inventing falsehoods about God. They have surely gone astray and are not guided.

And He it is who brings gardens into being: creepers and upright trees, the palm, and produce of various taste, and olives, and pomegranates alike and different. Eat of these fruits when they ripen and give away what is due upon the harvest day. But you shall not be prodigal; He does not love the prodigal.

Of the beasts you have, some are for carrying loads and others for slaughter. Eat of that which God has given you and do not walk in Satan's footsteps; he is your veritable foe. 6:142

Eight kinds of livestock: take a pair of sheep and a pair of goats. Say: 'Has He forbidden you the two males, the two females, or that which is in the wombs of the two females? Tell me with knowledge if you are truthful.' And a pair of camels and a pair of cattle. Say: 'Has He forbidden you the two males, the two females, or that which is in the wombs of the two females? Were you present when God gave you this commandment?'

Who is more wicked than he who, in ignorance, invents a falsehood about God to lead people astray? God does not guide the wrongdoers.

Say: 'I find nothing in what has been revealed to me that forbids anyone to eat of such food, unless it be carrion, running blood, or the flesh of swine – for that is an abomination – or any profane thing that has been consecrated to other than God. But whoever is driven by necessity, intending neither to sin nor to transgress – surely your Lord is forgiving and compassionate.' 6:145

6:146 To those who follow the Jewish Faith We forbade all animals with undivided hoofs[1] and the fat of sheep and oxen, except what is on their backs or their entrails, or what is mixed with the bone. Such is the penance We imposed on them for their misdeeds. What We declare is surely true. If they disbelieve in you, say: 'All-encompassing is the mercy of your Lord: and His punishment cannot be warded off from those that do wrong.'

The idolaters will say: 'Had God pleased, neither we nor our fathers would have served other gods besides Him; nor would we have declared anything unlawful.' In like manner did those who have gone before them disbelieve until they felt Our might.

Say: 'Have you any knowledge you can put before us? You believe in nothing but conjecture and follow nothing but falsehoods.'

Say: 'God alone has the conclusive proof. Had He so pleased He would have guided you all.'

6:150 Say: 'Bring me those witnesses of yours who can testify that God has forbidden this.' If they so testify, do not testify with them, nor follow the whims of those that deny Our revelations, disbelieve in the life to come, and set up other gods as equals with their Lord.

Say: 'Come, I will tell you what your Lord has made unlawful for you: that you shall serve no other gods besides Him; that you shall show kindness to your parents; that you shall not kill your children because you cannot support them: We provide for you and for them; that you shall not commit lewd acts, whether openly or in secret; and that you shall not kill – for that is forbidden by God – except for a just cause. Thus does He exhort you, that you may grow in wisdom.'

6:152 Do not tamper with the property of orphans, unless to improve their lot until they reach maturity. Give just weight and full measure; We never charge a soul with more than it can bear. Speak for justice, even if it affects your own kin. And be true to God's covenant. Thus does He exhort you, so that you may take thought.

1. Leviticus 11.

This path of Mine is straight. Follow it, and do not follow   6:153
other paths, for they will lead you away from His path. Thus
does He exhort you, so that you may fear Him.

We gave the Book to Moses, a perfect code for the righteous with precepts about all things, a guide and a blessing, so
that they might believe in meeting their Lord. And this Book
We have now revealed: truly blessed. Observe it and fear God,
so that you may find mercy and not say: 'The Book was
revealed only to two communities[1] before us; though of their
studies we were surely heedless'; or: 'Had the Book been
revealed to us, we would have been better guided than they.'

A veritable sign has now come to you from your Lord, a
guide and a blessing. And who is more wicked than he who
denies God's revelations and turns away from them? Those
that turn away from Our revelations We shall requite with
grievous torment for their turning.

Are they waiting for the angels to come to them, or for   6:158
your Lord to come, or for a sign of your Lord to come? On
the day some sign of your Lord does come, faith shall not
avail the soul that had no faith before or did not put its faith
to good uses.

Say: 'Wait if you will; we too are waiting.'

Have nothing to do with those who have split up their religion into sects. God will call them to account and declare to
them what they have done.

He that does a good deed shall be repaid ten of the like of
it; and he that does evil shall be rewarded only with the like.
None shall be wronged.

Say: 'My Lord has guided me to a straight path, to an
upright religion, to the faith of saintly Abraham, who was no
idolater.'

Say: 'My prayers and my devotions, my life and my death,
are all for God, Lord of the Universe: He has no peer. Thus
am I commanded, and I am the first of the Muslims.'

Say: 'Should I seek any but God for my Lord, when He is   6:164
the Lord of all things? Each soul shall reap the fruits only of

1. Jews and Christians.

its own deeds: no burdened soul shall bear another's burden. Then to your Lord shall you return, and He will resolve for you your differences.'

6:165 He has given you the earth for your heritage and exalted some of you in rank above others, that He might test you with what He has given you. Swift is your Lord in retribution; yet is He forgiving and compassionate.

THE HEIGHTS

In the Name of God, the Merciful, the Compassionate

7:1 ALIF *lām mīm ṣād*. A Book has been revealed to you – let not your heart be troubled about it – so that you may thereby give warning and admonish the faithful.

Observe that which is brought down to you[1] from your Lord and follow no other masters besides Him. But you seldom take warning.

How many cities have We obliterated! While sleeping Our scourge fell upon them, or at midday, when they were drowsing.

And when Our scourge fell upon them, their only cry was: 'We have indeed been wrongdoers.'

7:6 We will surely question those to whom the emissaries were sent, and We will surely question the emissaries themselves. With knowledge We will recount to them what they have done, for We were never away from them.

On that day all shall be weighed with justice. Those whose good deeds weigh heavy in the scales shall prosper, and those whose good deeds are light shall lose their souls, because they have reviled Our revelations.

We have given you power in the land and provided you with a livelihood: yet you are seldom thankful.

7:11 We created you and gave you form. Then We said to the angels: 'Prostrate yourselves before Adam.' They all

---

1. The Meccans.

prostrated themselves except Satan, who refused to prostrate himself.

'Why did you not prostrate yourself when I commanded you?' He asked.   7:12

'I am nobler than he,' he replied. 'You created me from fire, and You created him from clay.'

He said: 'Get you down hence! This is no place for your contemptuous pride. Away with you! Abject shall you henceforth be.'

He said: 'Reprieve me till the Day of Resurrection.'

'You are reprieved,' said He.

'Because You have led me into sin,' he said, 'I will waylay them as they walk on Your straight path, then spring upon them from before and from behind them, from their right and from their left. Then You will find the greater part of them ungrateful.'

'Get you hence!' He said. 'A despicable outcast shall you be. As for those that follow you, I will surely fill Hell with you all.

'And you Adam, dwell with your wife in Paradise, and eat   7:19 of any fruit you please; but never approach this tree or you shall both become wrongdoers.'

But Satan tempted them, so that he might reveal to them their shameful parts, which they had never seen before. And he said: 'Your Lord has forbidden you both to approach this tree only to prevent you from becoming angels or immortals.' Then he swore to them that he would give them friendly counsel.

Thus did he cunningly seduce them. And when they had eaten of the tree, their shame became visible to them, and they both hastened to cover themselves with the leaves of the Garden.

Their Lord called out to them, saying: 'Did I not forbid you both to approach that tree, and say to you that Satan was your veritable foe?'

They replied: 'Lord, we have wronged our own souls. Pardon us and have mercy on us, or we shall surely be among the lost.'

He said: 'Get you down hence, and may your descendants   7:24 be adversaries to each other. The earth will for a certain term

7:25 provide your dwelling and your comforts. There shall you live and there shall you die, and thence shall you be raised to life.'

Children of Adam! We have given you clothes to cover your shameful parts, and garments pleasing to the eye; but the robe of piety is the finest of them all. That is one of God's revelations. Perchance they will take thought.

Children of Adam! Let not Satan tempt you, as he seduced your parents out of Paradise. He stripped them of their garments to reveal to them both their shameful parts. He and his minions see you whence you cannot see them. We have made the demons patrons of the unbelievers.

When they commit a lewd act, they say: 'This is what our fathers used to do. God enjoined it.'

Say: 'God does not enjoin lewdness. Would you tell of God what you know not?'

Say: 'My Lord has enjoined justice. Turn your face to Him wherever you kneel down in prayer and call on Him with true devotion. Even as He created you, so shall you return.'

7:30 Some He has guided and some He has justly left in error; for they chose the demons for their patrons instead of God and deemed themselves on the right path.

Children of Adam! Dress well when you attend your mosques. Eat and drink, but do not indulge. He does not love the indulgent.

Say: 'Who has forbidden you to wear the decent clothes or to eat the wholesome things which God has provided for His servants?'

Say: 'These are for the enjoyment of the faithful in the life of this world, and they shall be theirs alone on the Day of Resurrection.'

Thus do We expound Our revelations to those endowed with knowledge. Say: 'My Lord has forbidden all lewd acts, whether overt or disguised, sin, and wrongful oppression; and He has forbidden you to worship what He did not sanction, or to tell of God what you know not.'

7:34 Every community has a term decreed; when their time is come, not for one hour shall they hold it back, nor can they go before it.

Children of Adam! When apostles of your own come to 7:35
proclaim to you My revelations, those that take warning and
mend their ways will have nothing to fear or to regret; but
those that deny and scorn Our revelations shall be the inmates
of the Fire, wherein shall they abide for ever.

Who is more wicked than he who invents a falsehood about
God or denies His revelations? Those shall have their share as
destined in the Book, and when Our emissaries come to claim
back their souls they shall say: 'Where are your idols now, those
whom you invoked besides God?' 'They have forsaken us,'
they will say, and will impeach themselves as unbelievers.

He will say: 'Enter, and join communities of jinn and
humankind that have gone before you into the Fire.'

As it enters, every community will curse the one that went
before it, and when all are gathered there, the last of them will
say of the first: 'These, Lord, have led us astray. Let their punishment be doubled in the Fire.'

He will say: 'All shall be doubly punished, though you may
know not.'

Then the first will say to the last: 'You were no better than 7:39
we. Taste then the torment, the penalty of your misdeeds.'

For those who have denied and scorned Our revelations
the gates of heaven shall not be opened; nor shall they enter
Paradise until the camel shall pass through the eye of a sewing
needle.[1] Thus shall We reward the transgressors.

Hell shall be their couch, and sheets of fire shall cover
them. Thus shall We requite the wrongdoers.

As for those that believe and do good works – We never
charge a soul with more than it can bear – they are the heirs of
Paradise, wherein shall they abide for ever.

We shall take away all rancour from their hearts. Rivers will 7:43
roll at their feet and they shall say: 'Praise be to God who has
guided us hither. Had He not given us guidance we would not
have been rightly guided. Our Lord's apostles have surely
preached the Truth.' And a voice will cry out to them: 'This is
the Paradise you inherited for what you did.'

1. Cf. Matthew 19:24; Mark 10:25; Luke 18:25.

7:44   Then the heirs of Paradise will cry out to the inmates of the Fire: 'What our Lord promised we have found to be true. Have you, too, found the promise of your Lord to be true?'

'Yes,' they will answer, and a herald will cry out among them: 'The curse of God be upon the wrongdoers who have debarred others from the path of God and sought to make it crooked, and who disbelieved in the life to come.'

A screen will divide them, and on the Heights there will be men who recognize each one by his look. To those in Paradise they shall say: 'Peace be upon you!' They shall not yet enter, though they long to be there.

And when they turn their eyes towards the inmates of the Fire they will cry: 'Lord, do not cast us among the wrongdoers!' Then, those on the Heights will say to men they recognize by their looks: 'Nothing have the riches you amassed and your scornful pride availed you. Are these the ones who you swore would never earn God's mercy? Come into Paradise. You have nothing to fear or to regret.'

7:50   And the inmates of the Fire will cry out to the heirs of Paradise: 'Give us some water, or some of that which God has given you.' They will say: 'God has forbidden both to the unbelievers, who made their religion a diversion and an idle sport, and who were seduced by their earthly life.'

On that day We will forget them as they forgot they would ever meet that day, and because they denied Our revelations.

And We have bestowed on them a Book We expounded with knowledge, a guide and a blessing to true believers. Are they waiting but for its fulfilment? On the day it is fulfilled, those that had forgotten it will say: 'Our Lord's apostles surely came to us with the Truth before. Could we but have intercessors to plead on our behalf! Could we but live our lives again, we would not do as we have done.' They shall forfeit their souls, and that which they invented will forsake them.

7:54   Your Lord is God, who created the heavens and the earth in six days and then ascended the throne. He throws the veil of night over the day; swiftly they follow one another. And the sun and the moon and the stars – all subservient to His will. His is the creation, His the command. Blessed be God, Lord of the Universe!

Pray to your Lord with humility and in secret. He does not love the transgressors. 7:55

Do not corrupt the earth after it has been purged of evil. Pray to Him with fear and hope; His mercy is within reach of the righteous.

He sends forth the winds as harbingers of His mercy, and when they have gathered up a heavy cloud, We drive it on to some dead land and let the water fall upon it, bringing forth all manner of fruit. Thus will We raise the dead to life. Perchance you will take thought.

Rich soil yields its crop by God's will; but poor soil yields nothing but what is poor and scant. Thus do We expound Our revelations to those who render thanks.

We sent forth Noah to his people. He said: 'Serve God, my people, for you have no god but Him. Beware the torment of a fateful day.'

But the elders of his people said: 'We can see that you are in palpable error.' 7:60

'I am not in error, my people,' he said, 'but am sent forth by the Lord of the Universe to deliver to you my Lord's messages and to give you friendly counsel; for I know of God what you know not. Do you think it strange that an Admonition should come to you from your Lord through a mortal like yourselves to warn you, so that you may fear God and be shown mercy?'

They denied him. So We saved him and all who were with him in the ark, and drowned those that denied Our revelations. Surely they were blind people.

And to the tribe of 'Ād We sent their kin Hūd. He said: 'Serve God, my people, for you have no god but Him. Will you not fear Him?'

The unbelievers among the elders of his tribe said: 'We can see you are a foolish man, and we surely think that you are lying.'

'Foolish I am not, my people,' he replied. 'I am sent forth by the Lord of the Universe to deliver to you my Lord's 7:68

7:69 messages and to give you honest counsel. Do you think it strange that an Admonition has come to you from your Lord through a mortal from among yourselves to warn you? Remember that He has made you the heirs of Noah's people and gave you greater power than He did to other creatures. Remember God's favours, that you may thrive.'

They said: 'Would you have us serve God alone and renounce the gods our fathers worshipped? Bring down the scourge you threaten us with, if what you say be true.'

He said: 'Your Lord's punishment and ire have already been decreed to visit you. Would you dispute with me about names which you and your fathers named, and for which God has revealed no sanction? Wait if you will; I will wait with you.'

We delivered him and those who were with him through Our mercy, and annihilated those that denied Our revelations. They were unbelievers all.

7:73 And to Thamūd We sent their kin Ṣāliḥ. He said: 'Serve God, my people, for you have no god but Him. A veritable proof has come to you from your Lord. Here is God's she-camel: a sign for you. Leave her to graze at will in God's own land and do not molest her, lest a woeful scourge should take you. And remember, He made you the heirs of 'Ād, and gave you power in the land. You have built mansions on its plains and hewn out houses into the mountains. Remember God's favours and do not corrupt the earth with wickedness.'

The haughty elders of his people said to the believers who were oppressed: 'Do you really believe that Ṣāliḥ is sent forth from his Lord?'

They answered: 'We do believe in the message he has been sent with.'

The haughty elders said: 'We deny all that you believe in.' They hamstrung the she-camel and defied the commandment of their Lord, saying to Ṣāliḥ: 'Bring down the scourge you threaten us with, if you have truly been sent.'

7:79 Thereupon the earthquake felled them, and when morning came they were crouching lifeless in their dwellings. He left them, saying: 'I conveyed to you, my people, the message of my Lord and gave you good counsel; but you had no love for those who give good counsel.'

And Lot, who said to his people: 'Will you persist in these lewd acts which no other nation has committed before you? You lust after men instead of women. Truly, you are a degenerate people.'   7:80

His people's only answer was: 'Banish them from your city. They are people who would keep themselves chaste.'

We delivered him and all his kin, except his wife, who stayed behind, and let loose a shower upon them. Consider the fate of the transgressors.

And to Midian, their kin Shu'aib. He said: 'Serve God, my people, for you have no god but Him. A veritable sign has come to you from your Lord. Give just weight and measure and do not defraud people of their possessions; do not corrupt the land after it has been purged of evil. That is best for you, if you are true believers.

'Do not squat down in every highway, threatening and debarring from the path of God those who believe in Him, and seeking to make that path crooked. Remember how He multiplied you when you were few in number. And consider the fate of the evil-doers.   7:86

'If there are some among you who believe in my message and some who disbelieve, be patient till God shall judge between us; He is the best of judges.'

The haughty elders of his tribe said: 'Return to our fold, Shu'aib, or we will banish you from our city, you and all your followers.'

'Even though we are averse to it?' he said. 'If we returned to your faith, from which God has delivered us, we should be false to God; we could only turn to it again by the will of God, our Lord. Our Lord encompasses all things with His knowledge, and in God we have put our trust. Lord, judge rightly between us and our people; You are the best of judges.'

And the infidel chieftains of his people said: 'If you follow Shu'aib, you shall indeed lose out.'

Thereupon the earthquake felled them, and when morning came they were crouching lifeless in their dwellings; as if   7:92

those that denied Shu'aib had never prospered there. It was
those that denied Shu'aib who did lose out.

7:93   He left them, saying: 'I conveyed to you, my people, the
messages of my Lord and gave you good counsel. How can I
grieve for an unbelieving people?'

And whenever We sent a prophet to a city We afflicted its
people with calamities and misfortunes so that they might
abase themselves. Then We changed adversity to good fortune, so that when they had multiplied they said: 'Our fathers
also had their sorrows and their joys.' And in their heedless-
ness We suddenly smote them.

And had the people of those cities believed and feared
God, We would have showered upon them blessings from
heaven and earth. But they disbelieved, and We punished
them for what they did.

Were the people of those cities secure from Our power
when it overtook them in the night while they were sleeping?

Or were the people of those cities secure from Our power
when it overtook them in the morning at their play?

7:99   Did they feel themselves secure from God's cunning?
None feels secure from God's cunning except the losers.

Or is it not plain to those that inherit the land after those
who once possessed it that, if We pleased, We could smite
them for their sins and set a seal upon their hearts, leaving
them bereft of hearing?

We have recounted to you the history of those cities. Their
apostles came to them with veritable proofs, yet they persisted
in their unbelief. Thus God seals up the hearts of the unbelievers.

We found the larger part of them untrue to their covenants; indeed, We found the larger part of them immersed in
evil.

Then after them We sent forth Moses with Our signs to
Pharaoh and his chieftains, but they too spurned them. Consider the fate of the evil-doers.

Moses said: 'Pharaoh, I am an apostle from the Lord of the
7:105   Universe, and may tell nothing of God but what is true. I

bring you a clear sign from your Lord. Let the Children of Israel depart with me.'

He said: 'If you have indeed brought a sign, show it to us if what you say be true.' 7:106

So he threw down his staff, and thereupon it changed to a veritable serpent. Then he drew out his hand, and it was white to all who saw it.

The elders of Pharaoh's people said: 'This man is but a skilful sorcerer who seeks to drive you from your land. What would you have us do?'

They said: 'Put them off awhile, him and his brother, and send forth criers to the cities to summon every skilful sorcerer to your presence.'

The sorcerers came to Pharaoh. They said: 'Shall we be rewarded if we win?'

'Yes,' he answered. 'And you shall be among the most favoured.'

They said: 'Moses, will you throw first, or are we the first to throw?' 7:115

'Throw,' he replied.

And when they threw, they bewitched the people's eyes and terrified them by a display of mighty sorcery.

Then We signalled to Moses: 'Throw down your staff.' And thereupon it swallowed up their false devices.[1]

Thus did the Truth prevail, and all their doings proved vain. Thus were they defeated and abased, and the sorcerers bowed down, and said: 'We now believe in the Lord of the Universe, the Lord of Moses and Aaron.'

Pharaoh said: 'Do you dare believe in Him before I give you leave? This is a plot you have contrived to turn the people out of their city. But you shall learn. I will cut off your hands and feet on alternate sides and then crucify you all!'

They said: 'We shall surely return to our Lord. You would punish us only because we believed in the signs of our Lord 7:126

1. Cf. Exodus 7:11 ff.

when they came to us. Lord, instil into us patience and let us die as Muslims.'

7:127 And the elders of Pharaoh's people said: 'Will you allow Moses and his people to perpetrate corruption in the land and to forsake you and your gods?'

He said: 'We will put their sons to death[1] and spare only their daughters. We shall surely triumph over them.'

Moses said to his people: 'Seek help in God and be patient. The earth is God's; He gives it to those of His servants whom He chooses. Happy shall be the lot of those that fear Him.'

They said: 'We were oppressed before you came to us, and still are we after your coming.'

He said: 'Your Lord will perchance destroy your enemies and give you the land to inherit. Then will He see how you will act.'

7:131 We afflicted Pharaoh's people with years of famine and dearth of fruitfulness, so that they might reflect. If good things came their way, they said: 'It is our due,' but if evil befell them they ascribed it to Moses and those who were with him. Yet it was God who had ordained their ills, though most of them did not know it.

And they said: 'Whatever miracle you work to enchant us with it, we will never believe in you.'

So We plagued them with the flood and with locusts, with lice and frogs and blood: miracles manifest, yet they scorned them all, for they were a sinful people.

And when each plague smote them, they said: 'Moses, pray to your Lord for us: invoke the promise He has made you. If you do lift the plague from us, we will believe in you and let the Israelites go with you.'

But when We had lifted the plague from them and the appointed time had come for them, they broke their promise. So We took vengeance on them and drowned them in the sea, for they had denied Our signs and paid no heed to them.

7:137 We gave the persecuted people dominion over the eastern and the western lands which We had blessed. Thus was your

---

1. Cf. Exodus 1:22.

Lord's gracious word fulfilled for the Israelites, because they had endured with fortitude; and We destroyed the edifices and the towers of Pharaoh and his people.

And We led the Israelites across the sea, and they came 7:138 upon a people who worshipped idols which they had. They said to Moses: 'Make us a god like the gods they have.'

He said: 'You are indeed an ignorant people. That which they follow is doomed, and all their works are vain. Am I to seek for you a deity other than God, when He has exalted you above the nations? We delivered you from Pharaoh's people, who had oppressed you cruelly, putting your sons to death and sparing only your daughters. Surely that was a great trial by your Lord.'

And We promised Moses thirty nights, to which We added ten nights more: so that the appointment with his Lord was after forty nights.[1]

And Moses said to his brother Aaron: 'Take my place among my people. Do what is right and do not follow the path of the wrongdoers.'

And when Moses came at Our appointed time and his 7:143 Lord communed with him, he said: 'Lord, reveal Yourself to me, that I may look upon You.'

He replied: 'You shall never see Me. But look upon the Mount; if it remains firm upon its base, then only shall you see Me.'

And when his Lord revealed Himself to the Mount, He levelled it to dust. Moses fell down senseless, and, when he had recovered, said: 'Glory be to You! I turn to You in penitence, and am the first of the believers.'

He said: 'Moses, I have chosen you above all mankind for My messages and My commandments. Take therefore what I have given you, and be thankful.'

And We inscribed for him upon the Tablets all manner of precepts, and instructions concerning all things, and said to him: 'Observe these steadfastly, and enjoin your people to observe what is best in them. I shall show you the abode of the ungodly. I will turn away from My signs those who lord it in the 7:146

---

1. Cf. Exodus 24:18.

land with arrogance and injustice, so that even if they witness each and every sign they shall not believe them. If they see the right path, they shall not walk upon it: but if they see the path of error, they shall choose it for their path; because they disbelieved Our signs and paid no heed to them.

7:147   'Vain are the deeds of those who disbelieve in Our signs and in the life to come. Shall they not be rewarded according only to their deeds?'

And in his absence the people of Moses made a calf from their ornaments, an image with a hollow sound. Did they not see that it could neither speak to them nor give them guidance? Yet they worshipped it and thus committed evil.

And when they repented and realized that they had strayed, they said: 'If our Lord does not have mercy on us and pardon us, we shall surely be among the lost.'

7:150   And when Moses returned to his people, angry and sorrowful, he said: 'Evil is the thing you did in my absence! Would you hasten the ordinance of your Lord?'

He threw down the Tablets and, seizing his brother's head, dragged him closer to him.

'Son of my mother,' Aaron said, 'the people overpowered me and almost did me to death. Do not let the enemy gloat over me; do not number me among the wrongdoers.'

'Lord,' said Moses, 'forgive me and forgive my brother. Admit us into Your mercy, for, of all those that show mercy, You are the most merciful.'

Those that worshipped the calf were to incur the anger of their Lord and servility in this life. Thus shall We reward those who fabricate falsehoods. But to those that do evil and later repent and believe, your Lord is forgiving and compassionate.

When his anger was allayed, Moses took up the Tablets, upon which was inscribed a pledge of guidance and of mercy
7:155   to those that fear their Lord. And Moses chose from among
.   his people seventy men[1] for Our appointed time and, when the quake shook them, said: 'Had it been Your will, Lord, You could have destroyed them long ago, and myself too. But

1. Cf. Exodus 24:1, 9.

would You destroy us because of what the fools among us did? That trial was ordained by You, to confound whom You willed and to guide whom You pleased. You alone are our guardian. Forgive us and have mercy on us: You are the best of those who forgive. Ordain for us what is good, both in this life and in the life to come; to You alone we turn.' 7:156

He said: 'My scourge I will visit upon whom I please: yet My mercy encompasses all things. I show it to those that fear God and give alms, and to those that in Our signs believe; to those that follow the Apostle – the Unlettered[1] Prophet – whom they shall find writ down for them in the Torah and the Gospel. He will enjoin righteousness on them and forbid them to do the reprehensible. He will make wholesome things lawful for them and foul things unlawful for them. He will relieve them of their burdens and of the shackles that weigh upon them. Those that believe in him and honour him, those that aid him and follow the light sent down with him, shall surely triumph.'

Say:[2] 'You people! I am God's emissary to you all; He that 7:158 has sovereignty over the heavens and the earth. There is no god but Him. He ordains life and death. Therefore have faith in God and His apostle, the Unlettered[1] Prophet, who believes in God and His commandments. Follow him, that you may be rightly guided.'

Yet among the people of Moses there are some who preach the Truth and act justly.

We divided them into twelve tribes, each a whole commu- 7:160 nity. And when his people demanded drink of him, We revealed Our will to Moses: 'Strike the rock with your staff.' Thereupon twelve springs gushed from it and each tribe knew its drinking-place.

We caused the clouds to draw their shadow over them and sent down for them manna and quails: 'Eat of the wholesome things We have given you.' They did Us no wrong, but they wronged themselves.

1. The word can also mean 'Gentile'.
2. These words are addressed to Muḥammad.

7:161 And when they were told: 'Dwell in this city, and eat from it whatever you please; pray for forgiveness and enter the gates bowing: We will forgive you your sins and bestow abundance on the righteous,' the wrongdoers among them changed what they were told to words that were not said to them; and We let loose on them a scourge from heaven as punishment for their wrongdoing.

Ask them about the city which overlooked the sea and what befell its people when they broke the Sabbath. On their Sabbath the fish came to them floating on the water, but on weekdays they never came near them. Thus did We test them because of the evil they did.

And when one of their tribes said: 'Why do you admonish a people for whom God has ordained destruction and grievous torment?' they replied: 'To be blameless in the sight of your Lord, and that they may fear God.' Therefore, when they forgot the warning they were given, We delivered those who had admonished against evil, and smote the wrongdoers with 7:166 punishment for their misdeeds. And when they scornfully persisted in their forbidden ways, We said to them: 'Turn into detested apes.'

Then your Lord declared that He would raise against them others who would oppress them grievously till the Day of Resurrection. Swift is the retribution of your Lord, yet is He forgiving and compassionate.

We dispersed them into communities throughout the earth – some were righteous, others were not – and tested them with blessings and misfortunes that they might return to the right path. Then others succeeded them who inherited the Book and took to these nether vanities. 'We shall be forgiven,' they said. And if such vanities came their way once more, they would again take to them.

Are they not committed in the Book to tell nothing of God but what is true? And they have studied it well; surely the world to come is better for those that fear God. Have you no sense?

7:170 As for those that strictly observe the Book and are steadfast in prayer, We shall not deny the righteous their reward.

And when We suspended the Mount over them as though 7:171
it were a shadow (they feared that it was falling down on them)
We said: 'Hold fast to that which We have given you and bear
in mind what it contains, that you may fear God.'

Your Lord brought forth descendants from the loins of
Adam's children, and made them testify against their own
souls. He said: 'Am I not your Lord?' They replied: 'Yes, we do
testify.' Lest you should say on the Day of Resurrection: 'We
had no knowledge of that,' or you should say: 'Our forefathers were, indeed, idolaters; but will You destroy us, their
descendants, on account of what the followers of falsehood did?'

Thus do We expound Our revelations that they may return
to the right path.

Tell them of the man to whom We vouchsafed Our signs
and who turned away from them: how Satan pursued him and
he went astray. Had it been Our will, We would have exalted 7:176
him through Our signs: but he clung to this earthly life and
succumbed to his desires. He can be compared to the dog
which pants if you chase it away, and pants still if you leave it
alone. Such are those that deny Our revelations. Recount to
them these parables, so that they may reflect.

Evil is the tale of those that denied Our revelations and
were unjust to their own souls.

He whom God guides is he who is rightly guided; but those
whom He confounds are they that will surely be lost.

We have predestined for Hell a multitude of jinn and
humans. They have hearts they cannot comprehend with; and
they have eyes they cannot see with; and they have ears they
cannot hear with. They are like beasts – indeed, they are more
misguided. Such are the heedless.

God has the Most Excellent Names; call on Him by them
and keep away from those that pervert them; they shall receive
their due for what they did.

Among those We created there is a community that gives
true guidance and acts justly. As for those that deny Our
revelations, We will lead them step by step whence they cannot tell; for though I bear with them, My stratagem is sure. 7:183

7:184 Has it never occurred to them that their compatriot[1] is no madman, but one who gives clear warning? Will they not ponder upon the kingdom of the heavens and the earth, and all the things that God created, and whether their hour is not drawing near? And in what other words after these will they believe?

None can guide those whom God confounds. He leaves them in their sinful ways, ever straying from the right path.

They ask you about the Hour: when will it come? Say: 'None but my Lord has knowledge of it.[2] Only He will reveal it – at the appointed time. A fateful hour shall it be, both in the heavens and on earth. It will but suddenly overtake you.'

They will put questions to you as though you were privy to it. Say: 'Only God has knowledge of it, but the greater part of mankind do not know this.'

7:188 Say: 'I have not the power to acquire benefits or to avert evil from myself, except by the will of God. Had I possessed knowledge of what is hidden, I would have availed myself of much that is good and no harm would have touched me. But I am no more than one who gives warning and joyful tidings to true believers.'

He it was who created you from a single being.[3] From that being He created his spouse, so that he might find comfort in her. And when he had lain with her, she conceived, and her burden was light. She carried it with ease, but when it grew heavy, they both called out to God their Lord: 'Grant us a goodly child and we will be truly thankful.'

Yet when He had granted them a goodly child, they both set up other gods besides Him in return for what He gave them. Exalted be God above their idols!

7:192 Will they worship those that can create nothing, and are themselves created? They cannot help them, nor can they help themselves.

1. Muḥammad.   2. Cf. Mark 13:32.   3. Literally, soul.

If you call them to the true guidance they will not follow you. It is the same whether you call to them or hold your peace.

Those whom you invoke besides God are, like yourselves, His creatures. Call on them, and let them answer you, if what you say be true!

Have they feet to walk with? Or have they hands to hold with? Or have they eyes to see with? Or have they ears to hear with?

Say: 'Call on your false gods and scheme against me. Give me no respite. Surely my guardian is God, who has revealed the Book; He acts as guardian of the righteous. Those on whom you call besides Him cannot help you, nor can they help themselves.'

If you call them to the right guidance, they will not hear. You find them looking towards you, but they cannot see.

Be tolerant, speak for what is right, and avoid the ignorant. If Satan presents you with a temptation, seek refuge in God; He hears all and knows all.

If the God-fearing are touched by a hint from Satan, they have but to reflect; and they shall see the light. As for their brothers, they would keep them long in error, nor would they ever desist.

When you have no *sūrah* to give them, they say: 'Have you not yet invented it?' Say: 'I follow only what is revealed to me by my Lord. This Book is a veritable proof from your Lord, a guide and a blessing to true believers.'

When the Koran is recited, listen to it in silence that you may be shown mercy. Remember your Lord deep in your soul with humility and awe, and without ostentation: in the morning and in the evening; and do not be heedless.

Those who dwell with your Lord do not disdain to worship Him; they give glory to Him and before Him they prostrate themselves.

THE SPOILS[1]

In the Name of God, the Merciful, the Compassionate

8:1 THEY ASK you about the spoils. Say: 'The spoils belong to God and the Apostle. Therefore fear God and end your differences. Obey God and His apostle, if you are true believers.'

The true believers are those whose hearts are filled with awe at the mention of God, and whose faith grows stronger when His revelations are recited to them. They are those who put their trust in their Lord, pray steadfastly, and give from what We gave them. Such are the true believers. They will be exalted to high ranks by their Lord, and forgiveness and a generous provision await them.

8:5 Just as your Lord bade you leave your home in the cause of Truth, and some of the faithful were reluctant, they argued with you about the Truth that had been revealed, as though they were being led to certain death while they looked on.

While God promised you victory over one of the two bands, it was your wish to take possession of the one that was unarmed.[2] God wished to vindicate the Truth by His words and to rout the unbelievers; to vindicate the Truth and to render falsehood vain, though the transgressors wished otherwise.

Remember when you prayed to your Lord for help and He answered: 'I am sending to your aid a thousand angels in their ranks.' By this good news God sought to reassure your hearts, for victory comes only from God; surely God is Almighty and wise.

8:11 You were overcome by sleep, a token of protection from

1. Of the Battle of Badr, in 624.
2. Muḥammad's plan was to attack an unarmed caravan belonging to the Quraysh of Mecca on its way from Syria to that city. An army of Meccans marched to its assistance. Some of the Muslims wished to attack the caravan, others the Meccan army. Muḥammad's forces, said to have been only 319 strong, routed the Meccans, who were nearly 1,000 in number.

Him. He sent down water from the sky to cleanse you and to purify you of Satan's abomination, to strengthen your hearts and to steady your footsteps.

Remember when God revealed His will to the angels: 'I am with you; so give courage to the believers. I shall cast terror into the hearts of the infidels. Strike off their heads, strike off the very tips of their fingers!' 8:12

That was because they defied God and His apostle; and he that defies God and His apostle shall be sternly punished by God. 'That is it: taste it.' The scourge of the Fire awaits the unbelievers.

Believers, when you encounter the infidels on the march, do not turn your backs to them in flight. If anyone on that day turns his back to them, except for tactical reasons, or to join another band, he shall incur the ire of God and Hell shall be his shelter: a wretched fate!

You did not slay them, but it was God who slew them. You did not smite them, but it was God who smote them so that He might richly reward the faithful. God hears all and knows all. Even so; God will surely frustrate the designs of the unbelievers. 8:17

If you[1] were seeking a judgement, now has a judgement come to you. If you desist, it will be best for you. And if you resume the fight, We will fight back, and your forces shall avail you nothing, superior though they be in number: for God is with the faithful.

Believers, obey God and His apostle, and do not forsake him, now that you have heard all. Do not be like those who say: 'We hear,' but pay no heed to what they hear.

The meanest beasts in God's sight are those that are deaf, dumb, and devoid of reason. Had God perceived any virtue in them, He would have surely made them hear. But even if He had made them hear, they would have turned away and refused to listen.

Believers, obey God and the Apostle when he calls you to 8:24

---

1. The Meccans.

that which gives you life. Know that God stands between man and his heart, and that in His presence shall you all be herded.

8:25 Guard yourselves against temptation.[1] The wrongdoers among you are not the only men who will be tempted; and know that God's punishment is stern.

And remember when you were few in number and persecuted in the land, ever fearing the onslaught of the people, how He gave you shelter. He made you strong with His help and provided you with wholesome things that you might render thanks.

Believers, do not betray God and the Apostle, nor knowingly betray your trust. Know that your worldly goods and your children are but a temptation, and that God's recompense is great.

Believers, if you fear God He will grant you salvation and cleanse you of your sins and forgive you. Supreme is God's bounty.

8:30 And remember how the unbelievers plotted against you,[2] seeking to take you captive or to have you slain or banished. They schemed – and God also schemed. God is the most adroit of schemers.

Whenever Our revelations are recited to them, they say: 'We have heard them. If we wished, we could say the like. They are but fables of the ancients.'

They also say: 'Lord, if this be indeed the Truth revealed from You, rain down upon us stones from heaven or bring us some woeful scourge to punish us.'

But God would not punish them while you were present in their midst. Nor would God punish them if they sought forgiveness.

And yet it is but just that God should punish them; for they have debarred others from the Sacred Mosque, although its guardian they are not. Its guardians are only those that fear God, but most of them have no knowledge.

8:35 Their prayers at the Sacred House are nothing but whist-

---

1. Thus Al-Jalālayn; *fitnah* can also mean sedition.
2. Muḥammad.

ling and clapping of hands. 'Taste then the scourge, because you disbelieved.'

The unbelievers expend their riches in debarring others from the path of God. Thus do they dissipate their wealth: but they shall rue it, and in the end be overthrown. The unbelievers shall into Hell be driven.

8:36

God will separate the wicked from the just. He will heap all the wicked one upon another and then cast them into Hell. These will surely be lost.

Tell the unbelievers that if they mend their ways their past shall be forgiven; but if they relapse, then theirs shall be the fate of bygone nations.

Fight them until idolatry[1] shall cease and God's religion shall reign supreme.[2] If they desist, God is cognizant of what they do; but if they pay no heed, know then that God is your protector; the noblest Protector and the noblest Helper.

And know that if you gain any spoils one-fifth of them shall belong to God, the Apostle, his kin, the orphans, the destitute, and the traveller in need; if you truly believe in God and what We revealed to Our servant on the Day of Salvation,[3] the day when the two armies met. God has power over all things.

8:41

You were on the nearer side of the valley and the unbelievers on the farther side, with the caravan below you. Had they offered battle, you would have surely declined; but God sought to accomplish what had been ordained, so that he that was destined to perish might by a clear sign die, and he that was destined to live might by a clear sign survive. Surely God hears all and knows all.

God made them appear to you in a dream as few; had He showed them to you as many, your courage would have failed you and discord would have triumphed in your ranks. But this God spared you. He has knowledge of man's innermost thoughts.

And when you met them, He made each appear to the other few in number, that God might accomplish what had been ordained. To God shall all things be returned.

8:44

1. Thus Al-Jalālayn; see p. 118, note 1.
2. Literally, all religion shall be God's.
3. Or: the day of victory, according to some commentators.

8:45   Believers, when you meet a troop stand firm and pray to God at all times, so that you may triumph. And obey God and His apostle and do not quarrel among yourselves, lest you lose courage and your resolve weaken. Have patience: God is with those that are patient.

Do not be like those who left their homes gloating and to be seen by people. They debar others from the path of God: but God has full knowledge of what they do.

Satan had made their deeds seem fair to them; and he said: 'No one shall conquer you this day. I shall be at hand to help you.' But when the two armies came within sight of each other, he took to his heels, saying: 'I am done with you, for I can see what you cannot. I fear God. God's punishment is stern.'

The hypocrites, and those whose hearts were tainted, said: 'Their religion has deceived them.' But he that puts his trust in God shall find that God is mighty and wise.

If you could see the angels when they carry off the souls of the unbelievers! They shall strike them on their faces and their backs, saying: 'Taste the torment of the Conflagration! This is the punishment for what your hands committed.' God is never unjust to His servants.

8:52   Like Pharaoh's people and those before them, they disbelieved God's revelations. Therefore God smote them for their sins; mighty is God and stern His retribution.

God does not change the blessings He has bestowed upon a people until they change what is in their hearts. And God hears all and knows all.

Like Pharaoh's people and those before them, they disbelieved their Lord's revelations. We destroyed them for their sins, and We drowned Pharaoh's people. They were wrongdoers all.

Surely the basest creatures in the sight of God are the blasphemers who will not believe; those who time after time violate their treaties with you and have no fear of God. If you capture them in battle discriminate between them and those that follow them, so that their followers may take warning.

8:58   If you fear treachery from any of your allies, you may fairly retaliate by breaking off your treaty with them. God does not love the treacherous.

And let not the unbelievers think they will ever get away;   8:59
they have not the power so to do. Muster against them all the
armed force and cavalry at your command, that you may strike
terror into the enemy of God and your own enemy, and
others besides them who are unknown to you but known to
God. All that you give in the cause of God shall be repaid to
you; and you shall not be wronged.

If they incline to peace, make peace with them, and put
your trust in God. Surely He it is who hears all and knows
all. And should they seek to deceive you, all-sufficient is God
for you. He it was who has made you strong with His help and
rallied the faithful round you, uniting their hearts. If you had
given away all the riches of the earth, you could not have so
united them: but God has united them. He is mighty and wise.

Prophet, sufficient is God for you, and sufficient are the
faithful who follow you.

Prophet, rouse the faithful to arms. If there are twenty   8:65
steadfast men among you, they shall vanquish two hundred;
and if there are a hundred, they shall rout a thousand unbelievers, for they are devoid of understanding.

God has now lightened your burden, for He knows that
you are weak. If there are a hundred steadfast men among
you, they shall vanquish two hundred; and if there are a thousand, they shall, by God's will, defeat two thousand. God is
with those that are steadfast.

A prophet may not take captives until he has fought and
triumphed in the land. You[1] seek the chance gain of this
world, but God desires for you the world to come. God is
mighty and wise. Had there not been a previous writ from
God, you would have been sternly punished for what you
took. Enjoy therefore the good and lawful things which you
have gained in war, and fear God. Surely God is forgiving and
compassionate.

Prophet, say to those you have taken captive: 'If God finds   8:70
goodness in your hearts, He will give you that which is better

---

1. Muḥammad's followers.

than what was taken from you, and He will forgive you. God is forgiving and compassionate.'

8:71 But if they seek to betray you, they have already betrayed God. Therefore He has made you triumph over them; God is all-knowing and wise.

Those that have embraced the Faith and left their land, and fought for the cause of God with their wealth and with their persons; and those that sheltered and helped, shall be as friends to each other.

Those that have embraced the Faith, but have not left, shall in no way be your friends until they leave. But if they seek your help in the cause of the Religion, it is your duty to assist them, except against a people with whom you have a treaty. And God is ever observant of what you do.

8:73 The unbelievers give aid and comfort to each other. If you fail to do likewise, there will be sedition in the land and great corruption.

Those that have embraced the Faith and fled their land and fought for the cause of God, and those that sheltered and helped – they are the true believers. Forgiveness and a gracious provision await them.

8:75 Those that have since embraced the Faith and left their land and fought with you – they too are your brothers; although according to the Book of God those who are bound by ties of blood are nearest to one another. Surely God has knowledge of all things.

REPENTANCE[1]

9:1 A DECLARATION of immunity from God and His apostle to the idolaters with whom you have made treaties:

9:2 For four months you shall go unmolested in the land. But

---

1. This is the only *sūrah* in the Koran which does not begin with the invocation 'In the Name of God, etc.' Traditional commentators regard it as a continuation of 'The Spoils'.

know that you shall not escape God's judgement, and that God will humble the unbelievers.

A proclamation to the people from God and His apostle on the day of the Greater Pilgrimage: 9:3

God and His apostle are under no obligation to the idolaters. If you repent, it shall be well with you; but if you pay no heed, know that you shall not be immune from God's judgement.

Proclaim a woeful punishment to the unbelievers, except to those idolaters who have honoured their treaties with you in every detail and aided none against you. With these keep faith, until their treaties have run their term. God loves the righteous.

When the sacred months[1] are over kill the idolaters wherever you find them. Arrest them, besiege them, and lie in ambush everywhere for them. If they repent and take to prayer and render the alms levy, allow them to go their way; God is forgiving and compassionate.

If an idolater seeks asylum with you, give him protection so that he may hear the Word of God, and then convey him to safety; for the idolaters are ignorant people. 9:6

How can God and His apostle repose trust in the idolaters, save those with whom you have made treaties at the Sacred Mosque? So long as they keep faith with you, keep faith with them. God loves the righteous.

How can you trust them? If they prevail against you, they will respect neither treaties nor ties of kin. They flatter you with their mouths, but their hearts reject you; and most of them are ungodly.

They sell God's revelations for a paltry price and debar others from His path. Evil is what they do; they break faith with the believers and set at nought all ties of kin. Such are the transgressors.

If they repent and take to prayer and render the alms levy, they shall become your brothers in the Faith. Thus do We expound Our revelations to those endowed with knowledge.

But if, after coming to terms with you, they break their 9:12

---

1. Shawwāl, Dhūl-Q'adah, Dhūl-Ḥajjah, and Muḥarram.

oaths, and revile your religion, then fight the leaders of unbelief – for no oaths are binding for them – so that they may desist.

9:13   Will you not fight against those who have broken their oaths and conspired to banish the Apostle? They were the first to attack you. Do you fear them? Surely God is more deserving of your fear, if you are true believers.

Fight them: God will chastise them at your hands and humble them. He will grant you victory over them and heal the spirit of the faithful. He will take away all rancour from their hearts: God shows mercy to whom He pleases. God is all-knowing and wise.

Or did you imagine you would be forsaken before God has recognized those of you who have fought valiantly and served none but God, His apostle, and the faithful? God is cognizant of what you do.

It ill becomes the idolaters to visit the mosques of God, for they are unbelievers, self-confessed. Vain shall be their works, and in the Fire shall they abide for ever.

9:18   None should visit the mosques of God except those who believe in God and the Last Day, attend to their prayers, and render the alms levy and fear none but God; these shall be rightly guided.

Do you pretend that he who gives a drink to the pilgrims and pays a visit to the Sacred Mosque is as worthy as the man who believes in God and the Last Day, and fights for God's cause? These are not held equal by God; God does not guide the wrongdoers.

Those that have embraced the Faith, and left their land, and fought for God's cause with their wealth and with their persons, are held in higher esteem by God; and it is they who shall triumph. Their Lord has promised them the joy of mercy from Himself and His pleasure, and Gardens of eternal bliss, wherein shall they abide for ever; God's recompense is great indeed.

9:23   Believers, do not befriend your fathers or your brothers if they choose unbelief in preference to faith; wrongdoers are those of you that befriend them.

Say: 'If your fathers, your sons, your brothers, your wives, your tribes, the property you have acquired, the merchandise you fear may not be sold, and the homes you love, are dearer to you than God, His apostle and the struggle for His cause, then wait until God shall pass His judgement. God does not guide the ungodly.' 9:24

God has aided you on many a battlefield. In the Battle of Hunain[1] you set great store by your numbers, but they availed you nothing: the earth, for all its vastness, seemed to close in upon you, and you turned your backs and fled. Then God caused His Divine Presence[2] to descend upon His apostle and the faithful: He sent to your aid warriors you did not see and sternly punished the unbelievers: that was the infidels' recompense.

Then God will after that show mercy to whom He will. God is forgiving and compassionate.

Believers! The idolaters are unclean. Let them not approach the Sacred Mosque after this year is ended. If you fear poverty, God, if He pleases, will enrich you through His own bounty; God is all-knowing and wise. 9:28

Fight those who believe in neither God nor the Last Day, who do not forbid what God and His apostle have forbidden, and do not embrace the Religion of Truth, from among those who were given the Book, until they render the tribute, by hand, in abject submission.

The Jews say Ezra is the son of God, and the Christians say Christ is the son of God. Such are the words they utter with their mouths, by which they emulate the infidels of old. God smite them! How perverse they are!

They make of their clerics and their monks, and of Christ, the son of Mary, Lords besides God; though they were ordered to serve but one God; there is no God but Him. Exalted be He above those they deify besides Him! 9:31

---

1. Fought in the year 630. The Muslim army was 12,000 strong, the Meccans 4,000.
2. See p. 26, note 1.

9:32   They would extinguish the light of God with their mouths: but God seeks only to perfect His light, though the infidels abhor it.

He it was who has sent forth His apostle with guidance and the Religion of Truth that he may exalt it above all religion, though the idolaters abhor it.

Believers, many are the clerics and the monks who defraud the people of their possessions and debar them from the path of God. To those that hoard up gold and silver and do not spend them in God's cause, proclaim a woeful punishment: the day when their treasures shall be heated in the fire of Hell, and their foreheads, sides, and backs branded with them. They will be told: 'These are the treasures that for yourselves you hoarded. Taste then the treasures that you hoarded.'

God ordained the months twelve in number when He created the heavens and the earth. Of these, four are sacred, according to the True Religion. Therefore do not sin against yourselves by violating them. But fight the idolaters in all these months, as they themselves fight you in all of them. And know that God is with the righteous.

9:37   The postponement of sacred months is a grossly impious practice, in which the unbelievers are misguided. They make it lawful one year and make it unlawful in the next, in order to make up for the months which God has sanctified; thus making lawful what God has forbidden. Their foul acts seem fair to them: God does not guide the unbelievers.

Believers, why is it that when you are told: 'March in the cause of God,' you linger slothfully in the land? Are you content with this life in preference to the life to come? Few indeed are the blessings of this life, compared with those of the life to come.

If you do not go on the march, He will mete out to you grievous punishment, and will replace you by other people. You will in no way harm Him: for God has power over all things.

9:40   If you do not help him,[1] God did help him when he was

---

1. Muḥammad.

driven out by the unbelievers with one other.[1] In the cave he said to his companion: 'Do not despair, God is with us.' God caused His Divine Presence[2] to descend upon him and sent to his aid warriors you did not see, so that He brought low the unbelievers' design: supreme is God's design. God is mighty and wise.

Whether lightly armed or well-equipped, march on and fight for the cause of God, with your wealth and with your persons. This will be best for you, if you but knew it.   9:41

Had the gain been immediate or the journey short, they would have followed you:[3] but the distance seemed too far to them. Yet they will swear by God: 'Had we been able, we would have marched with you.' They bring ruin upon themselves. God knows that they are surely lying.

God pardon you! Why did you give them leave before you discovered who was speaking the truth, and knew who was lying?

Those that believe in God and the Last Day will not beg you to exempt them from fighting with their possessions and with their persons. God best knows the righteous. Only those seek exemption who disbelieve in God and the Last Day, and whose hearts are filled with doubt. Because they doubt, they waver.   9:44

Had they intended to set forth, they would have prepared themselves for the march. But God was loath to let them go, and held them back. They were bidden to stay with those who stayed behind.

Had they taken the field with you, they would have only added to your burden. They would have wormed their way through your ranks, seeking to sow discord among you: and among you there were some who would have been willing listeners. God well knows the wrongdoers.

They had sought to sow dissension before this, and turned things topsy-turvy for you until the Truth prevailed and the will of God became manifest, averse to it though they were.   9:48

1. Abū-Bakr, later the first of the Rightly-guided Caliphs.
2. See p. 26, note 1.
3. Muḥammad.

9:49 Some among them say: 'Give us leave to stay behind, and do not expose us to temptation.' Surely they have already succumbed to temptation. Hell shall engulf the unbelievers.

If you meet with success, it grieves them; and if a disaster befalls you, they say: 'We have already taken our precautions.' And they turn away, rejoicing.

Say: 'Nothing will befall us except what God has ordained for us. He is our guardian. In God let the faithful put their trust.'

Say: 'Are you waiting for anything to befall us except victory or martyrdom? We are waiting for God's scourge to smite you, direct from Him or at our hands. Wait if you will; we will wait with you.'

Say: 'Whether you give willingly or with reluctance, your offerings shall not be accepted from you; for you are ungodly people.'

Their offerings shall not be accepted from them only because they have denied God and His apostle. They pray but half-heartedly and give only with reluctance.

9:55 So let neither their riches nor their children make you wonder. Through these God seeks to punish them in the life of this world, so that their souls shall perish while they are still in unbelief.

They swear by God that they are believers with you, and they are not with you. But they are afraid. If they could find a shelter or some caves, or any hiding-place, they would run in frantic haste to seek refuge in it.

And there are some among them who speak ill of you[1] concerning the distribution of alms. If a share is given them, they are content: but if they are not given a share, they grow resentful.

Would that they were satisfied with what God and His apostle have given them, and said: 'All-sufficient is God for us. God will provide for us from His own bounty, and so will His apostle. To God we will humbly submit.'

9:60 Alms shall be only for the poor and the destitute; for those that are engaged in the management of alms and those whose

1. Muḥammad.

128

hearts are sympathetic to the Faith; for the freeing of slaves and debtors; for the advancement of God's cause; and for the traveller in need. That is a duty enjoined by God; God is all-knowing and wise.

And there are some among them who speak ill of the Prophet, saying: 'He has an ear for everything.' Say: 'He has an ear only for what is good for you. He believes in God and puts his trust in the faithful. He is a blessing to the true believers among you. Those that speak ill of God's apostle have woeful punishment in wait for them.' 9:61

They swear by God in order to please you. But it is more just that they should please God and the Apostle, if they are true believers.

Are they not aware that whoever defies God and His apostle shall abide for ever in the fire of Hell? That surely is the supreme humiliation.

The hypocrites are afraid lest a *sūrah* be revealed to them, telling them what is in their hearts. Say: 'Scoff if you will; God will surely bring to light what you are dreading.'

If you question them, they will surely say: 'We were only jesting and making merry.' Say: 'Would you mock God, His revelations, and His apostle? Make no excuses. You have renounced the Faith after embracing it. If We pardon some among you, We will punish others, for they were transgressors.' 9:65

Be they men or women, the hypocrites are all alike. They enjoin the reprehensible, forbid the just, and tighten their fists. They forgot God, so God forgot them. Surely it is the hypocrites who are the ungodly.

God has promised the hypocrites, both men and women, and the unbelievers, the fire of Hell. Therein shall they abide for ever: a sufficient recompense. God has cursed them; and lasting torment awaits them.

Like those before you, mightier they were than you, and had greater riches and more offspring. Like them, you have enjoyed your earthly lot and, like them, you have engaged in idle talk. But vain were their works in this life, and vain shall they be in the life to come. These will surely be lost.

Have they not heard the histories of those who have gone 9:70

before them? The fate of Noah's people and of 'Ād and Thamūd; of Abraham's people and the people of Midian and the Ruined Cities? Their apostles came to them with veritable signs. God did not wrong them, but they wronged their own souls.

9:71 The true believers, both men and women, are friends to one another. They enjoin the just and forbid the reprehensible; they attend to their prayers, and render the alms levy, and obey God and His apostle. On these God will have mercy. God is mighty and wise.

God has promised the men and women who believe in Him Gardens watered by running brooks, wherein shall they abide for ever: goodly mansions in the Gardens of Eden: and, what is more, they shall have grace in God's sight. That is the supreme triumph.

Prophet, make war on the unbelievers and the hypocrites and deal rigorously with them. Hell shall be their home: a wretched fate!

9:74 They swear by God that they said nothing. Yet they uttered the word of blasphemy and renounced Islām after embracing it. They sought to do what they could not attain. Yet they had no reason to be spiteful; except perhaps because God and His apostle had enriched them through His bounty. If they repent, it will indeed be better for them; but if they pay no heed, God will torment them grievously, in this world and in the world to come. They shall have none on earth to protect or succour them.

Some among them pledged themselves to God: 'If He is bountiful to us, we will assuredly give alms and be among the righteous.' But when God had bestowed His bounty on them they tightened their fists and, turning their backs, hurried away. He has caused hypocrisy to reign in their hearts till the day they meet Him, because they have been untrue to the pledge they gave Him and because of the lies they told.

Are they not aware that God knows what they conceal and what they talk about in secret? That God knows what is hidden? As for those that taunt the believers who give freely, and deride those who give according to their means, God will deride them. Woeful punishment awaits them.

It is the same whether or not you beg forgiveness for them. 9:80
If seventy times you beg forgiveness for them, God will not
forgive them, for they have denied God and His apostle. God
does not guide the ungodly.

Those that stayed at home were glad that they were left
behind by God's apostle, for they had no wish to fight for the
cause of God with their wealth and with their persons. They
said: 'Do not go to war, the heat is fierce.'

Say: 'More fierce is the heat of Hell-fire!' Would that they
understood!

They shall laugh but little and shed many tears. Thus shall
they be rewarded for what they did.

If God brings you back in safety and some of them ask
leave to march with you, say: 'You shall never march with me,
nor shall you ever fight with me against an enemy. You chose
to stay at home on the first occasion; therefore you shall now
stay with those who will remain behind.'

You shall not pray for any of their dead, nor shall you 9:84
attend their burial. For they denied God and His apostle and
remained sinners to the last.

So let neither their riches nor their offspring rouse your envy.
Through these God seeks to punish them in the life of this
world, so that their souls shall perish while still in unbelief.

Whenever a *sūrah* was revealed, saying: 'Believe in God and
fight alongside His apostle,' the rich among them excused
themselves to you, saying: 'Leave us; we would rather be with
those who are to stay behind.'

They were content to be with those who stayed behind: a
seal was set upon their hearts, leaving them bereft of understanding. But the Apostle and the men who shared his faith
fought with their wealth and with their persons. These shall be
rewarded with good things. These shall surely prosper. God
has prepared for them Gardens watered by running brooks,
wherein shall they abide for ever. That is the supreme triumph. 9:90

Some Arabs of the desert turned up with excuses, begging
to be given leave; while those who denied God and His apostle
remained idle at home. A woeful scourge shall fall on those of
them that disbelieved.

9:91 It shall be no offence for the disabled, the sick, and those lacking the means, to stay behind: if they are true to God and His apostle. The righteous shall not be blamed: God is forgiving and compassionate. Nor shall those be blamed who, when they came to you demanding conveyances to mount to the battle-front and you said you could find none to carry them, went away in tears grieving that they could find nothing to contribute.

The offenders are those that seek exemption although they are men of wealth. They are content to be with those who stay behind. God has set a seal upon their hearts so that they are devoid of knowledge.

They will come up to you with excuses when you return to them. Say: 'Make no excuses: we will not believe you. God has revealed to us the truth about you. God will watch your actions, and so will His apostle. Then you shall return to Him who knows alike the unknown and the manifest, and He will declare to you what you have done.'

9:95 When you return they will appeal to you in God's name to let them be. So let them be: they are an abomination. Hell shall be their home, in requital for their misdeeds.

They will swear to you in order to gain your acceptance. But if you accept them, God will not accept the ungodly.

The desert Arabs surpass others in unbelief and hypocrisy, and have more cause to be ignorant of the laws which God has revealed to His apostle. But God is all-knowing and wise.

Some desert Arabs regard what they give as a compulsory fine and wait for some misfortune to befall you. May ill-fortune befall them! God hears all and knows all.

Yet there are some among the desert Arabs who believe in God and the Last Day, and regard what they give as a means of bringing them close to God and to the Apostle's prayers. Indeed, closer they shall be brought; God will admit them into His mercy; God is forgiving and compassionate.

9:100 As for those who led the way, the first of the *muhājirīn*[1] and the *ansār*,[2] and those who nobly followed them, God is pleased

---

1. Muḥammad's early followers who fled with him to Medina.
2. Muḥammad's supporters in Medina.

with them and they are pleased with Him. He has prepared for them Gardens watered by running brooks, wherein shall they abide for ever. That is the supreme triumph.

Some of the desert Arabs around you are hypocrites, and so are some of the citizens of Madīnah, who are indeed fanatical in their hypocrisy. You know them not, but We know them well. Twice We will chastise them: then shall they return to a grievous torment. 9:101

Others there are who have confessed their sins; they intermixed their good works with evil. Perchance God will pardon them: God is forgiving and compassionate. Take alms from their wealth, that they may thereby be cleansed and purified, and pray for them: for your prayers will give them comfort. God hears all and knows all.

Do they know not that God accepts repentance from His servants and welcomes alms, and that God pardons and is compassionate?

Say: 'Act as you will. God will behold your actions, and so will His apostle and the faithful; then shall you return to Him who knows alike the unknown and the manifest, and He will declare to you what you have done.' 9:105

And there are yet others who must await God's decree. He will either punish them or pardon them: God is all-knowing and wise.

And there are those who built a mosque from mischievous motives, to spread unbelief and disunite the faithful, in expectation of him[1] who had made war on God and His apostle. They swear their intentions were nothing but good, and God bears witness that they are lying. You shall not set foot in it; it is more fitting that you should pray in a mosque founded on piety from the very first, wherein you shall find men who love to keep themselves pure; God loves those that are purified.

Who is a better man, he who founds his house on the fear of God and His good pleasure, or he who builds on the brink of a crumbling precipice, so that his house will fall with him into the fire of Hell? God does not guide the wrongdoers. 9:109

1. Abū 'Āmir.

9:110   The edifice they built shall ever inspire their hearts with doubt, until their hearts are cut in pieces. God is all-knowing and wise.

God has purchased from the faithful their lives and worldly goods, and in return has promised them the Garden. They will fight for the cause of God, they will slay, and be slain. Such is the true promise He made in the Torah, the Gospel, and the Koran; and who is more true to his pledge than God? Rejoice then in the bargain you have made; that is the supreme triumph.

Those that repent and those that worship and praise Him; those that fast and those that kneel and prostrate themselves; those that enjoin justice, forbid the reprehensible, and observe God's commandments: proclaim joyful tidings to the faithful.

It is not for the Prophet or the believers to beg forgiveness for idolaters, even though they be related, after it has become manifest to them that they have earned the punishment of 9:114   Hell. Abraham prayed for his father only to fulfil a promise he had made him. But when he realized he was an enemy of God, he disowned him. Yet Abraham was a compassionate and tender-hearted man.

Nor will God confound men after He has given them guidance until He has manifested to them all that they should avoid; God has knowledge of all things.

God has sovereignty over the heavens and the earth; He ordains life and death. You have none besides God to protect or help you.

God pardoned the Prophet, the *muhājirīn* and the *anṣār*, who stood by him in the hour of adversity, when some among them were on the point of losing heart. He pardoned them; 9:118   He took pity on them and was compassionate. And to the three who had been left behind. So despondent were they that the earth, for all its vastness, and their own souls, seemed to close in upon them. They knew there was no refuge from God except in Him. Therefore He pardoned them, that they might repent: God pardons and is compassionate.

You believers, fear God and stand firm with those who 9:119
uphold the cause of Truth. No cause have the people of
Madīnah and the desert Arabs around them to forsake God's
apostle or to jeopardize his life so as to safeguard their own;
for they do not expose themselves to thirst or hunger or to
any ordeal in the cause of God, nor do they take any step
which may displease the unbelievers, nor do they inflict any
loss on an enemy but it shall be noted down for them as a
good deed: God will not deny the righteous their reward.
Each sum they give, be it small or large, and each valley they
traverse, shall be noted down, so that God may requite them
for their noblest deeds.

It is not right that all the faithful should go to war at once.
A band from each community should stay behind to instruct
themselves in the Religion and to admonish their people when
they return, so that they may be warned.

Believers, fight the infidels who dwell around you. Deal 9:123
firmly with them; and know that God is with those that fear
Him.

Whenever a *sūrah* is revealed, some among them ask:
'Which of you has had his faith increased by this?' It will
surely increase the believers' faith and give them joy. As for
those whose hearts are tainted, it will add abomination to
their abomination, so that they shall die while still in unbelief.

Do they not see how every year they were afflicted once or
twice? Yet they neither repent nor take warning. And whenever a *sūrah* is revealed, they glance at each other, asking: 'Is
anyone watching you?' Then they turn away. God has turned
away their hearts, for they are senseless people.

There has now come to you an apostle of your own, one
who grieves at your sinfulness and cares for you; one who is
benevolent and compassionate to the believers.

If they pay no heed, say: 'All-sufficient is God for me. 9:129
There is no god but Him; in Him I have put my trust. And He
is the Lord of the Glorious Throne.'

JONAH

In the Name of God, the Merciful, the Compassionate

10:1 ALIF *lām rā'*. These are the revelations of the Wise Book: Does it seem strange to people that We revealed Our will to a mortal from among themselves, saying: 'Give warning to the people, and proclaim joyful tidings to the faithful that they may have a tried and true footing with their Lord'?

The unbelievers say: 'This man[1] is a sorcerer manifest.' Yet your Lord is God, who in six days created the heavens and the earth and then ascended the throne, ordaining all things. None has power to intercede without His sanction. Such is God, your Lord: therefore serve Him. Will you not reflect?

To Him shall you all return: God's promise shall be fulfilled. He brings the Creation into being and will then restore it, so that He may justly recompense those who have believed and done good works. As for the unbelievers, scalding water shall they drink, and for their unbelief woeful punishment awaits them.

10:5 It was He that gave the sun his brightness and the moon her light, ordaining her phases that you may learn to compute the seasons and the years.[2] God created them only to manifest the Truth. He expounds His revelations to those endowed with knowledge.

In the alternation of night and day, and in all that God has created in the heavens and the earth, there are signs for the God-fearing.

Those who entertain no hope of meeting Us, being pleased and contented with the life of this world, and those who pay no heed to Our revelations, shall have the Fire as their abode in requital for their deeds.

As for those that believe and do good works, their Lord will guide them through their faith. Brooks will run at their
10:10 feet in the Gardens of Delight. Their prayer will be: 'Glory be

---

1. Muḥammad.
2. Cf. Genesis 1:14.

to You, Lord!' and their greeting: 'Peace!' 'Praise be to God, Lord of the Universe' will be the burthen of their plea.

Had God hastened what is ill for people as they would has- 10:11 ten what is good, their fate would have been sealed. Therefore We leave those who entertain no hope of meeting Us to their wrongdoing, ever straying from the right path.

When misfortune befalls man, he prays to Us lying on his side, sitting, or standing on his feet. But as soon as We relieve his affliction he carries on, as though he never prayed to Us to relieve the misfortune that touched him. Thus do their deeds seem fair to the transgressors.

We obliterated generations before you on account of the wrongs they did; their apostles had come to them with verit- able signs, but they would not believe. Thus do We requite the transgressors. We then made you their successors in the land, so that We might observe how you would act.

When Our clear revelations are recited to them, those who 10:15 entertain no hope of meeting Us say to you: 'Give us a Koran different from this, or change it.'

Say: 'It is not for me to change it, of my own accord. I fol- low only what is revealed to me, for I fear, if I disobey my Lord, the punishment of a fateful day.'

Say: 'Had God pleased, I would never have recited it to you, nor would He have made you aware of it. A whole life- time I dwelt among you before its coming. Will you not understand?'

Who is more wicked than he who invents a falsehood about God or denies His revelations? Truly, the transgressors shall not succeed.

They worship idols that can neither harm nor help them, and say: 'These will intercede for us with God.'

Say: 'Do you presume to tell God of what He knows to exist neither in the heavens nor on earth?' Glory be to Him! Exalted be He above the gods they serve besides Him!

There was a time when mankind were but one community. 10:19 Then they disagreed among themselves: and but for a Word from your Lord, long since decreed, their differences would have been surely resolved.

10:20 And they say: 'Why has no sign been sent down to him from his Lord?'

Say: 'God alone has knowledge of what is hidden. Wait if you will: I will wait with you.'

No sooner do We let people taste a blessing after some misfortune has afflicted them than they begin to scheme against Our revelations. Say: 'More swift is God's scheming. Our emissaries are recording your intrigues.'

He it is who guides them by land and sea. They embark: and as the ships set sail, rejoicing in a favourable wind, a raging tempest overtakes them. Billows surge upon them from every side and they fear they are encompassed by death. They call out to God, fervently dedicating all religion to Him: 'Deliver us from this peril and we will be truly thankful.'

Yet when He does deliver them, they perpetrate corruption in the land and act unjustly.

You people! It is your own souls that you are corrupting. Take your enjoyment in this life: to Us shall you then return, and We will declare to you all that you have done.

10:24 This present life is like the rich garment with which the earth adorns itself when watered by the rain We send down from the sky. Crops, sustaining man and beast, grow luxuriantly: but, as the earth's tenants begin to think themselves its masters, down comes Our scourge upon it, by night or by day, laying it waste, as though it did not blossom but yesterday. Thus do We expound Our revelations to people who reflect.

God invites you to the Abode of Peace; He guides whom He will to a straight path. Those that have done good works shall have a good recompense, and more besides. Neither blackness nor misery shall overcast their faces. They are the heirs of Paradise, wherein shall they abide for ever.

As for those that have done evil, evil shall be requited with like evil. Misery will oppress them (they shall have none to protect them from God), as though patches of the night's own darkness veiled their faces. These shall be the tenants of the Fire, wherein shall they abide for ever.

10:28 And on the day We herd them all together, We shall say to the idolaters: 'Keep to your places, you and your idols!' We will separate them one from another, and then their idols will say to them: 'It was not us that you worshipped. Sufficient is God as our witness, and your witness. Nor were we aware of your worship.'

Thereupon each soul will know what it did in days gone by. They shall be sent back to God, their true Lord, and the idols they invented will forsake them.

Say: 'Who provides for you from heaven and earth? Who has endowed you with hearing and sight? Who brings forth the living from the dead, and the dead from the living? Who ordains all things?'

They will say: 'God.'

Say: 'Will you not take heed, then? Such is God, your true Lord. That which is not true must needs be false. How then can you turn away?'

Thus is the Word of your Lord made true about the ungodly; they will not believe.

Say: 'Can any of your idols bring the Creation into being and then restore it?' Say: 'God brings the Creation into being and will then restore it. How is it that you are so misled?'

Say: 'Can any of your idols give guidance to the Truth?' Say: 'God gives guidance to the Truth. Who is more worthy to be followed: He that can give guidance to the Truth, or he that cannot and is himself in need of guidance? What has come over you that you so judge?'

Most of them follow nothing but mere conjecture. But conjecture is in no way a substitute for Truth. God is cognizant of what they do.

This Koran could not have been devised by any but God. Indeed, its confirmation of what was revealed before it, and its expounding of the Book, are beyond doubt from the Lord of the Universe.

If they say: 'He invented it himself,' say: 'Bring one *sūrah* like it. Call on whom you will besides God to help you, if what you say be true!'

Indeed, they disbelieve what they cannot grasp, for they have not yet seen its prophecy fulfilled. Likewise did those

10:29

10:34

10:39

before them disbelieve. But see what was the fate of the wrongdoers.

10:40 Some among them believe in it, and some among them do not believe in it. But your Lord best knows the evil-doers.

If they disbelieve you, say: 'My deeds are mine and your deeds are yours. You are not accountable for my actions, nor am I accountable for what you do.'

Some among them listen to you. But can you make the deaf hear you, incapable as they are of understanding?

Some among them look upon you; but can you show the way to the blind, bereft as they are of sight?

Indeed, in no way does God wrong people, but people wrong themselves.

The day He herds them all together, as though they had lingered but for an hour, they will acquaint themselves with each other and realize they shall lose out: those who denied they would ever meet God and did not follow the right path.

Whether We show you but some of the torment We threaten them with, or claim you back to Us before that, to Us they shall return, and God will then be witness to all their actions.

10:47 Each community has its own apostle. When their apostle comes, justice is done among them; they are not wronged.

They say: 'When will this promise be fulfilled, if what you say be true?'

Say: 'I have no control over any harm or benefit to myself, except by the will of God. A space of time is fixed for each community; when their time is come, not for one hour shall they delay: nor can they go before it.'

Say: 'Do but consider. Should His scourge fall upon you in the night or by the light of day, what punishment would the guilty hasten? Will you believe in it when it does overtake you, although it was your wish to hurry it on?'

Then will the wrongdoers be told: 'Feel the everlasting torment! Shall you not be rewarded according only to what you have earned?'

10:53 And they ask you if it is true. Say: 'Yes, by the Lord, it is certainly true! And you shall not escape.'

To redeem itself then, each soul would gladly give all that   10:54
the earth contains if it possessed it. They will rue in secret
when they behold the scourge; but judgement shall be fairly
passed upon them; they shall not be wronged.

Surely to God belongs all that the heavens and the earth
contain. Surely the promise of God is true, but most of them
have no knowledge. He it is who ordains life and death, and to
Him shall you be recalled.

You people! An Admonition has come to you from your
Lord, a cure for the mind, a guide and a blessing to the
believers.

Say: 'In God's grace and mercy let them rejoice, for these
are better than the worldly riches they amass.'

Say: 'Do but consider the provision God has sent down for
you. Some of it you pronounced unlawful and some, lawful.'
Say: 'Was it God who gave you leave, or do you invent falsehood about God?'

What will they think, those who invent falsehood about
God, on the Day of Resurrection? God is bountiful to mankind: yet most of them do not give thanks.

You shall engage in no affair, you shall recite no verse from   10:61
the Koran, you shall commit no act, but We shall be witnesses
over you when you engage in it. Not an atom's weight in earth
or heaven escapes your Lord, nor is there any object smaller
or greater, but is recorded in a veritable Book.

But surely the servants of God have nothing to fear or to
regret. Those that have faith and fear Him shall rejoice both
in this life and in the life to come: the words of God shall
never change. That is the supreme triumph.

Let not their words grieve you. All glory belongs to God;
He it is who hears all and knows all.

Surely to God belong all who are in the heavens and all
who are on the earth. Those that follow what they call gods
besides God follow nothing but idle fancies and preach
nothing but falsehoods.

He it is who has ordained the night for you to rest in and   10:67
given the day its light for you to see with. Surely in this there
are signs for attentive people.

10:68   They say: 'God has begotten a son.' Glory be to Him! Self-sufficient is He. His is all that the heavens and the earth contain. Have you any sanction for this? Would you say of God what you know not?

Say: 'Those that invent falsehood about God shall not succeed. They may take their ease in this life, but to Us they shall then return, and for their unbelief We will make them taste the grievous torment.'

And recount to them the tale of Noah. He said to his people: 'If it offends you, my people, that I should dwell in your midst and preach to you God's revelations (for in God I have put my trust), muster all your idols and decide on your course of action. Do not intrigue in secret. Execute your judgement and give me no respite. If you turn away, remember I demand of you no recompense. Only God will reward me. I am commanded to be a Muslim.'

But they disbelieved him. Therefore We saved him and those who were with him in the ark, so that they survived, and drowned those that denied Our revelations. Consider, then, the fate of those who were forewarned.

10:74   After him We sent apostles to their descendants. They brought them veritable signs, but they would not have faith in what they disbelieved before. Thus do We seal up the hearts of the transgressors.

Then We sent forth after them Moses and Aaron with Our signs to Pharaoh and his nobles. But they responded with scorn, for they were wicked people. And when the Truth had come to them from Us, they declared: 'Surely this is but sorcery manifest.'

Moses replied: 'Is this what you say of the Truth when it has come to you? Is this sorcery? Sorcerers shall never succeed.'

They said: 'Have you come to turn us away from the faith of our forefathers, that you two may lord it over the land? We will never believe in the pair of you.'

And Pharaoh said: 'Bring every learned sorcerer to my presence.'

And when the sorcerers attended, Moses said to them:
10:81   'Throw down what you wish to throw.' And when they had

thrown, Moses said: 'The sorcery that you have wrought, God will surely bring to nothing. God does not make good the work of those who do evil. By His words God vindicates the Truth, averse to it though the transgressors may be.' 10:82

Few of his[1] people believed in Moses, for they feared the persecution of Pharaoh and his nobles. Surely Pharaoh was a tyrant in the land, a man of rampant wickedness.

Moses said: 'If you believe in God, my people, in Him alone then put your trust if you are Muslims.'

They replied: 'In God we have put our trust. Lord, do not let us suffer at the hands of the wrongdoers. Deliver us, through Your mercy, from the unbelievers.'

We revealed Our will to Moses and his brother, saying: 'Build houses in Egypt for your people and make your homes places of worship. Conduct prayers and give good tidings to the faithful.'

'Lord,' said Moses, 'You have bestowed on Pharaoh and his nobles splendour and riches in this life, Lord, so that they may stray from Your path. Lord, wipe out their riches and harden their hearts, so that they shall persist in unbelief until they face the woeful scourge.' 10:88

He said: 'Your prayer shall be answered. Follow, both of you, the straight path and do not walk in the footsteps of those that have no knowledge.'

And We led the Israelites across the sea, and Pharaoh and his legions pursued them with wickedness and spite. But as he was drowning, Pharaoh said: 'Now I believe no god exists except the One in whom the Israelites believe. I am now a Muslim.'

'Only now! But before this you were a rebel and an evil-doer. We shall today save your body, so that you may become a sign for all posterity; a great many of mankind do not heed Our signs.'

We settled the Israelites in a secure land and provided them with wholesome things. Nor did they disagree among themselves until knowledge was given them. Your Lord will on the Day of Resurrection judge their differences. 10:93

1. Pharaoh's.

10:94 If you doubt what We have revealed to you, ask those who have read the Book before you. Truth has come to you from your Lord: therefore do not doubt it. Nor shall you deny God's revelations, for then you will be one of the lost.

Those for whom the Word of your Lord shall be fulfilled will not believe, even if every sign has come to them, until they face the woeful torment. Were it otherwise, every community, had it believed, would have profited from its faith. But it was so only with Jonah's people. When they believed, We spared them the punishment of disgrace in this nether life and suffered them to take their ease a while. Had your Lord pleased, all the people of the earth would have believed, one and all. Would you then force people to have faith?

None can have faith except by God's leave. He will visit abomination upon the senseless.

Say: 'Behold what the heavens and the earth contain!' But neither signs nor warnings will avail the unbelievers.

10:102 What can they wait for but the fate of those who have gone before them? Say: 'Wait if you will; I will wait with you.'

We shall save Our apostles and those who believe; it is but just that We should save the faithful.

Say: 'You people! Doubt my religion if you will, but never will I worship those that you worship besides God. I worship God, who will claim you back: for I am commanded to be a believer: "Dedicate yourself to the Religion in all uprightness and serve none besides God. You shall not pray to idols which can neither help nor harm you; for if you do, you will become a wrongdoer. If God afflicts you with a misfortune, none can remove it but Him; and if He bestows on you a good thing, none can withhold His bounty. He is bountiful to whom He will among His servants. He is the Forgiving One, the Compassionate."'

Say: 'You people! Truth has come to you from your Lord. He that follows the right path follows it for his own good, and he that strays from the right path strays at his own peril. I am not your keeper.'

10:109 Observe what is revealed to you, and have patience till God make known His judgement. He is the best of judges.

HŪD

In the Name of God, the Merciful, the Compassionate

ALIF *lām rā'*. A Book, whose verses are perfected and then   11:1
expounded, from Him who is wise and all-knowing:

Serve none but God. I am sent to you from Him to warn
you and to give good tidings.

Seek forgiveness of your Lord and turn to Him in penitence. A goodly provision He will make for you for an
appointed term, and will bestow His grace on each that has
merit. But if you pay no heed, then beware the torment of a
fateful day: to God shall you return. And He has power over
all things.

They cover up their bosoms to conceal their thoughts from
Him. But when they put on their garments, does He not know
what they conceal and what they reveal? He well knows their
innermost thoughts.

And there is not a creature on the earth but God provides   11:6
its sustenance. He knows its dwelling and its final resting-place.
All is recorded in a veritable Book.

Throned above the waters, He created the heavens and the
earth in six days, to find out which of you shall best acquit
yourselves.

When you[1] say: 'After death you shall be raised to life,' the
unbelievers declare: 'It is but sorcery manifest.' And if We put
off their punishment till an appointed time, they will surely
say: 'Why is it delayed?'

On the day it overtakes them, they shall not be immune
from it: the terrors at which they scoffed will encompass them.

If We let man taste a blessing from Ourself and then withhold it from him, he yields to despair and becomes ungrateful.   11:10
And if after adversity We let him taste good fortune, he will
surely say: 'Gone are my sorrows from me,' and grow jubilant
and boastful.

---

1. Muḥammad.

11:11 Not so the steadfast who do good works; forgiveness and a rich recompense await them.

You may chance to omit a part of what is revealed to you and be distressed because they say: 'Why has no treasure been sent down to him? And why has no angel come with him?'

But you are only to give warning; and God is the guardian of all things. Or do they say: 'He has invented it'?[1] Say: 'Produce ten *sūrahs* like it, all invented. Call on whom you will among your idols, if what you say be true. If they do not answer you, know then that it is revealed with God's knowledge, and that there is no god but Him. So will you be Muslims?'

Those that desire the life of this world and all its finery We shall reward for their deeds in their own lifetime: they shall not be given less. They are those who in the world to come shall have earned nothing but the Fire. Fruitless are their deeds, and vain are all their works.

11:17 Are they to be compared to those that have received a revelation from their Lord, recited by a witness from Him and heralded by the Book of Moses, a guide and a blessing? These have faith in it, but the factions who deny it shall be consigned to the Fire. Therefore do not doubt it. It is the Truth from your Lord: yet most people do not believe.

And who is more wicked than he who invents a falsehood about God? These shall be brought before their Lord; and witnesses will say: 'These are they who lied about their Lord.'

God's curse is on the wrongdoers, who debar others from the path of God and seek to make it crooked, and who deny the life to come. These shall not be impregnable in the land; there is none to protect them besides God. Their punishment shall be doubled, for they could neither hear nor see.

Such are those who shall forfeit their souls; their false 11:22 devices will forsake them, and in the life to come they will assuredly lose most.

1. The Koran.

As for those that believe and do good works and humble   11:23
themselves before their Lord, they are the heirs of Paradise,
wherein shall they abide for ever.

The two are like the blind and the deaf compared with
those that can see and hear. Are the two equal? So will you not
take thought?

We sent forth Noah to his people. He said: 'I have come to
warn you plainly. Serve none but God; beware the torment of
a woeful day.'

The unbelieving elders of his people said: 'We see you as
but a mortal like ourselves. Nor can we see you being followed
by any but the lowliest of our people: rash and undiscerning.
We see no superior merit in you: indeed we think that you are
lying.'

He said: 'Consider, my people! If my Lord has revealed to
me His will and bestowed on me a favour of His own, though
it be hidden from you, can we impose it on you, and you
averse to it? I seek of you no recompense for this, my people;   11:29
for none but God can reward me. Nor will I drive away the
faithful, for they will surely meet their Lord. But I can see that
you are ignorant people. And were I to drive them away, my
people, who would protect me from God? Will you not
reflect?

'I do not say to you that I possess God's treasuries, nor
have I knowledge of what is hidden; I do not claim to be an
angel, nor do I say to those your eyes disdain that God will not
be bountiful to them – God knows best what is in their
hearts – for then I should become a wrongdoer.'

'Noah,' they said, 'you have argued with us, and argued to
excess. Bring down the scourge you threaten us with, if what
you say be true!'

He said: 'God will bring it down upon you if He pleases:
nor shall you be immune. My counsel will not profit you if
God intends to confound you, willing though I am to offer
you counsel. He is your Lord, and to Him shall you be recalled.'

If they say: 'He has invented it himself,' say: 'If I have   11:35
indeed invented it, then may I be punished for my sin! I am
innocent of your imputations.'

And it was revealed to Noah: 'None of your people will believe in you save those who already believe. Do not grieve at what they do. Build the ark under Our watchful eyes, and with Our inspiration. You shall not plead with Me for those who have done wrong: they shall assuredly be drowned.'

So he built the ark. And whenever some elders of his people passed by him they mocked him. He said: 'If you mock us, we shall mock you just as you mock us. You shall learn who will be visited by a scourge that shall humiliate him, and be smitten by a scourge everlasting.'

And when Our judgement was passed and water welled out from the Oven, We said: 'Take into the ark a pair from every species, your kin (except for those already doomed), and the true believers.' But none believed with him except a few.

'Embark,' he said. 'In the name of God it shall set sail and cast anchor. Surely my Lord is forgiving and compassionate.'

And as the ark moved on with them amid the mountainous waves, Noah cried out to his son, who stood apart: 'Embark with us, my son; do not remain with the unbelievers.'

He replied: 'I shall seek refuge on a mountain, which will protect me from the water.'

He said: 'None shall be secure today from God's judgement but those who shall enjoy His mercy!' And thereupon the billows rolled between them, and Noah's son was drowned.

A voice cried out: 'Earth, swallow up your waters. Heaven, cease your rain!' The flood abated, and judgement was passed. The ark came to rest upon Al-Jūdī, and a voice declared: 'Gone are the wrongdoers.'

Noah called out to his Lord, saying: 'Lord, my son was my own flesh and blood. Your promise was surely true; You are the most just of judges.'

'Noah,' He said, 'he was no kin of yours: he had acted unjustly. Do not question Me about things you know nothing of. I admonish you lest you become an ignorant man.'

He said: 'I seek refuge in You, Lord, from asking You about things I know nothing of. Forgive me and have mercy on me, or I shall surely be among the lost.'

11:37

11:42

11:47

A voice said: 'Noah, land in peace with blessings from Ourself upon you and on *some* of the communities that are with you. Other communities We will suffer to take their ease, and will then visit them with a woeful scourge.' 11:48

That which We now reveal to you is secret history: it was unknown to you and to your people before this. Have patience; a joyful end awaits the righteous.

And to 'Ād We sent their kin Hūd. He said: 'Serve God, my people; you have no god but Him. False are your fabrications. I demand of you no recompense, my people, for none can reward me except my Creator. Will you not understand?

'My people, seek forgiveness of your Lord and turn to Him in penitence. He will send from the sky abundant rain upon you; He will add strength to your strength. Do not turn away from Him with wrongdoing.'

They said: 'Hūd, you have given us no evidence. We will not forsake our gods at your behest, nor will we believe in you. We can only suppose that one of our gods has afflicted you with evil.' 11:54

He said: 'God be my witness, and you are my witnesses too: I disown your idols. Scheme against me if you will, and give me no respite. I have put my trust in God, my Lord and your Lord. There is not a creature on the earth whose destiny He does not govern. Straight is the path of my Lord.

'If you pay no heed, I have made known to you what I was sent with, and my Lord will replace you by other people. You will in no way harm Him. My Lord is watching over all things.'

And when Our judgement came to pass, We delivered Hūd through Our mercy, together with those who shared his faith; We delivered them from a mighty scourge.

Such were 'Ād. They denied the revelations of their Lord, disobeyed His apostles, and did the bidding of every headstrong reprobate. Cursed were they in this world, and cursed shall they be on the Day of Resurrection.

'Ād denied their Lord. Gone are 'Ād, the people of Hūd.

And to Thamūd We sent their kin Ṣāliḥ. He said: 'Serve God, my people; you have no god but Him. It was He who brought you into being from the earth and gave you means to 11:61

dwell upon it. Seek forgiveness of Him, and turn to Him in penitence. My Lord is near at hand and answers all.'

11:62 'Ṣāliḥ,' they said, 'great were the hopes we placed in you before this. Would you now forbid us to serve the gods our fathers worshipped? Truly, we strongly doubt the faith to which you call us.'

He said: 'Do but consider, my people! If my Lord has revealed to me His will and bestowed on me His grace, who would protect me from God if I rebelled against Him? You would surely aggravate my ruin.

'My people, here is God's she-camel, a sign for you. Leave her to graze at will in God's own land, and do not molest her lest an instant scourge should fall upon you.'

Yet they hamstrung her. He said: 'You have but three days to take your ease in your dwellings: this prophecy shall not prove false.'

11:66 And when Our judgement came to pass, We delivered Ṣāliḥ through Our mercy from the ignominy of that day, together with those who shared his faith. Mighty is your Lord and all-powerful. The Cry took the wrongdoers, and when morning came they were crouching lifeless in their dwellings, as though they had never prospered there.

Thamūd denied their Lord. Gone are Thamūd.

Our messengers came to Abraham with joyful tidings. They said: 'Peace!' 'Peace!' he said, and hastened to bring them a roasted calf. But when he saw their hands being withheld from it, he mistrusted them and was afraid of them. They said: 'Have no fear. We are sent forth to the people of Lot.'

His wife, who was standing by, laughed.[1] We bade her rejoice in Isaac, and after Isaac, Jacob.

'Alas!' she said. 'How shall I bear a child when I am old and this, my husband, is well advanced in years? This is indeed a marvel.'

11:73 They said: 'Do you marvel at the ways of God? May God's mercy and blessings be upon you, dear hosts! Worthy of praise is He and glorious.'

---

1. Cf. Genesis 18:12.

And when awe left Abraham as he pondered the joyful tid- 11:74
ings, he pleaded with Us for the people of Lot. Abraham was
gracious, tender-hearted, and devout.

'Abraham, plead no more; Your Lord's will must needs be
done. Irrevocable is the scourge which shall smite them.'

And when Our emissaries came to Lot, he grew anxious
about them, and was distressed on their account. 'This is
indeed a day of woe,' he said.

His people, long addicted to evil practices, came hurrying
towards him. 'My people,' he said, 'here are my daughters:[1]
surely they are more wholesome to you. Fear God, and do not
shame me by insulting my guests. Is there not one right-minded
man among you?'

They said: 'You well know we have no need of your daughters; and you know full well what we are seeking.'

He said: 'Would that I had power enough to overcome you,
or could find refuge in a tower of strength!'

They said: 'Lot, we are the emissaries of your Lord: they 11:81
shall not touch you. Depart with your kin in the dead of night
and let none of you turn back, except your wife; she shall suffer the fate that they shall suffer. In the morning their hour
will come; is not the morning near?'

And when Our judgement came to pass, We turned their
city upside down and let loose upon it a shower of clay-stones
bearing the tokens of your Lord. The fate of the wrongdoers
was not far off.

And to the people of Midian We sent their kin Shu'aib. He
said: 'Serve God, my people; you have no god but Him. Do
not give short weight and measure. Prosperous though you
are, beware the torment of a fateful day.

'My people, give just weight and measure in all fairness. Do
not defraud people of their possessions, nor shall you corrupt
the land with evil. Better for you is God's recompense, if you
are true believers. I am not your keeper.'

'Shu'aib,' they said, 'do your prayers bid you we renounce 11:87
the gods our fathers worshipped and not conduct our affairs

1. Cf. Genesis 19:8.

in the manner we please? Truly, you are a kind and rightly-guided man!'

11:88 He said: 'Do but consider, my people! If my Lord has revealed to me His will and bestowed on me a gracious gift, should I not guide you? I do not wish to argue with you, only to practise myself what I forbid you. I seek only to reform you: as far as I am able. Nor can I succeed without God's help. In Him I have put my trust and to Him I turn in penitence.

'My people, let your dispute with me not bring upon you the doom which overtook the people of Noah, the people of Hūd, and the people of Ṣāliḥ; nor is it long since the people of Lot were punished. Seek forgiveness of your Lord and turn to Him in penitence. Compassionate and loving is my Lord.'

They said: 'Shuʻaib, much of what you say we cannot comprehend. We surely know how weak you are in our midst. But for your tribe, we should have stoned you. You shall on no account prevail against us.'

11:92 He said: 'My people, have you more regard for my tribe than for God? Dare you turn your backs upon Him? My Lord has knowledge of all your actions. Do what you will, my people, and so will I. You shall learn who will be punished and held up to shame, and who is lying. Watch if you will; I will watch with you.'

And when Our judgement was carried out We delivered Shuʻaib through Our mercy, together with those who shared his faith. The Cry took the wrongdoers, and when morning came they were crouching lifeless in their dwellings, as though they had never prospered there. Like Thamūd, gone are the people of Midian.

We sent forth Moses with Our signs and with manifest authority to Pharaoh and his nobles. But they followed the behest of Pharaoh; nor was Pharaoh's behest rightly guided. He shall stand at the head of his people on the Day of Resurrection, and shall lead them into the Fire. Evil is the place they shall be led to.

11:99 A curse followed them in this world, and on the Day of Resurrection an evil gift shall they receive.

The annals of those communities We recount to you: some have survived, while others have ceased to be. We did not wrong them, but they wronged themselves. The gods they called on besides God availed them nothing when your Lord's will was done; they only added to their ruin.

Such was the scourge with which your Lord scourged the communities while they sinned. Harrowing and relentless is His scourge.

Surely in this there is a sign for him that dreads the torment of the Hereafter. That will be a day on which all mankind shall be gathered; and that shall be a fateful day.

We shall defer it only for a time decreed. When that day is come, no soul shall speak but by His leave. Some shall be damned, and some shall be blessed. The damned shall be cast into the Fire, where, groaning and wailing, they shall abide as long as the heavens and the earth endure, unless your Lord ordain otherwise: your Lord shall accomplish what He will. As for the blessed, they shall abide in Paradise as long as the heavens and the earth endure, unless your Lord ordain otherwise: an endless recompense. Have no doubt as to what they worship; they worship what their fathers worshipped before them. Their deserts We shall requite, undiminished.

We gave the Book to Moses, but differences arose about it. And but for a Word from your Lord, already decreed, their fate would have long been sealed. Yet this they strongly doubt.

Your Lord will surely reward each according to his deeds; He has full knowledge of what they do. Follow then the straight path as you are bidden, together with those who have repented with you, and do not transgress. Surely He is ever observant of what you do.

Put no trust in the wrongdoers, lest the Fire should touch you. And none but God can protect or help you.

Attend to your prayers at the two ends of the day, and in part of the night-time too. Good deeds shall make amends for sins. This is an Admonition for those that reflect. And have patience; God will not deny the righteous their reward.

Was there, among the generations that have gone before you, a remnant that forbade corruption in the land, except the

11:117 few We had delivered from among them? The wrongdoers pursued their worldly pleasures and were sinful. The Lord would not have ruined the cities, without just cause, had their inhabitants been upright.

And had your Lord pleased, He would have united mankind in one community. They are still at odds, except for those to whom your Lord has shown mercy. To this end He has created them. The Word of your Lord shall be fulfilled: 'I will fill Hell with jinn and humans all.'

We recount to you the histories of those apostles to put courage into your heart. Through them Truth shall be revealed to you, with precepts and an Admonition for the faithful.

Say to the infidels: 'Do whatever lies within your power, and so shall we. Wait if you will; we too are waiting.'

11:123 God alone has knowledge of what the heavens and the earth conceal; to Him all things shall be referred. Worship Him, and put your trust in Him; your Lord is never heedless of what you do.

JOSEPH

In the Name of God, the Merciful, the Compassionate

12:1 ALIF *lām rā'*. These are the revelations of the veritable Book. We have revealed it an Arabic Koran, that you may grow in understanding.

In inspiring you with this Koran We recount to you the best of narratives, though before it you were heedless.

Joseph said to his father: 'Father, I dreamt of eleven stars and the sun and the moon; I saw them prostrate themselves before me.'[1]

'My son,' he replied, 'say nothing of this dream to your brothers, lest they plot evil against you: Satan is the sworn 12:6 enemy of man. Even thus shall you be chosen by your Lord. He will teach you to interpret visions, and will perfect His

1. Cf. Genesis 37:9.

favour to you and to the House of Jacob, as He perfected it to your forefathers Abraham and Isaac before you. Your Lord is all-knowing and wise.'

Surely in Joseph and his brothers there are signs for doubting men.

12:7

They said to each other: 'Surely Joseph and his brother[1] are dearer to our father than ourselves, though we are many. Truly, our father is much mistaken. Kill Joseph, or cast him away in some far-off land, so that you may have no rival in your father's love, and after that be honourable men.'

One of the brothers said: 'Do not kill Joseph; but, if you must, rather cast him into a dark pit. Some caravan will take him up.'

They said: 'Father, why do you not trust us with Joseph? Surely we wish him well. Send him with us tomorrow, that he may play and enjoy himself. We will take good care of him.'

He said: 'It would much grieve me to let him go with you; for I fear lest the wolf should eat him when you are off your guard.'

They said: 'If the wolf could eat him when we are so many, then we should surely be lost!'

12:14

So when they took him with them, they together resolved to cast him into a dark pit. We revealed to him Our will, saying: 'You shall tell them of all this when they will not know you.'

At nightfall they returned to their father, weeping. 'Father,' they said, 'we went off to compete together, and left Joseph with our packs. The wolf devoured him. But you will not believe us, though we speak the truth.' And they brought him their brother's shirt, stained with false blood.

'No!' he cried. 'Your souls have tempted you to something evil. Sweet patience! God alone can help me bear the loss you speak of.'

And a caravan passed by, who sent their water-bearer to the pit. And when he had let down his pail, he cried: 'Rejoice! Here is a boy!'

12:19

---

1. His full brother, Benjamin.

They concealed him as part of their merchandise. But God knew what they did. They sold him for a trifling price, for a few pieces of silver. They cared nothing for him.

The Egyptian who bought him said to his wife: 'Be kind to him. He may prove useful to us, or we may adopt him as our son.'

Thus We established Joseph in the land, and taught him to interpret dreams. God has power to accomplish His will, though most may not know it. And when he reached maturity We bestowed on him wisdom and knowledge. Thus do We reward the righteous.

The woman in whose house he served attempted to seduce him. She bolted the doors and said: 'Come!'

'God forbid!' he replied. 'My lord has treated me with kindness. Wrongdoers shall never prosper.'

She made for him, and he himself would have succumbed to her had he not seen the sign of his Lord. Thus did We shield him from evil-doing and lechery, for he was one of Our faithful servants.

They both rushed to the door. She tore his shirt from behind. And at the door they met her husband.

She said: 'Shall not the man who wished to violate your wife be thrown into prison or sternly punished?'

Joseph said: 'It was she who attempted to seduce me.'

'If his shirt is torn from the front,' said one of her people who was present, 'she is speaking the truth and he is lying. And if his shirt is torn from behind, then she is lying and he is speaking the truth.'

And when her husband saw that Joseph's shirt was rent from behind, he said to her: 'This is but one of your tricks. Your cunning is great indeed! Joseph, say no more about this. Woman, ask pardon for your sin. You have assuredly done wrong.'

In the city, women were saying: 'The Prince's wife has sought to seduce her servant. She has conceived a passion for him. We can see that she has clearly gone astray.'

When she heard of their intrigues, she invited them to a banquet prepared at her house. To each she gave a knife, and

12:20

12:25

12:30

12:31

ordered Joseph to present himself before them. When they saw him, they were amazed at him and cut their hands, exclaiming: 'God preserve us! This is no mortal, but a gracious angel.'

'This is he,' she said, 'on whose account you blamed me. I attempted to seduce him, but he was unyielding. If he declines to do my bidding, he shall be thrown into prison and shall be held in scorn.' 12:32

'Lord,' said Joseph, 'sooner would I go to prison than give in to their advances. Shield me from their cunning, or I shall yield to them and lapse into folly.'

His Lord answered his prayer and warded off their cunning from him. Surely He it is who hears all and knows all.

Yet, for all the evidence they had seen, they thought it right to jail him for a time.

Two young men entered the prison with him. One said: 'I dreamt that I was pressing grapes.' And the other: 'I dreamt I was carrying a loaf upon my head, and the birds came and ate of it. Tell us the meaning of these dreams, for we can see you are a man of virtue.'

He said: 'Whatever food you are provided with, I can divine for you its meaning, even before it reaches you. This knowledge my Lord has given me, for I have left the faith of those that disbelieve in God and deny the life to come. And I followed the faith of my forefathers, Abraham, Isaac, and Jacob. We are not to serve idols besides God. Such is the grace which God has bestowed on us and on mankind. Yet the larger part of mankind do not give thanks. 12:37

'Fellow prisoners! Are sundry gods better than God, the One who conquers all? Those you serve besides Him are nothing but names which you and your fathers have devised and for which God has revealed no sanction. Judgement rests only with God. He has commanded you to worship none but Him. That is the True Religion: but the larger part of mankind have no knowledge.

'Fellow prisoners, one of you will serve his lord with wine. The other will be crucified, and the birds will peck at his head. That is the answer to your question.' 12:41

12:42 And he said to the prisoner who he knew would survive: 'Remember me in the presence of your lord.'

But Satan made him forget to mention Joseph to his lord, so that he stayed in prison for several years.

The King said: 'I saw seven fatted cows which seven lean ones devoured; also seven green ears of corn and seven others dry. Tell me the meaning of this vision, my nobles, if you can interpret visions.'

They said: 'They are but a medley of dreams; nor are we skilled in the interpretation of dreams.'

Thereupon the man who had been freed remembered after all that time. He said: 'I shall bring you what it means. Give me leave to go.'

'Joseph,' he said, 'man of truth, tell us of the seven fatted cows which seven lean ones devoured; also of the seven green ears of corn and the other seven which were dry: so that I may go back to the people and inform them.'

12:47 He said: 'You shall sow for seven consecutive years. Leave in the ear the corn you reap, except a little which you may eat. There shall follow seven hungry years which will consume all but a little of what you stored. Then will come a year of abundant rain, in which the people will press the grape.'

He said: 'Bring this man before me.'

But when the envoy came to him, Joseph said: 'Go back to your master and ask him about the women who cut their hands. My master well knows their cunning.'

The King questioned the women, saying: 'What made you attempt to seduce Joseph?'

'God forbid!' they said. 'We know no evil of him.'

'Now the truth must come to light,' said the Prince's wife. 'It was I who attempted to seduce him. He has told the truth.'

'From this,' said Joseph, 'my lord will know that I did not betray him in his absence, and that God does not guide the
12:53 mischief of the treacherous. Not that I claim to be free from sin: man's soul is prone to evil, except his to whom my Lord has shown mercy. My Lord is forgiving and compassionate.'

The King said: 'Bring him before me. I will choose him for 12:54
my own.'

And when he had spoken with him, he said: 'You shall
henceforth dwell with us, honoured and trusted.'

Joseph said: 'Give me charge of the granaries of the land.
I know how to husband them wisely.'

Thus did We establish Joseph in the land, and he dwelt
there as he pleased. We bestow Our mercy on whom We will,
and never deny the righteous their reward. Surely better is the
recompense of the life to come for those who believe in God
and fear Him.

Joseph's brothers came and presented themselves before
him. He recognized them, but they knew him not. And when
he had given them their provisions, he said: 'Bring me a
brother of yours from your father. Do you not see that I give
just measure and am the best of hosts? If you refuse to bring
him to me, you shall have no measure here, nor shall you
come near me.'

They replied: 'We will endeavour to fetch him from his 12:61
father. This we will surely do.'

He said to his servants: 'Put their silver[1] into their packs, so
that they may discover it when they return to their people.
Perchance they will come back.'

When they returned to their father, they said: 'Father, corn
is henceforth denied us. Send our brother with us and we shall
have our measure. We will take good care of him.'

He said: 'Am I to trust you with him as I once trusted you
with his brother? But God is the best of guardians: and of all
those that show mercy He is the most merciful.'

When they opened their packs, they discovered that their 12:65
silver had been returned to them. 'Father,' they said, 'what
more can we desire? Here is our silver returned to us. We will
buy provisions for our people, and take good care of our
brother. We should receive an extra camel-load; a camel-load
should be easy enough.'

1. Literally, their merchandise.

12:66 He replied: 'I will not send him with you until you promise in God's name to bring him back to me, unless the worst befall you.'

And when they had given him their pledge, he said: 'God is the witness of what we say. My sons, do not enter from one gate; enter from different gates. In no way can I shield you from the might of God; judgement is God's alone. In Him I have put my trust. In Him let the trustful put their trust.'

And when they entered as their father bade them, he could in no way shield them from the might of God. It was but a wish in Jacob's soul which he had thus fulfilled. He was possessed of knowledge which We had given him. But the greater part of mankind have no knowledge.

When they went in to Joseph, he embraced his brother, and said: 'I am your brother. Do not grieve at what they did.'

And when he had provided them with their provisions, he hid a drinking-cup in his brother's pack.

Then a crier called: 'Travellers, you are surely thieves!'

12:71 They turned back to them, and said: 'What have you lost?'

'We miss the King's drinking-cup,' they said. 'He that brings it shall have a camel-load. I pledge my word for it.'

'In God's name,' they said, 'you know we did not come to do evil in the land. We are no thieves.'

They said: 'What punishment shall be his, if you prove to be lying?'

They said: 'He in whose pack the cup is found shall penalize himself for what he did. Thus do we punish the wrongdoers.'

He searched their bags before his brother's, and then took out the cup from his brother's bag.

Thus did we devise it for Joseph: by the King's law he had no right to seize his brother: but God willed otherwise. We exalt whom We will to a lofty station: and above those that have knowledge there is One who is all-knowing.

12:77 They said: 'If he has stolen – know then that a brother of his did steal before him.'

But Joseph kept his secret and revealed nothing to them.

He said: 'Your deed was worse. God best knows the things you speak of.'

They said: 'Noble Prince, he has an aged father; take one of us, instead of him. We can see you are a man of virtue.'

He said: 'God forbid that we should take any but the man with whom our property was found: for then we should surely be unjust.'

When they despaired of him, they went aside to confer in private. Their eldest said: 'Do you not know that your father took from you a pledge in God's name, and that long before you did your worst with Joseph? I will not stir from the land until my father gives me leave or God makes known to me His judgement: He is the best of judges. Return to your father and say to him: "Father, your son has stolen. We testify only to what we know: we could not guard against the unforeseen. Inquire at the city wherein we lodged, and from the caravan we travelled with. We surely speak the truth."'

'No!' cried their father. 'Your souls have tempted you to evil. But I will have sweet patience. God may bring them all to me: He alone is all-knowing and wise.' And he turned away from them, crying: 'Alas for Joseph!' His eyes went white with grief, and he was oppressed with silent sorrow.

They said: 'In God's name, will you not cease to remember Joseph until you ruin your health and die?'

He said: 'I complain only to God of my sorrow and sadness; God has made known to me things that you know not. Go, my sons, and seek news of Joseph and his brother. And do not despair of God's spirit; none but unbelievers despair of God's spirit.'

And when they went in to him, they said: 'Noble Prince, we and our people are scourged with famine. We have brought but little money. Give us our full measure, and be charitable to us: God surely rewards the charitable.'

'Do you know,' he said, 'what you did to Joseph and his brother? You are surely unaware.'

They said: 'Can you indeed be Joseph?'

'I am Joseph,' he said, 'and this is my brother. God has

been gracious to us. Those that fear God and endure with fortitude, God will not deny the virtuous their reward.'

12:91 'By the Lord,' they said, 'God has exalted you above us all. We have indeed done wrong.'

He said: 'None shall reproach you this day. May God forgive you: of all those that show mercy He is the most merciful. Take this shirt of mine and throw it over my father's face: he will recover his sight. Then return to me with your people all.'

When the caravan departed their father said: 'I feel the breath of Joseph, though you will not believe me.'

'By the Lord,' they said, 'you are surely under your old illusion.'

And when the bearer of joyful tidings arrived, he threw Joseph's shirt over the old man's face, and he regained his sight. He said: 'Did I not tell you, God has made known to me what you know not?'

They said: 'Father, implore forgiveness for our sins. We have indeed done wrong.'

12:98 He said: 'I shall implore my Lord to forgive you. He it is who is the Forgiving, the Compassionate One.'

And when they went in to Joseph, he embraced his parents and said: 'Welcome to Egypt, safe, if God wills!'

He helped up his parents to the throne, and they all fell on their knees and prostrated themselves before him.

'This,' he said to his father, 'is the meaning of my old vision: my Lord has fulfilled it. He has been gracious to me; He has released me from prison, and brought you out of the desert after Satan had stirred up strife between me and my brothers. My Lord is gracious to whom He will: He alone is all-knowing and wise.

'Lord, You have given me authority and taught me to interpret dreams. Creator of the heavens and the earth, my guardian in this world and in the world to come! Allow me to die a Muslim, and admit me among the righteous.'

12:102 That which We now reveal to you[1] is a tale of the unknown. You were not present when they conceived their plan, and

1. Muḥammad.

when they schemed together. Yet strive as you may, the greater 12:103
part of mankind will not believe.

And you demand of them no recompense for this: it is but
an Admonition to mankind.

Many are the marvels in the heavens and the earth; yet they
pass them by and pay no heed to them. The greater part of
them believe in God only if they can worship other gods
besides Him.

Are they confident they will not be overwhelmed by a
scourge from God, or that the Hour will not overtake them
unawares, without warning?

Say: 'This is my path. With sure knowledge I call on you to 12:108
have faith in God, I and all my followers. Glory be to God! I
am no idolater.'

Nor were those We sent before you other than men We
inspired from people of the cities.

Have they not travelled the land and seen what was the end
of those who disbelieved before them? Surely better is the life
to come for those that fear God. Can you not understand?

And when the apostles despaired and thought they were
denied, Our help came down to them, delivering whom We
pleased. The transgressors could not be saved from Our
power. Their annals point a moral to those that are of good 12:111
sense possessed.

This is no invented tale, but a confirmation of what came
before it, an explanation of all things, a guide and a blessing to
people who believe.

THUNDER

In the Name of God, the Merciful, the Compassionate

ALIF *lām mīm rā'*. These are the revelations of the Book: and 13:1
that which has been revealed to you from your Lord is Truth,
yet most do not believe.

It was God who raised the heavens without visible pillars. 13:2
He then ascended the throne and pressed the sun and the

moon into service, each pursuing an appointed course. He ordains all things: He makes plain His revelations, so that you may firmly believe in meeting your Lord.

13:3 It was He who spread out the earth and placed upon it mountains and rivers. He gave all plants their male and female parts and drew the veil of night over the day. Surely in these there are signs for people who reflect.

And in the land there are adjoining plots: vineyards and cornfields and groves of palm, the single and the clustered. Their fruits are nourished by the same water: yet We make the taste of some more favoured than the taste of others. Surely in this there are signs for people who understand.

If anything could make you marvel, then you should surely marvel at those who say: 'When we are dust, shall we be restored in a new creation?'

Such are those who deny their Lord. Their necks shall be bound with chains. Those are the tenants of the Fire, wherein shall they abide for ever.

13:6 And they bid you hasten evil rather than good. Yet many were those who were punished before them. Your Lord is forgiving to people, despite their wrongdoing: yet stern is your Lord in retribution.

And the unbelievers say: 'Why has no sign been sent down to him from his Lord?' But you are only to give warning; every nation has its mentor.

God knows what every female bears: He knows the wombs whose term falls short, and those that signify increase. For everything He has a finite measure.

He knows the unknown and the manifest: the Supreme One, the Most High.

It is the same whether you converse in secret or aloud, whether you hide under the cloak of night or walk about in 13:11 the light of day. Each has guardian angels before him and behind him, who preserve him by God's command.

God does not change a people's lot unless they change what is in their hearts. If God seeks to afflict them with a misfortune, none can ward it off. Besides Him, they have no protector.

He it is who makes the lightning flash upon you, inspiring 13:12
you with fear and hope, and gathers up the heavy clouds. The
thunder sounds His praises, and the angels, too, in awe of
Him. He hurls His thunderbolts at whom He pleases. Yet they
wrangle about God; and stern is His might.

To Him is the prayer of Truth. The idols to which they
pray give them no answer. They are like a man who stretches
out his hands to the water and bids it rise to his mouth: it cannot reach it. Vain are the prayers of the unbelievers.

All who dwell in the heavens and on the earth shall prostrate themselves before God: some willingly, some perforce,
and their very shadows, morning and evening.

Say: 'Who is the Lord of the heavens and the earth?'
Say: 'God.'
Say: 'Why then have you chosen other gods besides Him,
who, even to themselves, can do neither good nor harm?'

Say: 'Are the blind and the seeing equal? Is darkness equal
to the light?'

Or have their idols brought into being a creation like His,
so that both creations appear to them alike?

Say: 'God is the Creator of all things; He is the One who
conquers all.'

He sends down water from the sky which fills the riverbeds 13:17
to overflowing, so that the torrent bears a swelling foam, akin
to that which rises from smelted ore when men make ornaments and tools. Thus God depicts Truth and falsehood. The
scum is cast away, but that which is of use to man remains
behind. Even thus God speaks in parables.

Rich is the recompense of those that obey their Lord. But
those that disobey Him – if they possessed all that the earth
contains, and as much besides, they would gladly offer it for
their ransom. Theirs shall be a baleful reckoning. Hell shall be
their home, an evil resting-place.

Is then he who knows that the Truth has been revealed to
you from your Lord like him who is blind?

Truly, none will remember but those that are of good sense
possessed: those who keep faith with God and do not break
their pledge; who join together what God has bidden to be 13:21

13:22 united; who fear their Lord and dread a baleful reckoning; who for the sake of God endure with fortitude, attend to their prayers, and from what We gave them give in private and in public; and who ward off evil with good. These shall have the recompense of Paradise. They shall enter the Gardens of Eden, together with the righteous among their fathers, their spouses, and their descendants. From every gate the angels will come in to them, saying: 'Peace be to you for all that you have steadfastly endured; blessed is the recompense of Paradise.'

As for those who break God's covenant after confirming it, who put asunder what God has bidden to be united and perpetrate corruption in the land, the curse shall light on them; the scourge of Hell awaits them.

God gives abundantly to whom He will, and sparingly likewise. They rejoice in the life of this world: yet the life of this world is but a brief diversion compared with the life to come.

13:27 The unbelievers say: 'Why has no sign been sent down to him from his Lord?'

Say: 'God leaves in error whom He will, and guides to Himself those who repent and have faith; whose hearts find comfort in the remembrance of God. Surely in the remembrance of God all hearts are comforted. Blessed are those who believe and do good works; blissful is their final abode.'

Thus have We sent you forth to a community before whom other communities had passed away, that you may recite to them that with which We have inspired you. Yet they deny the Lord of Mercy. Say: 'He is my Lord. There is no god but Him. In Him I have put my trust, and to Him I shall return.'

13:31 And even if there be a Koran whereby the mountains could be set in motion, the earth rent asunder, and the dead communed with, surely all things are subject to God's will. Are the faithful unaware that, had God pleased, He could have guided all mankind?

As for the unbelievers, because of their misdeeds disaster shall not cease to afflict them or to crouch at their very doorstep until God's promise be fulfilled. God will not fail the appointed time.

Apostles were mocked before you: but, though I bore with the unbelievers, My scourge at length took them; and how terrible was My scourge! 13:32

Who is it that watches every soul and all its actions? Yet they set up other deities besides God. Say: 'Name them. Would you tell Him of that which is unknown to Him on the earth? Or are they merely empty words?'

Indeed, their foul devices seem fair to the unbelievers, for they are debarred from the right path. They have no guide, those whom God has led astray. Torment awaits them in this nether life: but more grievous is the torment of the life to come. From God they have no protector.

Such is the Paradise the righteous have been promised: it is watered by running brooks: eternal is its fruit, and eternal is its shade. Such shall be the end of the righteous; and the Fire shall be the fate of the unbelievers.

Those to whom We gave the Book rejoice in what is revealed to you, while some factions deny a part of it. Say: 'I am only commanded to serve God and to associate none with Him. To Him I pray, and to Him I shall return.' 13:36

Thus have We revealed it, a code of judgements in the Arabic tongue. If you succumb to their desires after the knowledge you have been given, from God you shall have no guardian or protector.

We sent forth apostles before you and gave them wives and descendants. Yet no apostle could work a miracle except by God's leave. Every age has a term decreed. God abrogates and confirms what He pleases. His is the Decree Eternal.

Whether We let you glimpse in some measure the scourge We promise them, or claim you back to Us, your mission is only to give warning: it is for Us to do the reckoning.

Do they not see how We invade their land and diminish its borders? If God decrees a thing, none can reverse it. And swift is His reckoning.

Those who have gone before them also schemed, but God is the master of all scheming: He knows what every soul has done. And the unbelievers will then learn for whom the blissful end is destined. 13:42

13:43 And the unbelievers say: 'You are not sent.' Say: 'Sufficient is God as my witness and your witness, and so are those who know the Book.'

ABRAHAM

In the Name of God, the Merciful, the Compassionate

14:1 ALIF *lām rā'*. A Book We have revealed to you so that, by their Lord's leave, you may lead the people from darkness to the light; to the path of the Mighty, the Praiseworthy One: the path of God, to whom belongs all that the heavens and all that the earth contain.

Woe betide the unbelievers, for they shall be grievously punished! Those who love the life of this world more than the life to come; who debar others from the path of God and seek to make it crooked: they have strayed far into error.

Each apostle We have sent has spoken only in the language of his own people, that he might clearly guide them. But God leaves in error whom He will and gives guidance to whom He pleases; He is the Almighty, the Wise One.

14:5 We sent forth Moses with Our signs: 'Lead your people out of the darkness into the light, and remind them of God's bounty.' Surely in this there are signs for every steadfast, thankful man.

And when Moses said to his people: 'Remember God's goodness to you when He delivered you from Pharaoh's nation, who had oppressed you cruelly, slaughtering your sons and sparing only your daughters; surely that was a grievous trial by your Lord. For your Lord had declared: "If you give thanks, I will bestow abundance upon you: but if you are thankless, My punishment is terrible indeed."'

And Moses said: 'If you and all who are on earth prove thankless, God does not need your thanks, though He deserves your praise.'

14:9 Have you not heard what befell those that have gone before you? The people of Noah, 'Ād, and Thamūd, and those who came after them? God alone knows their number. Their apostles came to them with veritable signs, but they bit their hands with their mouths[1] and said: 'We disbelieve your message. Indeed, we strongly doubt the faith to which you call us.'

Their apostles said: 'Is God, Creator of the heavens and the earth, to be doubted? He calls you that He may forgive you your sins and reprieve you till an appointed time.' 14:10

They said: 'You are but mortals like ourselves. You wish to turn us away from the gods our fathers worshipped. Bring us some clear authority.'

Their apostles said to them: 'We are indeed but mortals like yourselves; but God bestows His grace on such of His servants as He chooses. We cannot give you proof, except by God's leave; in God let true believers put their trust. And why should we not trust in God, when He has already guided us on to our paths? We will endure your persecution patiently. In God let the trusting put their trust.'

'Return to our fold,' the unbelievers said to their apostles, 'or we will banish you from our land.' 14:13

But their Lord revealed His will to them: 'We shall surely destroy the wrongdoers and shall surely give you the land to dwell in after them. Let him take heed who dreads My eminence and fears My threats.'

And they called for help; and every hardened sinner came to grief.

Hell will stretch behind him, and putrid water shall he drink: he will sip, but scarcely swallow. Death will assail him from every side, yet shall he not be dead. Harrowing torment awaits him.

The works of the unbelievers are like ashes which the wind scatters on a stormy day: they shall gain nothing from what they earn. That is surely the way to egregious error.

Do you not see that God created the heavens and the earth with Truth? He can remove you if He will and bring into being a new creation: that is no difficult thing for God. 14:20

---

1. I.e. with rage; thus Al-Jalālayn. Literally, they thrust their hands into their mouths.

14:21   All shall appear before God. The humble will say to those who thought themselves mighty: 'We were your followers. Can you protect us from God's punishment in any way?'

They will say: 'Had God given us guidance, we would have guided you. Neither panic nor patience will help us now. There is no escape for us.'

And when judgement had been passed, Satan will say to them: 'True was the promise which God made you. I too made you a promise, but did not keep it. Yet had I no power over you. I only called you, and you answered me. Do not now blame me, but blame yourselves. I cannot help you, nor can you help me. I never believed in that with which you associated me before.'

Grievous torment awaits the wrongdoers. And those that believe and do good works shall be admitted into Gardens watered by running brooks, wherein, by their Lord's leave, shall they abide for ever. Their greeting shall be: 'Peace!'

14:24   Do you not see how God compares a good word to a good tree? Its root is firm and its branches are in the sky; it yields its fruit in every season by its Lord's leave. God speaks in parables to people so that they may reflect. But an evil word is like a rotten tree torn out of the earth and shorn of all its roots.

God makes steadfast the faithful with His steadfast Word, both in this life and in the life to come. God leads the wrongdoers astray; God accomplishes what He pleases.

Have you not thought of those who repay the grace of God with unbelief and drive their people into the House of Perdition? In Hell shall they burn; and evil shall be their fate.

They set up equals to God to lead people away from His path. Say to them: 'Take your pleasure now: you are surely destined for the Fire.'

Tell My servants, those who are true believers, to be steadfast in prayer and from what We gave them to give in private and in public, before that day arrives when all trading shall cease and friendships be no more.

14:32   God it was who created the heavens and the earth. He sends down water from the sky wherewith He brings forth fruits for your sustenance. He has subdued the ships which, by His leave, sail the ocean in your service. He has subdued for you the rivers, and subdued for you the sun and the moon, which steadfastly pursue their courses. And He has subdued for you the night and the day. And of everything you have asked Him for He has given you some. If you reckoned up God's bounties you could not count them. Truly, man is wicked and thankless.

14:33

Abraham said: 'Lord, make this land[1] secure. Preserve me and my descendants from serving idols. Lord, many have they led astray. He that follows me shall become my brother, and if any turns against me, You are surely forgiving and compassionate.

'Lord, I have settled some of my offspring in a barren valley near Your Sacred House, so that they may observe true worship, Lord. Put in some people's hearts kindness towards them, and provide them with the earth's fruits; perchance they will give thanks.

'Lord, You have knowledge of all that we conceal and all that we reveal: nothing on earth or in heaven can be concealed from God.

14:38

'Praise be to God who has bestowed on me Ishmael and Isaac despite my old age! My Lord well hears all prayers.

'Lord, make me and my descendants steadfast in prayer. Lord, accept my prayer.

'Forgive me, Lord, and forgive my parents and all the faithful on the Day of Reckoning.'

Never think that God is unaware of the wrongdoers' actions. He only gives them respite till the day on which all eyes will stare with consternation. They shall rush in terror with heads uplifted; they shall stare, but see nothing; their hearts utterly vacant.

Forewarn the people of a day when the scourge will overtake them; when the wrongdoers will say: 'Lord, grant us respite for a short while. We will obey Your call, and follow the apostles.'

14:44

1. Mecca.

'Did you not once swear that you would never die away?

14:45 You lived in the dwellings of those who wronged their souls before you: yet you knew full well how We had dealt with them, and We spoke to you in parables about them.'

They schemed, but their schemes were known to God, even if their schemes could move mountains.

Never think that God will break the pledge He gave to His apostles. Mighty is God, and capable of revenge.

On the day when the earth is changed into a different earth and the heavens into new heavens, mankind shall stand before God, the One, who conquers all. On that day you shall see the guilty bound with chains, their garments pitch, and their faces covered with flames.

God will surely requite each soul according to what it earned. Swift is God's reckoning.

14:52 This is an exhortation to the people. Let them be warned thereby and know that He is but one God. Let them reflect, those that are of good sense possessed.

AL-ḤIJR

In the Name of God, the Merciful, the Compassionate

15:1 ALIF *lām rā'*. These are the revelations of the Book, and a veritable Koran:

The day will surely come when those who disbelieve will wish they were Muslims. Let them feast and make merry; and let their hopes beguile them. They shall learn.

Never have We destroyed a city whose term of life was not ordained and known beforehand. Communities cannot forestall their doom, nor can they retard it.

They say: 'You to whom the Admonition was revealed, you are surely possessed. Bring down to us the angels, if what you say be true.'

We shall send down the angels only with the Truth. Then shall they never be reprieved.

15:9 It was We that revealed the Admonition, and shall Ourself

preserve it. We have sent forth apostles before you to the   15:10
older nations: but they scoffed at each apostle We sent them.
Thus do We put doubt into the hearts of the guilty: they deny
him, despite the example of the ancients.

If We opened for them a gate in heaven and they ascended
through it higher and higher, still would they say: 'Our eyes
were dazzled: truly, we must have been bewitched.'

And We have decked the sky with constellations and made
them lovely to behold; and We guarded them from every
cursèd demon. Eavesdroppers are pursued by a fiery comet.

We have spread out the earth and set upon it immovable
mountains. We have planted it with every seasonable fruit,
providing sustenance for yourselves and for those you do not
provide for. We hold the store of every blessing and send it
down only in appropriate measure. We let loose the fertilizing
winds and bring down water from the sky for you to drink; its
stores are beyond your reach.

It is surely We who ordain life and death; We are the Heirs   15:23
of all things.

We surely know those who have gone before you, as We
surely know those who will come hereafter; and it is your
Lord who shall herd them all together. He is wise and all-
knowing.

We created man from dry clay, from black moulded loam,
and before him Satan from smokeless fire. Your Lord said to
the angels: 'I am creating man from dry clay, from black
moulded loam. When I have fashioned him and breathed My
spirit into him, kneel down and prostrate yourselves before
him.'

The angels, one and all, prostrated themselves, except
Satan: he refused to be with those who prostrated themselves.

He said. 'Satan, how is it that you are not with those who
prostrated themselves?'

He said: 'I was not to bow to a mortal whom You created
of dry clay, of black moulded loam.'

'Get you hence,' said He, 'you are accursed: and the curse
shall be on you till Judgement-day.'

'Lord,' he said, 'reprieve me till the Day of Resurrection.'   15:36

15:37 He said: 'You are reprieved till the Appointed Day.'

'Lord,' said Satan, 'since You have thus tempted me, I will seduce those on earth: I will surely tempt them all, except those among them who are Your faithful servants.'

He said: 'This is My straight path. You shall have no power over My servants, only the sinners who follow you: they are all destined for Hell. It has seven gates, and through each gate they shall come in separate bands. The righteous shall dwell among gardens and fountains; in peace and safety shall they enter them. We shall remove all rancour from their hearts, and they shall take their ease on couches face to face, a band of brothers. Toil shall not weary them, nor shall they ever be driven out.'

Tell My servants that I alone am the Forgiving One, the Compassionate; and that My scourge is the only woeful scourge.

And tell them of Abraham's guests: When they went in to him and said: 'Peace,' he said: 'We fear your intent.'

15:53 'Have no fear,' they said. 'We come to you with joyful tidings. You shall have a son endowed with knowledge.'

He said: 'Do you bring me such joyful tidings in my old age? What joyful tidings can you bring me?'

They said: 'We do gladden you with the Truth. Do not despair.'

He said: 'Who but the lost would despair of God's mercy? Envoys,' he said, 'what is your errand?'

They said: 'We are sent forth to a sinful people. The house of Lot alone we shall deliver, except his wife.' We had decreed that she should stay with those who were to stay behind.

And when the envoys came to the house of Lot, he said: 'No one knows you.'

'No,' they said. 'We bring you news of that concerning which they are in doubt. We bring you Truth, and what we say is true. Go with your kin in the dead of night; walk in their rear and let none turn round: go where you are commanded.'

Such was the command We gave him; those were to be obliterated next morning.

15:68 And the townsfolk came to him rejoicing. He said: 'These

are my guests; do not disgrace me. Fear God and do not 15:69
shame me.'

They said: 'Did we not forbid you to entertain strangers?'

He said: 'These are my daughters: take them, if you are
bent on doing the deed.'

By your life, they were reeling in their frenzy! At sunrise the
Cry took them. We turned their city upside down and let loose
a shower of clay-stones upon them.

Surely in this there are signs for prudent people. The road
on which it stood is trodden still. Surely in this there is a sign
for true believers.

Surely the dwellers of the Forest[1] also did wrong. On them,
too, We took vengeance, and made of both a manifest
example.

The people of Ḥijr[2] also denied the apostles. We gave them
Our signs, but they ignored them. They hewed their dwellings
out of the mountains and led their lives in safety. But one
morning the Cry took them. Nothing did their gains avail
them.

It was but to reveal the Truth that We created the heavens 15:85
and the earth and all that lies between them. The Hour is sure
to come: bear with them nobly. It is your Lord who is the
All-knowing Creator.

We have given you the seven oft-repeated verses[3] and the
Glorious Koran. Do not eye with envy what We have given
some among them to enjoy, nor grieve on their account. Show
kindness to the faithful, and say: 'I am he that gives veritable
warning.'

As surely will We punish the schismatics, those who have
broken up the Koran into bits and pieces.[4] By the Lord, We
will question them all about their doings.

Proclaim, then, what you are bidden and let the idolaters 15:94

1. The people of Midian.
2. Territory to the north of Medina, where the Thamūd are said to
have dwelt.
3. The seven verses of the *Fātiḥah*, or Exordium (p. xix).
4. 'Believing in some and denying others', according to Al-Jalālayn.

15:95 be. We will Ourself sustain you against those that mock you and serve other deities besides God. They shall learn.

We know you are distressed by what they say. Give glory in
15:99 praise of your Lord and prostrate yourself. Worship your Lord till the inevitable overtakes you.

THE BEE

In the Name of God, the Merciful, the Compassionate

16:1 GOD'S JUDGEMENT will surely come to pass: do not seek to hurry it on. Glory be to Him! Exalted be He above their idols!

By His will He sends down the angels with the Spirit to those among His servants whom He chooses, bidding them give warning: 'There is no god but Me: therefore fear Me.'

He created the heavens and the earth to manifest the Truth. Exalted be He above their idols!

He created man from a little germ: and yet is he openly contentious.

He created the beasts which give you warmth and food and other benefits. How pleasant they look when you bring them home to rest, and when you lead them out to pasture!

16:7 They carry your burdens to a land you could not otherwise reach except with painful toil. Surely kindly is your Lord, and compassionate.

Also horses, mules, and donkeys, for you to ride or put on show; and He creates other things beyond your knowledge.

God alone points to the right path. Some turn aside but, had He pleased, He would have given you guidance all.

It is He who sends down water from the sky, which provides you with your drink and brings forth the pasturage on which your cattle feed. And with it He brings forth corn and olives, dates and grapes and fruits of every kind. Surely in this there is a sign for people who can think.

16:12 He has pressed the night and the day, and the sun and the moon, into your service: the stars also serve you by His command. Surely in this there are signs for people who understand.

On the earth He has fashioned for you objects of various
hues: surely in this there is a sign for people who reflect.

He it is who has subdued the ocean, so that you may eat
from it fresh flesh and bring up from its depths ornaments to
wear. Behold the ships ploughing their course through it. All
this, that you may seek His bounty and may render thanks.

He set upon the earth firm mountains lest it should move
away with you; and rivers and roads, that you may be rightly
guided; by landmarks and the stars, too, they are directed.

Is He, then, who has created, like him who cannot create?
Will you, then, not ponder?

If you reckoned up God's blessings, you could not count
them. Surely God is forgiving and compassionate.

God has knowledge of what you conceal and what you
reveal. Those that they invoke besides God create nothing:
they are themselves created. Dead, not living; nor do they
know when they will be raised to life.

Your God is one God. Those that deny the life to come
have faithless hearts and are puffed up with pride. God surely
knows what they conceal and what they reveal. He does not
love the proud.

When they are asked: 'What has your Lord revealed?' they
say: 'Fables of the ancients!' They shall bear the full brunt of
their burdens on the Day of Resurrection, together with the
burdens of those who in their ignorance were misled by them.
Evil is that which they shall bear.

Those who had gone before them also schemed. But God
smote their edifice at its foundations, and its roof collapsed
upon their heads. The scourge overtook them whence they
did not perceive.

Then, on the Day of Resurrection He will hold them up to
shame, and He will say: 'Where are your idols now, the
theme of your disputes?' And those endowed with knowledge will say: 'Shame and sorrow shall this day smite the
unbelievers.'

Those whom the angels will claim back while steeped in sin
will offer their submission, saying: 'We have done no wrong!'
'Indeed! God well knows what you have done. Enter the gates

of Hell, wherein shall you abide for ever.' Evil is the abode of the arrogant.

16:30   But when the God-fearing are asked: 'What has your Lord revealed?' they will say: 'That which is best.' Good is the reward of those that do good works in this present life: but better is the abode of the life to come. Blessed is the abode of the God-fearing. The Gardens of Eden they shall enter, wherein brooks will roll at their feet; and wherein shall they have all that they desire. Thus shall God recompense the God-fearing, whom the angels will claim, in all their virtue, saying: 'Peace be on you. Come into Paradise, the reward of your labours.'

Are they only waiting for the angels to come down or for the fulfilment of your Lord's will? Those who had gone before them also waited. God did not wrong them, but they wronged their own souls: the evil which they did recoiled upon them, and the scourge at which they scoffed encompassed them.

16:35   The idolaters say: 'Had God pleased, we would not have worshipped any besides Him, neither we nor our forefathers; nor would we have declared anything unlawful without His sanction.' Such also was the plea of those who had gone before them. Yet what should apostles do but give veritable warning?

We raised an apostle in each community: 'Serve God and keep away from false gods.' Among them were some to whom God gave guidance, and among them were some doomed to go astray. Roam the earth and see what was the fate of the disbelievers!

Strive as you may to guide them, God will not guide those whom He confounds; there shall be none to help them.

They solemnly swear by God that God will never raise the dead to life. But that is a promise that shall be justly fulfilled, though most may not know it, so that He will resolve for them their differences, and that the unbelievers will know that they were lying. When We decree a thing, We need only say: 'Be,' and it is.

16:41   As for those who after persecution fled their homes in the cause of God, We will reward them well in this nether life: yet better still is the reward of the life to come, if they but knew it; those who bore ills with patience and put their trust in their Lord. 16:42

We sent none before you but men whom We inspired with revelations and with Psalms. Ask the People of the Admonition, if you know not. And to you also We have revealed the Admonition, so that you may proclaim to the people what was sent down for them, and that they may reflect.

Are those who plot evil so certain that God will not cause the earth to cave in beneath them, or that the scourge will not descend on them whence they do not perceive? Or smite them in the course of their journeys when they cannot escape, or give them over to slow destruction?[1] Yet is your Lord kindly and compassionate.

Do they not see how every object God created casts its shadow right and left, prostrating itself before God in all humility? To God bow all the creatures of the heavens and the earth, and the angels too. They are not disdainful; they fear their Lord on high and do as they are bidden. 16:48

And God has said: 'You shall not serve two gods, for He is but one God. Fear none but Me.'

His is what the heavens and the earth contain; His is the Religion everlasting. Would you then fear any but God?

There is no blessing you enjoy which does not come from God, and to Him you turn for help when misfortune befalls you. Yet no sooner does He remove your ills than some among you set up other gods besides their Lord, showing no gratitude for what We gave them. Take your pleasure now, and you shall learn.

To those they know nothing of, they assign a share of what We gave them. By the Lord, you shall be questioned about the lies you fabricated!

They foist daughters upon God (glory be to Him!), but for themselves they choose what they desire. When the birth of a female is announced to one of them, his countenance darkens 16:58

1. Thus Al-Baydāwī; an obscure verse. See also Arberry.

16:59 and he is mightily vexed. On account of the bad news he hides himself from people: should he put up with the shame or bury her in the earth? How ill they judge!

Evil are the ways of those who deny the life to come; and most sublime are the ways of God: He is the Almighty, the Wise One.

If God punished people for their sins, not one creature would He leave alive. He reprieves them till a time ordained; when their time is come, not for one hour shall they stay behind: nor can they go before it.

They foist upon God what they themselves abhor. Their tongues falsely claim that a good reward awaits them. But let there be no doubt: the Fire awaits them, and they have strayed into egregious error.

By the Lord, We have sent forth before you to other communities. But Satan made their deeds seem fair to them, and to this day he is their patron. Woeful punishment awaits them.

16:64 We have revealed to you the Book only that you may resolve their differences for them: a guide and a blessing to true believers.

And God sends down water from the sky wherewith He quickens the earth after its death. Surely in this there is a sign for people who can hear.

In cattle too you have a worthy lesson. We give you to drink of that which is in their bellies, between the bowels and the blood-streams: pure milk, pleasant for those who drink it.

And the fruits of the palm and the vine, from which you derive intoxicants and wholesome food. Surely in this there is a sign for those endowed with reason.

Your Lord inspired the bees, saying: 'Make your homes in the mountains, in the trees, and in the hives which men shall build for you. Then feed on every kind of fruit, and follow the trodden paths of your Lord.'

From its belly comes forth a syrup of different hues, a cure for humans. Surely in this there is a sign for those who would take thought.

16:70 God created you, and He will then reclaim you. Some

among you shall have their lives prolonged to abject old age, when all that they once knew they shall know no more. All-knowing is God, and Almighty.

In what He has provided, God has favoured some among you above others. Those who are so favoured will not allow their slaves an equal share in what they have. Would they deny God's goodness? 16:71

God has given you spouses from among yourselves and, through your spouses, children and grandchildren. And He has provided you with wholesome things: will they then in falsehood believe and deny God's bounty?

And they worship helpless idols which can confer on them no benefits from the heavens or the earth. Therefore compare God to none: God has knowledge, but you have not.

God makes this comparison: one a helpless slave, the property of his master; and one on whom We have bestowed a bounteous provision from which he gives in private and in public. Are the two equal? God be praised! But most of them have no knowledge.

And God makes this comparison: two men, one dumb and helpless, a burden on his master: wherever he sends him he comes back with nothing good. Is he equal to him who enjoins justice and is on a straight path? 16:76

To God belong the secrets of the heavens and the earth. The business of the Hour shall be accomplished in the twinkling of an eye, or in a shorter time. Surely God has power over all things.

And God brought you out of your mothers' wombs devoid of any knowledge, and gave you ears and eyes and hearts, so that you may give thanks.

Do they not see the birds that wing their way in heaven's vault? None but God sustains them. Surely in this there are signs for true believers.

And God has given you houses to dwell in, and has given you animals' skins for tents, that you may find them light when you travel and easy to pitch when you halt for shelter; while from their wool, fur, and hair, He has for a space of time provided you with comforts and domestic goods. 16:80

16:81   By means of that which He created, God has given you shelters from the sun; He has given you refuge in the mountains; He has given you garments to protect you from the heat, and coats of armour to shield you in your wars. Thus does He perfect His bounty to you, that you may turn to Islām.

But if they[1] pay no heed, your[2] mission is only to give clear warning.

They recognize God's bounty, yet they deny it. And most of them surely are ungrateful.

On the day We call to life a witness from each community, their pleas shall not avail the unbelievers, nor shall they be allowed to make amends. And when the wrongdoers face the scourge, it shall not be eased for them, nor shall they ever be reprieved.

16:86   When the pagans behold their idols, they will say: 'Lord, these are the idols to whom we prayed.' But their idols will retort: 'You are surely lying!' They shall proffer God submission on that day, and the gods of their own invention will forsake them.

Those that disbelieve and debar others from the path of God, We shall chastise all the more for their misdeeds; on the day We call to life a witness in each community from among themselves to testify against them. We shall call *you* to testify against these: for to you We have revealed the Book to manifest the Truth about all things, a guide, a blessing, and joyful tidings for the Muslims.

God enjoins justice, kindness, and charity to kin, and forbids lewdness, reprehensible conduct, and oppression. He admonishes you so that you may take thought.

Keep faith with God when you make a pledge. And you shall not break your oaths after you have sworn them, having made God thereby your surety. God has knowledge of what you do.

16:92   Do not, like the woman who unravels the thread she has firmly spun, take oaths with mutual deceit and break them on

---

1. The Meccans.   2. Muḥammad's.

finding yourselves superior in numbers. In this, God puts you to the proof. On the Day of Resurrection He will resolve your differences for you.

Had God pleased, He would have united you into one community. But He confounds whom He will and gives guidance to whom He pleases. And you shall surely be questioned over what you did. 16:93

And you shall not take oaths to deceive each other, lest a foot should slip after being rightly guided, and lest you taste misfortune for debarring others from the path of God: for then indeed you should incur a grievous punishment.

You shall not barter God's covenant for a trifling price. God's recompense is better for you, if you but knew it. Your worldly riches are transitory, but God's recompense is everlasting.

We shall recompense the steadfast according to their noblest deeds. Be they men or women, to those that embrace the Faith and do what is right We will surely grant a happy life; We shall reward them according to their noblest deeds.

When you read the Koran, seek refuge in God from accursèd Satan: no power has he over those who believe and who put their trust in their Lord. He has power only over those who befriend him and those who serve partners besides Him. 16:98

And if We change one *sūrah* for another (God knows best what He reveals), they say: 'You[1] are but an impostor.' Indeed most of them have no knowledge.

Say: 'The Holy Spirit brought it down from your Lord in Truth to reassure the faithful, and to give guidance and joyful tidings to Muslims.'

We do know that they say: 'A mortal taught him.' But the man[2] to whom they allude speaks a foreign tongue, while this is eloquent Arabic speech.

Those who disbelieve God's revelations God will not guide. Woeful punishment awaits them. 16:104

---

1. Muhammad.
2. Scholars differ as to the identity of this 'foreigner'. Some suppose him to be Salmān the Persian, others Ṣuhaib bin Sinān, and yet others 'Adas the Monk.

16:105   None invents falsehood save those who disbelieve God's revelations: it is they that are the liars.

Those who are forced to recant while their hearts remain loyal to the Faith shall be absolved; but those who open their bosoms to unbelief shall incur God's ire; and grievous punishment awaits them. That is because they love the life of this world more than the life to come; and God does not guide the unbelievers.

Such are those whose hearts and ears and eyes are sealed by God; such are the heedless. In the life to come they will assuredly be lost.

Your Lord – to those who after persecution left their land and fought and remained constant to the last – your Lord will be forgiving and compassionate on the day when every soul will plead for itself; when every soul will be requited for its deeds. They shall not be wronged.

16:112   God has made an example of a city[1] which was once safe and peaceful. Its provisions came to it abundantly from every quarter: but it denied God's favours. Therefore God afflicted it with famine and fear as punishment for what they did.

An apostle of their own did come to them, but they denied him; therefore the scourge smote them in their wrongdoing.

Eat of the good and lawful things which God bestowed on you, and give thanks for God's bounty if it is Him that you worship.

He has forbidden you carrion, blood, and the flesh of swine; also any flesh consecrated other than in the name of God. But whoever is driven by necessity, intending neither to sin nor to transgress, will find that God is forgiving and compassionate.

You shall not say, when your tongues utter falsehood: 'This is lawful, and that is forbidden,' in order to invent a falsehood about God. Those who invent falsehoods about God shall never succeed. Brief is their enjoyment, and woeful punishment awaits them.

16:118   To those who follow the Jewish Faith We have pronounced

1. Mecca.

unlawful what We recounted to you before. We never wronged them, but they wronged themselves.

To those who commit evil through ignorance, and then repent and mend their ways, your Lord is forgiving and compassionate. 16:119

Abraham was a paragon of piety, an upright man obedient to God: he was no idolater. He rendered thanks for His bounty, so that He chose him and guided him to a straight path. We bestowed on him a blessing in this world, and in the world to come he will assuredly dwell among the righteous.

And now We have revealed to you Our will: that you shall follow the faith of saintly Abraham, who was no idolater.

The Sabbath was ordained only for those who differed about it. On the Day of Resurrection your Lord will judge their differences. 16:124

Call people to the path of your Lord with wisdom and kindly exhortation. Reason with them in a manner most courteous. Your Lord best knows those who stray from His path, and He best knows the rightly guided.

If you punish, let your punishment be commensurate with the wrong that has been done you. But it shall be best for you to endure with patience.

Be patient, then: none but God will grant you patience. Do not grieve for them, nor distress yourself at their intrigues. God is with those who fear Him and do good works. 16:128

THE NIGHT JOURNEY

In the Name of God, the Merciful, the Compassionate

GLORY BE to Him who made His servant go by night from the Sacred Temple[1] to the farther Temple[2] whose surroundings 17:1

1. Of Mecca.
2. Of Jerusalem (and thence to the Throne of God, accompanied by the Angel Gabriel). Some Muslim commentators give a literal interpretation to this passage, others regard it as a vision.

We have blessed, that We might show him some of Our signs. He it is who hears all and observes all.

17:2   We gave Moses the Book and made it a guide for the Israelites: 'You shall take no guardian other than Myself. You are the descendants of those We carried in the ark with Noah: he was a truly thankful servant.'

In the Book We decreed to the Israelites: 'Twice shall you do evil in the land; and you shall commit great transgressions.'

And when the prophecy of the first came to be fulfilled, We sent against you servants of Ours, a formidable army[1] which ravaged your land and carried out the punishment that had been promised.

Then We once again granted you victory over them and multiplied your riches and your descendants, so that once 17:7 again you grew and multiplied. 'If you do good, it shall be to your advantage; and if you do evil, you shall sin against your own souls.'

And when the prophecy of the second came to be fulfilled, We sent another[2] to afflict you and to enter the Temple as the former entered it at first, utterly destroying all that they laid their hands on.

'Your Lord may yet be merciful to you. If you come back, We shall again come back. We have made Hell a prison-house for the unbelievers.'

Surely this Koran gives guidance to that which is most upright. It promises the faithful who do good works a rich recompense; and for those who deny the life to come We have prepared a woeful scourge. Yet man prays for evil as fervently as he prays for good. Truly, man is ever impatient.

17:12   We made the night and the day twin marvels. We enshrouded the marvel of the night with darkness and made the marvel of the day to see with, that you might seek the bounty of your Lord and learn to count the seasons and the years.[3] We have made all things manifestly plain to you.

---

1. The Assyrians.
2. The Romans.
3. Literally, and learn the number of the years and how to count.

And the fate of each man We have bound about his neck. 17:13
On the Day of Resurrection We shall confront him with a
Book he shall find wide open: 'Read your Book: enough for
you this day that your own soul should call you to account.'

He that seeks guidance shall have guidance for the good of
his own soul, and he that errs shall err at his peril. No burdened
soul shall bear another's burden. Nor do We punish until We
have sent forth an emissary.

When We resolve to raze a city, We first give warning to its
prodigals. If they persist in sin therein, judgement is passed,
and We destroy it utterly.

How many generations have We cut down since Noah's
time! Suffice it that your Lord is well aware of His servants'
sins and observes them all.

Whoever desires this fleeting life We shall quickly grant
him therein whatever We will and for whomever We please.
But then We have prepared Hell for him, wherein he shall
burn despised and rejected.

As for him that desires the life to come and strives for it as 17:19
he ought to, being a true believer, his endeavours shall be
richly recompensed.

On all – on these and those – We bestow the bounty of
your Lord: none shall be denied the bounty of your Lord.

Behold how We have exalted some above others. Yet the
life to come has higher ranks of honour and is more exalted.

Set up no other deity besides God, lest you incur disgrace
and ruin: your Lord has decreed that you shall worship none
but Him. And that you shall show kindness to your parents: if
either or both of them attain old age in your dwelling, show
them no sign of impatience, nor rebuke them; but speak to
them kind words. Treat them with humility and tenderness,
and say: 'Lord, be merciful to them, even as they nursed me
when I was an infant.'

Your Lord best knows what is in your hearts, and knows if
you are virtuous. He will surely forgive those that turn to Him
in penitence.

Give to the near of kin their due, and also to the destitute 17:26
and to the traveller in need. Do not squander your substance

17:27 wastefully, for the wasteful are Satan's brothers; and Satan is ever ungrateful to his Lord. And if, while hopefully seeking from your Lord some bounty, you lack the means to assist them, then speak to them kindly.

Be neither miserly nor prodigal, for then you should either earn reproach or be reduced to penury.

Your Lord gives abundantly to whom He will, and sparingly likewise. He knows and observes His servants.

You shall not kill your children for fear of poverty.[1] We will provide for them and for you. To kill them is a grievous sin.

You shall not commit adultery, for it is lewd and the way to evil.

You shall not kill any man God has forbidden you to kill, except for a just cause. If a man is slain unjustly, his heir shall be entitled to satisfaction. But let him not carry his vengeance to excess, for his victim is sure to be assisted and avenged.

17:34 And do not approach the property of orphans except with the best of motives, until they reach maturity. Keep your promises; you are accountable for all that you promise.

And give full measure, when you measure, and weigh with even scales; that is better and fairer in the end.

Do not follow what you know not. Man's eyes, ears, and heart – each of his senses shall be closely questioned.

And do not walk proudly on the earth. You cannot split the earth, nor can you rival the mountains in stature.

Evil is all this in the sight of your Lord, and odious.

These are but some of the wise precepts your Lord has inspired you[2] with. Serve no other deity besides God, lest you should be cast into Hell, condemned and rejected.

What! Has your Lord favoured *you*[3] with sons and Himself adopted females from among the angels? A monstrous blasphemy is that which you utter.

17:41 We have expounded Our revelations in this Koran so that

1. An allusion to the pre-Islamic custom of burying alive unwanted newborn girls.
2. Muḥammad.
3. The unbelievers.

they may remember. Yet it has only added to their aversion. Say: 'If, as they claim, there were other gods besides God, they would surely seek to dethrone Him.' 17:42

Glory be to Him! Exalted be He, high above their falsehoods!

The seven heavens, the earth, and all who dwell in them give glory to Him. All creatures celebrate His praises. Yet you cannot understand their praises. Benevolent is He and forgiving.

And when you recite the Koran, We place between you and those who deny the life to come a hidden screen. We have cast veils over their hearts lest they understand it, and made them hard of hearing. When you make mention of your Lord, alone, in the Koran they turn their backs with much aversion.

We well know what they wish to hear in it when they listen to you, and what they say when they converse in private; when the wrongdoers declare: 'The man you follow is surely bewitched.'

Behold what epithets they bestow upon you. They have surely gone astray and cannot find the right path. 17:48

And they say: 'What! When we are turned to bones and dust, shall we be restored in a new creation?'

Say: 'Whether you turn to stone or iron, or any other substance you may think unlikely to be given life.'

They will say: 'Who will restore us?'

Say: 'He that created you at first.'

They will shake their heads at you and say: 'When will this be?'

Say: 'It may well be near at hand. On that day He will summon you all, and you shall answer Him with praises. You shall think that you have lingered but a little while.'

And tell My servants to be courteous in their speech. Satan would sow discord among them; Satan is surely a veritable enemy of man.

Your Lord knows you best. He will show you mercy if He will, and punish you if He pleases.

We have not sent you to be their guardian. Your Lord is best aware of all who dwell in the heavens and the earth. 17:55

We have exalted some prophets above others. To David We gave Psalms.

17:56   Say: 'Pray if you will to those whom you deify besides Him.[1] They cannot relieve your distress, nor can they change it.'

Those to whom they pray, themselves seek to approach their Lord, vying with each other to be near Him. They crave His mercy and fear His punishment; for your Lord's punishment is to be feared indeed.

There is no city but We shall obliterate it before the Day of Resurrection, or grievously punish it: that is decreed in the Eternal Book.

And nothing hinders Us from sending signs except that the ancients disbelieved them. To Thamūd We gave the she-camel as a visible sign, yet they laid violent hands on her. We give signs only by way of warning.

17:60   We have told you that your Lord encompasses mankind. We have made the vision which We showed you, as well as the tree[2] cursed in the Koran, but a test for people's faith. We seek to put fear in their hearts, but this only makes their wickedness all the more outrageous.

And when We said to the angels: 'Prostrate yourselves before Adam,' they all prostrated themselves, except Satan, who said: 'Shall I bow to him whom You have made of clay?' And he said: 'Do You see this being whom You have exalted above me? If You give me respite till the Day of Resurrection, I will exterminate all but a few of his descendants.'

'Go!' said He. 'Hell is your reward, and the reward of those that follow you. An ample recompense it shall be. Rouse with your voice whomever you are able. Muster against them your battalions of horse and foot. Be their partner in riches and in offspring. Promise them what you will. (Satan promises them only to deceive them.) But over My true servants you shall have no authority. Sufficient is your Lord as a guardian.'

17:66   It is your Lord who drives for you the ships across the

---

1. The allusion is to worship of saints.
2. The Zaqqūm tree.

ocean, that you may seek His bounty. Surely He is ever compassionate towards you.

And when at sea a misfortune befalls you, all but Him of   17:67
those to whom you pray forsake you; yet when He brings you
safe to dry land you turn your backs: truly, man is ever thankless.

Are you confident He will not cause the earth to cave in
beneath you, or let loose a deadly sandstorm upon you? Then
you shall find none to protect you.

Or are you confident that when again He lets you put to sea
He will not blast you with a violent tempest and drown you
for being thankless? Then you shall find none to prosecute
your case against Us.

We have bestowed bounties on Adam's descendants and
carried them by land and sea. We have provided them with
wholesome things and exalted them above a great many of
Our creatures.

The day will surely come when We shall summon each   17:71
community with its leader. Those who are given their books
in their right hands will read their recorded doings, and shall
not in the least be wronged. And those who have been blind
in this life shall be blind in the life to come and more misguided.

They sought to entice you from Our revelations – they
nearly did – hoping that you might invent another in Our
name, and thus they would adopt you as an intimate friend.
Indeed, had We not strengthened your faith, you might have
made some compromise with them and We would thus have
made you taste a double punishment in this life and a double
punishment after death. Then you should have found none to
help you against Us.

And they sought to provoke you – they nearly did – and
thus drive you out of the land: and they then would have
scarcely survived your departure.

Such was Our way with the apostles We sent before you.
And you shall find no change in Our accustomed way.

Perform the prayer at sunset, at nightfall, and at the dawn
recital; the dawn recital has its witnesses; during the night as   17:79

well: an additional duty, for the fulfilment of which your Lord
may exalt you to a praiseworthy station.

17:80   Say: 'Lord, grant me a goodly entrance and a goodly exit,
and sustain me with Your own power.'

And say: 'Truth has come and Falsehood has been routed.
Falsehood was bound to be routed.'

That which We reveal in the Koran is a balm and a blessing
to true believers, although it only adds to the wrongdoers'
prospects of perdition.

When We bestow bounties on man, he turns his back and
holds aloof; and when evil befalls him, he grows despondent.

Say: 'Each man behaves after his own fashion. But your
Lord best knows who is more rightly guided.'

And they put questions to you about the Spirit. Say: 'The
Spirit is at my Lord's command. Little indeed is the knowledge
vouchsafed to you.'

If We pleased, We could take away that which We have
revealed to you: then you should find none to plead with Us
on your behalf except through a favour from your Lord. His
goodness to you has been great indeed.

17:88   Say: 'If men and jinn combined to produce a book akin to
this Koran, they would surely fail to produce its like, though
they helped one another as best they could.'

We have set forth for people in this Koran all manner of
arguments, yet most of them persist in unbelief. They say: 'We
will not believe in you until you make a spring gush from the
earth before our very eyes, or cause rivers to gush in a grove of
palms and vines; until you cause the sky to fall upon us in fragments, as you have claimed you would, or bring down God and
the angels in our midst; until you have for yourself a house of
gold, or ascend to heaven: nor will we believe in your ascent
until you have sent down for us a book which we can read.'

Say: 'Glory be to my Lord! Am I not but an emissary, made
of flesh and blood?'

Nothing prevents people from having faith when guidance
comes to them but the excuse: 'Can it be that God has sent a
human as an emissary?'

17:95   Say: 'Had the earth been safe enough for angels to walk on,

We would have sent down to them an angel from heaven as an emissary.'

Say: 'Sufficient is God as my witness, and your witness. He well knows and closely observes His servants.' 17:96

Those whom God guides are rightly guided; and those whom He confounds shall find no guardians besides Him. We shall herd them all on the Day of Resurrection, prostrate upon their faces, blind, dumb, and deaf. Hell shall be their refuge: whenever its flames die down We will rekindle them into a greater conflagration.

Thus shall they be rewarded: because they disbelieved Our revelations and said: 'When we are turned to bones and dust, shall we be restored in a new creation?'

Or do they not see that God, who has created the heavens and the earth, has power to create their like? Their term He preordained beyond all doubt. Yet the wrongdoers persist in unbelief.

Say: 'Had you possessed the treasures of my Lord's mercy, you would have covetously hoarded them. How niggardly is man!' 17:100

And to Moses We gave nine conspicuous signs. Ask the Israelites how he first appeared among them.

Pharaoh said to him: 'Moses, I can see that you are bewitched.'

'You know full well,' he replied, 'that none but the Lord of the heavens and the earth has revealed these visible signs. Indeed, Pharaoh, I can see that you are doomed.'

He sought to scare them out of the land: but We drowned him, together with those who were with him all. Then We said to the Israelites: 'Dwell in the land. When the promise of the Hereafter comes to be fulfilled, We shall herd you all together.'

With the Truth We revealed it, and with the Truth it has come down. We have sent you forth only to proclaim joyful tidings and to give warning; with a Koran that We divided into sections, that you may read it to the people with deliberation. We have imparted it by gradual revelation. 17:106

Say: 'It is for you to believe in it or to deny it. Those who 17:107

were endowed with knowledge before its revelation prostrate themselves when it is recited to them and say: "Glorious is our Lord. Our Lord's promise has surely been fulfilled." They fall down upon their faces, weeping; and as they listen, their awe increases.'

Say: 'You may call on God or you may call on the Merciful: by whatever name you call on Him, His are the most gracious names.'

Pray neither with too loud a voice nor in silence, but, between these extremes, seek a middle course. Say: 'Praise be to God who has never begotten a son; who has no partner in His Kingdom; who needs none to protect Him from humiliation.' Proclaim His greatness.

17:111

THE CAVE

In the Name of God, the Merciful, the Compassionate

18:1   PRAISE BE to God who has revealed the Book to His servant and made it flawless, unswerving from the Truth, that he may give warning of a dire scourge from Himself; proclaim to the faithful who do good works that a rich and everlasting recompense awaits them; and admonish those who say that God has begotten a son.[1] Surely of this they could have no knowledge, neither they nor their forefathers: a monstrous blasphemy is that which their mouths utter; they speak nothing but falsehood.

Yet, if they deny this revelation, you may destroy yourself with grief, sorrowing over them.

We have decked the earth with all manner of ornaments to test them as to who would acquit himself best. But We will surely reduce all that is on it to barren dust.

18:8

1. The noun *walad* in Classical Arabic can mean son/sons/daughter/ daughters or the collective 'offspring'.

Did you think the Sleepers of the Cave[1] and Al-Raqīm[2] a   18:9
wonder among Our signs?

When the youths sought refuge in the cave, they said:
'Lord, have mercy on us and guide us through our ordeal.'

We made them sleep[3] in the cave for many years, and then
awakened them to find out who could best tell the length of
their stay.

We recount to you their story in all truth. They were young
men who had faith in their Lord, and on whom We had lavished
Our guidance. We put courage in their hearts when they stood
up and said: 'Our Lord is the Lord of the heavens and the earth.
We call on no other god besides Him: for if we did we should
be blaspheming. Our people serve other gods besides Him,
though they have no convincing proof of their divinity. Who is
more wicked than he who invents a falsehood against God?

'And when you forsake them and those they worship
besides God, go to the cave for shelter. Your Lord will extend
to you His mercy and prepare for you a means of safety.'

You might have seen the rising sun decline to the right of   18:17
their cavern and, as it set, go past them on the left, while they
stayed within. That was one of God's signs. He whom God
guides is rightly guided; but he whom He confounds shall find
no friend to guide him.

And you might have thought them awake, though they
were sleeping. We turned them about to right and left, while
their dog lay at the cave's entrance with legs outstretched. Had
you looked upon them, you would have surely turned your
back and fled in terror.

Thus did We rouse them that they might question one   18:19
another. One of them asked: 'How long have you stayed
here?' They said: 'We have stayed one day, or part of a day.'
They said: 'Your Lord knows best how long you have stayed

1. The allusion is to the story of the Seven Sleepers. Cf. Gibbon's
account in *Decline and Fall of the Roman Empire*.
2. This may be the name of their dog, the tablet on which their names
were inscribed, or the mountain in which the cave was situated.
3. Literally, We sealed their ears.

here. Let one of you go to the city with this silver coin and bring you back whatever food he finds most wholesome there. Let him conduct himself with caution and not disclose your whereabouts to anyone. For if they find you out they will stone you to death, or force you back into their faith; then will you surely never succeed, ever.'

Thus did We reveal their secret, so that they might know that God's promise was true and that the Hour was not to be doubted.

People argued among themselves concerning them. Some said: 'Build a monument over their remains. Their Lord knows best who they were.' Those who were to win said: 'Let us build a place of worship over them.'

Some will say: 'They were three: their dog was the fourth.' Others, guessing at the unknown, will say: 'They were five: their dog was the sixth.' And yet others: 'Seven: their dog was the eighth.' Say: 'My Lord best knows their number. Only a few know them.'

Therefore, when you dispute about them, adhere only to that which is manifest and do not ask any of these concerning them.

Never say of anything: 'I will do this tomorrow,' without adding: 'If God wills.' When you forget, remember your Lord and say: 'May God guide me and bring me nearer to the Truth.'

Some say they stayed in their cave three hundred years and nine. Say: 'God knows best how long they stayed. His are the secrets of the heavens and the earth. Clear is His sight, and keen His hearing. They have no other guardian besides Him; He allows none to share His sovereignty.'

Proclaim what has been revealed to you from the Book of your Lord. None can change His Words. And you shall find no refuge besides Him.

And restrain yourself, you and those who pray to their Lord morning and evening, seeking His pleasure. Do not turn your eyes away from them in quest of the allurements of this life, nor obey him whose heart We have made heedless of Our remembrance; who follows his appetite and gives a loose rein to his desires.

Say: 'This is the Truth from your Lord. Let him who will,
believe in it, and him who will, deny it.'

For the wrongdoers We have prepared a fire which will
encompass them like the walls of a pavilion. When they cry
out for help they shall be showered with water as hot as molten brass, which will scald their faces; evil the drink, and evil
the resting-place.

As for those that believe and do good works, We shall not
deny the recompense of those whose deeds were good. The
Gardens of Eden shall be theirs, wherein brooks will roll at
their feet. Reclining there upon soft couches, they shall be
adorned with bracelets of gold, and arrayed in garments of
fine green silk and rich brocade: blissful the reward, and happy
the resting-place!

Coin for them a parable: Two men, to one of whom We
gave two vineyards set about with palm-trees and watered by
a running brook, with a cornfield lying in between. Each of
the vineyards yielded an abundant crop, and when their owner
had gathered in the harvest, he said to his companion while
conversing with him: 'I am richer than you, and my clan is
mightier than yours.'

And when, having thus wronged his soul, he entered his
vineyard, he said: 'I cannot think this will ever perish! Nor
do I think the Hour will ever come. Even if I returned to
my Lord, I should surely find a better place than this to go
back to.'

His companion replied, while still conversing with him:
'Have you no faith in Him who created you from dust, then
from a little germ, and then fashioned you into a man? As for
myself, God is my Lord, and I will associate none with my
Lord. When you entered your garden, why did you not say:
"What God has ordained must surely come to pass: there is
no strength except in God"? Though you see me poorer than
yourself and blessed with fewer children, yet my Lord may
give me a garden better than yours, and send down thunderbolts from heaven upon your vineyard, turning it into a barren
waste, or drain its water deep into the earth so that you will
find none of it.'

18:42 And his fruits were destroyed, and he wrung his hands with grief at all that he had spent on the garden: for the vines had tumbled down upon their trellises. 'Would that I had served no other gods besides my Lord!' he said. He had none to help him besides God, nor was he able to defend himself.

In such ordeals protection comes only from God, the true God. His is the best recompense and His the best requital.

And coin for them a simile about the life of this world. It is like the vegetation of the earth that thrives when watered by the rain We send down from the sky, soon turning into stubble which the wind scatters abroad. God has power over all things.

Wealth and children are the ornament of this life. But deeds of lasting merit are better rewarded by your Lord and hold for you a greater hope of salvation.

Tell of the day when We shall blot out the mountains and make the earth a barren waste; when We shall herd them all together, leaving not a soul behind.

18:48 They shall be ranged before your Lord: 'You have returned to Us as We created you at first. Yet you supposed We had not set for you a predestined time.'

The Book will be laid down, and you shall see the sinners dismayed at the content. They will say: 'Woe betide us! What can this Book mean? It omits nothing small or great: all is noted down!' and they shall find their deeds recorded there. Your Lord will wrong none.

And when We said to the angels: 'Prostrate yourselves before Adam,' all prostrated themselves except Satan, who was a jinnee disobedient to his Lord. Would you then serve him and his offspring as your masters rather than Myself, despite their enmity towards you? A sad substitute the wrongdoers have chosen!

I did not call them to witness at the creation of the heavens and the earth, nor at their own creation; nor was I to seek the aid of those who were to lead mankind astray.

On that day He will say: 'Call on those you claimed to be My partners.' They will invoke them, but they will make no
18:53 answer; for We shall place a deadly gulf between them. And

when the sinners behold the Fire they will realize that therein they shall be flung. Nor shall they ever escape from it.

In this Koran We have coined for mankind all manner of parables. But man is exceedingly contentious. 18:54

Nothing prevents people from having faith when guidance has been revealed to them, and from seeking their Lord's forgiveness: unless they are waiting for the fate of the ancients to overtake them or to behold the scourge with their own eyes.

We send the apostles only to proclaim joyful tidings and to give warning. But with false arguments the unbelievers seek to confute the Truth, deriding My revelations and My warnings.

Who is more wicked than he that, when reminded of his Lord's revelations, turns away from them and forgets what his own hands have done? We have cast veils over their hearts so that they cannot understand it,[1] and made them hard of hearing. Call them as you may to the right path, they shall never be guided.

And your Lord is the Forgiving One, the Merciful. Had it been His will to scourge them for what they did, He would have hurried on their punishment; but He has set for them a predestined time they cannot evade. 18:58

And all those cities! We destroyed them for the wrongs they did, and for their destruction We set a predestined time.

Moses said to his servant: 'I will journey on until I reach the land where the two seas meet, though I may march for ages.'

But when they came to the land where the two seas met, they forgot their fish, which made its way into the water, swimming at will.

And when they had journeyed farther on, he said to his servant: 'Bring us some food; we are worn out with this travelling.'

'Know,' he replied, 'that I forgot the fish when we were resting on the rock. It was only Satan who made me forget to mention this. It made its way miraculously into the sea.'

'This is what we have been seeking,' he said. They went back the way they came, and found one of Our servants to 18:65

1. The Koran.

199

whom We had vouchsafed Our mercy and whom We had
18:66 endowed with knowledge of Our own. Moses said to him:
'May I follow you, so that you may guide me by that which you
have been taught?'

'You will not bear with me,' said he. 'For how can you bear
with that which is beyond your knowledge?'

Moses said: 'If God wills, you shall find me patient: I shall
in no way cross you.'

He said: 'If you are bent on following me, you must not
question me about anything until I mention it to you myself.'

The two set forth, but as soon as they embarked, he bored
a hole in the bottom of the ship.

'Is it to drown her passengers that you have bored a hole in
her?' he said. 'A strange thing you have done.'

'Did I not tell you,' he said, 'that you would not bear
with me?'

'Pardon my forgetfulness,' said Moses. 'Do not be angry
with me on account of this.'

18:74 They journeyed on until they fell in with a certain youth.
He slew him, and Moses said: 'You have slain an innocent
man who has slain no one. Surely you have done a heinous
thing.'

'Did I not tell you,' he said, 'that you would not bear with
me?'

He said: 'If ever I question you again, abandon me; for
then I should deserve it.'

They travelled on until they came to a city. They asked its
people for some food, but they declined to receive them as
their guests. There they found a wall on the point of falling
down. He re-erected it, and Moses said: 'Had you wished, you
could have demanded payment.'

'Now has the time arrived when we must part,' he said. 'But
first I will explain to you those acts of mine which you could
not bear to watch with patience.

'As for the ship, it belonged to some poor fellows who had
laboured at sea. I wanted to damage it because at their rear
there was a king who was taking every ship by force.

18:80 'As for the youth, his parents both were true believers, and we feared lest he should plague them with wickedness and unbelief. It was our wish that their Lord should grant them 18:81 another in his place, a son more righteous and more filial.

'As for the wall, it belonged to two orphan boys in the city; beneath it a treasure of theirs was buried. Their father was an honest man. Your Lord decreed, as a mercy from your Lord, that they should dig up their treasure when they grew to manhood. What I did was not done by my will.

'That explains what you could not bear to watch with patience.'

They will ask you about Dhūl-Qarnayn.[1] Say: 'I will give you an account of him.

'We made him mighty in the land and gave him means to achieve all things. He journeyed on a certain road until he reached the West and saw the sun setting in a pool of black mud. Hard by he found a certain people.

'"Dhūl-Qarnayn," We said, "you must either punish them or show them kindness."

'He replied: "The wicked we shall surely punish. Then shall 18:87 they return to their Lord, who will torment them with grievous torment. As for those that have faith and do good works, we shall bestow on them a rich reward and deal indulgently with them."

'He then journeyed along another road until he reached the East and saw the sun rising upon a people whom We had exposed to its flaming rays.[2] So he did; and We had full knowledge of all the forces at his command.

'Then he journeyed along another road until he came between the Two Mountains and found a people who could barely understand a word. "Dhūl-Qarnayn," they said, "Gog and Magog are ravaging this land. Build a rampart between us, and we will pay you tribute."

'He replied: "The power my Lord has given me is better than any tribute. Lend me a force of men, and I will raise a rampart between you and them. Bring me blocks of iron." 18:96

1. Alexander the Great.
2. Literally, for whom We did not provide a veil to shield them from it.

'He dammed up the valley between the Two Mountains, and said: "Ply your bellows." And when the iron blocks were red with heat, he said: "Bring me molten brass to pour on them."

18:97 'Gog and Magog could not scale it, nor could they dig their way through it. He said: "This is a blessing from my Lord. But when my Lord's promise has been fulfilled, He will level it to dust; the promise of my Lord is ever true."'

And on that day We will let them come in tumultuous throngs. The Trumpet shall be blown and We will gather them all together.

On that day We shall lay Hell bare before the unbelievers, who have turned a blind eye to My Admonition and a deaf ear to My warning.

Do the unbelievers think that they can make My servants patrons besides Me? We have prepared Hell for the unbelievers to dwell in.

Say: 'Shall we tell you who will lose most through their
18:103 labours? Those whose endeavours in this world are misguided and who yet think that what they do is right; who disbelieve the revelations of their Lord and deny that they will ever meet Him.' Vain are the works of these. On the Day of Resurrection We shall give them no consequence.

Hell is their reward: because they disbelieved, and because they mocked My apostles and My revelations. As for those that have faith and do good works, they shall for ever dwell in the Gardens of Paradise, desiring no change.

Say: 'If the sea were ink with which to write the words of my Lord, the sea would surely run dry before the words of my Lord were finished, though we found another sea to replenish it.'

18:110 Say: 'I am but a mortal like yourselves. It is revealed to me that your God is one God. Let him that hopes to meet his Lord do what is right and worship none besides his Lord.'

MARY

In the Name of God, the Merciful, the Compassionate

Kāf *hā' yā' 'ain ṣād.* Remembering your Lord's goodness to   19:1
His servant Zacharias:

He invoked his Lord in secret, saying: 'Lord, my bones are
enfeebled, and my head glows silver with age. Yet never, Lord,
have I prayed to You in vain. I now fear my kin who will succeed me, for my wife is barren. Grant me, from Yourself, a
son who will be my heir and an heir to the House of Jacob,
and make him worthy, Lord, of Your pleasure.'

'Rejoice, Zacharias. We shall give you a son to rejoice in,
and his name shall be John; a name We have given no man
before him.'[1]

'Lord,' said Zacharias, 'how shall I have a son, when my
wife is barren, and I am well advanced in years?'

He replied: 'Thus did your Lord speak. That is easy for Me;   19:9
even as I brought you into being when you were nothing before.'

'Lord,' said Zacharias, 'give me a sign.'

'Your sign is that for three days and nights,' He replied,
'you shall be bereft of speech, though otherwise sound in
body.'

Then Zacharias came out from the Shrine and exhorted his
people to give glory morning and evening.

To John We said: 'Observe the Book with a firm resolve.'
We bestowed on him from Ourself wisdom, grace, and purity
while yet a child, and he grew up a righteous man; honouring
his father and mother, and neither arrogant nor rebellious.
Peace be on him on the day he was born and on the day of his
death and on the day he is raised to life.

And you shall recount in the Book the story of Mary: how
she left her people and betook herself to a solitary place to the
east.

We sent to her Our Spirit in the semblance of a full-grown   19:17

---

1. Cf. Luke 1:61.

19:18 man. And when she saw him she said: 'May the Merciful defend me from you! If you fear the Lord . . .'

'I am but your Lord's emissary,' he replied, 'and have come to give you a holy son.'

'How shall I bear a child,' she answered, 'when I have neither been touched by any man nor ever been unchaste?'

'Thus did your Lord speak,' he replied. '"That is easy enough for Me. We shall make him a sign to mankind and a blessing from Ourself. Our will shall be done."'

Thereupon she conceived him, and retired to a far-off place. And when she felt the throes of childbirth she lay down by the trunk of a palm-tree, crying: 'Oh, would that I had died before this, and passed into oblivion!'

But a voice from below called out to her: 'Do not despair. Your Lord has provided a brook that runs at your feet, and if you shake the trunk of the palm-tree it will drop fresh ripe dates in your lap. Therefore eat and drink and rejoice; and should you meet any mortal say to him: "I have vowed a fast to the Merciful and will not speak with anyone today."'

19:27 Carrying the child, she came to her people, who said to her: 'Mary, you have indeed done a shameful deed! Sister of Aaron,[1] your father was never a whoremonger, nor was your mother a harlot.'

She made a sign to them, pointing to the child. But they replied: 'How can we speak with a babe in the cradle?'

Whereupon he spoke and said: 'I am the servant of God. He has given me the Book and ordained me a prophet. His blessing is upon me wherever I go, and He has exhorted me to be steadfast in prayer and to give alms as long as I shall live. He has exhorted me to honour my mother and has purged me of vanity and wickedness. Peace be on me on the day I was born and on the day of my death and on the day I shall be raised to life.'

19:34 Such was Jesus son of Mary. That is the whole truth, which

---

1. It appears that Miriam, Aaron's sister, and Maryam (Mary), mother of Jesus, were, according to the Koran, one and the same person.

they still doubt. God forbid that He Himself should beget a
son! When He decrees a thing He need only say: 'Be,' and it is.

God is my Lord and your Lord: therefore serve Him. That
is a straight path.

Yet are the sects at odds among themselves. But when the
fateful day arrives, woe betide the unbelievers! Their hearing
and their sight will be sharpened on the day they appear before
Us. Truly, the wrongdoers are today in monstrous error.

And forewarn them of that woeful day, when Our decree
shall be fulfilled while they heedlessly persist in unbelief. We
Ourself shall inherit the earth and all who dwell upon it. And
to Us they shall be recalled.

You shall also recount in the Book the story of Abraham:

He was a saintly man and a prophet. He said to his father:
'Why do you worship a worthless idol, a thing that can neither
hear nor see?

'Father, things you know nothing of have come to my
knowledge: therefore follow me, that I may guide you along
an even path.

'Father, do not worship Satan; for Satan has rebelled against
the Lord of Mercy.

'Father, I fear that a scourge will fall upon you from the
Merciful, and you will become one of Satan's minions.'

He said: 'Do you dare renounce my gods, Abraham? Desist,
or I will stone you. Leave my house this instant!'

'Peace be with you,' said Abraham. 'I shall implore my Lord
to forgive you: for to me He has ever been gracious. But I will
not live with you or with your idols. I will pray to my Lord, and
may my prayers to my Lord not be in vain.'

And when Abraham had cast off his people and the idols
which they worshipped, We bestowed on him Isaac and Jacob.
Each of them We made a prophet, and We bestowed on them
gracious gifts and high renown.

In the Book tell also of Moses, who was a chosen man, an
apostle, and a prophet.

We called out to him from the right side of the Mount, and
when he came near We communed with him in secret. We gave
him, of Our mercy, his brother Aaron, himself a prophet.

19:54 And in the Book you shall tell of Ishmael: he, too, was a man of his word, an apostle, and a prophet.

He enjoined prayer and almsgiving on his people, and his Lord was pleased with him.

And in the Book tell of Idrīs:[1] he, too, was a saint and a prophet, whom We honoured and exalted.

Those were the men to whom God was gracious: the prophets from among the descendants of Adam and of those whom We carried in the ark with Noah; the descendants of Abraham, of Israel, and of those whom We have guided and chosen. For when the revelations of the Merciful were recited to them they fell down on their knees in tears and adoration.

But the generations who succeeded them neglected their prayers and succumbed to their desires. These shall assuredly be lost. But those that repent and embrace the Faith and do what is right shall enter Paradise and shall in no way be wronged: the Gardens of Eden, which the Merciful has promised on trust to His servants; His promise shall surely be fulfilled.

19:62 Therein shall they hear no idle talk, but only the voice of peace. And their sustenance shall be given them therein morning and evening. Such is the Paradise which We shall give the righteous among Our servants to inherit.

We descend only at the bidding of your Lord;[2] to Him belongs what is before us and behind us, and all that lies between.

And your Lord never forgets. The Lord of the heavens and the earth and all that is between them: worship Him, then, and be patient in His service; for do you know any other worthy of His name?

'What!' says man. 'When I am once dead, shall I be raised to life?'

19:67 Does man forget that We created him when he was nothing

---

1. Enoch.
2. Commentators say that these are the words of the Angel Gabriel, in reply to Muhammad's complaint of long intervals elapsing between periods of revelation.

before? By the Lord, We will assuredly herd them in company   19:68
with the demons and set them on their knees around the fire
of Hell: and then from every sect We will carry off its stoutest
rebels against the Lord of Mercy. And then We surely know
best who deserve most to be burnt in its flames.

There is not one among you who shall not pass through
it: such is the absolute decree of your Lord. We will deliver
those who fear Us, and therein leave the wrongdoers, on their
knees.

And when Our revelations are recited to them, manifest,
the unbelievers say to the faithful: 'Which of us two will have
a finer abode and better companions?'

And how many generations have We destroyed before
them, far greater in riches and in splendour!

Say: 'The Merciful will bear long with those in error until
they see the fulfilment of His promise: be it a worldly scourge
or the Hour itself. Then shall they learn whose is the worse
plight and whose the smaller following.'

God will increase His guidance to those that follow the right   19:76
guidance. Deeds of lasting merit shall earn you a better recompense in the sight of your Lord and a more auspicious end.

Mark the words of him who denies Our signs and who yet
boasts: 'I shall surely be given wealth and children!'

Has the future been revealed to him? Or has the Merciful
made him such a promise?

By no means! We will record his words and make his punishment long and terrible. All he speaks of he shall leave
behind and come before Us all alone.

They have chosen deities other than God to help them. By
no means! They will renounce their worship and turn against
them.

Behold how We send down to the unbelievers demons
who incite them to evil. Therefore do not hurry them on:
their days are numbered. The day will surely come when We
will gather the righteous in multitudes before the Lord of
Mercy, and drive the guilty to Hell in thirsty hordes. None has   19:87
power to intercede for them save him who has received the
sanction of the Merciful.

19:88 And they say: 'The Lord of Mercy has begotten a son.' You surely preach a monstrous falsehood, at which the very heavens might crack, the earth split asunder, and the mountains crumble to dust. That they should ascribe a son to the Merciful, when it does not become the Merciful to beget offspring!

There is none in the heavens or on earth but shall return to the Merciful in utter submission. He has kept strict count of them all, and one by one shall they come to Him on the Day of Resurrection. The Merciful will cherish those who believed and were charitable in their lifetime.

We have made it easy in your own tongue that you may thereby proclaim joyful tidings to the upright and give warning to a contentious people.

19:98 And how many generations have We destroyed before them! Can you find one of them still alive, or hear so much as a whisper from them?

ṬĀ' HĀ'

In the Name of God, the Merciful, the Compassionate

20:1 *Ṭā' hā'.*

It was not to distress you that We revealed the Koran to you, but to admonish the God-fearing. It is a revelation from Him who has created the earth and the lofty heavens, the Merciful who sits enthroned on high.

His is what the heavens and the earth contain, and all that lies between them and underneath the soil. You have no need to speak aloud; for He has knowledge of all that is secret, and all that is hidden.

He is God. There is no god but Him. His are the most gracious names.

Have you heard the story of Moses?

20:10 When he saw a fire, he said to his people: 'Stay here, for I can see a fire. Perchance I can bring you from it a lighted torch, or find a guide hard by the fire.'

When he came near, a voice called out to him: 'Moses, I am 20:11
your Lord. Take off your sandals, for you are now in the sacred
valley of Ṭuwā.

'And I have chosen you: so listen to what shall be revealed.

'I am God. There is no god but Me. Worship Me, and recite
your prayers in My remembrance.

'The Hour is sure to come. But I choose to keep it hidden,
so that every soul shall be rewarded according to its labours.
Let not those who disbelieve in it and yield to their desires
turn your thoughts from it, lest you perish. What is it you are
carrying in your right hand, Moses?'

He said: 'It is my staff; upon it I lean and with it I beat down
the leaves for my flock. And I have other uses for it besides.'

He said: 'Moses, cast it down.'

Moses threw it down, and thereupon it turned into a slithering serpent.

'Take it up and have no fear,' He said. 'We will change it 20:21
back to its former state. And now put your hand under your
armpit. It shall come out white, although unharmed: another
sign.

'We shall show you the most wondrous of all Our signs.
Go to Pharaoh; he has transgressed all bounds.'

'Lord,' said he, 'put courage into my heart, and make my
task easy. Free my tongue from its impediment, that men may
understand my speech. Appoint for me a helper from among
my kin, Aaron my brother. Grant me strength through him and
let him share my task, so that we may give glory to You always
and remember You always. You are surely watching over us.'

He said: 'Your request is granted, Moses. We had already
shown you bounty when we revealed Our will to your
mother, saying: "Put your child in the ark and let him be carried away by the river. The river will cast him on to the bank,
and he shall be taken up by an enemy of Mine and his." I
lavished My love on you, so that you might be reared under
My eye.

'Your sister went to them and said: "Shall I direct you to 20:40
one who will nurse him?"

'Thus did We restore you to your mother, so that her mind might be set at ease and that she might not grieve.

'And when you slew a man We delivered you from distress and then proved you by other trials.

20:41 'You stayed for years among the people of Midian, and you then came here, Moses, as was ordained. I have chosen you for Myself. Go, you and your brother, with My signs, and do not cease to remember Me. Go both of you to Pharaoh, for he has transgressed all bounds. Speak to him with gentle words; he may yet take thought and fear Us.'

'Lord,' they said, 'we dread his malevolence and tyranny.'

He said: 'Have no fear. I shall be with you. I hear all and see all. Go to him and say: "We are the emissaries of your Lord. Let the Israelites depart with us, and oppress them no more. We have come to you with a revelation from your Lord: peace shall be his that follows the right guidance. It is revealed to us that the scourge will fall on those who deny His signs and turn away from them."'

20:49 He said: 'And who is your Lord, Moses?'

'Our Lord,' he said, 'is He that gave all creatures their distinctive form and then rightly guided them.'

'How was it, then, with the early generations?' he said.

He said: 'My Lord alone has knowledge of that, recorded in a Book. My Lord does not err, neither does He forget. It is He who has made the earth your cradle and traced on it paths for you to walk on. It is He who sends down water from the sky with which We bring forth every kind of plant, saying: "Eat and graze your cattle. Surely in this there are signs for rational beings. From the earth We have created you, and to the earth We will restore you; and from it We will bring you back to life."'

We showed him all Our signs, but he denied them and paid no heed. He said: 'Have you come to drive us from our land with your sorcery, Moses? We will surely confront you with sorcery as powerful as yours. Appoint a day when both of us can meet, a tryst which neither we nor you shall fail to keep, and a place at an equal distance from us both.'

20:59 He said: 'Meet me on the day of the Feast, and let all the people come together before noon.'

Pharaoh withdrew; he gathered his sorcerers and then returned. 'Woe betide you!' said Moses to them. 'Invent no falsehoods against God, or He will obliterate you with a scourge. Those that invent falsehood have ever failed.'

They conferred among themselves, whispering to one another. They said: 'These two are sorcerers who intend to drive you from your land by their sorcery and do away with your best traditions. Muster all your forces and array them in their ranks; those who win today will surely triumph.'

They said: 'Moses, either you throw down, or we shall be the first to throw.'

'Throw you down,' he said.

And lo! by their sorcery their ropes and staffs appeared to Moses' eyes as though they were running.

Moses was much alarmed. We said: 'Have no fear; you shall surely win. Throw that which is in your right hand. It will swallow up their devices, for their devices are but the deceitful show of a sorcerer. And the sorcerer shall never prosper, wherever he has come from.'

The sorcerers prostrated themselves: they said: 'We now believe in the Lord of Aaron and Moses.'

'Do you dare believe in Him before I give you leave?' said Pharaoh. 'This man must be your master, who taught you witchcraft. I will cut off your hands and feet on alternate sides and crucify you on the trunks of palm-trees. You shall learn whose punishment is more terrible, and more lasting.'

They said: 'We cannot have greater faith in you than in the miracles which we have witnessed and in Him who has created us. Therefore do your worst; you can punish us only in this present life. We have put our faith in our Lord so that He may forgive us our sins and the sorcery you have imposed upon us. Better is God's recompense, and more lasting. He that comes before his Lord laden with sin shall be consigned to Hell, wherein he shall neither die nor live. But they that come before Him with true faith, having done good works, shall be exalted to the highest ranks: in the Gardens of Eden, watered by run- ning brooks, wherein shall they abide for ever. Such shall be the recompense of those that keep themselves pure.'

20:77 And We revealed Our will to Moses: 'Set forth with My servants in the night and strike for them a dry path across the sea. Have no fear of being overtaken, nor let anything dismay you.'

Pharaoh pursued them with his warriors, but the waters of the sea overwhelmed them. For Pharaoh misled his people: he did not guide them.

Children of Israel! We delivered you from your enemy and made a covenant with you on the right flank of the Mount. We sent down for you manna and quails. 'Eat of the wholesome things with which We have provided you and do not transgress, lest you should provoke My ire. He that provokes My ire shall assuredly be lost; and I will surely forgive him that repents and believes in Me, does a good deed, and follows the right path. But, Moses, why have you come with such haste from your people?'

He said: 'There they are, close behind me. I hastened to You, Lord, that I might earn Your pleasure.'

20:85 He said: 'We proved your people in your absence, but the Sāmirī¹ has led them astray.'

Moses went back to his people, angry and sorrowful. 'My people,' he said, 'did your Lord not make you a gracious promise? Did my absence seem too long to you, or was it to incur your Lord's anger that you failed me?'

They replied: 'We did not fail you of our own free will. We were made to carry the people's trinkets and cast them into the fire. The Sāmirī threw likewise, and forged for them a calf, an image with a hollow sound. "This," they said, "is your god and the god of Moses whom he has forgotten."'

Did they not see that it returned to them no answer, and that it could neither harm nor help them?

Aaron had said to them: 'My people, this is but a test for you. Your Lord is the Merciful. Follow me and do as I bid you.' But they had replied: 'We will not cease to worship it until Moses returns.'

20:93 He said to Aaron: 'Why did you not seek me out when you saw them go astray? Why did you disobey my bidding?'

---

1. It is not clear who the Sāmirī was.

'Son of my mother,' he replied, 'let go, I pray you, of my beard
and my head. I was afraid that you might say: "You have sown
discord among the Israelites and did not wait for my orders."'

'Sāmirī,' he said, 'what had come over you?'

He replied: 'I saw what they did not see. I took a handful of
dust from the trail of the Messenger and flung it away: thus
did my soul prompt me.'

'Go!' he said. 'An outcast shall you be in this life, nor shall
you escape your appointed doom. Behold this idol which you
have served with such devotion: we will burn it to cinders and
scatter its ashes far and wide over the sea.'

Your Lord is God, other than whom there is no god. His
knowledge encompasses all things.

Thus do We recount to you the history of events gone by.
An Admonition of Our own have We given you: those that
reject it shall bear a heavy burden on the Day of Resurrection.
For ever shall they bear it: an evil burden on the Day of Resurrection.

On the day when the Trumpet shall be blown; on that day
We shall herd all the sinners together. Their eyes blue with
terror, they shall murmur among themselves: 'You lingered
on the earth but ten days.'

We know full well what they will say. The most upright
among them will say: 'You lingered but one day.'

And they ask you about the mountains. Say: 'My Lord will
crush them to fine dust and reduce them to a desolate waste,
with no hollows nor jutting mounds to be seen.'

On that day men will follow their truthful summoner, their
voices hushed before the Lord of Mercy; and you shall hear
only the sound of marching feet. On that day no intercession
will avail except from him that has received the sanction of
the Merciful and whose word was pleasing to Him. He knows
what is before them and behind them, but of Him they have
no knowledge.

They will hang their heads with awe before the Living One,
the Ever-existent. Those who are burdened with sin shall
come to grief: but those who have believed and done good
works shall fear no tyranny or injustice.

20:113 And thus have We sent it down: a Koran in the Arabic tongue, and proclaimed in it warnings and threats, that they may fear God and be admonished. So, exalted be God, the True King!

Do not be quick to recite the Koran before its revelation is completed, but rather say: 'Lord, increase my knowledge.'

We had made a covenant with Adam, but he forgot, and We found him lacking in steadfastness. And when We said to the angels: 'Prostrate yourselves before Adam,' they all prostrated themselves except Satan, who refused.

'Adam,' We said, 'Satan is an enemy to you and to your wife. Let him not turn you both out of Paradise and plunge you into affliction. Here you shall not hunger or be naked; you shall not thirst, or feel the scorching heat.'

But Satan whispered to him, saying: 'Adam, shall I show you the Tree of Immortality and an imperishable kingdom?'

20:121 They both ate from it, so that they saw their shameful parts and began to cover themselves with the leaves of the Garden. Thus did Adam disobey his Lord and stray from the right path.

Then his Lord chose him; He relented towards him and rightly guided him.

'Get you down hence, both, all together,' He said, 'and may you be enemies to each other. When My guidance is revealed to you, he that follows it shall neither err nor grieve; but he that forsakes My remembrance shall live in woe and come before Us blind on the Day of Resurrection. "Lord," he will say, "why have You brought me blind before You when I had once been clear-sighted?"'

He will say: 'Just as Our revelations were declared to you and you forgot them, so on this day shall you be yourself forgotten.'

Thus shall We reward the transgressor who denies his Lord's revelations. But the scourge of the life to come is more terrible and more lasting.

20:128 Do they not comprehend how many generations We have destroyed before them? They walk amidst the very ruins wherein once they dwelt. Surely in this there are signs for those endowed with good sense.

But for a Word from your Lord, long since decreed, their destruction in this life would have been certain. Therefore bear with what they say. Give glory to your Lord before sunrise and before sunset. Praise Him night and day, so that you may find comfort.

20:129

Do not regard with envy what We have given some among them to enjoy – the flower of the present life – for with this We seek only to try them. Better is your Lord's provision, and more lasting.

Enjoin prayer on your people and be diligent in its observance. We demand of you no provision: We shall Ourself provide for you. Blessed shall be the end of the devout.

20:132

And they say: 'Why does he not bring us a sign from his Lord?' Have they not been given sufficient proof in previous scriptures?

Had We destroyed them with a scourge before his[1] coming they would have said: 'Lord, if only You had sent us an apostle! We would have followed Your revelations before we were humbled and disgraced.'

Say: 'All are waiting: so wait if you will. You shall learn who have followed the even path and who have been rightly guided.'

20:135

THE PROPHETS

In the Name of God, the Merciful, the Compassionate

THE DAY of Reckoning for mankind is drawing near, yet they blithely persist in unbelief. They listen with ridicule to each fresh warning that their Lord gives them: their hearts are set on pleasure.

21:1

21:3

In private the wrongdoers say to each other: 'Is this man not a mortal like yourselves? Would you follow witchcraft with your eyes open?'

1. Muḥammad's.

21:4   Say: 'My Lord has knowledge of whatever is said in heaven and earth. He it is who hears all and knows all.'

Some say: 'It[1] is but a medley of dreams.' Others: 'He has invented it himself.' And yet others: 'He is a poet: let him show us a miracle, as did the apostles in days gone by.'

Communities whom We destroyed before them did not believe either. Will *they* believe?

The apostles We sent before you were but men whom We inspired. Ask the People of the Book if you do not know this. The bodies We gave them could not dispense with food, nor were they immortal. Then We fulfilled for them Our promise: We delivered them and those We willed, and utterly destroyed the transgressors.

And now We have revealed a Book for your admonishment. Will you not understand?

Many a sinful city have We annihilated, and after that replaced by other people. And when they felt Our might they took to their heels and ran away. 'Do not run away; return to your comforts and to your habitations: you shall be questioned all.'

21:14   'Woe betide us, we have done wrong!' was their reply. And this they kept repeating until We mowed them down and put out their light.

And it was not in sport that We created the heaven and the earth and all that lies between them. Had it been Our will to find a diversion, We could have found one near at hand if such were Our intent.

Indeed, We will hurl Truth at Falsehood, until Truth shall triumph and Falsehood be no more. Woe betide you, for all the falsehoods you have uttered.

His are all who dwell in the heavens and on earth. Those who stand in His presence do not disdain to worship Him, nor are they ever wearied. They praise Him night and day, tirelessly.

Or have they chosen earthly deities? And can these deities
21:22   restore the dead to life? Were there other gods in heaven or earth besides God, both heaven and earth would be cor-

1. The Koran.

rupted. Exalted be God, Lord of the Throne, above their falsehoods!

None shall question Him about His works, but questioned they shall be. Or have they chosen other gods besides Him? Say: 'Show us your proof. Here are the Admonition of today and the Admonition of days gone by.' But most of them know not the Truth, and this is why they pay no heed.

No apostle have We sent before you without inspiring him: 'There is no god but Me. Therefore serve Me.'

And they say: 'The Merciful has begotten children.' God forbid! They are but His honoured servants. They do not speak till He has spoken: they act by His command. He knows what is before them and behind them. They intercede for none save those whom He accepts, and tremble for awe of Him. Whoever of them declares: 'I am a god besides Him,' We shall requite with Hell. Thus shall We requite the wrong-doers.

Are the disbelievers unaware that the heavens and the earth were but one solid mass which We tore asunder, and that We made every living thing from water? Will they not have faith?

We set firm mountains upon the earth lest it should move away with them, and hewed out highways in the rock so that they might be rightly guided.

We spread the heaven like a canopy and provided it with strong support: yet of its signs they are heedless.

And He it was who created the night and the day, and the sun and the moon: each moves swiftly in an orbit of its own.

No man before you[1] have We made immortal. If you yourself are doomed to die, will they live on for ever?

Every soul shall taste death. We will test you all with evil and good. And to Us shall you be recalled.

And when the unbelievers see you, they only mock you: 'Is this the one who denies your gods?' While against the remembrance of the Merciful they also blaspheme.

Impatience is the very stuff man is made of. I shall show you My signs: do not ask Me to hurry them on.

21:23

21:30

21:37

1. Muḥammad.

21:38   And they say: 'When will this promise be fulfilled, if what you say be true?'

If only the unbelievers knew the day when they shall strive in vain to shield their faces and their backs from the fire of Hell; the day when none shall succour them! Indeed, it will overtake them unawares and stupefy them. They shall have no power to ward it off, nor shall they be reprieved.

Other apostles were mocked before you; but those who derided them were felled by the very scourge they mocked.

Say: 'Who will protect you, by night and by day, from the Lord of Mercy?' Yet are they unmindful of their Lord's remembrance.

Or have they other gods to defend them? Their idols shall be powerless over their own salvation, nor shall they be protected from Our scourge.

Yet have We indulged them and their fathers, so that they have lived too long. Can they not see how We invade their land and diminish its borders? Is it they who will triumph?

21:45   Say: 'I warn you only by inspiration.' But the deaf can hear no plea when they are warned.

Yet if the lightest whiff from the vengeance of your Lord touched them, they would surely say: 'Woe betide us: we have done wrong!'

We shall set up just scales for the Day of Resurrection, so that no soul shall in the least be wronged. Actions as small as a grain of mustard seed shall be weighed out. Our reckoning shall suffice.

We bestowed Salvation upon Moses and Aaron, and a light and an Admonition for the righteous: those who fear their Lord, although unseen, and dread the terrors of the Hour.

And this[1] is a blessed Admonition We have sent down. Will you then reject it?

21:52   We formerly bestowed guidance on Abraham, for We knew him well. He said to his father and to his people: 'What are these images to which you are so devoted?'

---

1. The Koran.

They said: 'They are the gods our fathers worshipped.'   21:53

He said: 'Then you and your fathers have surely been in evident error.'

'Is it the Truth that you are preaching,' they said, 'or is this but a jest?'

'Indeed,' he said, 'your Lord is the Lord of the heavens and the earth. It was He that made them: to this I bear witness. By the Lord, I will overthrow your idols as soon as you have turned your backs.'

So he broke them all in pieces, except their supreme god, that they might return to him.

'Who has done this to our deities?' said some. 'He must surely be a wrongdoer.'

Others said: 'We have heard a youth called Abraham speak of them.'

They said: 'Then bring him here in sight of all the people, that they may act as witnesses.'

'Abraham,' they said, 'was it you who did this to our deities?'   21:62

'No,' he said. 'It was their chief who smote them. Ask *them*, if they can speak.'

Thereupon they turned their thoughts upon themselves and said to each other: 'Surely you are the ones who have done wrong.'

They were crestfallen: 'You know they cannot speak.'

He said: 'Would you then worship that, instead of God, which can neither help nor harm you? Shame on you and on your idols! Have you no sense?'

They said: 'Burn him and avenge your gods, if you must punish him!'

'Fire,' We said, 'be cool to Abraham and keep him safe.'

They sought to lay a snare for him, but it was they whom We ruined. We delivered him and Lot, and brought them to the land which We had blessed for all mankind.

We gave him Isaac, and then Jacob for a grandson; and We made each a righteous man. And We ordained them   21:73 leaders to give guidance at Our behest, and enjoined on them charity, prayer, and almsgiving. They served none but Ourself.

21:74   To Lot We gave wisdom and knowledge and delivered him from the city that had committed deeds of abomination; surely they were men of iniquity and evil. We admitted him to Our mercy: he was a righteous man.

And Noah, who invoked Us before him; We answered his prayer, and saved him and all his kin from the great calamity; and We delivered him from those who had denied Our revelations. Evil were they; We drowned them all.

And tell of David and Solomon: how they passed judgement regarding the cornfield in which strayed lambs of some people had grazed by night. We gave Solomon insight into the case and bore witness to their judgement.

We bestowed on both of them wisdom and knowledge, and caused the mountains and the birds to join with David in Our praise. All this We did.

We taught him the armourer's craft, so that you might have protection in your wars. Will you then give thanks?

21:81   To Solomon We subjected the raging wind: it sped at his bidding to the land which We had blessed. And of all things We had knowledge.

From among the demons We assigned to him some who dived for him into the sea and performed other tasks besides. We Ourself assured their preservation.

And tell of Job: how he called on his Lord, saying: 'I am sorely afflicted: and of all those that show mercy You are the most merciful.'

We answered his prayer and relieved his affliction. We restored to him his family and as many more with them: a blessing from Ourself and an Admonition to the devout.

And Ishmael, Idrīs,[1] and Dhūl-Kifl,[2] who all endured with patience. To Our mercy We admitted them, for they were upright men.

21:87   And of Dhūl-Nūn:[3] how he went away in anger, thinking

1. Enoch.
2. Ezekiel; his tomb is in the town of Kifl in southern Iraq, and is revered by both Jews and Muslims.
3. Jonah.

We had no power over him. But in the darkness he cried: 'There is no god but You. Glory be to You! I have done wrong.' We answered his prayer and delivered him from distress. Thus shall We save the true believers. _{21:88}

And Zacharias, who invoked his Lord, saying: 'Lord, let me not remain childless, though of all heirs You are the best.'

We answered his prayer and gave him John, curing his wife of sterility. They vied with each other in good works and called on Us with piety, fear, and awe.

And the woman who kept her chastity; We breathed into her Our spirit, and made her and her son a sign to all mankind.

Your community is but one community, and I am your only Lord. Therefore serve Me. They have divided themselves into factions, but to Us shall they all return. He that does good works in the fullness of his faith, his endeavours shall not be lost: We record them all.

It is ordained that no community We have destroyed shall ever rise again. But when Gog and Magog are let loose and rush headlong down every hill; when the true promise nears its fulfilment; the unbelievers' eyes shall stare in amazement: 'Woe betide us! Of this we have been heedless. We have assuredly done wrong.' _{21:95}

You and your idols shall be the fuel of Hell; therein shall you all go down. Were they true gods, they would not go there: but therein shall they abide for ever. They shall groan with anguish and be bereft of hearing.

But those to whom We have long since shown Our bounty shall be far removed from Hell. They shall not hear its hissing, but shall delight for ever in what their souls desire.

The Supreme Terror shall not grieve them, and the angels will receive them, saying: 'This is the day you have been promised.'

On that day We shall roll up the heaven like a scroll of parchment. Just as We brought the First Creation into being, so will We restore it. This is a promise We shall assuredly fulfil. _{21:104}

21:105   We wrote in the Psalms[1] after the Torah was revealed: 'The righteous among My servants shall inherit the earth.' That is an Admonition to those who serve Us.

We have sent you forth but as a blessing to mankind. Say: 'It is revealed to me that your God is one God. Will you then be Muslims?'

If they pay no heed, say: 'I have warned you all alike, though I cannot tell whether the scourge you are promised is imminent or far off. He knows your spoken words and knows your hidden thoughts. And for all I know, this may be a test for you and a short reprieve.'

21:112   Say: 'Lord, judge with fairness. Our Lord is the Merciful, whose help We seek against your blasphemies.'

THE PILGRIMAGE

In the Name of God, the Merciful, the Compassionate

22:1   YOU PEOPLE! Have fear of your Lord. The catastrophe of the Hour shall be terrible indeed.

The day you witness it, every suckling mother shall forsake her infant, every pregnant female shall cast her burden, and you shall see people reeling like drunkards although not drunk: but such shall be the horror of God's torment.

Yet there are some who in their ignorance dispute about God, and follow every rebellious demon doomed to seduce his follower and lead him to the scourge of the Conflagration.

22:5   You people! If you doubt the Resurrection remember that We had created you from dust, then from a living germ, then from a clot of blood,[2] and then from a half-formed lump of flesh, so that We might manifest to you Our power.

We cause to remain in the wombs whatever We please for an appointed term, and then We bring you forth as infants, that you may grow up and reach your prime. Some among you

1. Psalm 37:29.
2. *Alaq* can also mean a leech or a little worm.

die young, and some live on to abject old age when all that they once knew they know no more.

You sometimes see the earth dry and barren: but no sooner do We send the water down upon it than it begins to stir and swell, putting forth every kind of radiant bloom. That is because God is Truth: He resurrects the dead and has power over all things.

22:6

The Hour is sure to come – of this there is no doubt. And those who are in their graves God will raise to life.

Some wrangle about God, though they have neither knowledge nor guidance nor illuminating scripture. They turn away in scorn, to lead others astray from God's path: they shall incur disgrace in this life, and on the Day of Resurrection taste the torment of the Conflagration. 'This is the reward of your handiwork. God is never unjust to His servants.'

And among people there are some who profess to serve God and yet stand on the very fringe of the true faith. When blessed with good fortune they are content, but when an ordeal befalls them they turn upon their heels, forfeiting this life and the Hereafter. That way true perdition lies.

They call on idols which can neither harm nor help them. That is the extreme error.

22:11

They call on that which would sooner harm than help them: an evil master and an evil friend.

As for those that have faith and do good works, God will admit them to Gardens watered by running brooks. God's will is ever done.

If anyone thinks that God will not aid him in this world and in the world to come, let him stretch up a rope to the sky and hang himself. Then let him ponder if his cunning has done away with that which has enraged him.

And thus have We sent it down in clear revelations: God gives guidance to whom He will.

The true believers, those who follow the Jewish Faith, the Sabaeans, the Christians, the Magians, and the pagans, God will surely judge on the Day of Resurrection. Surely God is witness of all things.

Do you not see that those in the heavens and on the earth, 22:18

and the sun and the moon and the stars, the mountains and the trees, the beasts, and countless people – all do homage to God? Yet many have deserved the scourge. He who is humbled by God has none to honour him: God's will is ever done.

22:19 Here are two antagonists who contend about their Lord. Garments of fire have been prepared for the unbelievers. Scalding water shall be poured upon their heads, melting their skins and that which is in their bellies. They shall be lashed with rods of iron.

Whenever, in their anguish, they strive to escape from it, back shall they be dragged, and: 'Taste you the torment of the Conflagration!'

As for those that have faith and do good works, God will admit them to Gardens watered by running brooks. They shall be adorned with bracelets of gold and pearls, and arrayed therein in garments of silk. For they have been guided to the noblest of words; they have been guided to the path of Him who is worthy of praise.

22:25 The unbelievers who debar others from the path of God and from the Sacred Mosque which We provided for the people, natives and strangers alike, and those who seek to violate it sinfully – We shall make them taste a grievous torment.

When We prepared for Abraham the site of the Sacred Mosque We said: 'Worship none besides Me. Keep My House clean for those who walk around it, and those who stand upright, or kneel down in worship.'

Exhort all people to make the Pilgrimage. They will come to you on foot and on the backs of swift camels from every distant quarter; they will come to avail themselves of many a benefit, and to pronounce on the appointed days the name of God over the cattle which He has given them for food. Eat of their flesh, and feed the poor and the unfortunate.

Then let the pilgrims tidy themselves, make their vows, and
22:30 circle the Ancient House. Such is God's commandment. He that reveres the sacred rites of God shall fare better in the sight of his Lord.

The flesh of cattle is lawful for you, except for that which has been specified before. Guard yourselves against the abomination of idols; and avoid the utterance of falsehood.

Dedicated to God, and serving none besides Him: he that serves other deities besides God is like him who falls from heaven and is snatched off by the birds or carried away by the wind to some far-off region. Even such is he. 22:31

He that reveres the offerings made to God shows the piety of his heart. They are beneficial to you until a time decreed, then their place of sacrifice is by the Ancient House.

For every community We have ordained a ritual, that they may pronounce the name of God over the cattle which He has given them for food. Your God is one God: to Him submit. Give joyful tidings to the humble, whose hearts are filled with awe at the mention of God; who endure adversity with fortitude, attend to their prayers, and give from what We gave them.

And the camels We have made a part of God's rites. They are of much use to you. Pronounce over them the name of God as you draw them up in line for slaughter; and when they have fallen to the ground eat of their flesh and feed the uncomplaining beggar and the demanding supplicant. Thus have We subjected them to your service, so that you may give thanks. 22:36

Their flesh and blood does not reach God; it is your piety that reaches Him. Thus has He subjected them to your service, so that you may give glory to God for guiding you.

Give joyful tidings to the righteous. God will ward off evil from true believers; God does not love the treacherous and the thankless.

Permission to take up arms is hereby given to those who are attacked, because they have been wronged. Surely God has power to grant them victory: those who have been unjustly driven from their homes, only because they said: 'Our Lord is God.' Had God not defended some by the might of others, monasteries and churches, synagogues and mosques in which His praise is daily celebrated, would have been utterly destroyed. But whoever helps God shall surely be helped by Him: God is powerful and mighty: those who, if We make 22:41

them masters in the land, will attend to their prayers and render the alms levy, enjoin justice and forbid the reprehensible. God governs the destiny of all things.

22:42 If they disbelieve you, before them the people of Noah, 'Ād and Thamūd, the people of Abraham and the people of Lot, and the dwellers of Midian had also disbelieved: Moses was likewise disbelieved. I bore long with the unbelievers, and then I smote them. How awesome was the way I smote them!

How many cities, teeming with sin, have We laid waste! They lie in desolate ruin, their wells abandoned and their proud palaces empty.

Have they never journeyed through the land? Have they no hearts to reason with, or ears to hear with? It is their hearts, and not their eyes, that are blind.

They bid you hasten the scourge. And God will never fail His promise. Each day of your Lord's is like a thousand years in your reckoning.[1]

22:48 I bore long with many cities, teeming though they were with sin, and in the end I smote them. To Me shall all return.

Say: 'You people, I have been sent to warn you plainly. Those that accept the true faith and do good works shall be forgiven and richly provided for; and those that seek to confute Our revelations shall be the tenants of Hell.'

Never have We sent a single prophet or apostle before you with whose wishes Satan did not tamper. But God abrogates the interjections of Satan and God confirms His own revelations. God is all-knowing and wise. He makes Satan's interjections a temptation for those whose hearts are tainted, whose hearts are hardened – this is why the wrongdoers are in open schism – so that those who are endowed with knowledge may realize that this[2] is the Truth from your Lord and thus believe in it and humble their hearts towards Him. God will surely guide the faithful to a straight path.

Yet will the unbelievers never cease to doubt it, until the Hour overtakes them unawares, or the scourge of a baleful day descends upon them. On that day God will reign supreme;

22:56

---

1. Cf. Psalm 90:4.   2. The Koran.

He will judge them all. Those that believed and did good works shall enter the Gardens of Delight; but the unbelievers who have denied Our revelations shall receive an ignominious punishment. 22:57

And for those that have left their land in the cause of God and then died or were slain, God will surely make a generous provision: God is the most munificent Provider. He will surely admit them with a welcome that will please them. Omniscient is God, and gracious.

Thus shall it be. He that repays an injury in kind and then is wronged again shall be helped by God. God is merciful and forgiving.

Thus shall it be. God causes the night to pass into day, and the day to pass into night. God hears all and observes all.

Thus shall it be. God is Truth, and Falsehood all that they invoke besides Him. God alone is the Most High, the Supreme One.

Do you not see how God sends down water from the sky and forthwith the earth turns green? Gracious is God and all-knowing. 22:63

His is all that the heavens and the earth contain. Surely God is the Self-sufficient, the Praiseworthy One.

Do you not see that God has subdued for you all that is in the earth? And the ships which sail the sea at His bidding? He holds the sky from falling down upon the earth: this it shall not do except by His own leave. Kindly is God, and compassionate to mankind.

It is He who has given you life, and He who will cause you to die and make you live again. Surely man is ungrateful.

For every community We have ordained a ritual which they observe. Let them not dispute with you concerning this. Call them to the path of your Lord: you are rightly guided. If they argue with you, say: 'God knows best all that you do. On the Day of Resurrection God will judge your differences.'

Are you not aware that God has knowledge of what heaven and earth contain? All is recorded in a Book. That is easy enough for God.

Yet they worship besides God that for which no sanction is 22:71

revealed and of which they know nothing. The wrongdoers shall have none to help them.

22:72 And when Our revelations are recited to them in all their clarity, you will note denial in the faces of the unbelievers. Barely can they restrain themselves from assaulting those who recite Our revelations.

Say: 'Shall I tell you what is worse than that? The Fire which God has promised those who deny Him. A wretched fate!'

You people! Listen to this aphorism. Those whom you invoke besides God could never create a fly though they combined their forces. And if a fly stole aught from them, they could never retrieve it. Powerless is the supplicant, and powerless he whom he supplicates.

22:74 They do not render to God the homage due to Him; yet God is powerful and mighty.

God chooses emissaries from the angels and from people. Surely God hears all and observes all; He knows what is before them and behind them. And to God shall all things be recalled.

You that are true believers, kneel down and prostrate yourselves. Worship your Lord and do good works, so that you may succeed.

22:78 Fight for the cause of God with the devotion due to Him. *He* has chosen you, and laid on you no burdens in the observance of your Religion, the faith of your father Abraham. In this, as in former Scriptures, He has given you the name of Muslims, so that the Apostle may testify against you, and that you may yourselves testify against people.

Therefore attend to your prayers, render the alms levy, and hold fast to God; for He is your guardian. A gracious guardian and a gracious helper!

THE BELIEVERS

In the Name of God, the Merciful, the Compassionate

SUCCESSFUL ARE the believers, who are humble in their 23:1
prayers; who avoid profane talk, and give alms in earnest; who
restrain their carnal desires (except with their wives and
slave-girls, for with them they are blameless: transgressors are
those who lust after other than these); who are true to their
trusts and promises, and diligent in their prayers. These are
the heirs of Paradise, wherein shall they abide for ever.

We first created man from an essence of clay: then placed
him, a living germ, in a secure enclosure.[1] The germ We made
a clot of blood,[2] and the clot a lump of flesh. This We fashioned into bones, then clothed the bones with flesh, thus
bringing forth another creation. Blessed be God, the noblest
of creators.

Then you shall surely die hereafter, and then be restored to 23:16
life on the Day of Resurrection. We have created seven heavens[3] above you; of Our creation We were never heedless.

We sent down water from the sky in due measure, and lodged
it into the earth; but if We please, We can take it all away.

With it We caused palm-groves and vineyards to spring up,
yielding abundant fruit for your sustenance. The tree[4] which
grows on Mount Sinai gives oil and a condiment for all to eat.

In cattle, too, you have but an example and a lesson. We
give you to drink of that which is in their bellies, you eat their
flesh, and gain other benefits from them besides. By them, as
by the ships that sail the sea, you are carried.

We sent forth Noah to his people. 'Serve God, my people,' 23:23
he said, 'for you have no god but Him. Will you not take
heed?'

1. The womb.
2. See p. 222, note 2.
3. Literally, highways (Al-Jalālayn).
4. The olive.

229

23:24   The unbelieving elders of his people said: 'This man is but a mortal like yourselves, feigning to be your superior. Had God willed, He could have sent down angels. Nor did we hear that such a thing ever happened to our forefathers. He is surely but a man possessed. Keep an eye on him awhile.'

He said: 'Help me, Lord, for they disbelieve me.'

We revealed Our will to him, saying: 'Build the ark under Our watchful eyes, according to Our instructions. When Our judgement comes to pass and water wells out from the Oven, take aboard a pair from every species and the members of your household, except those of them already doomed. Do not plead with Me for those who have done wrong: they shall be drowned. And when you and your followers have gone aboard, say: "Praise be to God who has delivered us from the sinful people. Lord, let my landing be blessed. You alone can make me land in safety."'

Surely in that there were veritable signs. Thus did We put mankind to the test.

23:31   Then We raised a new generation, and sent forth to them an apostle of their own. 'Serve God,' he said, 'for you have no god but Him. Will you not take heed?'

But the unbelieving elders of his people, who denied the life to come and on whom We had lavished the good things of this life, said: 'This man is but a mortal like yourselves, nourished by the same food and drink. If you obey a mortal like yourselves, you shall indeed be lost. Does he promise you, when you are dead and turned to dust and bones, you will be raised to life? A foolish promise, indeed. There is no other life but this, our earthly life: we die and live, never to be restored to life. He is but a man who tells of God what is untrue. Never will we believe in him.'

He said: 'Help me, Lord, for they disbelieve me.'

He replied: 'Before long they shall rue it.' The Cry took them in all justice, and We swept them away like withered leaves. Gone are the sinful people.

After them We raised other generations – no community 23:44   can delay its doom or go before it – and sent forth Our apostles in succession. Yet time after time each community disbelieved its apostle, so that We destroyed them one by one and held them up as an example. Gone are a people who disbelieved.

Then We sent Moses and his brother Aaron, with Our 23:45 signs and with clear authority, to Pharaoh and his nobles. But they received them with contempt, for they were arrogant men. 'What!' said they. 'Are we to believe in two men like ourselves, whose people are our slaves?' They denied them, and thus incurred destruction. And We gave Moses the Book, that they might be rightly guided.

We made the son of Mary and his mother a sign, and gave them a shelter on a peaceful hillside watered by a fresh spring.

Apostles! Eat of that which is wholesome, and do good works: I have knowledge of all your actions. Your community is but one community, and I am your only Lord: therefore fear Me.

Yet they have divided themselves into factions, each rejoicing in its own doctrines. Leave them in their error till a time appointed.

Do they think that, in giving them wealth and children, 23:55 We are solicitous for their welfare? By no means! They lack perception.

Those who walk in fear of their Lord; who believe in the revelations of their Lord; who worship none besides their Lord; who give from what they were given with hearts filled with awe, knowing that they will return to their Lord: these vie with each other for salvation and shall be the first to attain it.

We charge no soul with more than it can bear. We have a Book which speaks the Truth: and none shall be wronged.

But their hearts are blind to all this; their deeds are of a different sort, and they are bent on doing them. But when We visit Our scourge upon those among them that live in affluence, they will howl for help. We shall say: 'Do not howl this day, for from Us you shall receive no help. My revelations were recited to you many a time, but you turned your backs in scorn, and passed the nights reviling them.'

Should they not heed the Word? 23:68

Was anything revealed to them that had not been revealed to their forefathers?

23:69 Or is it because they do not know their apostle that they deny him?

Do they say he is possessed?

Surely he has come to them with the Truth. But most of them abhor the Truth. Had the Truth followed their appetites, the heavens, the earth, and all who dwell in them, would have surely been corrupted. We have given them their Admonition: yet to their Admonition they pay no heed.

Are you seeking a recompense from them? Far better is your Lord's recompense: He is the most munificent Giver.

You have surely called them to a straight path, but those who deny the life to come will ever stray from the path.

And if We showed them mercy and relieved their misfortunes, they would persist in their insolent ways, ever straying blindly from the right path. We punished them, but they neither entreated their Lord nor humbled themselves before Him. And when We smote them with a grievous scourge, they yielded to utter despair.

23:78 He it was who gave you ears, eyes, and hearts: yet you are seldom thankful.

He it was who placed you on the earth, and before Him shall you be herded.

And He it is who ordains life and death, and He who alternates the night with the day. Can you not understand?

Indeed, they say what the ancients said before them. 'After our death, when we are dust and bones,' they say, 'shall we be raised to life? This we have been promised before, we and our forefathers. It is but a fable of the ancients.'

Say: 'Whose is the earth and all that it contains? If you really know?'

'God's,' they will say.

Say: 'Then will you not reflect?'

Say: 'Who is the Lord of the seven heavens, and of the Glorious Throne?'

23:87 'God,' they will say.

Say: 'Will you not fear Him, then?'

Say: 'In whose hands is the sovereignty of all things, pro- 23:88
tecting all, while against Him there is no protection? If you
really know?'

'In God's,' they will say.

Say: 'How then can you be so bewitched?'

But We have revealed to them the Truth, and they are surely
lying.

Never has God begotten a son, nor is there any other god
besides Him. Were this otherwise, each god would govern his
own creation, each holding himself above the other. Exalted
be God above their falsehoods!

He knows alike the unknown and the manifest. Exalted be
He above the gods they serve besides Him!

Say: 'Lord, if You will indeed let me see the scourge they
are promised, do not abandon me, Lord, among these wrongdoing people.' Indeed, We do have power enough to let you
see the scourge We promise them.

Requite evil with good. We know their slanders well. And
say: 'Lord, I seek refuge in You from the promptings of the
demons. Lord, I seek refuge in You from their presence.'

When death comes to one among them, he will say: 'Lord, 23:99
let me go back, that I may do good works in the world I have
left behind.'

Never! These are the very words which he will speak.
Behind them there shall stand a barrier till the Day of Resurrection. And when the Trumpet is blown, on that day their
ties of kin shall be broken, nor shall they ask help of one
another.

Those whose good deeds weigh heavy in the scales shall
triumph, but those whose good deeds are light shall forfeit
their souls and abide in Hell for ever. The fire will scorch their
faces and they will writhe in anguish.

'Were My revelations not recited to you, and did you not
deny them?'

'Lord,' they will say, 'fortune betrayed us and we were
people gone astray. Lord, deliver us from it; if we relapse, then
shall we indeed be wrongdoers.'

He will say: 'Stay here in shame and do not plead with Me. 23:108

23:109 Among My servants there were those who said: "Lord, we now believe. Forgive us and have mercy on us: You are the best of those that show mercy." But you derided them until they caused you to forget My warning; and you laughed at them. Today I shall requite them for their fortitude, for it is they who have triumphed.'

He will say: 'How many years did you linger on the earth?'

They will say: 'A day, or possibly less. Ask those who have kept count.'

23:114 He will say: 'Brief indeed was your sojourn, if you but knew it! Did you think We created you in vain and to Us you would never be recalled?'

Exalted be God, the True King. There is no god but Him, the Lord of the Glorious Throne.

He that invokes another god with God – a god of whose divinity he has no proof – his Lord will surely bring him to account. The unbelievers shall never succeed.

23:118 Say: 'Lord, forgive and have mercy. You are the best of those that show mercy.'

LIGHT

In the Name of God, the Merciful, the Compassionate

24:1 A *SŪRAH* We have revealed and sanctioned, proclaiming therein clear revelations, so that you may reflect.

The adulteress and the adulterer you shall give each a hundred lashes. Let no pity for either cause you to disobey God's Religion, if you truly believe in God and the Last Day; and let their punishment be witnessed by a number of believers.

The adulterer may marry only an adulteress or an idolatress; and the adulteress may marry only an adulterer or an idolater. This is forbidden to true believers.

24:4 Those that defame honourable women and cannot produce four witnesses you shall give eighty lashes. Do not accept their testimony ever after, for it is they who are the transgressors –

except those among them that afterwards repent and mend   24:5
their ways: God is forgiving and compassionate.

Those who accuse their wives but have no witnesses except
themselves, shall each swear four times by God that his charge
is true and in a fifth time call down upon himself the curse of
God if he is lying. But if his wife swears four times by God
that his charge is false and in a fifth time calls down His curse
upon herself if it be true, she shall receive no punishment.[1]

And but for God's grace and compassion for you, His
forgiveness and His wisdom . . .

Those who concocted that slander[2] were surely a clique
from among your own people. Do not regard it as a misfortune, for it has proved an advantage. Each one of them shall
be punished according to his sin. As for him who had the
greater share in it among them, his punishment shall be
terrible indeed.

When you heard it, why did the faithful, men and women,   24:12
not think well of their own people, and say: 'This is an evident
falsehood'? Why did they not produce four witnesses? If they
could not produce the witnesses, then they were surely lying
in the sight of God.

But for God's grace and mercy towards you in this life and
in the life to come, you would have been grievously punished
for your scandalmongering. You carried with your tongues
and uttered with your mouths what you knew not. You may
have thought it a trifle, but in the sight of God it was a grave
offence.

And when you heard it, why did you not say: 'It is not
proper for us to speak of this; glory be to God: this is a monstrous slander'?

God bids you never to repeat the like, if you are true believers. God makes plain to you the revelations. God is omniscient   24:18
and wise.

1. Cf. Numbers 5:11–31.
2. The reference is to the scandal instigated by the Prophet's political
   opponents involving Muḥammad's wife 'Ā'ishah with Ṣafwān b.
   al-Muʻaṭṭal.

24:19 Those who delight in spreading salacious slander against the faithful shall be grievously punished in this life and in the life to come. God knows, but you know not.

And but for God's grace and compassion for you, His kindliness and mercy . . .

You that are true believers, do not follow Satan's footsteps. He that walks in Satan's footsteps is incited by him to lewdness and everything reprehensible. But for God's grace and mercy, none of you would ever have kept himself pure. But God purifies whom He will; God hears all and knows all.

Let not the honourable and the rich among you swear to withhold their gifts from their kin, the destitute, and those who have fled their homes in the cause of God. Rather let them pardon and forgive. Do you not wish God to forgive you? God is forgiving and compassionate.

24:23 Those who defame honourable but careless believing women shall be cursed in this world and in the world to come. Grievous punishment awaits them on the day when their own tongues, hands, and feet will testify to what they did. On that day God will justly requite them in full; and they shall know that God is the veritable Truth.

Unclean women are for unclean men, and unclean men for unclean women. But good women are for good men, and good men for good women. These shall be cleared of calumny. Forgiveness, and a generous provision, await them.

Believers, do not enter dwellings other than your own until you have asked their owners' permission and wished them peace. That will be best for you; perchance you will remember.

If you find no one in them, do not go in till you are given leave. If you are refused admission, it is but more proper that you should go away. God has knowledge of all your actions.

It shall be no offence for you to seek shelter in empty dwellings. God knows what you reveal and what you hide.

Enjoin believing men to turn their eyes away from temptation and to preserve their chastity. This will make their lives purer. God has knowledge of all their actions.

24:31 Enjoin believing women to turn their eyes away from

temptation and to preserve their chastity; not to display their adornments (except such as are normally revealed); to draw their veils over their bosoms and not to display their finery except to their husbands, their fathers, their husbands' fathers, their sons, their stepsons, their brothers, their brothers' sons, their sisters' sons, their women-servants, and their slave-girls; male attendants lacking in natural vigour, and children who have no carnal knowledge of women. And let them not stamp their feet[1] when walking so as to reveal their hidden trinkets.

Believers, turn to God in penitence, all, that you may succeed.

And take in marriage those among you who are single and those of your male and female slaves who are honest. If they are poor, God will enrich them from His own bounty; God is munificent and all-knowing.   24:32

And let those who cannot afford to marry live in continence until God shall enrich them from His own bounty. As for those of your slaves who wish to buy their liberty, free them if you find in them any promise and bestow on them a part of the riches which God has given you.   24:33

And you shall not force your slave-girls into prostitution in order that you may enrich yourselves, if they wish to preserve their chastity. If anyone compels them, God will after their compulsion be forgiving and compassionate.

We have sent down to you discerning revelations; an account of those who have gone before you, and an Admonition to the righteous.

God is the light of the heavens and the earth. His light may be compared to a niche that enshrines a lamp, the lamp within a crystal of star-like brilliance. It is lit from a blessed olive tree neither eastern nor western. Its very oil would almost shine forth, though no fire touched it. Light upon light; God guides to His light whom He will.   24:35

God speaks in parables to mankind. God has knowledge of all things.

1. Cf. Isaiah 3:16, 18.

24:36   His light is found in temples God has sanctioned to be built for the remembrance of His name. In them, His praise is sung morning and evening, by men whom neither trade nor profit can divert from remembering God, from offering prayers, or from giving alms; who dread the day when hearts and eyes shall writhe with anguish; who hope that God will requite them for their noblest deeds and lavish His grace upon them. God gives without reckoning to whom He will.

As for the unbelievers, their works are like a mirage in a desert. The thirsty traveller thinks it is water, but when he comes near he finds that it is nothing. He finds God there, who pays him back in full. Swift is God's reckoning.

Or like darkness on a bottomless ocean spread with clashing billows and overcast with clouds: darkness upon darkness. If he stretches out his hand he can scarcely see it. Indeed the man from whom God withholds His light shall find no light at all.

24:41   Do you not see how God is praised by those in the heavens and those on earth? The very birds praise Him as they wing their way. He notes the prayers and praises of all His creatures; God has knowledge of all their actions.

It is God who has sovereignty over the heavens and the earth. To God shall all return.

Do you not see how God drives the clouds, then gathers and piles them up in masses through which you see the rain pour down in torrents? And from heaven's mountains He sends down the hail, pelting with it whom He will and turning it away from whom He pleases. The flash of His lightning almost snatches out men's eyes.

God makes the night succeed the day: surely in this there is a lesson for the clear-sighted.

God created every beast from water. Some creep upon their bellies, others walk on two legs, and others yet on four. God creates what He pleases. Surely God has power over all things.

We have sent down revelations demonstrating the Truth. God guides whom He will to a straight path.

24:47   They say: 'We believe in God and the Apostle and obey.'

But soon thereafter some among them turn their backs. Surely these are no believers.

And when they are called to God and His apostle that he may judge between them, some among them turn away. Had Truth been on their side they would have come to him in all obedience. 24:48

Is there a sickness in their hearts, or are they full of doubt? Do they fear that God and His apostle may deny them justice? Surely they are themselves the wrongdoers.

But when true believers are called to God and His apostle that he may judge between them, their only reply is: 'We hear and obey.' It is they that will surely succeed.

Those that obey God and His apostle, revere God and fear Him, will surely triumph.

They solemnly swear by God that if you order them, they will march forth. Say: 'Do not swear: your obedience, not your oaths, will count. Surely God is cognizant of what you do.'

Say: 'Obey God and obey the Apostle. If you do not, he is still bound to fulfil his obligations, and you are still bound to fulfil yours. If you obey him, you shall be rightly guided. The apostle's duty is but to give the veritable warning.' 24:54

God has promised those of you who believe and do good works to make them masters in the land as He made those who went before them, to strengthen the Religion He chose for them, and to change their fears to safety. Let them worship Me and serve none besides Me. Wicked indeed are they who after this deny Me.

And attend to your prayers, render the alms levy, and obey the Apostle, so that you may be shown mercy.

Never think that the unbelievers are immune on the earth. The Fire shall be their shelter: a wretched fate!

Believers, let your slaves and those who are under the age of puberty among you ask your leave on three occasions: before the dawn prayer, when you have put off your garments in the heat of noon, and after the evening prayer. These are the three occasions when none may intrude upon your privacy. At other times, it shall be no offence for you, or them, to go around visiting one another. Thus God makes plain to you the revelations: God is omniscient and wise. 24:58

24:59 And when they have reached the age of puberty, let your children still ask your leave as their elders do. Thus God makes plain to you His revelations: God is all-knowing and wise.

It shall be no offence for old spinsters who have no hope of marriage to discard their cloaks without revealing their adornments. Better if they do not discard them. God hears all and knows all.

It shall be no offence for the blind, the lame, the sick, and for yourselves to eat in your houses or the houses of your fathers, the houses of your mothers, the houses of your brothers, the houses of your sisters, the houses of your paternal uncles, the houses of your paternal aunts, the houses of your maternal uncles, the houses of your maternal aunts, or of your friends; or in houses with the keys of which you are entrusted. Nor shall it be an offence for you to eat together or apart.

And when you enter a house, salute one another with a greeting from God, devout and kindly. Thus God makes clear to you the revelations, that you may understand.

24:62 They only are true believers who have faith in God and His apostle, and who, when gathered with him upon a grave occasion, do not depart till they have begged his leave. Those who ask your leave are those who truly believe in God and His apostle. When they ask your leave to go away on any business of their own, grant it to whomever you please and implore God to forgive them; God is forgiving and compassionate.

Do not address the Apostle in the manner you address one another. God knows those of you who steal away, concealing themselves behind others. Let those who disobey his orders beware, lest some affliction or some woeful scourge be visited upon them.

24:64 Surely to God belongs what the heavens and the earth contain. He has knowledge of all you are up to. On the day when they return to Him, He will declare to them all that they have done. God has knowledge of all things.

SALVATION[1]

In the Name of God, the Merciful, the Compassionate

BLESSED BE He who has revealed Salvation to His servant,   25:1
that he may warn the nations; Sovereign of the heavens and
the earth, who has begotten no children and has no partner in
His sovereignty; who has created all things and ordained them
in due proportion.

And yet the unbelievers serve, besides Him, other gods
which can create nothing and were themselves created: which
can neither harm nor help themselves, and which have no
power over death or life, or the raising of the dead.

The unbelievers say: 'This[2] is but a forgery of his own
invention, in which others have helped him.' Unjust is what
they say and false.

And they say: 'Fables of the ancients he has written: they
are dictated to him morning and evening.'

Say: 'It is revealed by Him who knows the secrets of the heav-   25:6
ens and the earth. He is surely forgiving and compassionate.'

They also say: 'How is it that this apostle eats food and
walks about the market-squares? Why has no angel been sent
down to him to give warning with him? Why has no treasure
been given him, no garden to provide his sustenance?'

And the wrongdoers say: 'The man you follow is surely
bewitched.'

See what epithets they bestow upon you![3] They have gone
astray, and cannot return to the true path.

Blessed be He who, if He wills, can make for you better
things than these: Gardens watered by running brooks; and
He can make palaces for you.

Indeed, they deny the Hour. For those who deny the Hour
We have prepared a Conflagration. From far away they shall
hear it raging and roaring. And when, chained together, they   25:13
are flung into some narrow space, they will fervently call for

---

1. See p. 4, note 1.   2. The Koran.   3. Muḥammad.

25:14 death. But they will be told: 'Do not call today for one death; call for many deaths!'

Say: 'Which is better, this or the Paradise of Immortality which the righteous have been promised? It is their recompense and their retreat. Abiding there for ever, they shall find therein all that they desire. That is a promise which your Lord must needs fulfil.'

On the day He herds them together with their idols, He will say: 'Was it you who misled these My servants, or did they choose to go astray?'

They will answer: 'Glory be to You! We should never have chosen other guardians besides You. But You allowed them and their fathers the enjoyments of this life, so that they forgot the Admonition and became a people utterly extinct.'

'Your idols have denied your charges. You cannot avert your doom, nor can you be helped. Those of you who have done wrong We will grievously punish.'

25:20 And We have sent no apostles before you who did not eat food or walk about the market-squares. We test you by means of one another. Will you not have patience? Surely your Lord observes all.

Those who entertain no hope of meeting Us ask: 'Why have not the angels been sent down upon us? Why can we not see our Lord?' Arrogant they are, and mightily iniquitous.

On the day they behold the angels, the transgressors will not rejoice that day. The angels will say to them: 'You shall never cross that barrier.' Then We shall turn to that which they have done and render it as vain as scattered dust.

As for the heirs of Paradise, they shall on that day lodge in a more auspicious dwelling, and in a cooler resting-place.

On that day the sky with all its clouds shall be rent asunder and the angels sent down in their ranks. On that day the Merciful will truly reign supreme. A day of woe it shall be to the unbelievers.

On that day the wrongdoer will bite his hands and say: 'Would that I had walked in the Apostle's path! Oh, would 25:29 that I had never chosen so-and-so for my companion! It was he that made me stray from the Admonition after it had come to me. Satan is ever treacherous to man.'

And the Apostle says: 'Lord, my people have forsaken this 25:30 Koran.' Thus to every prophet We have assigned adversaries among the transgressors: but you need none besides your Lord to guide and help you.

And the unbelievers say: 'Why was the Koran not revealed to him entire in a single revelation?'

We have revealed it thus so that We may sustain your heart. We have imparted it by gradual revelation. No sooner will they come to you with an argument than We shall reveal to you the Truth, better expounded. Those who are dragged upon their faces into Hell shall have a viler place to dwell in, having strayed farther from the right path.

We gave the Book to Moses and assigned to him his brother Aaron as a helper. We sent them to those who had denied Our signs, and utterly destroyed them.

And Noah's people: when they denied the emissaries, We 25:37 drowned them and made of them an example to mankind; for the wrongdoers We prepared a woeful scourge.

And 'Ād and Thamūd, and those who dwelt in Al-Rass, and many generations in between: to each of them We gave examples, and each of them We exterminated.

They must surely have passed by the city which was destroyed by the fatal rain: have they never seen its ruins? Yet have they no faith in the Resurrection.

Whenever they see you they only deride you: 'Is this the man God has sent as an emissary? Had we not stood firm, he would have made us stray from our gods.' But when they face the scourge they shall realize who has strayed farther from the right path.

Have you considered him who has made a god of his own appetite? Would *you* be a guardian over him?

Or do you think most of them can hear or understand? They are but like cattle; indeed, even more misguided.

Do you not see how your Lord lengthens the shadow? Had 25:45

it been His will He could have made it constant. But We make the sun its guide; little by little We shorten it.

And He it was who made the night a mantle for you, and sleep a rest. He made each day a resurrection.

And He it is who drives the winds as harbingers of His mercy; and We send down pure water from the sky, so that We may give life to a dead land and quench the thirst of countless beasts and men We have created.

We have made it flow freely among them, that they may remember. Yet most decline to render thanks.

And had it been Our will, We could have sent to every city someone to give warning. So do not yield to the unbelievers, but fight them vigorously with this.[1]

And He it was who sent the two seas rolling, the one sweet and fresh, the other salt and bitter, and set a rampart between them, an insurmountable barrier.

And He it was who created man from water, and gave him kin of blood and of marriage. All-powerful is your Lord.

Yet they worship idols which can neither help nor harm them. Surely the unbeliever is an enemy to his Lord.

And We have sent you only to proclaim joyful tidings and to give warning. Say: 'I demand of you no recompense for this. Let him who will, take the right path to his Lord.'

Put your trust in the Ever-living who never dies. Celebrate His praise: He well knows all His servants' sins. In six days He created the heavens and the earth and all that lies between them, and then ascended the throne. He is the Lord of Mercy. Ask those who know, concerning Him.

When they are told: 'Bow down before the Merciful,' they ask: 'Who is the Merciful? Would you have us bow down to whatever you will?' And they grow more rebellious.

Blessed be He who decked the sky with constellations and therein set a lamp and a shining moon. And He it is who makes the night succeed the day: for those who would remember and render thanks.

True servants of the Merciful are those who walk humbly

1. The Koran.

on the earth and say: 'Peace!' to the ignorant who accost them; who pass the night standing and on their knees in adoration of their Lord; who say: 'Lord, ward off from us the torment of Hell, for its torment is everlasting: an evil dwelling and an evil resting-place'; who when they spend are neither extravagant nor niggardly, but keep the golden mean; who invoke no other deity besides God, and do not kill except for a just cause: manslaughter is forbidden by God; who do not commit adultery (he that does shall meet with evil: his punishment shall be doubled on the Day of Resurrection and in disgrace shall he abide for ever – unless he repent and believe and do good works, for then God will change his sins to good actions: God is forgiving and compassionate: he that repents and does good works shall truly return to God); who do not bear false witness, and who maintain their dignity when hearing profane abuse; who do not turn a deaf ear and a blind eye to the revelations of their Lord when they are reminded of them; who say: 'Lord, give us joy in our wives and children, and make us examples to those who fear You.' These shall be rewarded for their fortitude with the loftiest abode in Paradise. Therein shall they find a greeting and a welcome, and therein shall they abide for ever: a pleasant dwelling and a pleasant resting-place.

Say: 'Little cares my Lord if you do not invoke Him. Now that you have denied His revelations, His punishment is bound to overtake you.'

THE POETS

In the Name of God, the Merciful, the Compassionate

Ṭā' sīn mīm. These are the revelations of the veritable Book: you will perhaps fret yourself to death on account of their unbelief. If We will, We can reveal to them a sign from heaven before which they will bow their necks in utter humility.

They turned their backs on each fresh Admonition they

25:64

25:71

25:77

26:1

26:5

26:6 received from the Merciful: they disbelieved, but the truth of that which they have laughed to scorn will dawn upon them.

Do they not see the earth, how We have planted on it all kinds of beneficial plants? Surely in this there is a sign; yet most of them do not believe.

And surely your Lord is the Mighty One, the Compassionate. Your Lord called out to Moses, saying: 'Go to those wicked people, the people of Pharaoh. Will they not take heed?'

'Lord,' he said, 'I fear they will deny me. I may become impatient and stammer in my speech. Send for Aaron. They accuse me of a crime,[1] and I fear that they may put me to death.'

'Never fear,' said He. 'Go both of you with Our signs; We shall be with you and shall hear all. Go to Pharaoh and say to him: "We are messengers from the Lord of the Universe. Let the Israelites depart with us."'

Pharaoh said: 'Did we not bring you up when you were an infant? And did you not stay in our midst several years of your life? Yet you have done the deed you did; surely you are ungrateful.'

26:20 He said: 'I did that when I had gone astray. I fled from you because I feared you. But my Lord has given me wisdom and made me an apostle. And this is the favour with which you taunt me: you have made the Israelites your bondsmen.'

'Who is the Lord of the Universe?' said Pharaoh.

He said: 'The Lord of the heavens and the earth and all that lies between them. If only you believed!'

'Do you hear?' said he to those around him.

'Your Lord,' he went on, 'and the Lord of your forefathers.'

He said: 'The apostle who has been sent to you is surely possessed!'

'The Lord of the East and of the West,' said Moses, 'and all that lies between them. If only you could understand!'

'If you serve any other god but myself,' he said, 'I shall have you thrown into prison.'

'Even if I showed you a convincing sign?' he said.

26:31 He replied: 'Show it to us, if what you say be true.'

---

1. Moses had killed an Egyptian.

He threw down his staff and thereupon it changed to a ver- 26:32
itable serpent. Then he drew out his hand, and it was white to
all who saw it.

'This man,' he said to the nobles around him, 'is a skilful
sorcerer who seeks to drive you from your land by his sorcery.
What is your counsel?'

They said: 'Put them off awhile, him and his brother, and
send forth criers to the cities to bring every skilled enchanter
to your presence.'

The sorcerers were gathered on an appointed day, and the
people were asked: 'Are you all assembled? We may follow the
sorcerers if *they* win the day.'

And when the sorcerers came they said to Pharaoh: 'Shall
we be rewarded if we win?'

'Yes,' he answered, 'and you shall become my favoured
friends.'

Moses said to them: 'Throw down all that you wish to throw.'

They threw down their ropes and staffs, saying: 'By Phar- 26:44
aoh's glory, we shall surely win!'

Then Moses threw down his staff, and it swallowed up their
false devices. The sorcerers prostrated themselves, saying: 'We
now believe in the Lord of the Universe, the Lord of Moses
and Aaron.'

He said: 'Do you dare believe in Him before I give you
leave? He must surely be your master, who has taught you
witchcraft. But you shall see. I will cut off your hands and feet
on alternate sides and crucify you all.'

'That cannot harm us,' they replied, 'for to our Lord we
shall return. We hope our Lord will forgive us our sins, since
we are the first who have believed.'

Then We revealed Our will to Moses, saying: 'Set forth with
My servants in the night, for you will be pursued.'

Pharaoh sent forth criers to the cities. 'These,' they said,
'are but a puny band, who have provoked us much. But we are
a numerous army, well prepared.'

Thus did We make them leave their gardens and their fountains, their treasures and their sumptuous dwellings. Even 26:59
thus; and to the Israelites We gave those.

26:60 At sunrise the Egyptians followed them. And when the two multitudes came within sight of each other, Moses' companions said: 'We are surely undone!'

'No,' he said, 'my Lord is with me, and He will guide me.'

We bade Moses strike the sea with his staff, and the sea was cleft asunder, each part as high as a massive mountain. In between We made the others follow. We delivered Moses and all who were with him; and the others We drowned.

Surely in that there was a sign; yet most of them did not believe.

Surely your Lord is the Mighty One, the Compassionate. Recount to them the story of Abraham. He said to his father and to his people: 'What is that which you worship?'

They said: 'We worship idols and pray to them with all fervour.'

'Do they hear you when you pray?' he asked. 'Can they help you or do you harm?'

They said: 'This was what our forefathers did before us.'

26:75 He said: 'Do you see those you have worshipped, you and your forefathers of old? They are my enemies. Not so the Lord of the Universe, who has created me; who gives me guidance, food and drink; who, when I am sick, restores me; who will cause me to die and bring me back to life hereafter; who, I hope, will forgive me my sins on the Day of Judgement.

'Lord, bestow wisdom upon me, and admit me among the righteous. Endow me with a tongue of truthfulness among posterity and count me among the heirs of the Blissful Garden. Forgive my father, for he has gone astray. Do not hold me up to shame on the Day of Resurrection; the day when wealth and offspring will be of no avail, and when none shall be saved but him who comes before his Lord with a pure heart; when Paradise shall be brought within sight of the righteous and Hell be revealed to the erring. They will be asked: "Where are the idols which you worshipped besides God? Can they help you or help themselves?" And into Hell they shall be hurled, they and those who misled them, and Satan's legions all. "By the Lord," they will say, as they contend 26:98 with them, "we clearly erred when we made you equals with

the Lord of the Universe. It was but the transgressors who led   26:99
us astray. We have no intercessors now, no loving friend.
Could we but live our lives again we would be true believers.'''

Surely in that there was a sign, yet most of them did not
believe.

Surely your Lord is the Mighty One, the Compassionate.
The people of Noah disbelieved the emissaries. 'Will you not
fear God?' said Noah, their kin, to them. 'I am indeed your
truthful apostle. Fear God, then, and follow me. For this I
demand of you no recompense, for none can reward me
except the Lord of the Universe. Fear God, and follow me.'

They said: 'Are we to believe in you when your followers
are but the lowest of the low?'

'I have no knowledge of what they did,' he said. 'My Lord
alone can bring them to account. Would that you understood!
Nor will I drive away the true believers. I am sent forth only to
give plain warning.'

'Noah,' they said, 'desist, or you shall be stoned to death.'

He said: 'Lord, my people disbelieve me. Judge rightly   26:118
between us. Save me and the believers who are with me.'

᛫ So We delivered him and those who were with him in the
laden ark, and drowned the others thereafter.

Surely in that there was a sign; yet most of them did not
believe.

Surely your Lord is the Mighty One, the Compassionate.
'Ād disbelieved the apostles. Their kin Hūd had said to them:
'Will you not fear God? I am indeed your truthful apostle. Fear
God, then, and follow me. For this I demand of you no recom-
pense; none can reward me except the Lord of the Universe.
Will you erect a monument on every hill? Vain is your work.
You build strong fortresses, hoping that you may last for ever.
When you exercise your power, you act like cruel tyrants. Fear
God, and follow me. Fear Him who has given you all the things
you know. He has given you flocks and children, gardens and
fountains. Beware the torment of a fateful day.'

They said: 'We care nothing whether or not you preach
to us. This is but a myth of the ancients. Surely we shall not be   26:138
punished.'

26:139 They denied him, and thus We utterly destroyed them. Surely in that there was a sign; yet most of them did not believe.

Surely your Lord is the Mighty One, the Compassionate. Thamūd disbelieved the apostles. Their kin Ṣāliḥ had said to them: 'Will you not fear God? I am indeed your truthful apostle. Fear God and follow me. For this I demand of you no recompense; none can reward me except the Lord of the Universe. Are you to be left secure in this land, amid gardens and fountains, cornfields and palm-trees laden with fine fruit, hewing your dwellings out of the mountains and leading a wanton life? Have fear of God and follow me. Do not obey the bidding of transgressors who perpetrate corruption in the land and do no good at all.'

They said: 'Surely you are bewitched. You are but a mortal like ourselves. Show us a sign, if what you say be true.'

26:155 'Here,' he said, 'is this she-camel. She shall have her share of water as you have yours, each drinking on an appointed day. Do not harm her, or the scourge of a fateful day shall take you.'

Yet they hamstrung her, and in the morning were repentant. The scourge took them.

Surely in that there was a sign. Yet most of them did not believe.

Surely your Lord is the Mighty One, the Compassionate. Lot's people disbelieved the apostles. Their kin Lot had said to them: 'Will you not fear God? I am indeed your truthful apostle. Fear God and follow me. For this I demand of you no recompense; none can reward me except the Lord of the Universe. Will you fornicate with the males of humans and eschew the wives whom God has created for you? Surely you are a sinful people.'

'Lot,' they said, 'desist or you shall be banished.'

He said: 'I abhor your ways. Lord, deliver me and my kin from their practices.'

26:172 We delivered him and his kindred all, save for one old woman who stayed behind, and the others We utterly

destroyed. We pelted them with rain, and evil was the rain   26:173
which fell on those who were forewarned.

Surely in that there was a sign. Yet most of them did not
believe.

Your Lord is the Mighty One, the Compassionate. The
dwellers of the Forest[1] disbelieved the apostles. Shu'aib had
said to them: 'Will you not fear God? I am indeed your truthful apostle. Fear God and follow me. For this I demand of you
no recompense: none can reward me except the Lord of the
Universe. Give just measure and defraud none. Weigh with
even scales and do not cheat the people of what is rightly
theirs; nor shall you corrupt the land with evil. And fear Him
who created you and the earlier generations.'

They said: 'You are surely bewitched. You are but a mortal
like ourselves. Indeed, we believe that you are lying. Bring
down upon us a fragment of the sky if what you say be true.'

He said: 'My Lord has better knowledge of what you do.'   26:188
They disbelieved him, and thus the scourge of the Day of
Darkness smote them; it was surely the scourge of a fate-
ful day.

Surely in that there was a sign; yet most of them did not
believe.

Your Lord is the Mighty One, the Compassionate. This is
surely revealed by the Lord of the Universe. The Faithful
Spirit has brought it down into your heart, that you may give
warning in eloquent Arabic speech. It was surely foretold in
the Scriptures of the ancients. Is it not sufficient proof for
them that the doctors of the Israelites recognize it? If We had
revealed it to a foreign man, and he had recited it to them,
they still would not have believed. Thus do We put unbelief in
the hearts of the guilty: they shall not believe in it until they
see the woeful scourge, which shall suddenly smite them when
they are heedless. And then they will say: 'Shall we ever be
reprieved?'

Is it their wish to hurry on Our scourge? Think! If We let
them live in ease for many years, and then the promised   26:206

1. The people of Midian.

26:207 scourge does fall upon them, of what avail will their past enjoyments be to them?

Never have We destroyed a city We did not warn and admonish beforehand. We are never unjust.

It was not the demons who brought this down: it is neither in their interest nor in their power. Indeed, they are too far away to overhear it.

Therefore call on no other god besides God, lest you suffer torment. Admonish your nearest kin and show kindness to those of the believers who follow you. If they disobey you, say: 'I am not accountable for what you do.'

26:217 Put your trust in the Mighty One, the Compassionate, who observes you when you stand upright and when you walk among the worshippers. He it is who hears all and knows all.

Shall I tell you on whom the demons descend? They descend on every lying sinner. They eagerly listen, but most of them are liars.

Poets are followed by erring men. Behold how aimlessly they rove in every valley, preaching what they never practise.

26:227 Not so the true believers, who do good works and remember God with fervour and defend themselves only when wronged. The wrongdoers will then learn to what end they will be overturned.

THE ANT

In the Name of God, the Merciful, the Compassionate

27:1 *Ṭā' sīn.* These are the revelations of the Koran, a veritable Book; a guide and joyful tidings to true believers, who attend to their prayers and render the alms levy and firmly believe in the life to come.

As for those that deny the life to come, We make their deeds seem fair to them, so that they blindly stray from the
27:5 right path. Such are those who shall be grievously punished and in the life to come lose most.

You have surely received the Koran from Himself, from Him who is wise and all-knowing. Tell of Moses, who said to his people: 'I can descry a fire. I will go and bring you news and a lighted torch to warm yourselves with.'

And when he came near, a voice called out to him: 'Blessed be He who is in the fire and all around it! Glory to God, Lord of the Universe! Moses, I am God, the Almighty, the Wise One. Throw down your staff.'

And when he saw it slithering like a serpent, he turned and fled, without a backward glance.

'Moses, do not be afraid,' said He. 'My apostles are never afraid in My presence. As for those who sin and then do good after evil, I am forgiving and compassionate.

'Put your hand into your pocket. It will come out white, although unharmed. This is but one of the nine signs for Pharaoh and his people; surely they are a sinful people.'

But when Our visible signs did come to them, they said: 'This is sorcery manifest.' They denied them in their wickedness and their pride, although their souls knew them to be true. Consider the fate of the evil-doers.

We bestowed knowledge on David and Solomon. The two said: 'Praise be to God who has exalted us above many of His believing servants.'

And Solomon succeeded David. He said: 'Know, you people, we have been taught the tongue of birds and endowed with all good things. Surely this is the signal favour.'

His forces of jinn and men and birds were called to Solomon's presence, and ranged in battle array. When they came to the Valley of the Ants, an ant said: 'Go into your dwellings, ants, lest Solomon and his warriors should unwittingly crush you.'

He smiled, laughing at her words, and said: 'Inspire me, Lord, to render thanks for the favours with which You have favoured me and my parents, and to do good works that will please You. Admit me, through Your mercy, among Your righteous servants.'

He inspected the birds and said: 'Why is it that I do not see the lapwing? Is he not here? I shall grievously punish him or even slay him if he does not offer me a veritable excuse.'

27:22 The bird, who was not long in coming, said: 'Things have come to my knowledge that are unknown to you. With truthful news I come to you from Sheba, where I found a woman reigning over them. She is possessed of every virtue and has a splendid throne. I found that she and her subjects worship the sun instead of God. Satan has seduced them and debarred them from the right path, so that they might not be guided to the worship of God, who brings to light all that is hidden in the heavens and the earth and knows what you conceal and what you reveal. God; there is no god but Him, the Lord of the Glorious Throne.'

He said: 'We shall soon see if what you say be true or false. Go and deliver to them this message of mine. Then turn aside and await their answer.'

27:29 The Queen of Sheba said: 'Know, my nobles, that I have received a gracious message. It is from Solomon: "In the Name of God, the Merciful, the Compassionate. Do not exalt yourselves above me, but come to me as Muslims." Nobles, let me hear your counsel, for I make no decision without your consent.'

They said: 'We are a valiant and mighty people. It is for you to decide; so consider what you should command.'

She said: 'When kings invade a city they ravage it and abase the mightiest of its people. These men will do the same. But I shall send them a present and see with what reply the envoys will return.'

And when her envoy came to Solomon, he said: 'Is it gold that you would give me? That which God has bestowed on me is better than all the riches He has given you. Yet you glory in your gift. Go back to them: we will march against them with forces they cannot oppose, and drive them from their land humbled and in abject submission.'

And to his nobles he said: 'Which of you will bring to me her throne, before they sue for peace?'

27:39 An ifrit from among the jinn said: 'I will bring it to you before you rise from your seat. I am strong enough and faithful.'

But he who was deeply versed in the Book,[1] said: 'I will bring it to you in a twinkling of your eye.' 27:40

And when he saw it set before him, he said: 'This is a bounty from my Lord with which He would test my gratitude. He that gives thanks gives them for his own soul; but he who is ungrateful . . . All-sufficient and gracious is my Lord.'

Then he said: 'Let her throne be altered, so that we may see whether she will recognize it or be at a loss.'

And when she came to Solomon, she was asked: 'Is your throne like this?' And she said: 'It looks as though it were the same.'

He said: 'Before her we were endowed with knowledge, and were assuredly Muslims. Her false gods have debarred her, for she comes from an unbelieving people.'

She was bidden to enter the palace; and when she saw it she thought it was a pool of water, and bared her legs. But Solomon said: 'It is a palace paved with glass.'

'Lord,' she said, 'I have sinned against my own soul. Now I submit with Solomon to God, Lord of the Universe.'

And to Thamūd We sent their kin Ṣāliḥ. He said: 'Serve none but God.' But they divided themselves into two discordant factions. 27:45

'My people,' he said, 'why do you wish to hasten evil rather than good? If you seek forgiveness of God, you may be shown mercy.'

They said: 'We presage evil from you and from those who are with you.'

He said: 'The evil you presage can come only from God; you are a people put to the proof.'

In the town there was a band of nine men, who did evil in the land and nothing that was good. They said: 'Let us swear in the name of God to kill him in the night, together with all his household. And we will say to his next of kin: "We did not witness his family's murder. It is the truth we are telling."'

Thus they plotted: but We too plotted, while they were unaware. And behold the consequence of their plot! We 27:51

---

1. Assaf ben Berachia, according to the commentators.

27:52 destroyed them utterly, together with their people all. Because they sinned, their dwellings are desolate ruins. Surely in this there is a sign for prudent people. And We delivered the true believers and those who kept from evil.

And tell of Lot. He said to his people: 'Do you commit lewdness with your eyes open, lustfully seeking men instead of women? Surely you are an ignorant people.'

Yet this was his people's only reply: 'Banish the house of Lot from your city. They are people who would keep themselves chaste.'

So We delivered him and his household, except his wife, whom We caused to stay behind, and pelted the others with pouring rain; and evil was the rain which fell on those who were forewarned.

27:59 Say: 'Praise be to God, and peace upon His servants whom He has chosen! Who is more worthy, God or the idols they serve besides Him? He who created the heavens and the earth, and sent down water from the sky for you, bringing forth gardens of delight? Try as you may, you cannot cause such trees to grow.' Another god besides God? Yet they make other deities His equals.

He who has established the earth and watered it with running rivers; who has set mountains upon it and placed a barrier between the two seas?[1] Another god besides God? Indeed, the greater part of them have no knowledge.

He who answers the oppressed when they cry out to Him, and relieves their affliction? He who has given you the earth to inherit? Another god besides God? How little you reflect!

He who guides you in the darkness of land and sea, and sends the winds as harbingers of His mercy? Another god besides God? Exalted be God above their idols!

27:64 He who brought the Creation into being and will then restore it; who gives you sustenance from heaven and earth? Another god besides God? Say: 'Give us your proof, if what you say be true!'

---

1. Salt water and fresh water.

Say: 'No one in the heavens or on earth has knowledge of   27:65
what is hidden except God. Nor shall they ever know when
they will be raised to life.'

Have they attained a knowledge of the life to come? By no
means! They are in doubt about it and their eyes are sealed.

And the unbelievers say: 'When we and our fathers are
turned to dust, shall we be raised to life? We were promised
this once before, we and our fathers. It is but a fable of the
ancients.'

Say: 'Roam the earth and see what was the fate of the transgressors.' Do not grieve for them, nor be distressed at their
intrigues.

And they say: 'When will this promise be fulfilled, if what
you say be true?'

Say: 'A part of what you challenge may well be near at
hand.'

Surely your Lord is bountiful to mankind: yet most of
them do not give thanks.

Your Lord surely knows what their bosoms hide and what   27:74
they say in public. There is no secret in heaven or earth but is
recorded in a veritable Book.

Surely this Koran expounds to the Israelites most of that
over which they disagree. It is surely a guide and a blessing to
true believers. Your Lord will rightly judge them. He is the
Almighty, the All-knowing. Therefore put your trust in God;
yours is surely the path to the veritable Truth.

You cannot make the dead hear you, nor can you make the
deaf hear your call if they turn their backs and pay no heed;
nor can you guide the blind out of their error. None shall give
ear to you save those who believe in Our revelations, and have
become Muslims.

On the day when the Judgement smites them, We will bring
out from the earth a monster that shall speak to them. Truly,
people had no faith in Our revelations.

On that day We shall herd from each community a multitude of those who disbelieved Our revelations. They shall be
led in separate bands, and, when they come, He will say: 'You   27:84
denied My revelations although you knew nothing about

27:85 them. What was it you were doing?' The Judgement will smite them in their sins, and they shall be dumbfounded.

Do they not see how We have made the night for them to rest in, and the day to give them light? Surely there are signs in this for true believers.

On that day the Trumpet shall be blown and all who dwell in the heavens and on earth shall be seized with consternation, except for those whom God will choose to spare. And all shall come to Him in utter humility.

The mountains, solid though you may think them, will pass by as the clouds pass by. Such is the handiwork of God, who has perfected all things. He surely has full knowledge of what you do.

27:89 Those that come with a good deed shall have what is better, and from the terrors of that day they shall be secure. But those that come with a vile deed shall be hurled headlong into the Fire. Shall you not be rewarded according only to your deeds?

I am commanded to serve the Lord of this City, which He has made sacred. All things are His. And I am commanded to be a Muslim, and to proclaim the Koran. He that takes the right path shall take it for the good of his own soul. And to him who strays from the right path, say: 'I am only to give warning.'

27:93 And say: 'Praise be to God! He will show you His signs and you will recognize them. Your Lord is never heedless of what you do.'

THE STORY

In the Name of God, the Merciful, the Compassionate

Ṭā' sīn mīm. These are the revelations of the veritable Book. 28:1
In all truth We shall recount to you the tale of Moses and
Pharaoh for the instruction of the faithful.

Now Pharaoh made himself a tyrant in the land. He divided his people into castes, one group of which he oppressed,
slaughtering their sons and sparing only their daughters. Surely
he was an evil-doer.

But it was Our will to favour those who were oppressed in
the land and to make them leaders among men, to bestow on
them a heritage and to give them power in the land; and to
show Pharaoh, Haman,[1] and their warriors the very scourge
they dreaded.

We revealed Our will to Moses' mother, saying: 'Give him 28:7
suck, but if you are concerned about his safety, then put him
down on to the river. Have no fear, nor be dismayed; for We
shall restore him to you and shall invest him with a mission.'

Pharaoh's household picked him up, though he was to
become their adversary and their scourge. For Pharaoh,
Haman, and their warriors were sinners all.

His wife said to Pharaoh: 'This child may bring joy to us
both. Do not slay him. He may show promise, and we may
adopt him as a son.' But they little knew what they were doing.

Moses' mother's heart was sorely troubled. She would have
revealed who he was, had We not strengthened her heart so
that she might become a true believer. She said to his sister:
'Go, and follow him.'

She watched him from a distance, unseen by others. We 28:12
had earlier caused him to refuse the nurses' breasts, so his sister

---

1. In the Koran, Haman is one of Pharaoh's ministers; in the Bible
   (Esther 3:8), Haman is Chief Minister of Ahasuerus (Xerxes I),
   king of Persia.

said: 'Shall I direct you to a family who will bring him up for you and take good care of him?'

28:13 Thus did We restore him to his mother, so that she might rejoice in him and grieve no more, and that she might know that God's promise was true. But most of them had no knowledge.

And when he had reached maturity and grown to manhood We bestowed on him wisdom and knowledge. Thus do We reward the righteous.

He entered the town unnoticed by its people, and found two men at each other's throats, the one of his own race, the other an enemy. The Israelite appealed for Moses' help against his enemy, so that Moses struck him with his fist and killed him. 'This is the work of Satan,' he said. 'He is a veritable enemy of man and seeks to lead him astray. Forgive me, Lord,' he said, 'for I have sinned against my soul.'

And God forgave him; for He it is who is the Forgiving One, the Compassionate. He said: 'By the favour You have shown me, Lord, I vow that I will never lend a helping hand to wrongdoers.'

28:18 Next morning he was walking in the town in fear and caution, when lo, the man who sought his help the day before cried out to him again for help. 'Clearly,' said Moses, 'you are a quarrelsome man.'

And when he was about to lay his hands on him who was an enemy of them both, he said: 'Moses, would you kill me as you killed a man yesterday? You are surely seeking to be a tyrant in the land, not seeking to be an upright man.'

And a man came running from the farthest quarter of the city. 'Moses,' he said, 'the elders are plotting to kill you. Fly for your life; I am one that gives you good counsel!'

He left it in fear and caution, saying: 'Lord, deliver me from the wrongdoing people.' And as he made his way towards Midian, he said: 'May the Lord guide me to an even path.'

28:23 When he came to the well of Midian he found around it a multitude of people watering their flocks, and beside them he found two women keeping back their sheep. 'What is it that troubles you both?' he asked.

They said: 'We cannot draw water until the shepherds have driven away their flocks. Our father is an elderly man, well advanced in years.'

He drew water for them and then retired to the shade, saying: 'Lord, I surely stand badly in need of the blessing You have sent me.' 28:24

One of the two girls came bashfully towards him and said: 'My father calls you. He wishes to reward you for drawing water for us.'

And when he went and recounted to him his story, the old man said: 'Fear nothing. You are now safe from the wrong-doing people.'

One of the girls said: 'Father, take him into your service. A man who is strong and honest is the best that you can hire.'

He said: 'I wish to give you in marriage one of these two daughters of mine if you stay eight years in my service; but if you wish it, you may stay ten. I shall not deal harshly with you; you shall find me, God willing, an upright man.'

He said: 'So be it between us. Whichever term I shall fulfil, I trust I shall not be wronged. God is witness of what we say.' 28:28

And when he had fulfilled his term and was journeying with his family, Moses descried a fire on the mountainside. He said to his people: 'Stay here, for I can see a fire. Perhaps I can bring you news of it, or a torch from the fire to warm yourselves with.'

When he came near it, a voice called out to him from a bush in a blessed spot on the right side of the valley, saying: 'Moses, I am God, Lord of the Universe. Throw down your staff.'

And when he saw it slithering like a serpent, he turned and fled without a backward glance.

'Moses, approach and fear not; you are safe. Put your hand into your pocket: it will come out white, although unharmed. Now draw back your arm, and do not stretch it out in terror. These are two proofs from your Lord for Pharaoh and his elders. Surely they are an ungodly people.' 28:32

28:33 'Lord,' said he, 'I have killed one of their number and fear that they will kill me. Aaron my brother is more fluent of tongue than I; send him with me that he may help me and confirm my words, for I fear they will reject me.'

He replied: 'We will strengthen your arm with your brother, and will bestow such power on you both, that none shall reach you. Set forth, with Our signs. You, and those who follow you, shall surely triumph.'

And when Moses came to them with Our veritable signs, they said: 'This is nothing but sorcery contrived; nor have we heard of the like among our forefathers.'

Moses said: 'My Lord knows best the man who brings guidance from His presence and gains the recompense of the life to come. The wrongdoers shall never succeed.'

'Nobles,' said Pharaoh, 'you have no other god that I know of except myself. Make me, Haman, bricks of clay, and build for me a tower that I may climb up to the god of Moses. I am convinced that he is lying.'

28:39 Pharaoh and his warriors conducted themselves with arrogance and injustice in the land, thinking they would never be recalled to Us. But We seized him and his warriors, and We cast them into the sea. Consider the fate of the wrongdoers.

We made them leaders who invited to the Fire, but on the Day of Resurrection they shall not be helped. In this world We laid a curse on them, and on the Day of Resurrection they shall be among the damned.

After We had destroyed the early generations We gave Moses the Book as a beacon for mankind, a guide and a blessing, so that they might take thought.

You[1] were not present on the western side when We charged Moses with his commission, nor did you witness the event. But We raised many generations after him whose lives were prolonged. You did not dwell among the people of Midian, nor did you recite to them Our revelations; but it was We who sent you forth.

28:46 You were not present on the mountainside when We called

---

1. Muḥammad.

out. Yet have We sent you forth, as a blessing from your Lord, to forewarn a nation to whom no one before you had been sent to warn them, so that they may reflect and may not say, when evil befalls them on account of their misdeeds: 'Lord, had You sent us an apostle, we should have obeyed Your revelations and believed in them.'

28:47

And now that they have received the Truth from Us, they ask: 'Why is he not given the like of what was given to Moses?' But did they not deny what was formerly given to Moses? They say: 'Two works¹ of sorcery complementing one another!' And they declare: 'We will believe in neither of them.'

Say: 'Bring down from God a scripture that is a better guide than these and I will follow it, if what you say be true!'

If they make you no answer, know that they are led by their desires. And who is in greater error than he who is led by his desires, without guidance from God? God does not guide the wrongdoers.

We have caused the Word to reach them so that they may take thought. Those to whom We gave the Book before this believe in it. When it is recited to them they say: 'We believe in it; it is the Truth from our Lord. Before its coming we were Muslims.'

28:51

Twice shall their reward be given them, because they have endured with fortitude, requiting evil with good and giving from what We gave them; and because they pay no heed to profane talk, and say: 'We have our actions and you have yours. We wish you peace. We will have nothing to do with ignorant men.'

You cannot guide whomever you please: but it is God who guides whom He will. He best knows those who yield to guidance.

And they say: 'If we follow your guidance, we shall be dispossessed of our land.' But have We not given them a sanctuary of safety² to which fruits of every kind are brought as a provision from Ourself? But most of them have no knowledge.

28:57

1. The Torah and the Koran.
2. At the Ka'bah.

28:58   How many cities have We destroyed that once flourished in
wanton ease! The dwellings they left behind are but scarcely
inhabited; We Ourself were the only heirs.

Nor did your Lord obliterate the cities until He had sent
apostles to their capital proclaiming to them Our revelations.
Nor did We obliterate the cities unless their inhabitants were
wrongdoers.

That which you have been given is but the enjoyment and
the gaudy show of this present life. Better is God's recompense and more lasting. Have you no sense to reason with?

Can he who has received Our gracious promise, and will
see it fulfilled, be compared with him to whom We have given
the enjoyment of this life and who will be summoned on the
Day of Resurrection?

On that day He will call to them, saying: 'Where are the
gods whom you alleged to be My partners?'

Those on whom the Judgement has been passed will say:
'Lord, these are the men whom we misled. We led them astray
as we ourselves were led astray. We disown them before You;
it was not us that they worshipped.'

28:64   Then they will be told: 'Call to your idols!' And they will
call to them, but they shall get no answer. They shall behold
the scourge and wish that they were rightly guided.

On that day He will call to them, saying: 'What answer did
you give those who were sent?' And on that day they will be so
confused that they will ask no questions. But those that
repented and embraced the Faith and did what was right may
hope for salvation.

Your Lord creates what He will and chooses freely, but
they have no power to choose. Glorified and exalted be He
above their false gods!

And your Lord knows what their bosoms hide and what
they say in public. He is God: there is no god but Him. Praise
be His in the first world and in the last. His is the Judgement,
and to Him shall you be recalled.

28:71   Say: 'Think! If God should enshroud you in perpetual
night till the Day of Resurrection, what other god could give
you light? Will you not hear?'

Say: 'Think! If God should give you perpetual day until the 28:72
Day of Resurrection, what other god could bring you a night
to rest in? Will you not see?'

Of His mercy He has given you the night to rest in, and the
day that you may seek His bounty and give thanks.

On that day He will call out to them, saying: 'Where are the
gods whom you alleged to be My partners?' From each community We will seize a witness, and We shall say: 'Show Us
your proof.' Then shall they learn that the Truth is God's, and
the deities of their own invention will forsake them.

Korah[1] was one of Moses' people, but he treated them
unjustly. We had given him such treasures that their very keys
would have weighed down a band of sturdy men. His people
said to him: 'Do not exult; God does not love the exultant. But
seek, by means of that which God has given you, to attain the
Abode of the Hereafter. Do not forget your share in this world.
Be good to others as God has been good to you, and do not
strive for evil in the land, for God does not love the evil-doers.'

He said: 'I was given this on account of the knowledge I 28:78
possess.'

Did he not know that, from among the generations gone
before him, God had obliterated some who were mightier and
possessed of much more wealth than he? The wrongdoers
shall not be questioned about their sins.

And when he went out among his people in all his finery,
those who loved this nether life said: 'Would that we had the
like of what Korah has been given! He is indeed a man of
great good fortune.'

But those who were endowed with knowledge said: 'Alas
for you! Better is God's recompense for him that has faith and
does good works; but none shall attain it save those who have
endured with fortitude.'

We caused the earth to swallow him up, him and his dwelling, so that he found none besides God to help him; nor was
he able to help himself. And those who on the day before 28:82
had coveted his lot next morning said: 'Behold! God gives

1. Cf. Numbers 16.

265

abundantly to whom He will among His servants, and sparingly also. But for the grace of God to us, He could have caused the earth to swallow us. Behold! The ungrateful shall never succeed.'

28:83 That Final Abode We shall assign to those who seek neither grandeur on the earth nor evil-doing. The righteous shall have a blessed end.

He that comes with a good deed shall have what is better; and they that commit vile deeds shall be requited only according to what they did.

28:85 He who has committed the Koran to your keeping will surely bring you home[1] again. Say: 'My Lord best knows him who has brought guidance and him who is in manifest error.'

Never did you expect the Book to be revealed to you except through your Lord's mercy. Therefore give no support to the unbelievers. Let no one turn you away from God's revelations, now that they have been revealed to you. Call men to your Lord, and serve none besides Him.

28:88 Invoke no other god together with God. There is no god but Him. All things shall perish except His Face. His is the Judgement, and to Him shall you be recalled.

THE SPIDER

In the Name of God, the Merciful, the Compassionate

29:1 ALIF *lām mīm*. Do people think that once they say: 'We are believers,' they will be left alone and not be tested?

We tested those who have gone before them. God surely knows the truthful, and He surely knows the liars.

Or do the evil-doers think they will escape Our reach? How ill they judge!

29:5 He that aspires to meet God must know that God's appointed time is sure to come. He alone hears all and knows all.

1. To Mecca.

He that fights for God's cause fights for himself. God 29:6
needs the help of none. Those that have faith and do good
works We shall surely cleanse of their sins and requite according to their noblest deeds.

We have enjoined man to show kindness to his parents. But
if they bid you serve besides Me deities you know nothing of,
do not obey them. To Me you will all return, and I shall declare
to you all that you have done. Those that believe and do good
works We shall assuredly admit among the righteous.

Some profess to believe in God, yet when they suffer in
God's cause they confuse the persecution of man with the
punishment of God. But if your Lord gives you victory, they
are sure to say: 'We were on your side.'

Does not God know best the thoughts of people? God
well knows the true believers, and He well knows the hypocrites.

The unbelievers say to the faithful: 'Follow us, and we will 29:12
bear the burden of your sins.' But they will bear none of their
sins. They are surely lying.

They shall bear their own burdens, and other burdens
besides their burdens; and on the Day of Resurrection they
shall surely be questioned about the lies they fabricated.

We sent forth Noah to his people, and he dwelt among
them for a thousand years less fifty.[1] Then in their sinfulness
the Flood took them. But We delivered him and those who
were in the ark, and made the event a sign for mankind.

And tell of Abraham. He said to his people: 'Serve God
and fear Him. That would be best for you, if you but knew it.
You worship idols besides God and fabricate falsehoods.
Those whom you serve besides God cannot give you your
daily bread. Therefore seek your daily bread from God, and
worship Him. Give thanks to Him, for to Him you shall
return.

'If you disbelieve, other communities before you likewise 29:18
disbelieved. Yet the apostle's duty is only to render the
warning.'

1. Cf. Genesis 9:29.

29:19 Do they not see how God brings the Creation into being, and then restores it? Surely that is easy enough for God.

Say: 'Roam the earth and see how God has brought the Creation into being. Then will God initiate the Latter Creation. God has power over all things; He punishes whom He will and shows mercy to whom He pleases. To Him shall you be recalled.'

Neither on earth nor in heaven shall you escape His reach: nor have you any besides God to protect or help you.

Those that disbelieve God's revelations and deny that they will ever meet Him shall despair of My mercy. Woeful punishment awaits them.

His people's only reply was: 'Kill him!' or 'Burn him!'

But from the fire God delivered him. Surely in this there are signs for true believers.

29:25 He said: 'You have chosen idols instead of God, but your love of them will last only in this nether life. On the Day of Resurrection you shall disown one another, and you shall curse one another. Your abode shall be the Fire, and none shall succour you.'

Lot believed in him. He said: 'I will fly this land whither my Lord bids me.[1] He is the Almighty, the Wise One.'

We gave him Isaac and Jacob and bestowed on his descendants prophethood and the Book. We gave him his reward in this life, and in the life to come he shall dwell among the righteous.

And Lot: he said to his people: 'You commit lewd acts which no other nation has committed before you. You lust after men and assault them on your highways. At your gatherings you perpetrate abominations.'

But his people's only answer was: 'Bring down the scourge of God upon us, if what you say be true.'

'Lord,' said he, 'deliver me from these degenerate people.'

29:31 And when Our emissaries brought Abraham the joyful tidings,[2] they said: 'We are to destroy the people of this city, for its people have done wrong.'

---

1. Thus Al-Jalālayn.
2. The birth of a son in his old age.

He said: 'But Lot dwells in it.'   29:32

'We well know who dwells in it,' they said. 'We shall deliver him and all his household, except his wife, who shall remain behind.'

And when Our emissaries came to Lot, he was troubled and distressed on their account. They said: 'Have no fear, and do not grieve. We shall deliver you and all your household, except your wife, who shall remain behind. We shall bring down a scourge from heaven upon the people of this city to punish them for their sins.'

Surely the ruins We left of that city are a veritable sign for those that can understand.

And to the people of Midian, their kin Shu'aib. He said: 'Serve God, my people. Look forward to the Last Day. Do not corrupt the earth with wickedness.'

But they denied him. The earthquake took them, and when morning came they were crouching lifeless in their homes.

And 'Ād and Thamūd: this is vouched for by their dwellings.   29:38
Satan had made their deeds seem fair to them and debarred them from the right path, keen-sighted though they were.

And Korah, Pharaoh, and Haman! Moses came to them with veritable signs, but they behaved arrogantly in the land, powerless though they were to escape Us: and in their sinfulness, one and all, We smote them. On some We sent down a violent whirlwind; others the Cry overtook; some We caused to be swallowed up by the earth, and yet others We overwhelmed by the Flood. God did not wrong them, but they wronged themselves.

Those who serve other masters besides God may be compared to the spider which builds a cobweb for itself. Surely the spider's is the frailest of all dwellings, if they but knew it. God knows whatever they invoke besides Him; He is the Almighty, the Wise One.

Such are the comparisons We make for the instruction of people; but none will grasp their meaning save those that have knowledge.

God created the heavens and the earth with Truth. Surely   29:44
in this there is a sign for true believers.

29:45 Proclaim the portions of the Book that have been revealed to you and be steadfast in prayer: prayer fends off all that is foul and reprehensible. But your foremost duty is to remember God. God has knowledge of what you do.

And be courteous when you argue with the People of the Book, except with those among them who do wrong. Say: 'We believe in that which has been revealed to us and was revealed to you. Our God and your God is one. To Him we submit as Muslims.'

Thus have We revealed the Book to you. Those to whom We gave the Book believe in it, as do some of your own people. Only the unbelievers deny Our signs.

Never have you[1] read a book before this, nor have you ever transcribed one with your right hand. Had you done either, the unbelievers might have doubted. But to those who were given knowledge it is a veritable sign. Only the wrongdoers deny Our signs.

29:50 They say: 'Why have no signs been sent down to him from his Lord?' Say: 'Signs are in the hands of God. My mission is only to give clear warning.'

Is it not sufficient for them that We have revealed to you the Book for their instruction?[2] Surely in this there is a blessing and an Admonition for true believers.

Say: 'Sufficient is God as my witness, and your witness. He knows all that is in the heavens and the earth. Those who believe in falsehood and deny God will surely be the losers.'

And they challenge you to hasten on the scourge. Had there not been a time appointed, the scourge would have long since taken them. Indeed, it will come down upon them suddenly, and catch them unawares.

They challenge you to hasten on the scourge. But Hell will encompass the unbelievers, when the scourge will assail them from above and from beneath their feet, and God will say: 'Taste the reward of your own deeds.'

29:56 You that are true believers among My servants, My earth is

1. Muḥammad.   2. Literally, to be recited to them.

vast. Therefore serve Me. Every soul shall taste death, and then to Us shall you be recalled. 29:57

Those that embrace the true Faith and do good works We shall lodge for ever in the mansions of Paradise, where rivers will roll at their feet. Blessed is the reward of those who labour patiently and put their trust in their Lord.

Countless are the beasts that cannot fend for themselves. God provides for them, as He provides for you. He alone hears all and knows all.

If you ask them who it is that has created the heavens and the earth, and subdued the sun and the moon, they will surely say: 'God.' How then can they turn away from Him?

God gives abundantly to whom He will among His servants, and sparingly also. God has full knowledge of all things.

And if you ask them who it is that sends down water from the sky and thus resurrects the earth after its death, they will surely say: 'God.' Say: 'Praise, then, be to God!' But the greater part of them are senseless. 29:63

The life of this world is but a sport and a diversion. It is the life to come that is the true life: if they but knew it.

When they embark they pray to God with all religious fervour; but when He brings them safe to land, behold how they serve other gods besides Him, showing ingratitude for what We gave them and revelling in wanton ease. But they shall learn.

Do they not see how We have given them a sanctuary of safety,[1] while all around them people are carried off by force? Would they believe in falsehood and deny God's goodness?

And who is more wicked than the man who invents a falsehood about God and denies the Truth when it is declared to him? Is there not in Hell a resting-place for the unbelievers?

Those that fight for Our cause We will surely guide to Our own paths. Surely God is with the righteous. 29:69

---

1. At the Ka'bah.

THE GREEKS OF BYZANTIUM

In the Name of God, the Merciful, the Compassionate

30:1 ALIF *lām mīm.* The Greeks have been defeated[1] in a neighbouring land. But in a few years they shall themselves gain victory: such being the will of God before and after.

On that day the believers will rejoice in God's help. He gives victory to whom He will. And He is the Mighty One, the Compassionate.

That is God's promise; God will never break His promise. Yet most do not know it.

They know the outward show of this nether life, but of the life to come they are heedless. Have they not pondered within their own minds that God created the heavens and the earth and all that lies between them only for a worthy end, and for an appointed term? Yet many deny they will ever meet their Lord.

30:9 Have they never journeyed through the land and seen what was the fate of their forebears? Far mightier were they; they tilled the land and built upon it more than these have ever built. And to them, too, their apostles came with undoubted signs. God did not wrong them but they wronged themselves. Evil was the end of those who did evil, because they had disbelieved God's revelations and derided them.

God brings the Creation into being and will then restore it. To Him shall you be recalled.

On the day the Hour strikes, the wrongdoers will be speechless with despair. None of their idols will intercede for them: indeed, they will deny their idols.

On the day the Hour strikes, mankind will divide. Those who have embraced the Faith and done good works will 30:16 rejoice in a fair Garden; but those who have disbelieved and denied Our revelations and the life to come, shall be delivered up for punishment.

---

1. By the Persians, in Syria – in 615. Muḥammad's sympathies were with the Christians, not with the idolatrous Persians.

So glory be to God in your evenings and in your mornings; 30:17 and to Him be praise in the heavens and the earth, at your twilights and at your noons.

He brings forth the living from the dead, and brings forth the dead from the living: He resurrects the earth after its death. Likewise shall you be raised to life.

By one of His signs He created you from dust; and, behold, you became humans and multiplied throughout the earth. By another of His signs He created for you spouses from among yourselves, that you might live in peace with them, and between you planted love and kindness. Surely there are signs in this for people who reflect.

And among His signs are the creation of the heavens and the earth, and the diversity of your tongues and colours. Surely in this there are signs for all mankind.

By another sign of His you sleep at night and seek by day His bounty. Surely there are signs in this for those who can hear.

Lightning is yet another of His signs, inspiring you with 30:24 fear and hope. He sends down water from the sky, and with it He quickens the earth after its death. Surely in this there are signs for those that are of sense possessed.

And by another of His signs heaven and earth stand firm at His bidding. Then, when with one shout He summons you out of the earth, lo, you shall be raised.

To Him belongs whosoever is in the heavens and the earth: all are obedient to Him.

And He it is who brings the Creation into being, and will then restore it: that is easier for Him.

His is the most exalted attribute in the heavens and the earth; and He is the Almighty, the Wise One.

He makes you this comparison, drawn from your own lives. Do your slaves share with you on equal terms what We have given you? Do you fear them as you fear one another? Thus do We expound Our revelations to people who understand.

Indeed, the wrongdoers are led unwittingly by their own appetites. And who can guide those whom God has led astray? There shall be none to succour them.

Therefore, stand firm in your devotion to the True Religion, 30:30

which God created for mankind to embrace. God's Creation cannot be changed. This is surely the Upright Religion, but most do not know it.

30:31 Turn to Him and fear Him; be steadfast in prayer and serve no other god besides Him. Do not divide your Religion into sects, each exulting in its own doctrines.

And when a misfortune befalls people, they turn in prayer to their Lord. But no sooner does He let them taste a blessing from Himself than some among them take up other gods besides their Lord, showing no gratitude for what We gave them. Take your pleasure now, and you shall learn.

Have We revealed to them a sanction enjoining them to serve idols?

And when We give people the taste of a good thing they rejoice in it, but when evil befalls them through their own fault, they grow despondent. Do they not see that God gives abundantly to whom He will, and sparingly also? Surely there are signs in this for true believers.

30:38 Therefore give their due to the next of kin, to the destitute, and to the traveller in need. That is best for those that strive to please God; such men will surely prosper.

People's wealth you seek to increase by usury will not increase in the sight of God; but the alms you give for the love of God shall be repaid many times over.

God it is who has created you and given you your daily bread. He will cause you to die hereafter and will then bring you back to life. Can any of your idols do the least of these? God forbid! Glory to Him, and exalted be He above their false gods!

Corruption is now manifest on land and at sea in consequence of what the hands of mankind did: that they may taste the fruit of what they did and mend their ways.

Say: 'Roam the earth and see what was the fate of those who came before you. The greater part of them worshipped idols.'

30:43 Therefore stand firm in your devotion to the Upright Religion before that day arrives which none may put off against the will of God. On that day mankind will be parted in two:

the unbelievers shall answer for their unbelief, and the right- 30:44
eous will have done well for themselves: for then He will of
His bounty recompense those who have believed and done
good works. He does not love the unbelievers.

By another of His signs He sends the winds as bearers of
good tidings, so that He may give you a taste of His mercy and
that the ships may sail at His bidding; so that you may seek His
bounty and render thanks.

We sent before you apostles to their peoples, and they
brought them veritable signs. We took vengeance on those
who sinned, and rightly succoured the true believers.

God it is who drives the winds that stir the clouds. He
spreads them as He will in the heavens and breaks them up, so
that you can see the rain falling from their midst. When He
sends it down on such of His servants as He chooses, behold,
they are elated with joy, though before its coming they had
lost all hope.

Behold then the tokens of God's mercy; how He resurrects 30:50
the earth after its death. It is He who will assuredly resurrect
the dead; He has power over all things.

Yet if We let loose a searing wind, and they beheld
their crops turn yellow, they would after that persist in
unbelief.

You surely cannot make the dead hear you, nor can you
make the deaf hear your call if they turn their backs and pay
no heed; nor can you guide the blind out of their error. None
shall give ear to you save those who believe in Our revelations,
and are now Muslims.

God creates you weak: after weakness He gives you
strength, and after strength infirmity and grey hairs. He creates whatever He will: He is the Omniscient, the Almighty.

On the day the Hour strikes, the wrongdoers will swear
that they had lingered but one hour. Thus are they ever
deceived.

But those to whom knowledge and faith have been given 30:56
will say: 'You lingered there, as God ordained, till the Day of
Resurrection. This is the Day of Resurrection: yet you did not
know it.'

30:57 On that day their pleas shall not avail the wrongdoers, nor shall they be asked to make amends.

In this Koran we have set forth for people all manner of arguments. Yet if you recite to them a single verse, the unbelievers will surely say: 'You preach nothing but falsehoods.' Thus God seals the hearts of the ignorant.

30:60 Therefore have patience. God's promise is true. Let not those who disbelieve drive you to despair.

LUQMĀN

In the Name of God, the Merciful, the Compassionate

31:1 ALIF *lām mīm.* These are the revelations of the Wise Book, a guide and a blessing to the righteous, who attend to their prayers, render the alms levy, and firmly believe in the life to come. These are rightly guided by their Lord, and will surely succeed.

Some there are who would indulge in frivolous talk, so that they may without knowledge lead men away from the path of God and hold it up to ridicule. For these there shall be shameful punishment.

When Our revelations are recited to them, they turn their backs in scorn, as though they never heard them: as though their ears were sealed. To these proclaim a woeful punishment.

31:8 But those that believe and do good works shall enter the Gardens of Delight, wherein shall they abide for ever. God's promise shall be fulfilled: He is the Almighty, the Wise One.

He raised the heavens with no visible pillars, and set firm mountains on the earth lest it should shake with you. He dispersed upon it all manner of beasts; and We sent down water from the sky with which We caused all kinds of goodly plants to grow.

31:11 Such is God's Creation: now show Me what your other gods created. Surely, the unbelievers are in evident error.

We bestowed wisdom on Luqmān,[1] saying: 'Give thanks to   31:12
God. He that gives thanks has much to gain for his own soul,
but if anyone is thankless, God is self-sufficient and worthy
of praise.'

Tell of Luqmān, who admonished his son, saying: 'My son,
serve no other deity besides God, for idolatry is an abominable sin.'

We enjoined man to show kindness to his parents, for with
much pain his mother bears him, and he is not weaned before
he is two years of age. We said: 'Give thanks to Me and to
your parents. To Me shall all return. But if they press you to
serve besides Me deities you know nothing of, do not obey
them. Be kind to them in this world, and follow the path of
those who turn to Me. To Me shall you return, and I will
declare to you what you have done.'

'My son, if it be as small as a grain of mustard seed, be   31:16
it hidden inside a rock or in the heavens or in the earth,
God will bring it to light. Surely gracious is God and all-
knowing.

'My son, be steadfast in prayer, enjoin justice, and forbid
the reprehensible. Endure with fortitude whatever befalls
you. That is a duty incumbent on all.

'Do not treat people with scorn, nor walk exultant on the
earth: surely God does not love the arrogant and the vainglorious. Rather let your stride be modest and your voice low:
the most hideous of voices is the braying of the ass.'

Do you not see how God has subjected to you all that the
heavens and the earth contain, and lavished on you His
bounty, visible and unseen? Yet some among people still argue
about God, without knowledge or guidance or illuminating
scripture.

And when they are told: 'Follow what God has revealed,'
they say: 'We will follow the faith our fathers practised.' Yes,
even though Satan invites them to the torment of the Conflagration.

He that submits his face to God and leads a righteous life   31:22

---

1. A sage who, we are told, was a grandson of a sister or an aunt of Job.

31:23 stands on the firmest ground.[1] To God shall all return. As for those that disbelieve, let not their disbelief grieve you. To Us shall they return and We will declare to them what they have done. God has knowledge of their innermost thoughts.

We suffer them to take their ease awhile, and will then subject them to a grievous scourge.

If you say to them: 'Who has created the heavens and the earth?' they will surely say: 'God.' Say: 'Praise, then, be to God!' But the greater part of them have no knowledge.

His is what the heavens and the earth contain. Surely God alone is self-sufficient and worthy of praise.

If all the trees of the earth were pens, and the sea, replenished by seven other seas, were ink, the words of God could not be finished still. Almighty is God, and wise.

You were created but as one soul, and as one soul you shall be raised to life. God hears all and observes all.

31:29 Do you not see how God causes the night to pass into the day and the day to pass into the night? And He has pressed the sun and the moon into His service, each running for an appointed term. God is cognizant of what you do. Because God is the Truth, and false are the idols they invoke besides Him. And surely God is the Most High, the Supreme One.

Do you not see how the ships speed upon the ocean by God's grace, so that He may reveal to you some of His wonders? Surely in this there are signs for every steadfast, thankful person.

When the waves, like a giant shadow, envelop them, they pray to God, consecrating their religion to Him. But no sooner does He bring them safe to land than some among them falter between faith and unbelief. None denies Our revelations except the treacherous and the ungrateful.

31:33 You people! Fear your Lord, and fear the day when no parent shall avail his child nor any child his parent. God's promise is surely true. Let the life of this world never deceive you, nor let the Dissembler trick you about God.

---

1. Literally, grasps the firmest handle.

God alone has knowledge of the Hour. He sends down the 31:34
abundant rain and knows what every womb contains.

No mortal knows what he will earn tomorrow; no mortal
knows on which ground he will breathe his last. God alone is
omniscient and well aware.

PROSTRATION

In the Name of God, the Merciful, the Compassionate

ALIF *lām mīm.* The revelation of the Book, of which there is 32:1
no doubt, is from the Lord of the Universe.

Do they say: 'He[1] has invented it himself'?

Surely it is the Truth from your Lord, that you may forewarn a people none has warned before you, and that they may
be rightly guided.

It was God who in six days created the heavens and the
earth and all that lies between them, and then ascended the
throne. You have no guardian or intercessor besides Him.
Will you not reflect?

He governs all, from heaven to earth. And all will ascend to
Him in a single day, a day whose space is a thousand years by
your reckoning.

He knows the unknown and the manifest. He is the 32:6
Almighty, the Merciful, who excelled in everything He created. He first created man from clay, then made his offspring
from a drop of humble fluid. Then He moulded him and
breathed His spirit into him. He made for you ears and eyes
and hearts: yet you are seldom thankful.

And they say: 'Once lost into the earth, shall we be in a new
creation?' Indeed, they deny they will ever meet their Lord.

Say: 'The angel of death in charge of you will claim you
back. Then to your Lord shall you be recalled.'

Would that you could see the wrongdoers when they hang 32:12
their heads before their Lord! They will say: 'Lord, we now see

1. Muḥammad.

and hear. Send us back and we will do good works. Now we are firm believers.'

32:13   Had it been Our will, We could have given every soul its guidance. But My Judgement shall be fulfilled: 'I will surely fill Hell with jinn and humans all. Taste this, for you forgot you would ever meet this day. We, too, will forget you. Taste the eternal torment, which you have earned by what you did.'

Indeed, none believes in Our revelations save those who, when reminded of them, prostrate themselves in adoration and give glory to their Lord in all humility; who forsake their beds to pray to their Lord in fear and hope; who give from what We gave them. No mortal knows what bliss will be in store for these as a reward for their labours.

Can he, then, who is a true believer, be compared to him who is ungodly? Surely they are not equal.

As for those that believe and do good works, they shall be lodged in the Gardens of Paradise in recompense for their 32:20 labours. But those that do evil, the Fire shall be their home. Whenever they wish to emerge from it they shall be driven back, and shall be told: 'Taste the torment of the Fire, which you persistently denied.'

We will surely make them taste the lighter torment of this world before the greater torment of the world to come, that they may perchance return to the right path. And who is more wicked than he that pays no heed to the revelations of his Lord when he is reminded of them? We will surely take vengeance on the transgressors.

We gave the Book to Moses (never doubt that you[1] will meet him) and made it a guide for the Israelites. And when they grew steadfast and firmly believed in Our revelations, We appointed leaders from among them who gave guidance at Our bidding. On the Day of Resurrection your Lord will resolve their differences for them.

32:26   Or do they not know how many generations We have destroyed before them? They walk among their ruined dwell-

---

1. Muḥammad.

ings. Surely in this there are conspicuous signs. Have they no ears to hear with?

Do they not see how We drive the water to the parched land and bring forth crops which they and their cattle eat? Have they no eyes to see with? 32:27

They say: 'When will this judgement[1] come, if what you say be true?'

Say: 'On the Day of Judgement their faith shall not avail the unbelievers, nor shall they be reprieved.'

Therefore pay no heed to them, and wait as they are waiting. 32:30

THE CONFEDERATES

In the Name of God, the Merciful, the Compassionate

PROPHET, HAVE fear of God and do not yield to the unbelievers and the hypocrites. God is all-knowing and wise. 33:1

Obey what is revealed to you from your Lord, for God is cognizant of all your actions, and put your trust in God. Sufficient is God as a guardian.

God has never put two hearts within one man's body. He does not regard the wives whom you divorce as your mothers,[2] nor your adopted sons as your own sons. These are mere words which you utter with your mouths: but God speaks the Truth and gives guidance to the right path.

Name your adopted sons after their fathers; that is more just in the sight of God. If you do not know their fathers, regard them as your brothers in the Faith and as your cousins. Your unintentional errors shall be overlooked, but not the errors your hearts intended. God is ever forgiving and compassionate. 33:5

1. Or: victory.
2. An allusion to the formula: 'Be to me as my mother's back', accepted among pagan Arabs as a declaration of divorce.

33:6 The Prophet has a greater claim on the faithful than they have on each other. His wives are their mothers.

God ordains that blood relations are closer to one another than to other believers or *muhājirīn*,[1] although you are permitted to do your friends a kindness.[2] That is in the Book decreed.

Tell of the covenant We made with the prophets; with you, with Noah and Abraham, with Moses and Jesus son of Mary. A solemn covenant We made with them, that He might question the truthful about their truthfulness. But for the unbelievers He has prepared a woeful punishment.

Believers, remember God's goodness to you when you were attacked by your enemy's army. We unleashed against them a violent wind and invisible warriors: God observed all that you were doing.

They attacked you from above and from below, so that your eyes were blurred, your hearts leapt up to your throats, and you thought ill of God's design. There the faithful were
33:12 put to the proof; there they were grievously shaken. The hypocrites and the faint-hearted said: 'God and His apostle made us promises only to deceive us.' Some among them said: 'People of Yathrib,[3] you cannot stand much longer. Go back to your city.' And yet others sought the Prophet's leave, saying: 'Our homes are defenceless,' while defenceless they were not. They only wished to flee.

Had the city been entered from every quarter, and had they been roused to rebellion, they would have surely rebelled. But they would have occupied it only for a little while.

Surely before that, they swore to God never to turn their backs in flight. And an oath to God must needs be answered for.

Say: 'Nothing will your flight avail you. If you escaped from death or slaughter you would enjoy this world only for a little while.'

33:17 Say: 'Who can protect you from God if it is His will to scourge

1. See p. 132, note 1.
2. By leaving them bequests.
3. The old name of Medina.

you? And who can prevent Him from showing you mercy?' They shall find none besides God to protect or help them.

God well knows those of you who hold the others back; who say to their comrades: 'Join our side,' and seldom take part in the fighting, being ever reluctant to assist you. When fear overtakes them they look to you[1] for help, their eyes rolling, like someone in the agony of death. But once they are out of danger they assail you with their sharp tongues, covetously demanding the richest part of the booty. Those never had faith, and God will bring their acts to nothing: that is easy enough for God. 33:18

They thought the confederates would never withdraw. Indeed, if the confederates should come again, they would sooner be in the desert among the wandering Arabs. There they would ask news of you, but were they with you they would take but little part in the fighting.

There is a good example in God's apostle for those of you who look to God and the Last Day and remember God always.

When the true believers saw the confederates, they said: 'This is what God and His apostle have promised us; God and His apostle have spoken the Truth.' And this only increased their faith and submission. 33:22

Among the believers there are men who have been true to their covenants with God. Some have died, and some await their end, yielding to no change. God will surely requite the faithful for their faith and sternly punish the hypocrites – or show them mercy if He will: God is ever forgiving and compassionate.

God turned back the unbelievers in their rage, and they went away empty-handed. God helped the faithful in the stress of war: Almighty is God, and all-powerful.

He brought down from their strongholds those who had supported them from among the People of the Book[2] and cast terror into their hearts, so that some you slew and some you took captive.

He made you heirs of their land, their houses, and their 33:27

1. Muḥammad.   2. The Jews of Banī Qurayẓah; 600–900 men were beheaded and the women and children sold into slavery (Al-Bayḍāwī).

goods, and of yet another land[1] on which you had never set foot before. Truly, God has power over all things.

33:28 Prophet, say to your wives: 'If you seek this nether life and its vanities, come, I will make provision for you and release you honourably. But if you seek God and His apostle and the Abode of the Hereafter, God has prepared a rich recompense for those of you who do good works.'

Wives of the Prophet! Those of you who commit a veritable lewd act shall be doubly punished. That is easy enough for God. But those of you who obey God and His apostle and do good works shall be doubly recompensed; for them We have made a rich provision.

Wives of the Prophet! You are not like other women. If you fear God, do not be too complaisant in your speech, lest the lecherous-hearted should lust after you. Show discre-
33:33 tion in what you say. Stay in your homes and do not display your finery as women used to do in the days of ignorance.[2] Attend to your prayers, give alms, and obey God and His apostle.

Women of the Household, God seeks only to remove abomination from you and to purify you. Commit to memory the revelations of God and the wise sayings that are recited in your dwellings. Gracious is God and all-knowing.

Be they men or women, those who are Muslims and have faith; who are devout, sincere, patient, humble, charitable, and chaste; who fast and are ever mindful of God – on these God will bestow forgiveness and a rich recompense.

It is not for true believers – men or women – to order their own affairs if God and His apostle decree otherwise. He that disobeys God and His apostle strays grievously into error.

33:37 You[3] said to the man[4] whom God and yourself have favoured: 'Keep your wife and have fear of God.' You sought

---

1. Khaybar.
2. Pre-Islamic days.
3. Muḥammad.
4. Zayd, Muḥammad's adopted son.

to hide in your heart what God was to reveal.[1] You were afraid of man, although it would have been more proper for you to fear God. And when Zayd divorced her, We gave her to you in marriage, so that it should become legitimate for true believers to wed the wives of their adopted sons if they had divorced them. God's will must needs be done.

No blame shall be attached to the Prophet for doing what   33:38 is sanctioned for him by God. Such was the way of God with those who went before him: God's decrees are ever pre-ordained; those who convey God's commandments, fearing Him and fearing none besides God. Sufficient is God's reckoning.

Muḥammad is the father of no man among you.[2] He is the Apostle of God and the Seal of the Prophets. Surely God has knowledge of all things.

Believers, be ever mindful of God: praise Him morning and evening. It is He and His angels that bless you, so that He may lead you from darkness to the light. To believers He is ever compassionate.

Their greeting on the day they meet Him shall be: 'Peace!'   33:44 A rich reward He has prepared for them.

Prophet, We have sent you forth as a witness, a bearer of joyful tidings, and an emissary to warn them; one who shall call men to God by His leave and by a shining light.

Tell the faithful that God has prodigious blessings in store for them. Do not yield to the unbelievers and the hypocrites: disregard their insolence. Put your trust in God; sufficient is God as a guardian.

Believers, if you marry believing women and divorce them before the marriage is consummated, you are not required to observe a waiting period. Provide well for them and release them honourably.

Prophet, We have made lawful for you the wives to whom   33:50 you have granted dowries and the slave-girls whom God has given you as booty; the daughters of your paternal and maternal

---

1. Your intention to marry Zayd's wife.
2. Muḥammad left no male heirs.

uncles and of your paternal and maternal aunts who fled with you; and any believing woman who gives herself to the Prophet and whom the Prophet wishes to take in marriage. This privilege is yours alone, being granted to no other believer.

We well know the duties We have imposed on them concerning their wives and their slave-girls: so that none may blame you. God is ever forgiving and compassionate.

33:51   You may put off any of your wives you please and take to your bed any of them you please. Nor is it an offence for you to receive any of those whom you have temporarily set aside. That is more proper, so that they may be contented and not vexed, and may all be pleased with what you give them.

God knows what is in your[1] hearts. Surely God is all-knowing and gracious.

It shall be unlawful for you[2] to take more wives or to change your present wives for other women, though their beauty please you, unless they are slave-girls whom you own. God takes cognizance of all things.

33:53   Believers, do not enter the houses of the Prophet for a meal without waiting for the proper time, unless you are given leave. But if you are invited, enter; and when you have eaten, disperse. Do not engage in familiar talk, for this would annoy the Prophet and he would be ashamed to bid you go; but of the truth God is not ashamed. If you ask his wives for anything, speak to them from behind a curtain. This is more chaste for your hearts and their hearts.

You must not speak ill of God's apostle, nor shall you ever wed his wives after him; this would surely be a grave offence in the sight of God. Whether you reveal a thing or conceal it, God has knowledge of all things.

It shall be no offence for the Prophet's wives to be seen unveiled by their fathers, their sons, their brothers, their brothers' sons, their sisters' sons, their women, or their slave-girls. Women, have fear of God; surely God observes all things.

The Prophet is blessed by God and His angels. Bless him, then,
33:56   you that are true believers, and greet him with a worthy salutation.

---

1. The believers'.   2. Muḥammad.

Those who speak ill of God and His apostle shall be cursed   33:57
by God in this life and in the life to come. And He has prepared for them a shameful punishment.

Those who traduce believing men and believing women
undeservedly shall bear the guilt of slander and grievous sin.

Prophet, enjoin your wives, your daughters, and the wives
of true believers to draw their veils close round them. That is
more proper, so that they may be recognized and not be
molested. God is ever forgiving and compassionate.

If the hypocrites and those who have tainted hearts and
the scandalmongers of Madīnah do not desist, We will rouse
you against them, and their days therein will be numbered.
Cursed wherever they are found, they shall be seized and put
to death without mercy.

Such has been God's way with those who have gone before
them. And you shall find no change in the way of God.

People ask you about the Hour. Say: 'God alone has know-   33:63
ledge of it. And how are you to know? The Hour may well be
near at hand.'

God has laid His curse upon the unbelievers and prepared
for them a Conflagration. Abiding therein for ever, they shall
find none to protect or help them.

On the day when their heads roll about in the Fire, they
shall say: 'Would that we had obeyed God and obeyed the
Apostle!' And they shall say: 'Lord, we obeyed our masters
and our great ones, but they led us away from the right path.
Lord, mete out to them a double scourge; lay on them a
mighty curse.'

Believers, do not behave like those who slandered Moses.
God cleared him of their calumny, and he was exalted by
God. Believers, fear God and speak the Truth. He will bless
your works and forgive you your sins. Those who obey God
and His apostle shall win a signal victory.

We offered Our trust to the heavens, to the earth, and to
the mountains, but they refused the burden and were afraid
to receive it. Man undertook to bear it, but he has proved a
sinner and a fool.

God will surely punish the hypocrites and the idolaters,   33:73

both men and women; but to believing men and to believing women He will turn in mercy. God is ever forgiving and compassionate.

SHEBA

In the Name of God, the Merciful, the Compassionate

34:1 PRAISE BE to God, to whom belongs all that the heavens and the earth contain! Praise be to Him in the world to come. He is the Wise One, the All-knowing.

He has knowledge of all that goes into the earth and all that springs up from it; all that comes down from heaven and all that ascends to it. He is the Compassionate, the Forgiving One.

The unbelievers say: 'The Hour will never come upon us.' Say: 'Yes, by the Lord, it is surely coming! He knows all that is hidden. Not an atom's weight in the heavens or the earth escapes Him; nor is there anything smaller or greater but is 34:4 recorded in a veritable Book. He will surely recompense those who have faith and do good works; they shall be forgiven and a rich provision shall be made for them. But those who strive to confute Our revelations shall suffer the torment of a harrowing scourge.'

Those endowed with knowledge can see that what has been revealed to you from your Lord is the Truth, leading to the path of the Almighty, the Praised One.

The unbelievers say: 'Shall we show you a man[1] who would have you know that when you have been torn into shreds you will be raised in a new creation? Has he invented a falsehood about God, or is he a man possessed?' Truly, those who deny the life to come are doomed to torment, and they have strayed far into error.

34:9 Do they not see what is before them and behind them in heaven and earth? If We will, We can cause the earth to cave

---

1. Muḥammad.

in beneath their feet or let fragments of the sky fall upon them. Surely there is a sign in this for every penitent man.

On David We bestowed Our bounty. We said: 'Mountains, and you birds, echo his songs of praise.' We made iron pliant to him, saying: 'Make coats of mail and measure their links with care. Do what is right: I am watching all your actions.' **34:10**

And to Solomon We subjected the wind, travelling a month's journey on a morning and a month's journey on an evening. We gave him a spring flowing with molten brass, and jinn who served him by leave of his Lord. Those of them who did not do Our bidding We shall chasten with the torment of the Conflagration. They made for him whatever he pleased: shrines and statues, basins as large as watering-troughs, and built-in cauldrons. We said: 'Give thanks, House of David.' Yet few of My servants are truly thankful.

And when We had decreed his death, they did not know that he was dead until they saw a worm eating away his staff. And when his corpse fell down, the jinn realized that had they had knowledge of the unknown, they would not have remained in shameful torment.

For the natives of Sheba there was indeed a sign in their dwelling-place: a garden on their right and a garden on their left. We said to them: 'Eat of what your Lord has given you and render thanks to Him. Pleasant is your land and forgiving is your Lord.' **34:15**

But they paid no heed. So We let loose upon them the waters of the dam and replaced their gardens by two others bearing bitter fruit, tamarisks, and a few nettles. Thus did We punish them for their ingratitude: do We punish any but the ungrateful?

Between them and the cities that We have blessed, We placed roadside hamlets so that they could journey to and fro in measured stages. We said: 'Travel through them by night and by day in safety.'

But they said: 'Lord, make the stages of our travel longer.' They sinned against their souls; so We held them up as an example and tore them into shreds. Surely there is a sign in this for every steadfast, thankful person. **34:19**

34:20 Satan had judged them rightly; they followed him all, except for a band of true believers. Yet had he no power over them: Our only aim was to recognize those who believed in the life to come and those who were in doubt. Your Lord takes cognizance of all things.

Say: 'Call on those whom you deify besides God. They do not control an atom's weight in the heavens nor on the earth; nor have they any share in either. Nor has He any helpers among them.'

None can intercede with God save him who has received His sanction. When fear is banished from their hearts, they shall ask each other: 'What has your Lord ordained?' 'The Truth,' they shall answer. 'He is the Most High, the Supreme One.'

Say: 'Who provides for you from the heavens and the earth?'

Say: 'God. Either we or you are right, or clearly in the wrong.'

Say: 'You are not accountable for our sins, nor are we accountable for your actions.'

34:26 Say: 'Our Lord will bring us all together, then He will rightly judge between us. He is the All-knowing Judge.'

Say: 'Show me those whom you have named with Him as partners. Never. God alone is the Almighty, the Wise One.'

We have sent you forth to all mankind, that you may give them joyful tidings and forewarn them. But the larger part of mankind have no knowledge. And they say: 'When will this promise be fulfilled, if what you say be true?'

Say: 'Your day is already appointed. Not for one hour can you hold it back, nor can you hurry it on.'

And the unbelievers say: 'We will never believe in this Koran, nor in what had come before it.'

If only you could see the wrongdoers when they are brought before their Lord! Bandying charges with one another, those who were despised will say to those who deemed themselves mighty: 'But for you, we would have been believers.'

34:32 Then those who deemed themselves mighty will say to those who were despised: 'Was it we who debarred you from God's guidance after it was given you? No! You yourselves were wrongdoers.'

'By no means,' the others will rejoin. 'You have plotted,   34:33
night and day, bidding us disbelieve in God and set up rivals
to Him.'

And they will repent in secret when they see the scourge.
We will put chains round the necks of the unbelievers. Shall
they not be rewarded but according to their deeds?

We have sent no apostle to any city whose message was not
denied by its affluent people. The unbelievers say: 'We have
been given greater wealth and more children than the faithful.
Surely we shall not be punished.'

Say: 'My Lord gives abundantly to whom He will, and sparingly also. But most do not know it.'

Neither your riches nor your children shall bring you one
jot nearer to Us. Those that have faith and do what is right
shall be doubly rewarded for their deeds: in the High Pavilions
they shall dwell in peace. But those that strive to confute Our
revelations shall be summoned up.

Say: 'My Lord gives abundantly to whom He will of His   34:39
creatures, and sparingly also. Whatever you give in alms He will
recompense you for it. He is the most munificent Provider.'

On the day He herds them all together, He will say to the
angels: 'Was it you that they worshipped?'

'Glory be to You!' they will say. 'You are our defender
against them! They worshipped jinn, and it was in jinn that
most of them believed.'

On that day you shall be powerless to help or harm one
another. To the wrongdoers We shall say: 'Taste the torment
of the Fire, which you persistently denied.'

When Our clear revelations are recited to them, they say:
'This is but a man who would turn you away from the gods
your fathers worshipped.' And they say: 'This[1] is nothing but
an invented falsehood.' While those who denied the Truth
when it was given them say: 'This is but sorcery manifest.'

Yet have We given them no scriptures to study, nor have
We sent before you any apostle to warn them.

Those who have gone before them likewise denied Our   34:45

---

1. The Koran.

revelations. They were ten times as prosperous and mighty:[1] yet they rejected My apostles. And then how terrible was the way I rejected them!

34:46 Say: 'With one thing I admonish you: stand up before God in pairs or singly and ponder whether your compatriot[2] is indeed possessed. He is sent forth only to forewarn you of a grievous scourge.'

Say: 'I demand no recompense of you: keep it for your-selves. None but God can reward me; and He is the witness of all things.'

Say: 'My Lord hurls forth the Truth. He has knowledge of all that is hidden.'

34:49 Say: 'Truth has come. Falsehood has vanished and shall return no more.'[3]

Say: 'If I am in error, the loss is surely mine; but if I am in the right, it is thanks to that which my Lord has revealed to me. He hears all and is near at hand.'

If you could only see the unbelievers when they are seized with terror! There shall be no escape; they shall be taken from their graves.[4] They will say: 'We believe in Him.' But how will they attain the Faith when they are far away, since they at first denied it, and sneered at the unseen when they were far away?

34:54 They shall be barred from their desires, as were those before them; they, too, were perplexed with doubt.

---

1. Literally, they (the Meccans) scarcely possess one-tenth of what We gave them (their predecessors).
2. Muḥammad.
3. Thus Al-Jalālayn. Or: Falsehood cannot bring aught into being, neither can it restore it.
4. Literally, from a place near at hand (Al-Jalālayn).

THE CREATOR

In the Name of God, the Merciful, the Compassionate

PRAISE BE to God, Creator of the heavens and the earth. He   35:1
sends forth the angels as His messengers, with two, three, or
four pairs of wings. He multiplies His creatures according to
His will. And God has power over all things.

The blessings God bestows on people none can withhold;
and what He withholds none can bestow after Him. He is the
Almighty, the Wise One.

You people! Bear in mind God's goodness to you. Is there
any other creator who provides for you from heaven and earth?
There is no god but Him. How then can you turn away?

If they deny you, other apostles have been denied before
you. To God shall all things revert.

You people! The promise of God is true. Let not the life of   35:5
this world ever deceive you, nor let the Dissembler ever
deceive you about God. Satan is your foe: therefore treat him
as a foe. He tempts his followers, that they may become the
heirs of the Conflagration.

The unbelievers shall have grievous torment, but those
that believe and do good works shall have forgiveness and a
rich recompense.

And what of him whose foul deeds are made to seem fair
to him? God leaves in error whom He will and guides whom
He pleases. Do not destroy yourself[1] with sighs on their
account: God has full knowledge of what they do.

God it is who sends forth the winds which set the clouds in
motion. We drive them on to some dead land and give fresh
life to the earth after it has died. Such is the Resurrection.

If anyone seeks glory, let him know that glory is God's   35:10
alone. The good word ascends to Him, and the good deed is
exalted by Him. But those that plot evil shall be grievously
punished; and their plots shall come to nothing.

1. Muḥammad.

35:11   God created you from dust, then from a little germ. Into two sexes He divided you. No female conceives or gives birth without His knowledge. No one grows old or has his life cut short but in accordance with what a Book decrees. This is easy enough for God.

The two seas are not alike. The one is fresh, sweet, and pleasant to drink from, and the other is salt and bitter. From both you eat fresh fish and from both you bring out ornaments to wear. Behold how the ships plough their course through them as you sail away to seek His bounty. Perchance you will give thanks.

He causes the night to pass into the day, and He causes the day to pass into the night. He has pressed the sun and the moon into His service, each running for an appointed term. Such is God, your Lord. His is the sovereignty: the idols whom you invoke besides Him have power over nothing. If you pray to them they cannot hear your prayer, and even if they hear you they cannot answer you. On the Day of Resurrection they will deny that you ever served them. None can make known to you the Truth like the One who is all-knowing.

35:15   You people! It is you who stand in need of God. God it is who needs none and is worthy of praise. He can do away with you if He will and replace you with a new creation; this is no impossible thing for God.

No burdened soul shall bear another's burden. If a laden soul cries out for help, not even a near relation shall share its burden.

You shall admonish none but those who fear their Lord though they cannot see Him, and are steadfast in prayer. He that keeps himself pure surely keeps pure for his own soul. To God is the final return.

The blind and the seeing are not equal, nor are the darkness and the light. The shade and the heat are not equal, nor are the living and the dead. God can cause whom He will to hear Him, but you cannot make those who are in their graves hear you.

35:24   Your only duty is to give warning. We have sent you with the Truth to proclaim joyful tidings and to give warning; for there is no community that has not had an emissary to warn it. If they disbelieve you, those who have gone before them also disbelieved. Their apostles came to them with veritable signs, with Scriptures, and with the light-giving Book. But in the end I smote the unbelievers: and how terrible was the way I disowned them! _{35:25}

Do you not see that God has sent down water from the sky with which We bring forth fruits of different hues? In the mountains there are streaks of various shades of white and red, and jet-black rocks. Humans, beasts, and cattle have their different colours, too.

From among His servants, only those fear God who know that God is mighty and forgiving.

Surely those who recite the Book of God and attend to their prayers and give from what We gave them, in private and in public, may hope for imperishable gain. He will give them their rewards and enrich them from His own abundance. He is forgiving and bountiful in His rewards.

What We have revealed to you in the Book is the Truth confirming what had come before it. God knows and observes His servants. _{35:31}

Then We bestowed the Book on those of Our servants whom We have chosen. Some among them sin against their souls, some follow a middle course, and some, by God's leave, vie with each other in charitable works: this is the supreme virtue.

The Gardens of Eden they shall enter, wherein they shall be decked with bracelets of gold and pearls, and arrayed in robes of silk. They will say: 'Praise be to God who has taken away from us all sorrow; our Lord is forgiving and bountiful in His rewards. Through His grace He has admitted us into the Eternal Mansion, wherein we shall endure no toil, and shall endure no weariness.'

As for the unbelievers, the fire of Hell awaits them. Death shall not deliver them; and its torment shall never be eased for them. Thus shall We requite the thankless.

Therein they will cry out: 'Lord, get us out, and we will do good works unlike what we used to do.' 'Did We not make _{35:37}

your lives long enough for anyone who would be warned to take warning? Besides, someone *did* come to warn you: have a taste of it then. None shall succour the wrongdoers.'

35:38   God knows the mysteries of the heavens and the earth. He well knows people's innermost thoughts.

He it is who has given you the earth to inherit. He that disbelieves shall bear the burden of his disbelief. In disbelieving, the unbelievers earn nothing but odium in the sight of their Lord; their disbelief earns the unbelievers nothing but perdition.

Say: 'Behold your other gods on whom you call besides God. Show me what part of the earth they have created! Have they a share in the heavens?'

Or have We given them a scripture affording them a veritable proof? Truly, vain are the promises the wrongdoers give each other.

It is God who keeps the heavens and the earth from falling asunder. Should they fall, none could hold them back after Him. Gracious is He, and forgiving.

35:42   They solemnly swore by God that if someone came to warn them, they would accept his guidance more readily than did other communities. Yet when someone did come to warn them, they turned away from him with greater aversion, behaving arrogantly in the land and plotting evil. But evil shall recoil only on those that plot evil.

Are they awaiting any but the way the ancients were dealt with? But you will find no change in the ways of God; nor will you find in the ways of God any alteration.

Have they never journeyed through the land and seen the fate of those who went before them, who were far mightier than they?

Surely there is nothing in the heavens or the earth beyond the power of God. All-knowing is He, and mighty.

35:45   Were it God's will to bring people to account for what they did, not one creature would He have left on the earth's surface. But He respites them till an appointed time. And when their time is come, God has been watching all His servants.

YĀ' SĪN

In the Name of God, the Merciful, the Compassionate

Yā' sīn. By the Wise Koran, you are surely one sent forth upon a straight path. 36:1

A revelation from the Almighty, the Forgiving: that you may forewarn a people who, because their fathers were not warned before them, are now heedless. On most of them judgement has been passed; yet still they disbelieve.

We have bound their necks with chains of iron reaching up to their chins, so that they cannot bow their heads. We have put a barrier before them and a barrier behind them and covered them over, so that they cannot see.

It is the same for them whether or not you warn them: they will not believe. You shall warn only those who observe the Admonition and fear the Merciful, though they cannot see Him. To these give joyful tidings of pardon and a rich reward.

It is We who will resurrect the dead. We record their deeds and the vestiges they leave behind: We keep account of all things in a veritable Book. 36:12

You shall cite, as a case in point, the people of the city[1] to which the emissaries made their way. We first sent to them two, but when they rejected both We strengthened them with a third. They said: 'We have been sent to you as emissaries.' But they said: 'You are but mortals like ourselves. The Merciful has revealed nothing: you are only lying.'

They said: 'Our Lord knows that we are true emissaries. Our only duty is to give clear warning.'

They said: 'Your presence bodes but evil for us. Desist, or we will stone you or inflict on you a painful scourge.'

They said: 'The evil you forebode can come only from yourselves. Will you not take heed? Surely you are great transgressors.' 36:19

---

1. Probably Antioch, to which, we are told, Jesus sent two disciples, and then a third.

36:20 Thereupon a man came running from the far quarter of the city. 'My people,' he said, 'follow those who have been sent to you. Follow those who ask no recompense of you and are rightly guided. Why should I not serve Him who has created me and to whom you shall be recalled? Should I serve other gods than Him? If it is the will of the Merciful to afflict me, their intercession will avail me nothing, nor will they save me. Indeed, I should then be in evident error. I believe in your Lord; so hear me.'

He was told: 'Enter Paradise'; and he said: 'Would that my people knew how gracious my Lord has been to me, how highly He has honoured me!'

After him, We sent down no host from heaven against his people: this We never do. There was but one shout – and, behold, they were lifeless.

Alas for My bondsmen! They laugh to scorn every apostle that comes to them. Do they not see how many generations We have destroyed before them? Never shall they return to them: all shall be brought before Us.

36:33 Let the once-dead earth be a sign for them. We gave it life, and from it produced grain for their sustenance. We planted it with gardens of the palm and the vine, and watered it with gushing springs, that they might feed on its fruit. It was not their hands that made all this.[1] Should they not give thanks?

Glory be to Him who made all things in pairs: the plants of the earth, mankind themselves, and things they know nothing of.

Another sign for them is the night. From the night We sheer off the day – and lo, they are plunged in darkness.

And the sun hastens to its own resting-place: its course is laid by the Almighty, the All-knowing.

And for the moon We have ordained phases; it wanes, until it returns like a bent old twig.

36:40 The sun is not to overtake the moon, nor does the night outpace the day. Each in its own orbit swims.

1. Or: so that they might feed on its fruit and what their hands have made.

Another sign for them is that We carried their offspring in   36:41
the laden ark. And similar vessels We have made for them to
ride on. We drown them if We will: none can help or rescue
them, except through Our mercy and unless enjoyment is
allowed for a time.

When they are told: 'Have fear of that which is before you
and behind you, that you may be shown mercy,' they turn
away from every sign that comes to them from their Lord.

And when they are told: 'Give from that which God has
given you,' the unbelievers say to the faithful: 'Are we to feed
those whom God can feed if He chooses? Surely you are in
glaring error.' And they say: 'When will this promise be fulfilled, if what you say be true?'

They must be waiting but for a single blast, which will take
them while they are still disputing. They will have no time to
make a will, nor shall they return to their kin.

The Trumpet will be blown and, behold, from the graves   36:51
they will stand before their Lord. 'Woe betide us!' they will
say. 'Who has roused us from our resting-place? This is
what the Lord of Mercy promised: the apostles have told
the truth!' And with but one blast they shall be gathered all
before Us.

On that day no soul shall suffer the least injustice. You shall
be rewarded only according to your deeds.

On that day the tenants of Paradise will be busy with their
joys. They and their spouses in shady groves upon soft
couches they shall recline; therein shall they have fruits, and all
that they call for.

'Peace!' shall be the word from a compassionate God.
'Keep yourselves apart, you sinners, this day! Children of
Adam, did I not charge you never to worship Satan, your veritable foe, but to worship Me? That is a straight path. Yet has
he led from among you many a generation astray. Had you no
sense? This is the Hell you have been promised. Burn therein
this day on account of your disbelief.'

On that day We shall seal their mouths. Their hands will
speak to Us, and their very feet will testify to what they did.
Had it been Our will, We could have put out their eyes: yet   36:66

even then they would have rushed headlong upon their wonted path. But how could they see their error?

36:67 Had it been Our will, We could have transformed them where they stood, so that they could neither go forward nor retrace their steps.

We reverse the growth of those to whom We give long life. Have they no sense?

We have taught him[1] no poetry, nor would poetry befit him. This is but an Admonition: an eloquent Koran to exhort the living and to pass judgement on the unbelievers.

Or have they not considered how, among the things Our hands have made, We have created for them the beasts of which they are masters? We have subjected these to them, that they may ride on some and eat the flesh of others; they drink their milk and put them to other uses. Will they not give thanks?

36:74 They have set up other gods besides God, hoping they may be helped. They cannot help them: yet they stand like warriors ready to defend their idols.

So let not their words grieve you. We have knowledge of what they conceal and what they reveal.

Has not man considered that We created him from a little germ? Yet is he brazenly contentious. He answers Us back with arguments, and forgets his own creation. He says: 'Who will give life to rotten bones?'

Say: 'He who first brought them into being will give them life again: He has knowledge of every creature; He who gives you from the green tree a flame, and lo! you light a fire.'

Or has He who created the heavens and the earth no power to create others like them? That He surely has. He is the all-knowing Creator. When He decrees a thing He need only say: 'Be,' and it is.

36:83 So glory be to Him who with His hands holds sovereignty over all things, and to whom shall you be recalled.

---

1. Muhammad.

THE RANKS

In the Name of God, the Merciful, the Compassionate

BY THOSE who range themselves in ranks; by those who cast 37:1
out demons;[1] and by those who recite an Admonition: your
God is One: the Lord of the heavens and the earth and all that
lies between them: the Lord of the Eastern Regions.

We have decked the lower heaven with constellations,
guarding it against every rebellious demon, so that they may
not listen in to those on high. Meteors are hurled at them
from every side; then, driven away, they are consigned to an
eternal scourge. Eavesdroppers are pursued by fiery comets.

Ask them if they deem themselves of a nobler make than
the rest of Our creation. Of coarse clay We created them.

You marvel, while they scoff. When they are warned they
heed no warning. When they are shown a sign they mock at it
and say: 'This is but sorcery manifest. What! When we have
died and turned to dust and bones, shall we be raised to life,
we and our forefathers?'

Say: 'Yes. And you shall be utterly humbled.' 37:18

One blast will sound, and they shall see it all. 'Woe betide
us!' they will say. 'This is the Day of Reckoning; this is the
Judgement-day which you denied.'

But We shall say: 'Herd up the sinners, their spouses, and
the deities they worshipped besides God, and lead them to the
path of Hell. Hold them there for questioning.

'What has come over you that you cannot help each other?'

But on that day they will submit. They will reproach each
other, saying: 'You have imposed upon us!' – 'No! It was you
who would not be believers. We had no power over you: you
were sinners all. Just is the verdict our Lord has passed upon
us; we shall surely taste the scourge. We seduced you, but we
ourselves have been seduced.'

On that day they will all share in the torment. Thus shall 37:34

---

1. One of the interpretations given by Al-Baydāwī.

37:35 We deal with the wrongdoers, for when they were told: 'There is no deity but God,' they said with scorn: 'Are we to renounce our gods for the sake of a mad poet?'

Surely he has brought the Truth, confirming those who were sent before. You shall all taste the grievous torment: you shall be requited only according to your deeds.

But God's true servants shall be well provided for, feasting on fruits, and honoured in the Gardens of Delight. Reclining face to face upon soft couches, there shall be passed among them a goblet filled at a gushing fountain, white, and delicious to those who drink it. It will neither dull their senses nor befuddle them. They shall sit with bashful, dark-eyed virgins, as chaste as hidden pearls.[1]

With questions they will approach each other. One will say: 'I had a friend who used to say: "Do you really believe? When we have died and turned to dust and bones, shall we ever be brought to judgement?"' And he will say: 'Come, will you 37:55 look down?' He will look down and see his friend in the very midst of Hell. 'By the Lord,' he will say, 'you almost ruined me! But for the grace of my Lord I should have surely been summoned myself. Shall we never die again, having died once, and shall we never be scourged at all?'

Surely that is the supreme triumph. To this end let everyone labour.

Is this not a better welcome than the Zaqqūm tree? We have made this tree a scourge for the unjust. It grows in the nethermost part of Hell, bearing fruit like demons' heads: on it they shall feed, and with it they shall cram their bellies, together with draughts of scalding water. Then to Hell shall they surely return.

They found their fathers erring, yet they eagerly followed in their footsteps. Most of the ancients went astray before them, though We had sent emissaries to give them warning. So consider the fate of those who had been warned: except God's true servants.

37:76 Noah called to Us, and he was graciously answered. We

1. As 'if they were the sheltered eggs of ostriches' is another interpretation.

delivered him, and his household, from the great calamity, and made his descendants the sole survivors. We bestowed on him the praise of later generations: 'Peace be on Noah among all mankind!'

Thus do We reward the righteous: he was one of Our believing servants. The others We peremptorily drowned.

Of the selfsame faith was Abraham, who came to his Lord with a pure heart. He said to his father and to his people: 'What are these that you worship? Would you serve false deities instead of God? What think you of the Lord of the Universe?'

He lifted up his eyes to the stars and said: 'I am sick!' And his people turned their backs and went off.

He stole away to their idols and said: 'Will you not eat? Why do you not speak?' With that he fell upon them, striking them down with his right hand.

The people came running to the scene. 'Would you wor- ship that which you have carved with your own hands,' he said, 'when it was God who created you and all that you have made?'

They said: 'Build up a pyre and cast him into the blazing hell.' Thus did they scheme against him: but We abased them all.

He said: 'I will take refuge with my Lord; He will give me guidance. Lord, grant me a righteous son.'

We gave him joyful tidings of a gentle son. And when he reached the age when he could work with him, his father said to him: 'My son, I dreamt that I was sacrificing you. Tell me what you think.'

He said: 'Father, do as you are bidden. God willing, you shall find me steadfast.'

And when they had both submitted, and he had laid him down upon his brow, We called out to him, saying: 'Abraham, you have confirmed the vision.' Thus do We reward the righteous. That was indeed the veritable test. We ransomed him with a noble sacrifice and left for him the praise of later generations: 'Peace be on Abraham!'

Thus do We reward the righteous. He was one of Our believing servants.

37:112   We gladdened him with the news of Isaac, a saintly prophet, and blessed him and Isaac. Among their descendants were some who did good works and some who clearly sinned against their souls.

We showed favour to Moses and to Aaron and delivered them both, with their people, from the great calamity. We succoured them, and it was they who were the victors. We gave them the Illuminating Book and guided them to the straight path. We left for them both the praise of later generations: 'Peace be on Moses and Aaron!'

Thus do We reward the righteous. They were two of Our believing servants.

Elias[1] also was one of those sent forth. He said to his people: 'Have you no fear? Would you invoke Baal and forsake the most gracious of creators? God is your Lord and the Lord of your forefathers.'

37:127   But they rejected him, and will thus be called to account. Not so God's true servants. We bestowed on him the praise of later generations: 'Peace be on Elias!'

Thus do We reward the righteous. He was one of Our believing servants.

Lot also was one of those sent forth. We delivered him and his kindred all, except for an old woman who stayed behind, and utterly destroyed the others. You pass by their ruins in the morning and at night: have you no sense?

Jonah also was one of those sent forth. He fled to the laden ship, cast lots, and was condemned. The whale swallowed him, for he had sinned; and had he not devoutly praised the Lord he would have stayed in its belly till the Day of Resurrection. We cast him, gravely ill, upon a desolate shore and caused a gourd-tree to grow over him. We sent him to a hundred thousand, or even more; they believed in him, and We let them live in ease for a certain time.

37:150   Ask them if it be true that your Lord has daughters, and they sons. Or did We create the angels females; and were they

1. Elijah. Cf. 1 Kings 18:17–21.

witnesses? Surely they lie when they assert: 'God has given birth.' 37:151

Would He choose daughters, rather than sons? What has come over you that you should so judge?

Will you not take thought? Have you a veritable proof? Bring us your scripture, if what you say be true!

They assert kinship between Him and the jinn. But the jinn well know that they will be called up to account. Exalted be God above their imputations! Not so God's true servants.

Neither you nor your idols shall deceive any about God save him who is destined to be burnt in Hell. We[1] each have our appointed place. It is we who range ourselves in ranks, and we are they that give glory.

And they say: 'Had we received an Admonition from the ancients, we would have become God's true servants.' Yet they disbelieve; and they shall learn. 37:168

Before then We promised Our servants who were sent forth they would be helped and Our armies would surely be the victors. So pay no heed to them awhile: you will surely see their downfall as they shall see your triumph.

Do they wish to hurry on Our scourge? Evil shall be that morning when it smites them in their courtyards, forewarned though they have been.

So pay no heed to them awhile. You will surely see their downfall as they shall see your triumph. Exalted be your Lord, the Lord of Glory, above their imputations!

And peace be on those who were sent forth, and praise to God, Lord of the Universe! 37:182

---

1. The angels.

ṢĀD

In the Name of God, the Merciful, the Compassionate

38:1 *Ṣād.* BY the Koran, proclaiming the Admonition! Surely the unbelievers are imbued with arrogance and perverseness.

How many generations have We destroyed before them! They all cried out for mercy, when it was too late to escape.

They marvel that one of their own should come to warn them. 'This is a sorcerer, a teller of lies,' the unbelievers say. 'Does he claim the gods are one god? This is indeed a strange thing.'

Their elders go about saying: 'Go, and stand firm in the worship of your gods: it is a binding duty. We have not heard of this[1] in the Christian Faith.[2] It is nothing but a false invention. What! Was the Admonition sent down to him alone among us?'

Indeed, they are in doubt about My Admonition; indeed, they have not yet tasted My scourge.

38:9 Do they possess the treasures of the mercy of your Lord, the Almighty, the Munificent One? Is theirs the sovereignty over the heavens and the earth and all that lies between them? Then let them climb up to the sky by ropes! There, none shall be found but factions of defeated warriors.

Before them the people of Noah, 'Ād, and Pharaoh, who impaled his victims upon the stakes; Thamūd, the people of Lot, and the dwellers of the Forest[2] – they disbelieved, they were all those factions: all charged the apostles with imposture. And My punishment justly smote them.

Yet these are waiting but for a single cry – which none may retard. They say: 'Lord, hasten our doom before the Day of Reckoning!'

Bear with what they say, and remember Our servant David,
38:18 who was both a mighty and a penitent man. We made the

---

1. Monotheism.   2. Literally, the last Faith.
3. The people of Midian.

mountains[1] join with him in praise evening and morning, and the birds, too, in all their flocks; all were obedient to him. We made his kingdom strong, and gave him wisdom and discriminating judgement.

Have you heard the story of the litigants who entered his chamber by climbing over the wall? When they went in to David and saw that he was alarmed, they said: 'Fear not. We are two litigants, one of whom has wronged the other. Judge rightly between us and do not be unjust; guide us to the right path.

'My brother here has ninety-nine ewes, but I have only one ewe.[2] He demanded that I should entrust it to him, and got the better of me in the dispute.'

He said: 'He has certainly wronged you in seeking to add your ewe to his flock. Many partners are unjust to one another; but not so those that have faith and do good works, and they are few indeed.'

David realized that We were only testing him. He sought forgiveness of his Lord and fell down penitently on his knees. We forgave him that, and in Our presence he shall be honoured and well received. 'David, We have made you master in the land. Rule with justice among the people and do not yield to lust, lest it turn you away from God's path. Because they forget the Day of Reckoning, those that stray from God's path shall be grievously punished.'

It was not in vain that We created heaven and earth and all that lies between them. That is what the unbelievers think. But woe betide the unbelievers when they are cast into the Fire!

Are We to equate those that have faith and do good works with those that perpetrate corruption in the land? Are We to equate the righteous with the ungodly?

This Book We have revealed to you with Our blessing, that those that are of good sense possessed might ponder its revelations and take warning.

---

1. Cf. Psalm 148:9–10.
2. The allusion is to Uriah's wife.

38:30 And We gave Solomon to David; and he was a good and penitent servant. When, one evening, his prancing steeds were ranged before him, he said: 'My love for good things has distracted me from the remembrance of my Lord, until the sun disappeared behind the veil of darkness. Bring me back my chargers!' And with this he fell to hacking their legs and necks.

We put Solomon to the proof and placed a body upon his throne, so that he at length repented. He said: 'Forgive me, Lord, and bestow upon me such sovereignty as shall belong to none after me. You are the Bountiful Giver.'

We subjected the wind to him, so that it blew softly at his bidding wherever he directed it; and the demons, too, every builder and diver and others bound with chains. 'This is Our giving. It is for you to bestow or to withhold, without reckoning.' In Our presence he shall be honoured and well received.

And tell of Our servant Job. He called out to his Lord, saying: 'Satan has afflicted me with anguish and torment.'

38:42 'Stamp your feet; here is a cool spring for you to wash in and to drink from.'

We restored to him his household and as many more with them: a blessing from Ourself and an Admonition to those that are of good sense possessed.

'Take a bunch of twigs and beat with it; do not break your oath.'[1] We found him steadfast; a good and penitent man.

And tell of Our servants Abraham, Isaac, and Jacob: men of might and vision We made pure with the thought of the Hereafter. They shall dwell with Us among the chosen and the righteous.

And tell of Ishmael, Elisha, and Dhūl-Kifl,[2] who were all among the just.

38:49 This is but an Admonition. The righteous shall return to

1. Job had sworn to give his wife a hundred blows. The oath was kept by his giving her one blow with a bunch of a hundred twigs. Commentators quote this passage as permitting any similar release from an oath rashly taken.
2. Ezekiel; see p. 220, note 2.

a blessed retreat: to the Gardens of Eden, whose gates shall   38:50
open wide to receive them. Reclining therein, they will call for
abundant fruit and drink with bashful virgins for companions.

All this you are promised for the Day of Reckoning; this is
Our gift: a gift unending.

But doleful shall be the return of the transgressors. In Hell
shall they burn, an evil resting-place. Therein let them taste
their drink: scalding water, festering blood, coupled with other
putrid things.

'This band shall be thrown in headlong with you. No welcome shall await them; they shall be promptly cast into the
Fire.'

'No welcome for you either! It was you who prepared this
for us, an evil plight.'

Then will they say: 'Lord, inflict on those who brought this
fate upon us a twofold torment in the Fire.' And they will say:
'But why do we not see men whom we deemed wicked and
whom we laughed to scorn? Or have our eyes missed them?'

All this shall come to pass. The inmates of the Fire will   38:64
wrangle among themselves.

Say: 'I am only to give warning. There is no divinity but
God, the One who conquers all. He is the Lord of the heavens and the earth and all that lies between them: the Almighty,
the Forgiving One.'

Say: 'This is a fateful message: yet you pay no heed to it. I
had no knowledge of those on high when they wrangled
among themselves. It was revealed to me, only that I might
warn you plainly.'

Tell of your Lord when He said to the angels: 'I am creating man from clay. When I have fashioned him and breathed
My spirit into him, kneel down and prostrate yourselves
before him.'

The angels prostrated themselves one and all, except Satan,
who was too proud and was an unbeliever.

'Satan,' said He, 'what prevented you from bowing to him   38:75
whom I created with My own hands? Are you too proud, or
do you deem yourself superior?'

38:76 He said: 'I am nobler than he. You created me from fire, but him from clay.'

'Get you out hence, you are accursed!' said He. 'And My curse shall remain on you until the Day of Reckoning.'

He said: 'Reprieve me, Lord, till the Day of Resurrection.'

He said: 'Reprieved you shall be till the Day of the time appointed.'

'I swear by Your glory,' said he, 'that I will seduce them all except Your faithful servants.'

He said: 'Learn the Truth, then, and I speak nothing but the Truth: I will surely fill Hell with your offspring and those from among your followers, all.'

Say: 'I demand of you for this no recompense. Nor do I pretend to be what I am not. This is but an Admonition to 38:88 mankind; in a while you shall learn about it all.'

THE THRONGS

In the Name of God, the Merciful, the Compassionate

39:1 THE REVELATION of the Book is from God, the Almighty, the Wise One. We have revealed to you the Book with the Truth: therefore worship God, consecrating your religion to Him.

Is it not to God that True Religion belongs? As for those who set up other patrons[1] besides Him, saying: 'We serve them only that they may bring us nearer to God,' God Himself will resolve their differences for them. God does not guide the disbelieving liar.

Had it been God's will to adopt a son, He would have chosen whom He pleased out of His own Creation. Exalted be He! He is God, the One, who vanquishes all.

39:5 It was with Truth that He created the heavens and the earth. He causes the night to succeed the day and causes the day to overtake the night. He made the sun and the moon

1. The allusion is to the worship of saints, and to Christian doctrines.

subservient to Him, each running for an appointed term. He is surely the Almighty, the Forgiving One.

He created you from a single soul, then from it He created 39:6 its spouse. He sent down to you four different pairs of cattle.[1] He moulds you in your mothers' wombs by stages in threefold darkness.

Such is God, your Lord. His is the sovereignty; there is no god but Him. How, then, can you be turned away from Him?

If you render Him no thanks, God does not need you; yet His servants' ingratitude does not please Him; if you are thankful, your thanks will please Him.

No burdened soul shall bear another's burden. To your Lord shall you then return and He will declare to you what you have done. He well knows one's innermost thoughts.

When evil befalls man, he prays to his Lord and turns to Him in penitence; yet no sooner does He bestow on him a favour than he forgets what he had prayed for and makes other deities God's equals, in order to lead others away from His path.

Say: 'Enjoy your unbelief awhile; but you shall be among 39:9 the tenants of the Fire. Can he who passes the night in adoration, standing or on his knees, who bewares the life to come and hopes to earn the mercy of his Lord, . . . ?' Say: 'Are they equals, those that have knowledge and those that have none?' Truly, none will take thought but those that are of good sense possessed.

Say: 'You, My servants, that are true believers, fear your Lord. Those who do good in this life shall receive a good reward. God's earth is vast. But those that endure with fortitude He will recompense without reckoning.'

Say: 'I am commanded to worship God, consecrating my religion to Him; I am commanded to be the first of Muslims.'

Say: 'I fear, if I disobey my Lord, the torment of a fateful day.'

Say: 'God I worship, consecrating my religion to Him. As 39:15 for yourselves, worship what you will besides Him.'

1. Camels, cows, sheep, and goats, according to the commentators.

Say: 'They shall lose much, those who will forfeit their souls and their kin on the Day of Resurrection. That will surely be the ultimate loss. Above them there shall be sheets of fire, and sheets of fire shall be beneath them. By this, God puts fear into His servants' hearts.' Fear Me, then, My servants.

But those who keep from idol-worship and turn to God in penitence shall rejoice; give joyful tidings to My servants who listen to precepts and follow what is best in them. It is these whom God has guided; it is these that are of good sense possessed.

Can you rescue from the Fire those on whom the Word of torment was pronounced? As for those who truly fear their Lord, they shall be lodged in mansions towering high, set about with running brooks. Such is God's promise: God never fails His promise.

Do you not see how God sends down water from the sky which penetrates the earth and gathers in springs beneath? With it He then brings forth plants of various hues. They wither, they turn yellow, and then He turns them into dust. Surely in this there is an admonition for those that are of good sense possessed.

He whose bosom God has opened to Islām shall receive light from his Lord. But woe betide those whose hearts are hardened against the remembrance of God! They are in evident error.

God has now revealed the best of Scriptures, a Book uniform in style proclaiming promises and warnings. Those who fear their Lord tremble with awe at its revelations, and their skins and hearts melt at the remembrance of God. Such is God's guidance: He guides whom He will. But he whom God confounds shall have none to guide him.

Can he who with his face strives to ward off the terrors of the Resurrection . . . ? And the wrongdoers will be told: 'Taste the punishment which you have earned.'

Those who have gone before them also disbelieved, so that the scourge overtook them unawares. God made them taste dishonour in this life, but the torment of the life to come shall be more terrible, if they but knew it.

39:16

39:21

39:26

We have given mankind in this Koran all manner of para- 39:27
bles, that they may take thought: a Koran in the Arabic tongue,
free from any flaw, that they may fear God.

God makes this comparison: a man who has many masters
who are ever at odds among themselves; and a man devoted
to one master. Are they to be held equal? God be praised! But
most of them have no knowledge.

You[1] are doomed to die, and they are doomed to die. Then,
on the Day of Resurrection, in your Lord's presence you[2] shall
still dispute.

So who is more wicked than he who invents a falsehood
about God and denies the Truth when it is declared to him? Is
there not a home in Hell for the unbelievers?

Those who proclaim the Truth, and those who give cre-
dence to it – they surely are the God-fearing. Their Lord will
give them all that they desire. Thus shall the righteous be
rewarded.

God will expunge their foulest deeds and reward them 39:35
according to their noblest actions.

Is God not all-sufficient for His servant? Yet they threaten
you with those they serve besides Him. He whom God confounds has none to guide him; and he whom God guides
none can lead astray. Is God not mighty and capable of
revenge?

And if you ask them who created the heavens and the
earth, they will surely reply: 'God.' Say: 'Do you think then
that, if God be pleased to afflict me, your idols could relieve
my affliction; or that if He be pleased to show me mercy, they
could withhold His mercy?'

Say: 'God is my all-sufficient patron. In Him let the trustful
put their trust.'

Say: 'My people, do as best you can and so will I. You shall
learn who will be seized by a scourge that will disgrace him,
and be smitten by a scourge everlasting.'

We have revealed to you the Book with the Truth, for the 39:41
instruction of the people. He that follows the right path shall

---

1. Muḥammad.   2. The unbelievers.

follow it for his own good; and he that strays shall do so at his own peril. You are not their keeper.

39:42 God claims back every soul upon its death, and the souls of the living when they are asleep. Those that are doomed to die He keeps, and lets the others go for a time ordained. Surely in this there are signs for people that reflect.

Have they chosen others besides God to intercede for them? Say: 'Even though they have no power nor understanding?'

Say: 'Intercession is wholly in the hands of God. His is the sovereignty over the heavens and the earth. Then to Him shall you be recalled.'

When God alone is named, the hearts of those who deny the Hereafter shrink with aversion; but when their other gods are named, they are filled with joy.

Say: 'Lord, Creator of the heavens and the earth, who has knowledge of the unknown and the manifest, You alone can judge Your servants' differences.'

39:47 If the wrongdoers possessed all the treasures of the earth and as much besides, they would gladly offer it to redeem their souls from the harrowing scourge on the Day of Resurrection. For God will show them what they have never reckoned with. And the evil of their deeds will manifest itself to them, and that which they derided will encompass them.

And when evil befalls man he calls out to Us; but when, instead, We vouchsafe him a favour from Ourself, he says: 'It is my due.' By no means! It is but a test: yet most of them do not know it.

The same was said by those before them: but they gained nothing from what they did, and the very evil of their deeds recoiled upon them.

And the wrongdoers among these[1] shall also have the evil of their deeds recoil upon them: nor shall they ever be immune.

39:52 Do they not know that God gives abundantly to whom He

---

1. The Meccans.

will, and sparingly also? Surely in this there are signs for true believers.

Say: 'You that serve Me, who have sinned against your souls, do not despair of God's mercy; assuredly God forgives all sins. He it is who is the Forgiving One, the Compassionate. Turn in penitence to your Lord, and submit to Him before the scourge overtakes you; for then there will be none to help you. Follow the best of what is revealed to you by your Lord before the scourge suddenly smites you, when you are unaware; lest any soul should say: "Alas! I neglected my duty to God and scoffed with the scoffers." Or should say: "If God had guided me I would have feared Him." Or should say, when it sees the scourge: "Could I but live again, I would lead a righteous life."

'"Yes, indeed. My revelations did come to you; but you denied them. You were arrogant and a blasphemer."'

And on the Day of Resurrection you shall see their faces blackened, those who uttered falsehoods about God. Is there not in Hell a resting-place for the arrogant?

But God will deliver those who fear Him, for they have earned salvation. Evil shall not strike them, nor shall they ever grieve.

God is the Creator of all things, and of all things He is the Guardian. His are the keys of the heavens and the earth. And those that deny God's revelations will surely be lost.

Say: 'Would you bid me serve a deity other than God, you ignorant people?'

You have been warned, you and those who have gone before you, that if you worship other deities besides God, your works will come to nothing and you will surely be among the lost. Therefore serve God and render thanks.

They underrate the might of God. But on the Day of Resurrection He will hold the entire earth in His grasp and fold up the heavens in His right hand. Glory be to Him! Exalted be He above their idols!

And the Trumpet shall be blown, and all who are in the heavens and on earth shall fall down in shock, except those that shall be spared by God. Then the Trumpet will be blown

39:53

39:61

39:68

39:69 again, and lo! they shall rise and gaze around them. The earth will shine with the light of her Lord, and the Book will be laid open. The prophets and the witnesses shall be brought in, and all shall be judged with fairness: none shall be wronged. Every soul shall be recompensed according to its deeds, for He best knows all that they did.

And in throngs the unbelievers shall be led to Hell. When they draw near, its gates will be opened, and its keepers will say to them: 'Did there not come to you apostles of your own who proclaimed to you the revelations of your Lord and fore-warned you of this day?'

39:72 'Yes,' they will say. And thus the promised scourge will smite the unbelievers. They will be told: 'Enter the gates of Hell and stay therein for ever.' Evil is the dwelling-place of the arrogant.

And in throngs those who fear their Lord shall be led to Paradise. When they draw near, its gates will be opened, and its keepers will say to them: 'Peace be to you; you have led good lives. Enter Paradise and abide therein for ever.'

And they will say: 'Praise be to God who has made good to us His promise and given us the earth to inherit, that we may dwell in Paradise wherever we please.' Blessed is the reward of the righteous.

39:75 And you shall behold the angels circling about the Throne, giving glory to their Lord. They shall be judged with fairness, and all shall say: 'Praise be to God, Lord of the Universe!'

THE BELIEVER[1]

In the Name of God, the Merciful, the Compassionate

40:1 *Ḥā' mīm.* The revelation of the Book is from God, the Mighty
40:3 One, the All-knowing, who forgives sin and accepts repentance; whose punishment is stern, and bounty infinite. There is no god but Him. All shall return to Him.

1. This *sūrah* is also known by another title: 'The Forgiving One'.

None but unbelievers dispute God's revelations. Do not be 40:4
deceived by their prosperous dealings in the land. Before
them Noah's people also disbelieved, and so did the factions
after them. Each community strove to lay hands on their
apostle, seeking with false arguments to refute the Truth; but
I smote them, and how stern was My retribution! Thus shall
your Lord's judgement be passed on the unbelievers: they are
assuredly the inmates of the Fire.

Those who bear the Throne and those who stand around it
give glory to their Lord and believe in Him. They implore forgiveness for the faithful, saying: 'Lord, You embrace all things
with Your mercy and Your knowledge. Forgive those that
have repented and followed Your path. Shield them from the
scourge of Hell. Admit them, Lord, into the Gardens of
Eden which You have promised them, together with all the
righteous among their forefathers, their spouses, and their
descendants. You are the Mighty One, the Wise One. Shield
them from all evil; he whom You shield from evil on that day
will surely earn Your mercy. That is the supreme triumph.'

To the unbelievers a voice will call: 'God's abhorrence of 40:10
you is greater than your abhorence of yourselves. You were
called to the Faith, but you denied it.'

They shall say: 'Lord, twice You made us die, and twice
You gave us life. We now confess our sins. Is there no way
out?'

'This is because when God was invoked alone, you disbelieved; but when bidden to serve other gods besides Him you
did believe. Today judgement rests with God, the Most High,
the Supreme One.'

It is He who reveals His signs to you, and sends down sustenance from the sky for you. Yet none takes thought except
the repentant. Pray, then, to God and consecrate your religion
to Him, however much the unbelievers may dislike it.

Exalted and throned on high, He lets the Spirit descend at
His behest on those of His servants whom He chooses, that
He may warn them of the day when they shall meet Him; the 40:16
day when they shall rise up from their graves with nothing

hidden from God. And who shall reign supreme on that day? God, the One, who vanquishes all.

40:17 On that day every soul shall be recompensed according to what it did; on that day none shall be wronged. Swift is God's reckoning.

Forewarn them of the approaching day, when men's hearts will leap up to their throats and choke them; when the wrong-doers will have neither friend nor intercessor to be listened to. He knows the furtive look and the hidden thought. God will judge with fairness, but the idols to which they pray besides Him can judge nothing. Surely God alone hears all and observes all.

Have they never journeyed through the land and seen what was the fate of those who have gone before them, far greater in prowess? God smote them for their sins, and from God they had no protector. That was because their apostles had come to them with veritable signs and they disbelieved. So God smote them. Mighty is God, and stern His retribution.

40:23 We sent forth Moses with Our signs and with veritable authority to Pharaoh, Haman, and Korah. But they said: 'A sorcerer, a teller of lies.'

And when he brought them the Truth from Ourself, they said: 'Put to death the sons of those who share his faith, and spare only their daughters.' Futile were the schemes of the unbelievers.

And Pharaoh said: 'Let me kill Moses, and then let him invoke his god! I fear that he will change your religion and spread disorder in the land.'

Moses said: 'I take refuge in my Lord and your Lord from every tyrant who denies the Day of Reckoning.'

And one of Pharaoh's kin, who in secret was a true believer, said: 'Would you kill a man merely because he says: "My Lord is God"? He has brought you veritable signs from your Lord. If he is lying, may his lie be on his head; but if he is speaking the truth, some of what he threatens you with will smite you. 40:29 God does not guide a lying transgressor. Today you are the masters, my people, illustrious throughout the land. But who will save us from the might of God when it bears down upon us?'

Pharaoh said: 'I have told you what I think. I will surely guide you to the right path.'

And he who was a true believer said: 'I warn you, my people, against the fate which overtook the factions: the people of Noah, 'Ād, and Thamūd, and those that came after them. God does not seek to wrong His servants. 40:30

'I warn you, my people, against the day when you will cry out to one another, the day when you will turn and flee, with none to defend you against God. And he whom God confounds will have none to guide him. Before this, Joseph came to you with veritable signs, but you never ceased to doubt them; and when he died you said: "After him God will never send another apostle." Thus God confounds the doubting transgressor. Those who dispute God's revelations, with no authority vouchsafed to them, are held in deep abhorrence by God and by the faithful. Thus God seals up the heart of every scornful tyrant.'

And Pharaoh said: 'Haman, build me a tower that I may reach the highways – the very highways – of the heavens, and look upon the god of Moses. I am convinced that he is lying.' 40:36

Thus was Pharaoh seduced by his foul deeds and was turned away from the right path; Pharaoh's cunning led only to perdition.

And he who was a true believer said: 'Follow me, my people, and I shall guide you to the right path. My people, the life of this world is but a fleeting pleasure; the life to come is the everlasting mansion. Those that do evil shall be rewarded with like evil; but those that have faith and do good works, be they men or women, shall enter Paradise and therein receive blessings without number.

'My people, how is it that I call you to salvation, and you call me to the Fire? You bid me deny God and serve other gods I know nothing of; and I call you to the Mighty One, the Forgiving One. Indeed, the gods to whom you call me can be invoked neither in this world nor in the world to come. Our return shall be to God. The transgressors shall be the inmates of the Fire. 40:43

40:44 'Bear in mind what I have told you. To God I commend myself. God is cognizant of all His servants.'

God delivered him from the evils which they plotted, and a grievous scourge encompassed Pharaoh's people. To the Fire they shall be exposed morning and evening, and on the day the Hour strikes, a voice will cry: 'Admit Pharaoh's people to the most grievous torment.'

And when they argue in the Fire, the humble will say to those who deemed themselves mighty: 'We have been your followers: will you now ward off from us some of the flames?' But those who deemed themselves mighty will say: 'We are all in it now; God has judged His servants.'

And those in the Fire will say to the keepers of Hell: 'Implore your Lord to relieve our torment for a single day!'

They will say: 'But did your apostles not come to you with veritable signs?'

'Yes,' they will say. Their keepers will say: 'Then offer your prayers.' But vain shall be the prayers of the unbelievers.

40:51 We will surely help Our apostles and the true believers both in this world and on the day when the witnesses rise to testify; the day when no excuse avails the wrongdoers. The Curse shall be their lot, and theirs the evil abode.

We gave Moses Our guidance and the Israelites the Book to inherit: a guide and an Admonition to those that are of good sense possessed. Therefore have patience; God's promise is surely true. Implore forgiveness for your sins, and celebrate the praise of your Lord evening and morning.

As for those who dispute God's revelations, with no authority vouchsafed to them, they nurture in their hearts ambitions they shall never attain. Therefore seek refuge in God; He it is who hears all and observes all.

Surely, the creation of the heavens and the earth is greater than the creation of man; yet most have no knowledge.

The blind and the seeing are not equal, nor are the wicked the equals of those that have faith and do good works. Yet do you seldom take thought.

40:59 The hour is sure to come: of this there is no doubt; yet most do not believe.

And your Lord has said: 'Call on Me and I will answer you. 40:60 Those that disdain My worship shall enter Hell in abject humility.'

It was God who made for you the night to rest in and the day to give you light. God is bountiful to people, yet the larger part of the people do not give thanks.

Such is God, your Lord, the Creator of all things. There is no god but Him. How then are you led astray? Yet, even thus, those who deny God's revelations are led astray.

God it is who has made the earth a dwelling-place for you, and the sky a ceiling. He has moulded your bodies into comely shapes and provided you with wholesome things.

Such is God, your Lord. Blessed be God, Lord of the Universe.

He is the Living One; there is no god but Him. Pray to Him, then, consecrating your religion to Him. Praise be to God, Lord of the Universe!

Say: 'I am forbidden to serve your idols, now that veritable 40:66 proofs have come to me from my Lord. I am commanded to submit to the Lord of the Universe.'

He it was who created you from dust, then from a little germ, and then from a clot of blood.[1] He brings you out as infants into the world; you reach manhood, then decline into old age though some of you die young, that you may serve your appointed term and perchance grow in understanding.

He it is who ordains life and death; if He decrees a thing, He need only say: 'Be,' and it is.

Do you not see how those who dispute God's revelations are turned away from the right path? Those who have denied the Book and the message We sent through Our apostles will learn hereafter: when, with shackles and chains round their necks, they shall be dragged through scalding water and then burnt in the Fire.

Then they will be told: 'Where are the gods whom you have served besides God?' 40:74

'They have forsaken us,' they will say. 'Indeed, they were

---

1. See p. 222, note 2.

nothing, those gods to whom we prayed.' Thus God confounds the unbelievers.

40:75 And they will be told: 'That is because on earth you took delight in falsehoods, and led a wanton life. Enter the gates of Hell and stay therein for ever. Evil is the home of the arrogant.'

Therefore have patience: God's promise is surely true. Whether We let you[1] glimpse in some measure the scourge We promise them, or claim you back before We smite them, to Us shall they be recalled.

We sent forth apostles before you; of some We have already told you, of others We have not yet told you. None of those apostles could bring a sign except by God's leave. And when God's will was done, justice prevailed, and there and then the deniers lost.

40:79 It is God who has provided you with beasts, that you may ride on some and eat the flesh of others. You put them to many uses; they take you where you wish to go, carrying you by land as ships carry you by sea.

And He reveals to you His signs. Which of God's signs do you deny?

Have they never journeyed through the land and seen what was the fate of those who have gone before them? They were more numerous than them, and far greater in prowess and in splendour in the land; yet all their gains proved of no avail to them.

When their apostles brought them veritable signs they proudly boasted of their own knowledge; but soon the scourge they mocked encompassed them. And when they beheld Our might they said: 'We now believe in God alone. We deny the idols which we served besides Him.'

40:85 But their new faith was of no avail to them, when they beheld Our might: such being the way of God with His creatures; and there and then the unbelievers lost.

1. Muḥammad.

WELL EXPOUNDED

In the Name of God, the Merciful, the Compassionate

Ḥā' mīm. Sent down from the Merciful, the Compassionate: a 41:1
Book of revelations well expounded, an Arabic Koran for
those endowed with knowledge.

It proclaims joyful tidings and a warning: yet most of them
turn their backs and hear not. They say: 'Our hearts are proof
against that to which you call us. Our ears are stopped, and a veil
stands between ourselves and you. Do as you will, and so will we.'

Say: 'I am but a mortal like yourselves. It is revealed to me
that your God is one God. Therefore take the straight path to
Him and implore His forgiveness. Woe betide those who
serve other gods besides Him; who give no alms and disbelieve in the life to come. As for those who have faith and
do good works, an endless recompense awaits them.'

Say: 'Do you indeed disbelieve in Him who created the
earth in two days? And do you make other gods His equals?
The Lord of the Universe is He.'

He set therein mountains towering high above it; He pro- 41:10
nounced His blessing upon it, and in four days provided it
with sustenance for all alike. Then, turning to the sky, which
was but a cloud of vapour, He said to it and to the earth:
'Come forward both, willingly or perforce.'

And they both said: 'Come we will, obediently.' He decreed
them to be seven heavens in two days, and to each heaven He
assigned its task. We decked the lowest heaven with lamps and
guarded them. Such is the design of the Mighty One, the
All-knowing.

If they pay no heed, say: 'I have given you warning of a
thunderbolt, like the thunderbolt which struck 'Ād and
Thamūd. When apostles came to them from before them and
from behind them, saying: "Serve none but God," they said:
"Had it been our Lord's will He would have sent down angels.
We will never believe in your message."'

And as for 'Ād, they conducted themselves with arrogance 41:15

323

in the land, without justice. 'Who is mightier than we?' they used to say. Could they not see that God, who had created them, was mightier than they? Yet they denied Our revelations.

41:16 So, over a few ill-omened days We let loose on them a howling gale, to make them taste the scourge of shame in this nether life; but more shameful still will be the scourge of the life to come. There shall be none to succour them.

And as for Thamūd, We offered them Our guidance, but they preferred blindness to guidance. Therefore the thunderbolt of a humiliating scourge struck them for their misdeeds; and We delivered those who believed and those who feared God.

Forewarn them of the day when God's enemies will be herded into the Fire, so that when they are sorted out, their ears, their eyes, and their very skins will testify to what they did. And to their skins they will say: 'Why did you testify against us?' and their skins will say: 'God, who gives speech to all things, has made us speak. It was He who in the beginning 41:22 created you, and to Him shall you be recalled. You did not hide yourselves, so that your ears and eyes and skins could not be made to testify against you; yet you thought that God did not know much of what you did. It was the thoughts you entertained about your Lord that ruined you, so that you are now among the lost.'

If they persist, the Fire shall be their home: and if they sue for pardon, their suit shall not be granted.

We have assigned to them companions who make their past and present seem fair and right to them. Well have they deserved the fate of bygone races of jinn and humans. They shall assuredly be lost.

The unbelievers say: 'Do not listen to this Koran. Cut short its recital with frivolous chatter, so that you may gain the upper hand.'

41:28 We will surely make the unbelievers taste grievous torment, and pay them back for the worst of their misdeeds. Thus shall God's enemies be recompensed. The Fire shall for ever be their home, because they have denied Our revelations.

And the unbelievers will say: 'Lord, show us those among
the jinn and humans who made us go astray. We will trample
them under our feet and make them the lowest of the low.'

As for those who say: 'Our Lord is God,' and then follow
the straight path, the angels will descend upon them, saying:
'Fear not, and do not grieve. Rejoice in the Paradise you have
been promised. We are your guardians in this world and in the
world to come. Therein shall you have all that your souls
desire and shall have all that you can ask for: a rich provision
from a God forgiving and compassionate.'

And who speaks better than he who calls others to the
worship of God, does what is right, and says: 'I am a Muslim'?

Good deeds and evil deeds are not equal. Requite evil with
what is better and lo, he who is your enemy now will become
as if your intimate friend. But none will attain this attribute
save those who patiently endure; and none will attain it save
those who are immensely fortunate.

If Satan tempts you, seek refuge in God. He it is who hears
all and knows all.

Among His signs are the night and the day, and the sun and
the moon. But do not prostrate yourselves before the sun or
the moon; rather prostrate yourselves before God, who created them both, if you would truly serve Him.

If they[1] disdain His service, let them remember that those
who dwell with God give glory to Him night and day and are
never wearied.

And yet another of His signs is that you behold the earth
humble and desolate: but when We send down the rain upon
it, it stirs and swells. He that gives it life will surely raise the
dead to life. He has power over all things.

Those that deny Our revelations are not hidden from Our
view. Is he who is cast into the Fire better off than he who
emerges safe on the Day of Resurrection? Do as you will, He
observes whatever you do.

Those who deny the Admonition when it is preached to
them – and surely it is a momentous Book: falsehood cannot

1. The pagans.

reach it from before or from behind. It is a revelation from a wise and praiseworthy God.

41:43 Nothing is said to you that has not been said to other apostles before you. Your Lord is forgiving, but stern in retribution.

Had We revealed it a Koran in a foreign tongue they would have said: 'If only its verses were expounded! Why in a foreign tongue, and he an Arabian?'

Say: 'To true believers it is a guide and a healing balm. But those who deny it are deaf and blind: they are called to from a far-off place.'

We gave the Book to Moses, but contentions arose about it. And but for a Word from your Lord, long since decreed, judgement would have been passed among them; grave is their doubt about it.

He that does good does it for his own soul; and he that commits evil does so at his own peril. Never is your Lord unjust to mortals.

41:47 He alone has knowledge of the Hour. No fruits come out of their pods, no female conceives or is delivered, but with His knowledge.

On the day He calls out to them: 'Where are those fellow-gods of Mine?' 'We confess,' they will say, 'that none of us can vouch for them.' The idols to which they prayed before will vanish from them, and they shall learn there is no escape.

Man never wearies of praying for good things. But when evil befalls him he loses hope and grows despondent. And if after affliction We vouchsafe him a favour from Ourself, he is sure to say: 'This is my own. I do not think the Hour will ever come. And even if I do return to my Lord, He will surely reward me well.' We shall tell the unbelievers what they did, and We will surely visit upon them a grievous scourge.

When We show favour to man, he turns his back and holds aloof; but when evil befalls him he is loud in prayer.

41:52 Say: 'Do but consider: if this Koran is indeed from God and you deny it, who can err more than he who openly defies Him?'

We will show them Our signs across the horizons and in their own souls, until they clearly see that it is the Truth. Does it not suffice that your Lord is the witness of all things? 41:53

Yet they still doubt that they will ever meet their Lord. Yet surely He encompasses all things. 41:54

COUNSEL

In the Name of God, the Merciful, the Compassionate

Ḥā' mīm: 'ain sīn qāf. Thus God, the Mighty One, the Wise One, inspires you as He inspired those before you. 42:1

His is what the heavens and the earth contain. And He is the Most High, the Almighty, the Supreme One.

The heavens above well-nigh split asunder as the angels give glory to their Lord and beg forgiveness for those on earth. Surely God is the Forgiving One, the Compassionate.

As for those that serve other masters besides Him, God Himself is watching them; you are not their keeper.

Thus have We revealed to you an Arabic Koran, that you may warn the mother-city[1] and those who dwell around it; that you may forewarn them of the day that shall indubitably come: when all are brought together, some in Paradise and some in the Conflagration. 42:7

Had it been God's will, He could have united them into one community. But God admits whom He will into His mercy; the wrongdoers have none to befriend or succour them.

Or have they set up other guardians besides Him? But surely it is God who is the Guardian. He resurrects the dead, and He has power over all things.

Whatever the subject of your disputes, the final word belongs to God. Such is God, my Lord: in Him I have put my trust, and to Him I turn in penitence.

Creator of the heavens and the earth, He has given you spouses from among yourselves, and cattle male and female; it 42:11

---

1. Mecca.

is thus that He multiplies you. Nothing can be compared to Him. He alone hears all and sees all.

42:12 His are the keys of the heavens and the earth. He gives abundantly to whom He will, and sparingly also. He has knowledge of all things.

He has ordained for you such religion as He enjoined on Noah, which We have now revealed to you; which We enjoined on Abraham, Moses, and Jesus: 'Observe the Religion and do not divide.' Hard for the pagans is that to which you call them. God chooses for it whom He will, and guides to it those that repent.

Yet they did not divide themselves, through their own wickedness, until knowledge was given them. And but for a Word that had already gone forth from your Lord reprieving them for an appointed term, judgement would have surely been passed among them. And those who inherited the Book after them have their grave doubts too.

42:15 Therefore preach and keep to the straight path as you are commanded. Do not be led by their desires, but say: 'I believe in all the Scriptures that God has revealed. I am commanded to exercise justice among you. God is our Lord and your Lord. We have our works and you have your works; let there be no argument between us. God will bring us all together, and to Him shall be the final return.'

As for those who argue about God after pledging obedience to Him, their arguments will have no weight with their Lord. Ire will fall upon them, and grievous punishment awaits them.

God it is who has revealed the Book with Truth and Justice. And how do you know? The Hour may be fast approaching.

Those who deny it seek to hurry it on; but the true believers dread its coming, and know it is the Truth. Indeed, those who doubt the Hour have strayed far into error.

Benign is God towards His servants; He is bountiful to whom He will. He is the Invincible One, the Almighty.

42:20 Whoever seeks the harvest of the world to come, to him We will give in great abundance; and whoever desires the harvest of this world, a share of it shall We give him: but in the world to come he shall have no share at all.

Have they idols which in the practice of their faith have made lawful to them what God has not allowed? Had the Decisive Word not been pronounced already, judgement would have surely been passed among them. Woeful punishment awaits the wrongdoers. 42:21

You shall behold the wrongdoers aghast at what they earned, which will surely smite them. But those that have faith and do good works shall dwell in the fair Gardens of Paradise, and shall receive in their Lord's presence all that they desire. That will be the supreme grace.

Such is God's joyful promise to His servants who believe and do good works. Say: 'For this I ask of you no recompense, except to love your kin.' He that does a good deed We shall repay many times over. Surely God is forgiving and bountiful in His rewards.

Or do they say: 'He has framed a falsehood about God'? But if God pleased, He could set a seal upon your heart. God will bring falsehood to nothing and vindicate the Truth by His Words. He surely knows one's innermost thoughts. 42:24

He it is who accepts His servants' repentance, and pardons their sins. He has knowledge of what you do.

And he answers those who believe and do good works, and enriches them through His bounty. But grievous punishment awaits the unbelievers.

Had God bestowed abundance upon His servants, they would have committed much injustice in the land. But He gives what He will in due measure; He well knows and observes His servants.

He it is who sends down the rain when they have lost all hope, and spreads abroad His mercy. He is the Guardian worthy of praise.

And among His signs is the creation of the heavens and the earth, and the living things He has dispersed over them. If He will, He can gather them all together.

Whatever misfortune befalls you, it is the fruit of your own labours. He forgives much. 42:30

42:31 And on the earth you cannot escape, nor have you any besides God to protect or help you.

And among His signs are the ships which sail like mountains upon the ocean. If He will, He calms the wind, so that they lie motionless upon its bosom:[1] surely there are signs in this for the steadfast who render thanks; or He causes them to founder as punishment for their misdeeds.[2] Yet He forgives much.

Those who dispute Our revelations shall realize that they have no escape.

That which you have been given is but the fleeting pleasure of this life. Better and more enduring is God's recompense to those who believe and put their trust in their Lord; who eschew grievous sins and lewd acts and, when angered, are willing to forgive; who obey their Lord, attend to their prayers, and conduct their affairs by mutual counsel; who give in alms from what We gave them and, when oppressed, seek to redress their wrongs.

42:40 Let evil be requited with like evil. But he that forgives and seeks reconcilement shall be recompensed by God. He does not love the wrongdoers.

Those who seek to redress their wrongs incur no guilt. But great is the guilt of those who oppress their fellow men and conduct themselves with wickedness and injustice in the land. Woeful punishment awaits them.

To endure with fortitude and to forgive is a duty incumbent on all. He whom God confounds has no protector after Him.

And you shall see the wrongdoers when they behold the 42:45 scourge, say: 'Is there no way back?' And you shall see them ranged before it: awed and humiliated, they shall look with furtive glances. And the true believers will say: 'The lost are those who lost their souls and all their kin on the Day of Resurrection.'

The wrongdoers shall surely suffer everlasting torment;

1. Literally, back.
2. The misdeeds of those who sail in them.

they shall have no friends besides God to help them. He   42:46
whom God confounds shall be lost indeed.

Obey your Lord before a day arrives which none can put
off against the will of God. There shall be no refuge for you
on that day, nor can there be any denials.

If they pay no heed, know that We have not sent you[1] to be
their keeper. Your only duty is to give warning.

When We give man a taste of Our mercy, he rejoices in it;
but when evil befalls him because of what his hands committed, man is ungrateful.

God's is the sovereignty over the heavens and the earth. He   42:49
creates what He will; He gives daughters to whom He will and
sons to whom He pleases. Or He gives both sons and daughters, and He makes sterile whom He will. Omniscient is God,
and Almighty.

It is not vouchsafed to any mortal that God should speak
to him except by inspiration, or from behind a veil, or through
a messenger sent and authorized by Him to make known His
will. Exalted is He, and wise.

And thus have We inspired you[1] with a spirit of Our will
when you knew nothing of the Book or belief; but We made it
a light whereby We guide those of Our servants whom We
please. You will surely guide them to a straight path: the path of   42:53
God, to whom belongs all that is in the heavens and all that is in
the earth. Surely to God shall all things in the end return.

ORNAMENTS

In the Name of God, the Merciful, the Compassionate

Ḥā' mīm. By the veritable Book!   43:1

We have revealed it an Arabic Koran, that perchance you
may understand it. It is a transcript of the Eternal Book in
Our keeping, sublime, and full of wisdom.

Should We hold back the Admonition from you simply   43:5

1. Muḥammad.

43:6 because you are a prodigal people? Many a prophet did We send forth to the ancients: but no prophet did arise among them that they did not mock. We obliterated them, though they were mightier than these.[1]

Such then, was the example of the ancients. Yet, if you ask them[1] who created the heavens and the earth, they are bound to say: 'The Almighty, the All-knowing, created them.'

He it is who has made the earth a cradle for you and traced out routes upon it that you may find your way; who sends down water from the sky in due measure and thereby We resurrect a dead land: even thus shall you be raised to life; who has created all living things in pairs and made for you the ships and beasts on which you ride, so that, as you rest upon their backs, you may recall the goodness of your Lord and say: 'Glory to Him who has subjected these to us. But for Him we could not be their masters. To our Lord we shall surely return.'

43:15 Yet they[1] assign to Him some from among His servants. Surely man is monstrously ungrateful. Would God choose daughters for Himself from what He created and favour you with sons?[2]

And yet when the birth of a female[3] is announced to any of them his countenance darkens and he is grievously vexed. Or would they ascribe to God females who adorn themselves with trinkets and are powerless in disputation?

They make females the angels who are the Merciful's servants: did they witness their creation? Their testimony shall be noted down; and they shall be closely questioned.

They say: 'Had it been the will of the Merciful, we should never have worshipped them.' Surely of this they have no knowledge: they are only lying.

43:21 Or have We given them a scripture before this, so that they should hold fast to it?

1. The Meccans.
2. The pagan Arabs believed that the angels, and their own goddesses, were daughters of Allāh.
3. Literally, the birth of what they liken to the Merciful.

Indeed, they say: 'This was the faith our fathers practised; 43:22
and we are merely guided by their footsteps.'

Thus, never did We send forth before you to a city one to
give warning, but those who lived therein in opulence said:
'This was the faith our fathers practised; and we are merely
following in their footsteps.'

Each of them said: 'What if I bring you a faith more
enlightened than your fathers'?' But they said: 'We reject the
message you have been sent with.' So We took vengeance on
them; and consider the fate of those who disbelieved.

And tell of Abraham, who said to his father and to his
people: 'I renounce the gods you worship, except Him who
created me, for He will rightly guide me.' He made this an
abiding precept among his descendants, that they might for
ever turn to Him.

Indeed, I made things pleasant for these and for their 43:29
fathers until there came to them the Truth and an undoubted
Apostle. But now that the Truth has come to them, they say:
'This is sorcery. We utterly reject it.' They also say: 'Why has
this Koran not been revealed to some important man from
the two cities?'[1]

Is it they who apportion your Lord's blessings? It is We
who deal out to them their livelihood in this world, exalting
some in rank above others, so that the one may take the other
into his service. Better is your Lord's mercy than all their
hoarded treasures.

But for the chance that humankind might have become
one race of unbelievers, We would have given those who denied
the Lord of Mercy mansions with silver roofs, and stairs to
ascend on; mansions with silver gates and silver couches to
recline on; and ornaments of gold: for all these are but the
baubles of this life. It is the life to come that your Lord
reserves for those who fear Him.

He that does not observe the remembrance of the Merciful
shall have a demon for his companion: they turn people away 43:36
from the right path, though they may think themselves rightly

---

1. Mecca and Medina.

43:38 guided. And when he comes before Us, he will say:[1] 'Would that we were as far apart as the East is from the West.' Evil indeed is that companion.

But on that day, because you have done wrong, the thought that you will share the scourge with others will not console you.

Can you make the deaf hear, or guide the blind or those in grievous error? Whether We take you hence or let you live to see Our promises fulfilled, of them We shall surely be avenged: for We have power absolute over them.

Therefore hold fast to that which was revealed to you: you are surely on a straight path. It is an Admonition to you and to your people: and you shall be questioned all.

Ask those of Our apostles whom We sent before you if We ever appointed gods besides the Merciful to be worshipped.

43:46 We sent forth Moses with Our signs to Pharaoh and his nobles. He said: 'I am the apostle of the Lord of the Universe.' But when he came to them with Our signs they laughed at them; yet each fresh sign We revealed to them was but more powerful than the one that came before it. We therefore smote them with the scourge, so that they might return to the right path.

'You, sorcerer,' they said, 'pray for us to your Lord and invoke the promise He has made you. We will accept your guidance.'

But when We removed the scourge from them, they broke their pledge.

And Pharaoh made a proclamation to his people. 'My people,' said he, 'is the kingdom of Egypt not mine, and are these rivers which flow at my feet not mine also? Can you not see? Am I not better than this despicable wretch, who can scarcely make his utterance clear? Why have no bracelets of gold been given him, or angels sent down to accompany him?'

Thus did he incite his people: and they obeyed him, for 43:55 they were degenerate people. And when they provoked Us,

---

1. To his companion.

We took vengeance on them and drowned them all, as a pre- 43:56
cedent and an example to those who succeeded them.

And when Mary's son is cited as an example, your people
turn away and say: 'Who is better, he or our gods?' They cite
him to you merely to provoke you. They are indeed a contentious people.

He was but a mortal whom We favoured and made an
example to the Israelites. Had it been Our will, We could have
turned you into angels, your successors on the earth.

He is a portent of the Hour: have no doubt about its coming and follow Me. This is a straight path: let not Satan debar
you, for he is your veritable foe.

And when Jesus came with evident signs, he said: 'I have
come to give you wisdom, and to make plain to you some of
the things you differ about. Fear God and follow me. God is
my Lord and your Lord: therefore serve Him. That is a straight
path.'

Yet the factions disagreed among themselves. But woe 43:65
betide the wrongdoers, for they shall suffer the anguish of a
woeful day.

Are they only waiting for the Hour to overtake them suddenly when they are unaware? Friends shall on that day become
enemies to one another, except the God-fearing.

But you, My servants, who have believed in Our revelations
and are become Muslims, shall on that day have nothing
to fear or to regret. Enter Paradise, you and your spouses,
rejoicing. You shall be served around with golden dishes
and golden goblets. Therein shall abound what every soul
desires and every eye delights in; and therein shall you abide
for ever.

And such is the Paradise you shall inherit by virtue of your
good deeds. Therein your sustenance shall be abundant fruit.

But the transgressors shall endure for ever the torment of 43:74
Hell, which for them shall not be assuaged; they shall be
speechless with despair. We did not wrong them, but it was 43:76
they who did wrong.

43:77 'Mālik,'[1] they will call out, 'let your Lord make an end of us!' But he will say: 'Here you shall remain!'

We have made known to you the Truth, but most of you the Truth abhor.

If they are resolved to ruin you,[2] We are resolved to ruin them. Or do they think We cannot hear their secret talk and private converse? Yes! Our emissaries, at their side, record it all.

Say:[3] 'If the Lord of Mercy had a son, I would be the first to worship him.'

Exalted be the Lord of the heavens and the earth, the Lord of the Throne, above their falsehoods! Let them paddle, let them play, until they face the day they are promised.

43:84 And He it is who in heaven is God and on earth is God; He is the Wise One, the All-knowing. Blessed be He who has sovereignty over the heavens and the earth and all that lies between them! He alone has knowledge of the Hour, and to Him shall you be recalled.

Those to whom they pray besides Him have not the power to intercede for them, save those who testify to the Truth and have knowledge of it.

Yet if you ask them who created them, they will surely say, 'God.' How then can they be so misled?

And he can only say: 'Lord, these are surely people that do not believe.'

43:89 So bear with them and wish them peace; they shall learn.

---

1. One of the keepers of Hell. 2. Muḥammad.
3. To the Christians.

SMOKE

In the Name of God, the Merciful, the Compassionate

Ḥā' mīm. By the veritable Book, We revealed it[1] on a blessed   44:1
night, intending to give warning; on a night when every wise
commandment was expounded as a commandment from
Ourself. We it was who sent it down as a blessing from your
Lord; surely He it is who hears all and knows all: the Lord of
the heavens and the earth and all that lies between them. Mark
this, if you are true believers. There is no god but Him. He
ordains life and death; He is your God and the God of your
forefathers. Yet they divert themselves with doubt.

Watch for the day when the sky will pour down palpable
smoke, enveloping mankind: a woeful scourge. Then will they
say: 'Lord, lift the scourge from us. We are now believers.' But
how will their remembrance help them, when a true apostle
did come to them and they denied him, and said: 'A well-taught
madman!'

Yet if We but slightly ease your torment, you will return to   44:15
unbelief. On the day We bring down the supreme scourge We
will surely be avenged.

Before them, We tested Pharaoh's people. A gracious apostle had come to them, saying: 'Hand over to me God's servants.
I am an honest emissary. And do not hold yourselves above
God. I bring you clear authority. I adjure you by Him who is
my Lord and your Lord not to stone me. If you have no faith
in me, leave me well alone.'

Then he cried out to his Lord, saying: 'Surely these are a
sinful people.'

'Set forth with My servants in the night, for you will be
pursued. Leave the sea at rest behind you. They are warriors
doomed to be drowned.'

How many gardens and fountains they left behind! Cornfields, and noble palaces, and good things in which they took   44:27

---

1. The Koran.

44:28 delight. All this We gave to others to inherit. Neither heaven nor earth shed tears for them; nor were they reprieved. We saved the Israelites from the degrading scourge, from Pharaoh, who surely was a tyrant and a transgressor, and chose them knowingly above the nations. We showed them such miracles as manifestly tested them.

Yet there are those who say: 'We shall die but one death, nor shall we ever be raised to life again. Bring back to us our forefathers, if what you say be true.'

Are they better than the people of Tubba'[1] and those who thrived before them? We destroyed them all, for they too were wicked men.

It was not in jest that We created the heavens and the earth and all that lies between them. We created them both only to reveal the Truth. But of this the larger part of them have no knowledge.

44:40 The Day of Judgement is the appointed time for them all. On that day no friend shall help a friend; none shall be helped save those to whom God shows mercy. He is the Mighty One, the Compassionate.

The Zaqqūm tree shall provide the sinner's food. Like dregs of oil, like scalding water, it shall simmer in his belly. 'Seize him and drag him into the depths of Hell. Then pour out the scourge of scalding water over his head: "Taste this, you illustrious and honourable man! This is the very fate you always doubted."'

Surely the righteous shall be lodged in a mansion secure amid gardens and fountains face to face, arrayed in rich silks and fine brocade. Even thus; and We shall wed them to dark-eyed houris. Secure against all ills, they shall call for every kind of fruit; and, having died once, they shall never die again. Your Lord will in His mercy shield them from the scourge of Hell. That will be the supreme triumph.

We have made it easy in your own tongue, that they may
44:59 remember. Wait, then; they too are waiting.

---

1. The people of Himyar, in Arabia.

KNEELING

In the Name of God, the Merciful, the Compassionate

Ḥa' mīm. The revelation of the Book is from God, the Mighty One, the Wise One. 45:1

Surely in the heavens and the earth there are signs for the faithful; in your own creation, and in the beasts He scatters far and near, signs for firm believers; in the alternation of night and day, in the sustenance God sends down from the sky with which He resurrects the earth after its death, and in the marshalling of the winds, signs for those who can understand.

Such are God's revelations: We recite them to you in all Truth. But in what words will they believe, if not in God Himself and all His signs?

Woe betide every untruthful sinner! He hears God's revelations recited to him and then, as though he never heard them, persists in scorn. Forewarn him of a woeful scourge. And if he knew a little of Our signs, he would deride them: such men shall suffer degrading torment. 45:8

Hell is at their rear. Their gains shall not avail them, nor shall the masters they have served besides God. Grievous punishment awaits them.

This is true guidance. Those that deny their Lord's revelations shall suffer the anguish of a woeful scourge.

God it is who has subdued for you the ocean, that the ships may sail upon it at His bidding; that you may seek His bounty and render thanks.

He has subjected to you what the heavens and the earth contain; all is from Him. Surely in this there are signs for people who reflect.

Tell the believers to pardon those who cannot wish for the days of God,[1] when He will requite people according to what they did. He that does a good deed does it for his own soul; 45:15

---

1. I.e. the days of victory.

and he that commits evil does so at his own peril. Then to your Lord shall you be recalled.

45:16   To the Israelites We gave the Book and bestowed on them judgement and prophethood. We provided them with wholesome things and exalted them above the nations. We gave them explicit commandments: yet it was not till knowledge had been vouchsafed them that they disagreed, maliciously, among themselves. Your Lord will on the Day of Resurrection judge what they differ about.

We then set for you a law to the right path. Follow it, and do not yield to the desires of those that are devoid of knowledge; for they can in no way shelter you from God. The wrongdoers are protectors of each other; but the righteous have God Himself for their protector.

This is an Admonition to mankind; a guide and a blessing to firm believers.

Or do those who committed evil deeds think they are equal in Our sight to those who believe and do good works, and likewise their lives and deaths? How ill they judge!

45:22   God created the heavens and the earth to manifest the Truth, and to recompense each soul according to its deeds. They shall not be wronged.

Do but consider: who, besides God, can guide him who makes his lust his god, whom God deliberately confounds, setting a seal upon his ears and heart, and drawing a veil over his eyes? Will you not take thought?

They say: 'There is but one life in this world and no other. We die and live; nothing but Time destroys us.' Surely of this they have no knowledge. They are merely guessing.

And when Our veritable revelations are recited to them, their only argument is: 'Bring back our forefathers, if what you say be true!'

Say: 'God it is who gives you life and then causes you to die; He will then gather you all on the Day of Resurrection, of which there is no doubt; yet most do not know it.'

45:27   God it is who has sovereignty over the heavens and the earth. On the day the Hour strikes, those who have denied His revelations will assuredly lose all.

You shall see each community on its knees. Each commu-   45:28
nity shall be summoned to its Book: 'You shall this day be
requited for your deeds. This Book of Ours speaks with Truth
against you. We have recorded what you did.'

As for those who believe and do good works, their Lord will
usher them into His mercy. That shall be the veritable triumph.

As for the unbelievers: 'Were My revelations not declared
to you? Did you not scorn them and commit evil? When you
were told: "God's promise is true: the Hour is sure to come,"
you said: "We know nothing of the Hour. It is but a vain conjecture, nor are we convinced."'

The evil of their deeds will manifest itself to them, and the   45:33
scourge at which they scoffed will encompass them. They will
be told: 'We will this day forget you, as you yourselves forgot
you would meet this day. The Fire shall be your shelter, and
none will help you. That is because you scoffed at God's
revelations and were seduced by your earthly life.'

On that day there shall be no way out for them; nor shall
they be asked to make amends.

Praise, then, be to God, Lord of the heavens and Lord of
the earth, Lord of the Universe. Supremacy be His in the heav-   45:37
ens and on earth. He it is who is the Mighty One, the Wise One.

THE SAND DUNES

In the Name of God, the Merciful, the Compassionate

Ḥā' mīm. The revelation of the Book is from God, the Mighty   46:1
One, the Wise One.

It was but to manifest the Truth that We created the heavens
and the earth and all that lies between them: to last for an appointed term. Yet the unbelievers pay no heed to Our warning.

Say: 'Have you pondered on those whom you invoke   46:4
besides God? Show me what part of the earth they have created! Have they a share in the heavens? Bring me a scripture
revealed before this, or some other vestige of divine knowledge, if what you say be true.'

46:5 Who is in greater error than he who prays to idols which will never hear him till the Day of Resurrection – which are, indeed, unaware of his prayers; which, when mankind are herded up together, will declare themselves their enemies and will disown their worship?

When Our revelations are recited to them, veritable as they are, the unbelievers say of the Truth when it is declared to them: 'This is sorcery manifest.'

Or do they say: 'He has fabricated it[1] himself'?

Say: 'If I have indeed fabricated it, then there is nothing you can do to shield me from the ire of God. He well knows the way you fulminate about it. Sufficient is He as my witness and your witness. And it is He who is the Forgiving One, the Compassionate.'

Say: 'I am nothing new among the apostles; nor do I know what will be done with me or you. I follow only what is revealed to me, and my only duty is to give clear warning.'

46:10 Say: 'Do but consider: if it[1] is indeed from God and you reject it; if an Israelite[2] has vouched for it and believed in it, while you yourselves deny it with disdain: surely God does not guide the wrongdoers.'

And the unbelievers say of the faithful: 'Had there been any good in it they would not have believed in it before us.' And since they reject its guidance, they say: 'This is an ancient falsehood.'

And before it, was the Book of Moses: a guide and a blessing. And this Book confirms it in the Arabic tongue, to forewarn the wrongdoers and to give joyful tidings to the righteous.

Those that say: 'Our Lord is God,' and follow the straight
46:14 path shall have nothing to fear or to regret. They are the heirs of Paradise, therein to abide for ever as a reward for their labours.

---

1. The Koran.
2. 'Abdullāh b. Salām, according to the commentators.

And We have enjoined man to show kindness to his par- 46:15
ents. With much pain his mother bears him, and with much
pain she brings him into the world. He is born and weaned in
thirty months. When he grows to manhood and attains his
fortieth year, let him say: 'Inspire me, Lord, to give thanks for
the favours You have bestowed on me and on my parents, and
to do good works that will please You. Grant me good
descendants. To You I turn and to You I submit as a Muslim.'

Such are those from whom We will accept their noblest
works and whose misdeeds We shall overlook. We shall admit
them among the heirs of Paradise: true is the promise that has
been given them.

But he that says to his parents: 'Fie on you both! Do you
threaten me with a resurrection, when generations have
passed away before me?' – he that, when they pray for God's
help and say: 'Woe betide you! Have faith; the promise of
God is true,' says: 'This is but a fable of the ancients' – these
shall justly deserve the fate of bygone races of jinn and
humans: they shall assuredly be lost.

There are rewards for all, according to their deeds, that He 46:19
may duly requite them for their works. They shall not be
wronged.

The day the unbelievers are exposed before the Fire, We
shall say to them: 'You squandered away your precious gifts in
your earthly life, and took your fill of pleasure from them.
Today your recompense will be degrading torment, because
you acted with arrogance and injustice in the land and committed evil.'

And tell of 'Ād's kin who warned his people in the Valley
of the Sand Dunes; and there have been other emissaries
before and since his time, saying: 'Serve none but God.
Beware the torment of a fateful day.'

They said: 'Have you come to turn us falsely away from our
gods? Bring down what you threaten us with, if what you say
be true!'

He said: 'God alone has knowledge of it. I am here only to 46:23
deliver to you the message I have been sent with. But I can see
that you are ignorant people.'

46:24 And when they saw a passing cloud heading for their valleys, they said: 'This is a passing cloud that will bring us rain.'

'By no means!' he said. 'It is what you have sought to hasten: a hurricane bringing a woeful scourge; it shall lay everything waste at the bidding of its Lord.'

And when morning came there was nothing to be seen besides their ruined dwellings. Thus do We reward the wrongdoers.

We had made them as powerful as yourselves,[1] and given them ears and eyes and hearts. Yet nothing did their ears, their eyes, or their hearts avail them since they denied the revelations of God. That which they mocked encompassed them.

We destroyed the cities which had once flourished around you, and made plain the revelations, that they might return to the right path. Why did their gods not help them, gods they had set up besides God to bring them close to Him? Indeed, they utterly forsook them. Such were their lies, and such their false inventions.

46:29 And tell how We dispatched to you a band of jinn who, when they came and listened to the Koran, said to each other: 'Hush! Hush!' And as soon as it was ended they betook themselves to their people to give them warning. 'Our people,' they said, 'we have just been listening to a Book revealed since the time of Moses, confirming what had come before it and guiding to the Truth and to a straight path. Our people, answer the call of God's summoner and believe in Him. He will forgive you your sins and deliver you from a woeful scourge. Those that pay no heed to God's summoner shall not go unpunished on the earth. There shall be none to protect them besides Him. Surely they are in evident error.'

Do they not see that God, who created the heavens and the earth and was not wearied by their creation, has power to raise the dead to life? Yes. He has power over all things.

46:34 The day the unbelievers are arrayed before the Fire they shall be asked: 'Is this not real?' 'Yes, by the Lord,' they will

1. The Meccans.

say. 'Then taste the torment,' He will say, 'for you did not believe.'

Bear up then with patience, as did the steadfast apostles 46:35 before you, and do not seek to hurry on their doom. The day they behold the scourge they are promised, their life on earth will seem to them no longer than one hour of a day.

That is a warning. Shall any be destroyed but the ungodly?

MUHAMMAD

In the Name of God, the Merciful, the Compassionate

THOSE WHO disbelieve and debar others from God's path He 47:1 will bring their deeds to nothing. And the faithful who do good works and believe in what has been revealed to Muhammad – which is the Truth from their Lord – He will forgive their sins and ennoble their estate.

This, because the unbelievers follow falsehood, while the faithful follow the Truth from their Lord. Thus God lays down for mankind their rules of conduct.

When you meet the unbelievers strike off their heads and, 47:4 when you have wreaked widespread slaughter among them, bind your captives firmly. Then either grant them their freedom or take a ransom from them, until War shall lay down her burdens.

Thus shall you do. Had God willed, He could Himself have punished them; but thus shall it be that He may test you, the one by the other.

As for those who are slain in the cause of God, He will not bring their deeds to nothing. He will vouchsafe them guidance and ennoble their estate; He will admit them into the Paradise He has made known to them.

Believers, if you help God, He will help you and make you strong. But the unbelievers shall be consigned to perdition, and He will bring their deeds to nothing. Because they have abhorred God's revelations, He will frustrate their works.

Have they never journeyed through the land and seen what 47:10

was the fate of those who have gone before them? God destroyed them utterly; and a similar fate awaits the unbelievers, because God is the protector of the faithful: and because the unbelievers have no protector.

47:11

God will surely admit those who believe and do good works to Gardens watered by running brooks. The unbelievers take their fill of pleasure and eat as cattle eat: but the Fire shall be their resting-place.

How many cities were mightier than your own city, which has cast you[1] out! We obliterated them, and there was none to succour them.

Can he who follows the guidance of his Lord be compared to him who is led by his desires and whose foul deeds seem fair to him?

Such is the Paradise which the righteous have been promised: therein shall flow rivers of water undefiled, and rivers of milk for ever fresh; rivers of wine delectable to those that drink it, and rivers of clarified honey. Therein shall they have of every fruit, and forgiveness from their Lord. Are they to be compared to those who shall abide in Hell for ever, and drink scalding water that will tear their bowels to pieces?

47:16

Some of them indeed listen to you, but no sooner do they leave your presence than they ask those endowed with knowledge: 'What did he say just now?' Such are those whose hearts are sealed by God, and who follow their base desires.

As for those who follow the right path, He will increase their guidance and show them the way to righteousness.

Are they waiting for the Hour to overtake them suddenly? Its portents have already come. How else will they be reminded when it does overtake them?

Know that there is no deity but God. Implore Him to forgive your sins and to forgive the true believers, men and women. God knows your busy haunts and resting-places.

47:20

And the faithful say: 'If only a *sūrah* were revealed!' But when a forthright *sūrah* is revealed and fighting is mentioned therein, you see the infirm of heart staring at you as though they are

---

1. Muḥammad.

346

fainting away for fear of death. Yet obedience and courteous
speech would become them better. Indeed, should fighting be
ordained, it would be better for them to be true to God.

If you[1] renounced the Faith, would you not do evil in the
land and violate the ties of blood? Such are those whom God
has cursed, leaving them deaf and sightless.

Will they not ponder on the Koran? Or are there locks
upon their hearts?

Those who return to unbelief after God's guidance has
been revealed to them are seduced by Satan and inspired by
him. That is because they say to those who abhor the Word of
God: 'We shall obey you in *some* matters.' God knows their
secret talk.

What will they do when the angels carry off their souls,
striking their faces and their backs?

Because they follow what has provoked the ire of God
and abhor what pleases Him, He will bring their works to
nothing.

Or do the feeble-hearted think that God will not reveal
their malice? If We pleased, We could point them out to you
and you would recognize them promptly by their looks: but
you will surely recognize them from the tenor of their speech.
God has knowledge of all your actions.

We shall put you to the proof until We know the valiant
and the resolute among you; and We will test all that is said
about you.

The unbelievers who debar others from the path of God
and disobey the Apostle after they have seen the light shall in
no way harm God. He will bring their works to nothing.

Believers, obey God and obey the Apostle, and let not your
labours come to nothing.

Those that disbelieve and debar others from the path of
God and in the end die unbelievers God will never forgive.
Therefore do not falter or sue for peace when you have gained
the upper hand. God is on your side and will not grudge you
the recompense of your labours.

1. The hypocrites.

47:36 The life of this world is but a sport and a diversion. He will give you your deserts if you believe in Him and fear Him. He does not demand your wealth; if He demanded all and strongly pressed you, you would grow niggardly, and this would show your malice.

47:38 It is you who are being called upon to give in the cause of God. Some among you are ungenerous; yet whoever is ungenerous to His cause is ungenerous only to his own soul. Indeed, God does not need you, but you need Him. If you pay no heed, He will replace you by other people unlike you.

VICTORY

In the Name of God, the Merciful, the Compassionate

48:1 WE HAVE given you[1] a signal victory,[2] so that God may forgive you your past and future sins, and perfect His goodness to you; that He may guide you on to a straight path; and that God may bestow on you His mighty help.

He it was who sent down the Divine Presence[3] into the hearts of the faithful, so that their faith might grow stronger – God's are the legions of the heavens and the earth: God is all-knowing and wise; that He may admit the believers, both men and women, into Gardens watered by running brooks, therein to abide for ever; that He may forgive them their sins – this, in God's sight, is a glorious triumph; and that He may punish the hypocrites and the idolaters, men and women, who think evil thoughts about God. A turn of evil shall befall them, for God is angry with them. He has laid on them His curse and made Hell ready for them: a wretched fate!

48:7 God's are the legions of the heavens and the earth. God is mighty and wise.

1. Muḥammad.
2. The taking of Mecca in 630, or the Jewish settlement of Khaybar a year earlier.
3. See p. 26, note 1.

We have sent you[1] forth as a witness and as a bearer of joyful tidings and warnings, so that you[2] may have faith in God and His apostle and that you may assist Him, honour Him, and praise Him morning and evening. 48:8

Those that swear fealty to you, surely swear fealty to God Himself. The Hand of God is above their hands. He that breaks his oath breaks it at his own peril, but he that keeps his pledge to God shall be richly recompensed by Him.

The desert Arabs who stayed behind[3] will say to you: 'We were occupied with our goods and families. Implore God to pardon us.' They will say with their tongues what they do not mean in their hearts.

Say: 'Who can intervene on your behalf with God if it be His will to do you harm or good? Indeed, God is ever cognizant of what you do.'

No! You[4] thought the Apostle and the believers would never return to their people; and with this fancy your hearts were delighted. You harboured evil thoughts and thus incurred damnation. 48:12

As for those that disbelieve in God and His apostle, for the unbelievers We have prepared a Conflagration. It is God who has sovereignty over the heavens and the earth; He pardons whom He will and punishes whom He pleases. And God is ever forgiving and compassionate.

Those that stayed behind when you set forth to take some spoils will say: 'Let us come with you.'

They seek to change the Word of God. Say: 'You shall not come with us. So God has said beforehand.'

They will say: 'You are surely jealous of us.' But how little they understand!

Say to those of the desert Arabs who stayed behind: 'You shall be called upon to fight a people possessed of overwhelming might, unless they willingly embrace Islām. If you 48:16

1. Muḥammad.
2. The Meccans.
3. Away from the fighting.
4. The desert Arabs.

prove obedient, God will reward you well. But if you turn away, as you did turn away before this, He will inflict on you a woeful punishment.'

48:17 It shall be no offence for the blind, no offence for the lame, and no offence for the sick to stay behind. He that obeys God and His apostle shall be admitted into Gardens watered by running brooks; but on him that turns and flees He will inflict a woeful punishment.

God was well pleased with the faithful when they swore allegiance to you under the tree; He knew what was in their hearts. Therefore He sent down the Divine Presence[1] upon them, and rewarded them with a speedy victory and with abundant spoils to take. Almighty is God and wise.

48:20 God has promised you abundant spoils to take, and has given you this[2] with all promptness. He has stayed your enemies' hands, so that He may make your victory a sign to true believers and guide you along a straight path.

And God knows of other spoils which you have not yet taken. God has power over all things.

If the unbelievers join battle with you, they shall be put to flight. They shall find none to protect or help them.

Such was the way of God in days gone by: nor shall you ever find change in the way of God.

And He it was who ended hostilities between you in the Valley of Mecca[3] after He had given you victory over them. God was watching all your actions.

48:25 It was they who disbelieved and debarred you from the Sacred Mosque and prevented your offerings from reaching their destination. But for the fear that you might have trampled underfoot believing men and women unknown to you and thus incurred unwitting guilt on their account, He ordained it thus that He might admit whom He will into His mercy. Had they stood apart from them, We would have inflicted a woeful punishment on those of them who were unbelievers.

1. See p. 26, note 1.
2. The spoils taken at Khaybar.
3. The allusion is probably to the Peace of Ḥudaybiyya, in 628.

And while bigotry – the bigotry of ignorance – was hold-   48:26
ing sway in the hearts of the unbelievers, God sent down His
Divine Presence[1] on His apostle and on the faithful and made
the word of piety binding on them, for they were most worthy
and deserving of it. God has knowledge of all things.

God has in all truth fulfilled His apostle's vision: 'If God   48:27
wills, you shall enter the Sacred Mosque secure and fearless,
with hair cropped or shaven.' He knew what you knew not;
and what is more, He granted you a speedy victory.

He it is that has sent forth His apostle with guidance and
the Religion of Truth, that he may exalt it above all religion.
Sufficient is God as a witness.

Muḥammad is God's apostle. And those who follow him   48:29
are ruthless to the unbelievers but merciful to one another.
You behold them worshipping on their knees, seeking grace
from God and His good will. Their marks are on their faces,
the traces of their prostrations. Thus are they described in the
Torah, and are described in the Gospel:[2] they are like the seed
which puts forth its shoot and strengthens it, so that it rises
stout and firm upon its stalk, delighting the sowers. Through
them He seeks to enrage the unbelievers. Yet to those of them
who will embrace the Faith and do good works God has
promised forgiveness and a rich recompense.

THE CHAMBERS

In the Name of God, the Merciful, the Compassionate

BELIEVERS, DO not behave presumptuously in the presence   49:1
of God and His apostle. And fear God: surely God hears all
and knows all.

Believers, do not raise your voices above the voice of the
Prophet, nor shout aloud when speaking to him as you do to
one another, lest your labours should come to nothing without your knowledge. Those who speak softly in the presence   49:3

1. See p. 26, note 1.   2. Cf. Mark 4:26–9.

of God's apostle are those whose hearts God has tested for piety. Forgiveness and a rich reward await them.

49:4 Those who call out to you[1] while you are in your chambers are for the most part devoid of understanding. If they waited until you went out to them, it would be better for them. But God is forgiving and compassionate.

Believers, if a mischief maker brings you a piece of news, inquire first into its truth, lest you should wrong people unwittingly and then regret your action.

And be aware that God's apostle is among you. If he obeyed you in many matters, you would surely come to grief. But God has endeared the Faith to you and beautified it in your hearts, making unbelief, wrongdoing, and disobedience abhorrent to you. Such are those who are rightly guided through God's grace and bounty. God is all-knowing and wise.

49:9 If two parties of believers take up arms the one against the other, make peace between them. If either of them unjustly attacks the other, fight the aggressors till they submit to God's judgement. When they have submitted, make peace between them in equity and fairness; God loves those who exercise fairness.

The believers are a band of brothers. Make peace among your brothers and fear God, that you may be shown mercy.

Believers, let no people mock other people, who may perhaps be better than themselves. And let no women mock other women, who may perhaps be better than themselves. Do not defame one another, nor call one another by nicknames. It is an evil thing to be called by a bad name after embracing the Faith. Those that do not repent are themselves the wrongdoers.

Believers, avoid immoderate suspicion, for in some cases suspicion is a crime. Do not spy on one another, nor backbite one another. Would any of you like to eat the flesh of his dead brother? Surely you would loathe it. And fear God; God pardons and is compassionate.

49:13 You people! We have created you from a male and a female,

1. Muḥammad.

and made you into communities and tribes, that you might get to know one another. The noblest of you in God's sight is he who fears Him. God is all-knowing and conversant with all.'

The Arabs of the desert say: 'We are believers.' Say: 'Believ- 49:14 ers you are not. Rather say: "We profess Islām," for faith has not yet found its way into your hearts. If you obey God and His apostle, He will in no way deny you the reward of your labours. Surely God is forgiving and compassionate.'

The true believers are those that believe in God and His apostle, and never doubt afterwards; and who fight with their wealth and with their persons in the cause of God. Such are those whose faith is true.

Say: 'Would you instruct God in your religion, when God 49:16 knows what the heavens and the earth contain? When God has knowledge of all things?'

They think they have conferred on you a favour by embracing Islām. Say: 'In accepting Islām you have conferred on me no favour. It was God who bestowed a favour on you in guiding you to the true Faith. Admit this, if you are truthful. God 49:18 knows all that is hidden in the heavens and the earth. God is cognizant of what you do.'

QĀF

In the Name of God, the Merciful, the Compassionate

Qāf. By the Glorious Koran! 50:1

They indeed marvel that one of their own has come to warn them; so that the unbelievers say: 'This is indeed a wondrous thing. When we are dead and turned to dust . . . ?[1] Such a return is most improbable!'

We know how the earth consumes them. We hold a Book which records all.

Indeed, they denied the Truth when it had come to them, 50:5

1. '[. . . shall we be raised to life]?'

353

50:6 and now they are perplexed. Have they never observed the sky above them, how We built it up and furnished it with ornaments, leaving no crack in its expanse?

And We spread out the earth and set upon it immovable mountains. We brought forth from it all kinds of delectable plants. A lesson and an Admonition to every penitent mortal.

We send down blessed water from the sky with which We bring forth gardens and the harvest grain, and tall palm-trees laden with clusters of dates, a sustenance for humankind; thereby giving new life to a dead land. Such shall be the Resurrection.

Long before these the people of Noah and the dwellers of Al-Rass[1] denied the Truth; and so did Thamūd and 'Ād, Pharaoh and the kin of Lot, the dwellers of the Forest[2] and the people of Tubba';[3] all disbelieved the apostles and were thus visited by My threatened scourge.

50:15 Were We worn out by the First Creation? Yet they are in doubt about a new creation.[4]

We created man; We know the promptings of his soul, and are closer to him than his jugular vein.

When the twin keepers receive him, seated on his right, and on his left, no word he utters but shall be noted down by a vigilant guard.

And when the agony of death comes upon him with the Truth, they will say: 'This is the fate you endeavoured to avoid.' And the Trumpet shall be blown: that is the promised day.

Each soul shall come attended by one who will drive it on, and another to testify against it: 'Of this you have been heedless; now we have removed your veil, so that today your sight

50:23 is keen.' And his companion will say: 'My testimony is ready to hand.'

1. Commentators are disagreed as to the identity of this place name. Some say it is a town in Yamāmah, others a well in Midian.
2. The people of Midian.
3. The people of Himyar, whose kings bore the title of Tubba'.
4. The Resurrection.

'Cast, you two, into Hell every hardened unbeliever, every   50:25
opponent of good, every doubting transgressor who has set
up another deity besides God. Hurl him, you two, into the
harrowing scourge!'

His companion[1] will say: 'Lord, I did not mislead him. He
had already strayed far into error.'

He will say: 'Do not dispute in My presence. I did forewarn
you; My word cannot be changed, nor am I unjust to mortals.'

On that day, We shall say to Hell: 'Are you now full?' And
Hell will say: 'Are there any more?'

And, not far thence, Paradise shall be brought close to the
righteous: 'Here is what you were promised: for every penitent and honest man, who fears the Merciful though unseen,
and comes before Him with a contrite heart. Enter it in peace.
This is the day of immortality.'

Therein shall they have all that they desire; and We have yet   50:35
more.

How many generations, far greater in prowess, have We
wiped out before them! They searched the entire land: but
could they find a refuge? Surely in this there is a lesson
for everyone who is of a heart possessed, and can hear
and see.

In six days We created the heavens and the earth and all
that lies between them; nor were We ever wearied.

Bear then with what they[2] say. Give glory to your Lord
before sunrise and before sunset. In the night praise Him, and
make the additional prostrations.

Listen on the day when the Crier will call from near; the
day when they will hear the cry of Truth. On that day they will
rise up from their graves. It is We who ordain life and death;
and to Us shall all return.

On that day the earth will be rent asunder over them, and   50:44
from it they shall emerge in haste. To herd them all is easy
enough for Us.

---

1. The demon who is chained to him.
2. The unbelievers.

50:45 We well know what they say. You shall not use coercion with them. Admonish with the Koran whoever fears My threat.

THE WINDS

In the Name of God, the Merciful, the Compassionate

51:1 BY THE dust-scattering winds and the heavily-laden clouds; by the smoothly-gliding ships, and by the angels who deal out as commanded; that which you are promised shall truly be fulfilled, and the Last Judgement shall surely come to pass!

By the heaven with its starry highways, the words you utter are inconsistent! None but the perverse turn away from the Truth. Perish the liars, who dwell in darkness and are heedless of the life to come!

'When will the Day of Judgement be?' they ask. On that day they shall be scourged in the Fire: 'Taste this, the punishment you sought to hasten!'

51:15 The righteous shall dwell amidst gardens and fountains, and shall receive what their Lord will give them. For they did good works before, sleeping but little in the night-time, praying at dawn for God's pardon, and sharing their goods with the beggars and the dispossessed.

On earth there are signs for firm believers and in your own souls. Can you not see?

Heaven holds your sustenance and all that you are promised. I swear by the Lord of heaven and earth that this is true, as true as you are speaking now!

Have you heard the story of Abraham's honoured guests?[1]

They went in to him and said: 'Peace!' 'Peace!' he said and, seeing that they were strangers, betook himself to his family and returned with a fatted calf. He placed it before them, saying: 'Will you not eat?'

51:28 He grew afraid of them, but they said, 'Have no fear,' and told him he was to have a son endowed with knowledge.

1. Cf. Genesis 18.

His wife came crying and beating her face. 'Surely I am a 51:29
barren old woman,' she said.

'Such is the will of your Lord,' they said. 'He surely is the
Wise One, the All-knowing.'

'Messengers,' said he, 'what is your errand?'

They said: 'We are sent forth to a perverted people, that we
may bring down on them a shower of clay-stones marked by
your Lord for the destruction of the sinful.'

We led all the believers out of the town – We found but
one household of true Muslims – and left therein a sign for
those who fear the woeful scourge.

And in Moses there was a sign. We sent him forth to Pharaoh with manifest authority, but he turned his back, he and his
nobles, saying: 'A sorcerer, or a man possessed.' So We seized
him and his warriors, and cast them into the sea. Indeed, he
deserved much blame.

In the fate of 'Ād there was another sign. We let loose on 51:41
them a blighting wind, which pounded into dust all that it
swept before it.

And in Thamūd. They had been told: 'Enjoy yourselves till
a time decreed'; but they disobeyed the commandment of
their Lord. The thunderbolt struck them as they looked on;
they could not rise up from their fall, nor did they gain their
end.

And the people of Noah before them. Surely they too were
a degenerate people.

The heaven We built with mighty hands, giving it a vast
expanse, and stretched the earth beneath it: gracious is He
who spread it out. And all things We have made in pairs, so
that you may take thought.

Therefore seek God. From Him I come to you with a clear
warning. You shall not set up another deity besides God.
From Him I come to you with a clear warning.

Thus no apostle ever came to those before them[1] but that
they said: 'Sorcerer!' or 'A man possessed!' Have they handed 51:53

1. The Meccans.

this down from one generation to the next? Surely they are transgressors all.

51:54 Pay no heed to them; you shall incur no blame. Exhort them; exhortation helps the true believers.

I created the jinn and mankind only that they might worship Me. I demand no livelihood of them, nor do I ask that they should feed Me.

God alone is the Munificent Giver, the Mighty One, the Invincible. The wrongdoers' sins are like the sins of those that 51:60 sinned before them; so let them not hurry Me on. Woe betide then the unbelievers when their promised day is come!

THE MOUNT

In the Name of God, the Merciful, the Compassionate

52:1 BY THE Mount,[1] and by a Book penned on unrolled parchment; by the Visited House,[2] the Lofty Vault,[3] and the swelling sea, your Lord's punishment shall surely come to pass! No power shall ward it off.

On that day the heaven will shake and reel, and the mountains move and pass away. Woe betide on that day the unbelievers, who now divert themselves with profane talk.

On that day they shall be hurled into the fire of Hell: 'This is the Fire which you denied.

52:15 'Is this sorcery, or can you not see? Burn in its flames. It is the same whether or not you show forbearance. You shall be recompensed according only to your deeds.'

But in fair Gardens the righteous shall dwell in bliss, rejoicing in what their Lord will give them. Their Lord will shield them from the scourge of Hell. 'Eat and drink to your hearts' content, in recompense for what you did.'

They shall recline on couches ranged in rows. To dark-eyed houris We shall wed them.

52:21 We shall unite the true believers with those of their des-

1. Mount Sinai.   2. The Ka'bah.   3. The sky.

cendants who follow them in their faith, and shall not deny them the reward of their good works; each man is the hostage of his own deeds.

Fruits We shall give them, and such meats as they desire. They will pass from hand to hand a cup inspiring no idle talk, no sinful urge; and there shall wait on them young boys of their own, as fair as virgin pearls. 52:22

They will approach one another, asking questions. 'When we were living among our kin,' they will say, 'we were troubled by many fears. But God has been gracious to us; He has preserved us from the fiery scourge, for we prayed to Him in days gone by. He alone is the Beneficent One, the Compassionate.'

Therefore give warning. By the grace of God, you are neither soothsayer nor madman.

Or do they say: 'He is but a poet: we are waiting for the uncertainty of Fate to befall him'? Say: 'Wait if you will; I will wait with you.'

Or does their reason bid them say this? Or is it that they are wicked people? 52:32

Or do they say: 'He has invented it[1] himself'? Indeed, they have no faith. Let them produce a scripture like it, if what they say be true!

Or were they created out of the void? Or were they their own creators?

Or did *they* create the heavens and the earth? Surely they have no faith!

Or do they hold the treasures of your Lord, and have control absolute?

Or have they a ladder by means of which they overhear Him? Let their eavesdropper bring a positive proof!

Is He to have the daughters and you[2] the sons?

Or are you[3] demanding payment of them, that they should fear to be weighed down with debts?

Or have they knowledge of what is hidden? Can they write it down? 52:41

---

1. The Koran.   2. The unbelievers.   3. Muḥammad.

52:42 Or are they scheming? It is the unbelievers' schemes that shall come to nothing.

Or have they a deity other than God? Exalted be God above their idols!

And if they saw a piece of heaven falling down, they would still say: 'It is but a pile of clouds!'

So let them be, until they face the day when they shall stand dumbfounded; the day when their schemes shall be of no avail to them; and they shall not be helped.

And besides this a scourge awaits the wrongdoers, though most of them do not know it.

Await with patience the judgement of your Lord: you are ever in Our sight. And give glory to your Lord when you rise,

52:49 in the night-time praise Him, and at the setting of the stars.

THE STAR

In the Name of God, the Merciful, the Compassionate

53:1 BY THE star when it declines, your compatriot[1] is not in error, nor is he deceived!

He does not speak out of his own fancy. This is a revelation inspired. He is taught by one who is powerful and mighty.[2]

He stood on the uppermost horizon; then, drawing near, he came down within two bows' length or even closer, and revealed to His servant that which He revealed.

His[3] own heart did not deny his vision. Do you[4] doubt, then, what he beholds?

He beheld him once again at the sidra tree, beyond which no one may pass. Nearby is the Garden of Repose.

53:17 When that tree was covered with what covered it, his eyes

1. Muḥammad.
2. Gabriel.
3. Muḥammad's.
4. The unbelievers.

did not wander, nor did they turn aside: he beheld some of his 53:18
Lord's mightiest signs.

Have you thought on Al-Lāt and Al-'Uzzā, and on Manāt,
the third other?[1] Are you to have the male, and He the female?
This is indeed an unfair distinction!

They are but names which you and your forefathers have
invented; God has vested no authority in them. The unbelievers follow but vain conjectures and the whims of their own
souls, although the guidance of their Lord had long since
come to them.

Or is man to attain all that he desires? To God belongs the
life to come, and this first life.

Numerous are the angels in the heavens; yet their intercession shall avail nothing until God give leave to whom He wills
and accepts.

Those that disbelieve in the Hereafter call the angels by the
names of females. Yet of this they have no knowledge: they
follow mere conjecture, and conjecture is no substitute for
Truth.

Pay no heed, then, to those who ignore Our Admonition 53:29
and seek only the life of this world. This is the sum of their
knowledge. Your Lord best knows who has strayed from His
path, and He best knows who has followed the right guidance.

And to God belongs what the heavens and the earth contain. He will requite the evil-doers according to their deeds,
and richly recompense those who do good works.

To those who avoid the grossest sins and indecencies and
commit only small offences, your Lord will show abundant
forgiveness. He knew you well when He created you from
earth and when you were still in your mothers' wombs. Do
not pretend to purity; He best knows those who fear Him.

Have you considered him who turns his back, giving little
at first and then nothing at all? Does he know, and can he see,
what is hidden? Or has he not been told of what is writ in
the Scriptures of Moses and Abraham, who was true to his 53:37

1. Names of Arabian idols, claimed by the pagans of Mecca to be
daughters of God.

53:38 covenant: that no burdened soul shall bear another's burden, and that man shall be judged only by his labours; that his labours shall be scrutinized, and that he shall be justly requited for them; that all things shall in the end return to your Lord; that it is He who moves to laughter and to tears, and He who ordains death and life; that God created the two sexes, the male and the female, from a drop of ejaculated semen, and will bring about the other creation; that it is He who bestows and 53:49 enriches, He who is the Lord of Sirius;[1] that it was He who obliterated 'Ād at first and then Thamūd, sparing no one, and before them the people of Noah, who were more sinful and more rebellious. The Mu'tafikah[2] He also doomed, so that they were smitten by the scourge that smote them.

Which then of your Lord's blessings would you deny? He that now warns you is just like those who warned the others before you. That which is coming is near at hand; none but God can disclose the Hour.

Do you marvel then at this revelation, and laugh instead of 53:62 weeping? Making merry still? Rather prostrate yourselves before God, and worship.

THE MOON

In the Name of God, the Merciful, the Compassionate

54:1 THE HOUR is drawing near, and the moon is cleft in two. Yet, when they behold a sign, the unbelievers turn their backs and say: 'Sorcery unceasing!'

They deny the truth, and follow their own fancies. But in the end all issues shall be laid to rest.

Cautionary tales, profound in wisdom, have been narrated to them: but warnings are unavailing.

Let them be. The day the Crier summons them to the dread 54:7 account, they shall come out from their graves with downcast

---

1. The Dog Star, worshipped by the pagan Arabs.
2. The Ruined Cities, where Lot's people lived.

eyes, and rush towards him like swarming locusts. The un- 54:8 believers will say: 'This is indeed a doleful day!'

Before them, the people of Noah disbelieved. They disbelieved Our servant, and called him madman. Rejected and contemned, he cried out to his Lord, saying: 'Help me, I am overcome!'

We opened the gates of heaven with pouring rain and caused the earth to burst with gushing springs, so that the waters met for a predestined end. We carried him in a vessel built with planks and nails, which drifted on under Our eyes: a recompense for him who had been disbelieved.

This We have left as a sign: but is there any that will remember? How grievous was My scourge, and warning!

We have made the Koran easy to remember: but is there any that will remember?

'Ād, too, did not believe. How grievous was My scourge, and warning! On a day of unremitting woe, We let loose on them a howling wind which snapped people off like trunks of uprooted palm-trees. How grievous was My scourge, and warning!

We have made the Koran easy to remember: but is there 54:22 any that will remember?

Thamūd, too, disbelieved the warnings. They said: 'Are we to follow a mortal, alone among us? That would surely be error and madness. Did he alone among us receive the Admonition? He is indeed an impudent liar.'

'Tomorrow they shall learn who is the impudent liar. We are sending the she-camel to test them. Observe them closely and have patience. Tell them they must share their drink with her, and that for every draught they must attend in person.'

They called their friend, who took a knife and hamstrung her. How grievous was My scourge, and warning! A single cry was heard, and they became like the dry twigs of the sheepfold builder.

We have made the Koran easy to remember: but is there any that will remember?

The people of Lot disbelieved the warnings. We let loose 54:34 on them a stone-charged whirlwind: only the house of Lot at

54:35 dawn did We deliver, through Our mercy. Thus do We reward the thankful.

He had warned them of Our onslaught, but they doubted the warnings. They demanded his guests of him; so We put out their eyes: 'Taste My punishment, now that you have scorned My warnings!' And at daybreak a long-lasting scourge smote them. 'Taste My punishment, now that you have scorned My warnings!'

We have made the Koran easy to remember: but is there any that will remember?

To Pharaoh's people came the warnings. But they disbelieved all Our signs, and We smote them with the scourge of the Almighty, the Omnipotent.

Are your unbelievers better than those? Or have you immunity in the Scriptures?

54:44 Or do they say: 'We are a victorious army'? The army shall be routed and put to flight.

The Hour is their time appointed; and more calamitous, and more doleful, shall be the Hour.

Yet the wrongdoers persist in error and madness. On the day they are dragged into the Fire with faces down: 'Feel the touch of Hell!'

We have surely created all things according to a measure. We command but once: Our will is done in the twinkling of an eye.

We have destroyed many a people like yourselves: is there any that will remember?

All they did is in the Scriptures: every action, small or great, is noted down. The righteous shall dwell in Gardens watered 54:55 by running brooks, honourably seated in the presence of a Mighty King.

THE MERCIFUL[1]

In the Name of God, the Merciful, the Compassionate

IT IS the Merciful who has taught the Koran.   55:1

He created man and taught him articulate speech. The sun and the moon pursue their ordered course. The plants and the trees bow down in adoration.

The heaven He raised on high and set the Balance of all things, that you might not transgress that Balance. Give just weight and full measure, and do not cheat the Balance.

And the earth He laid for His creatures, with all its fruits and blossom-bearing palm, chaff-covered grain, and scented herbs. So which of your Lord's blessings would you[2] deny?

He created man from potter's clay, and the jinn from smokeless fire. So which of your Lord's blessings would you deny?

The Lord of the two easts[3] is He, and the Lord of the two   55:17
wests. So which of your Lord's blessings would you deny?

He has let loose the two seas:[4] they meet one another. Yet between them stands a barrier which they cannot overrun. So which of your Lord's blessings would you deny?

Pearls and corals come out from both. So which of your Lord's blessings would you deny?

His are the ships that sail like mountains upon the ocean. So which of your Lord's blessings would you deny?

All that live on earth are doomed to die. But the Face of your Lord will abide for ever, in all its majesty and glory. So which of your Lord's blessings would you deny?

All who dwell in heaven and earth entreat Him. Each day   55:29

1. Cf. this *sūrah* with Psalm 136.
2. The pronoun is in the dual number (i.e. the two of you), the words being addressed to mankind and the jinn. This refrain is repeated no fewer than 31 times.
3. The points at which the sun rises in summer and in winter.
4. Salt water and fresh water.

55:30 some mighty task engages Him. So which of your Lord's blessings would you deny?

Jinn and mankind, We shall surely find the time to judge you. So which of your Lord's blessings would you deny?

You race of jinn and mankind, if you have power to penetrate the confines of heaven and earth, then penetrate them. But this you shall not do except with Our own authority. So which of your Lord's blessings would you deny?

Flames of fire shall be lashed at you, and molten brass. There shall be none to help you. So which of your Lord's blessings would you deny?

When the sky splits asunder, and reddens like a rose or stainèd leather (so which of your Lord's blessings would you deny?), on that day neither man nor jinnee will be asked about his sins. So which of your Lord's blessings would you deny?

The transgressors will be known by their looks; they shall be seized by their forelocks and their feet. So which of your Lord's blessings would you deny?

55:44 That is the Hell the transgressors deny. They shall wander between fire and water fiercely seething. So which of your Lord's blessings would you deny?

But for those that fear the majesty of their Lord there are two Gardens (so which of your Lord's blessings would you deny?) planted with shady trees. So which of your Lord's blessings would you deny?

Each is watered by a flowing spring. So which of your Lord's blessings would you deny?

Each bears every kind of fruit in pairs. So which of your Lord's blessings would you deny?

They shall recline on couches lined with rich brocade, and within reach will hang the fruits of both Gardens. So which of your Lord's blessings would you deny?

Therein are bashful virgins whom neither man nor jinnee will have touched before. So which of your Lord's blessings would you deny?

55:59 Virgins as fair as corals and rubies. So which of your Lord's blessings would you deny?

Shall the reward of goodness be anything but good? So 55:61
which of your Lord's blessings would you deny?

And beside these there shall be two other Gardens (so
which of your Lord's blessings would you deny?) of darkest
green. So which of your Lord's blessings would you deny?

A gushing fountain shall flow in each. So which of your
Lord's blessings would you deny?

Each planted with fruit-trees, the palm and the pomegran- 55:68
ate. So which of your Lord's blessings would you deny?

In each there shall be virgins chaste and fair. So which of
your Lord's blessings would you deny?

Dark-eyed virgins, sheltered in their tents (so which of
your Lord's blessings would you deny?), whom neither man
nor jinnee will have touched before. So which of your Lord's
blessings would you deny?

They shall recline on green cushions and fine carpets. So
which of your Lord's blessings would you deny?

Blessed be the name of your Lord, the Lord of Majesty 55:78
and Glory!

THAT WHICH IS COMING

In the Name of God, the Merciful, the Compassionate

WHEN THAT which is coming comes – and no soul shall then 56:1
deny its coming – some shall be abased and others exalted.

When the earth shakes and quivers, and the mountains
crumble away and scatter abroad into fine dust, you shall be
divided into three multitudes: those on the right (blessed shall
be those on the right); those on the left (damned shall be
those on the left); and those to the fore (foremost shall be
those). Such are they that shall be brought near to their Lord
in the Gardens of Delight: a whole multitude from ages past,
and but a few from the latter age.

They shall recline on jewelled couches face to face, and
there shall wait on them immortal youths with bowls and
ewers and a cup of purest wine (that will neither pain their 56:19

56:20 heads nor take away their reason); with fruits of their own choice and flesh of fowls that they relish. And theirs shall be dark-eyed houris, chaste as virgin pearls: a guerdon for what they did.

Therein they shall hear no idle talk, no sinful speech, but only the greeting, 'Peace! Peace!'

Those on the right hand – happy shall be those on the right hand! They shall recline on couches raised on high in the shade of thornless sidrs and clusters of ṭalḥ;[1] amidst gushing waters and abundant fruits, never-ending, unforbidden.

We created the houris and made them virgins, loving companions for those on the right hand: a multitude from ages past, and a multitude from the latter age.

As for those on the left hand (wretched shall be those on the left hand!) they shall dwell amidst scorching winds and seething water: in the shade of pitch-black smoke, neither cool nor refreshing. For they have lived in comfort and persisted in the heinous sin,[2] saying: 'What! When we are dead and turned to dust and bones, shall we be raised to life? And our forefathers, too?'

56:49 Say: 'Those from ages past, and those from the latter age, shall be brought together at the time of an appointed day. Then, as for you who err and disbelieve, you shall eat from the Zaqqūm tree and fill your bellies with its fruit. You shall drink scalding water: yet you shall drink it as the thirsty camel drinks.'

Such shall be their fare on the Day of Reckoning.

We created you: why then will you not believe?

Behold the semen you discharge: did you create it, or were We its Creators?

It was We that ordained death among you. Nothing can hinder Us from replacing you by others like yourselves or transforming you into beings you know nothing of.

You surely know of the First Creation. Why, then, do you not reflect? Consider the earth you till. Is it you that sow the
56:65 seeds, or are We the Sowers? If We pleased, We could turn

---

1. Probably the banana tree.   2. Idolatry.

your harvest into chaff, so that you would keep forlornly jesting: 'We are laden with debt! Why, we have been robbed!'   56:67

Consider the water which you drink. Was it you that sent it
down from the cloud, or were We the Senders? If We pleased,
We could turn it bitter. Why, then, do you not give thanks?

Consider the fire which you light. Was it you that made the
timber, or were We the Makers? A reminder for man We made
it, and for the traveller a comfort.

Praise, then, the name of your Lord, the Supreme One.

I swear by the shelters of the stars (a mighty oath, if you
but knew it) that this is a holy Koran, safeguarded in a Book
which none may touch except the purified; a revelation sent
down from the Lord of the Universe.

Would you scorn a Scripture such as this, and earn your   56:82
daily bread denying it?

When under your very eyes a dying man's soul leaps up to
his throat (We are nearer to him than you, although you cannot see), why do you not restore it, if you are not to be judged
hereafter? If what you say be true?

Thus, if he is favoured, his lot will be repose and plenty,
and a Garden of Delight. If he is one of those on the right
hand, he will be greeted with 'Peace be with you!' by those on
the right hand.

But if he is an erring disbeliever, his welcome shall be a
downpour of scalding water, and incineration in a hell.

This is surely the veritable Truth. Praise, then, the name of   56:96
your Lord, the Supreme One.

IRON

In the Name of God, the Merciful, the Compassionate

ALL THAT is in the heavens and on the earth gives glory to   57:1
God. He is the Almighty, the Wise One.

He it is that has sovereignty over the heavens and the earth.   57:2
He ordains life and death, and has power over all things.

57:3 He is the First and the Last, the Visible and the Unseen. He has knowledge of all things.

He it was who created the heavens and the earth in six days, and then seated Himself upon the throne. He knows all that goes into the earth and all that comes out from it, all that descends from heaven and all that ascends to it. And He is with you wherever you are. God is cognizant of what you do.

He has sovereignty over the heavens and the earth. To God shall all things return. He causes the night to pass into the day, and causes the day to pass into the night. He has knowledge of one's innermost thoughts.

Have faith in God and His apostle and give from that which He has made your inheritance; for whoever of you believes and gives shall be richly recompensed.

And what cause have you not to believe in God, when the Apostle calls on you to believe in your Lord, with whom you have made a covenant, if you are true believers?

57:9 He it is who sends down clear revelations to His servant, that he may lead you out of darkness into the light. Surely God is benignant to you and compassionate.

And why should you not give in the cause of God, when God alone will inherit the heavens and the earth? Those of you that gave before the victory, and took part in the fighting, shall receive greater honour than those who gave and fought thereafter. Yet God has promised you all a good reward; God has knowledge of what you do.

Who will give a generous loan to God? He will pay him back twofold, and his shall be a noble recompense.

The day when you behold the believers, men and women, with their light shining before them and on their right hands: 'Rejoice this day, in Gardens watered by running brooks, wherein shall you abide for ever.' That is the supreme triumph.

On that day the hypocrites, men and women, will say to the believers: 'Wait for us, that we may borrow some of your light.' They will be told: 'Go back, and seek a light!'

57:14 A wall with a gate shall be set before them. Inside there shall be mercy, and without, to the fore, the torment. They will call out to them, saying: 'Were we not on your side?' 'Yes,' they will reply, 'but you tempted yourselves, you bided your time, you doubted, and were seduced by vain desires until God's will was done and the Dissembler misled you about God. Today no ransom shall be accepted from you, nor from the unbelievers. The Fire shall be your refuge: justly have you earned it, a wretched end!' 57:15

Is it not time for true believers to submit with humble hearts to God's remembrance and to the Truth He has revealed, that they may not be like those who were given the Book before this, whose days were prolonged and whose hearts were hardened? Many of them are ungodly.

Know that God restores the earth to life after its death. We have made Our revelations clear to you, that you may understand.

Those that give alms, be they men or women, and those that give a generous loan to God, shall be repaid twofold. Theirs shall be a noble recompense.

And those that believe in God and His apostles are the 57:19 men of Truth who shall testify in their Lord's presence. They shall have their guerdon and their light. But those that disbelieve Our revelations and deny them are the heirs of Hell.

Know that the life of this world is but a sport and a diversion, a show and an empty boast among you, a quest for greater riches and more children. It is like the plants that flourish after rain: the unbelievers rejoice to see them grow; but then they wither and turn yellow, soon becoming worthless stubble. In the life to come there is a grievous scourge, forgiveness from God and good pleasure. The life of this world is but a pleasurable delusion.

Therefore vie for the pardon of your Lord, and for a Paradise as vast as heaven and earth, prepared for those who believe in God and His apostles. Such is the grace of God: He bestows it on whom He will. God's grace is infinite.

No misfortune befalls the earth, or your own persons, but is ordained before We bring it into being. That is easy enough for God; so that you may not grieve for the good things you miss, 57:23 or be overjoyed at what you gain. God does not love the

57:24 haughty, the vainglorious; nor those who, being niggardly themselves, enjoin people to be niggardly. As for him that pays no heed – God alone is self-sufficient and worthy of praise.

We have sent Our apostles with signs manifest, and with them sent down the Book and the Balance, that people might conduct themselves with fairness. We have sent down iron, with its mighty strength and diverse uses for mankind, that God may recognize those who aid Him, though unseen, and His apostles. Strong is God, and mighty.

We sent forth Noah and Abraham, and bestowed on their offspring prophethood and the Book. Some were rightly 57:27 guided, but many were degenerate. In their trail We sent Our apostles, and after those Jesus son of Mary. We gave him the Gospel, and put compassion and mercy in the hearts of his followers. As for monasticism, they instituted it themselves (for We had not enjoined it on them), seeking thereby to please God; but they did not observe it faithfully. We rewarded only those who believed; many of them were degenerate.

Believers, fear God and put your trust in His apostle. He will grant you a double share of His mercy, He will bestow on you a light to walk in, and He will forgive you: God is forgiving and compassionate.

57:29 Let the People of the Book recognize that they have no control over anything within the grace of God, and that grace is in His hands alone; He vouchsafes it to whom He will, and God's grace is infinite.

SHE WHO PLEADED

In the Name of God, the Merciful, the Compassionate

58:1 GOD HAS surely heard the words of her[1] who pleaded with you against her husband and made her plaint to God. God has

---

1. Khawlah, daughter of Tha'labah, who had been divorced by the formula: 'Be to me as my mother's back', which was accepted as a declaration of divorce among pagan Arabs.

heard what you two said to each other. Surely God hears all and observes all.

Those of you who divorce their wives by declaring them to be their mothers' backs should know that they are *not* their mothers. Their mothers are only those who bore them. The words they utter are unjust and false: but God pardons and forgives. 58:2

Those that divorce their wives by so saying, and afterwards retract their words, shall free a slave[1] before they touch each other again. This you are enjoined to do: God is cognizant of what you do. He that has no slave shall fast two successive months before they touch one another. He that cannot shall feed sixty of the destitute. Thus it is, so that you may believe in God and His apostle. Such are the bounds set by God. Woeful punishment awaits the unbelievers.

Those that oppose God and His apostle shall be brought low, as have been those before them. We have sent down distinct revelations. Shameful punishment awaits the unbelievers.

On the day when God restores them all to life He will tell them what they did. God had counted their deeds, and they forgot them. God is witness of all things. 58:6

Are you not aware that God knows what the heavens and the earth contain? If three confer in secret, He is their fourth; if five, He is their sixth; whether fewer or more, He is with them wherever they be. Then, on the Day of Resurrection, He will inform them of their doings. God has knowledge of all things.

Have you not seen those who, though forbidden to intrigue in secret, defiantly intrigue together in sin and enmity and disobedience to the Apostle? When they come to you, they salute you in words which God does not greet you with, and ask themselves: 'Why does God not punish us for what we say?' Hell is scourge enough for them: in its flames they shall burn, a wretched fate!

Believers, when you converse in private do not speak in sin and enmity and disobedience to the Apostle, but with justice 58:9

1. As a penalty.

and with piety; and fear God, before whom you shall be herded.

58:10   Intrigue is the work of Satan, who means to vex the faithful. Yet he can harm them not at all, except by the will of God. In God let the faithful put their trust.

Believers, make room[1] in your assemblies when you are bidden so to do: God will make room for you hereafter. Again, rise up when you are told to rise: God will raise to high ranks those of you that believe and those endowed with knowledge. God is cognizant of what you do.

You believers, when you confer with the Apostle, give alms before such conference. That is better and more righteous for you. But if you lack the means, God is forgiving and compassionate.

Do you hesitate to offer alms before you confer with him? If you do not (and God will pardon your offence), then at least recite your prayers and render the alms levy and obey God and His apostle. God is cognizant of what you do.

58:14   Do you see those that have befriended a people with whom God is angry? They belong neither to you nor to them. They knowingly swear to falsehood. God has prepared for them a grievous scourge. Evil indeed is that which they have done.

They use their faith as a disguise, and debar others from the path of God. Shameful punishment awaits them.

Their wealth and children shall in no way protect them from God. They are the inmates of the Fire, wherein shall they abide for ever.

On the day when God restores them all to life, they will swear to Him as they now swear to you, imagining that their oaths will help them. Surely it is they who are lying.

Satan has gained possession of them, and caused them to forget God's Admonition. They are the confederates of Satan; but Satan's confederates will surely be the losers.

Those that oppose God and His apostle shall be brought
58:21   low. God has decreed: 'I will surely triumph, Myself and My apostles.' Powerful is God, and mighty.

---

1. For the Prophet, or for your fellow-Muslims.

You shall find no believers in God and in the Last Day on 58:22
friendly terms with those who oppose God and His apostle,
even though they be their fathers, their sons, their brothers, or
their nearest kin. God has inscribed the Faith in their very
hearts, and strengthened them with a spirit of His own. He will
usher them into Gardens watered by running brooks, wherein
shall they abide for ever. God is well pleased with them, and
they are well pleased with Him. They are the confederates of
God: and God's confederates will surely triumph.

EXILE

In the Name of God, the Merciful, the Compassionate

ALL THAT is in the heavens and on the earth gives glory to 59:1
God. He is the Omnipotent, the Wise One.

He it was that drove the unbelievers among the People of
the Book out of their dwellings into the first exile.[1] You did
not think that they would go; and they, for their part, fancied
that their strongholds would protect them from God. But
God smote them whence they did not expect, casting such
terror into their hearts that their dwellings were destroyed by
their own hands as well as by the faithful. Learn from their
example, you that have eyes.

Had God not decreed exile[2] for them, He would have 59:3
surely punished them in this world. But in the world to come
the torment of the Fire awaits them, because they had set
themselves against God and His apostle; and he that sets himself against God should know that God is stern in retribution.

It was by God's leave that you cut down or spared their
palm-trees, so that He might humiliate the ungodly. As for 59:6
those spoils of theirs which God has assigned to His apostle,
you spurred neither horse nor camel to capture them: but

1. An allusion to Muḥammad's expedition against the Jews of Banu
al-Naḍīr in Arabia.
2. Mostly to Syria.

375

God gives His apostles authority over whom He will; and God has power over all things.

59:7 The spoils taken from the town-dwellers and assigned by God to His apostle shall belong to God, to the Apostle and his kin, to orphans, to the destitute and to the traveller in need; they shall not become the property of the rich among you. Whatever the Apostle gives you, take it; and whatever he forbids you, abstain from it. Fear God; God is stern in retribution.

They shall also be for the poor among the *muhājirīn*[1] who have been driven from their homes and their possessions, who seek God's grace and pleasure and who help God and His apostle; these are the true believers.

Those who stayed in their own city[2] and embraced the Faith before them, love those who have sought refuge with them; they do not covet what they are given, but rather prize them above themselves, though they are in want. Those that preserve themselves from their own greed shall surely prosper.

59:10 Those that came after them say: 'Forgive us, Lord, and forgive our brothers who embraced the Faith before us. Remove from our hearts any rancour towards the faithful. Lord, You are benignant and compassionate.'

Do but consider the hypocrites. They say to their fellow-unbelievers among the People of the Book: 'If you are driven out, we will go with you. We will never obey anyone who seeks to harm you. If you are attacked, we will certainly help you.'

God bears witness that they are lying. If they are driven out, they will not go with them, nor, if they are attacked, will they help them. Indeed, if they do go to their help, they will take to their heels and leave them in the lurch.

Their dread of you is more intense in their hearts than their fear of God: so devoid are they of understanding.

They will never fight against you in a body except in fortified cities and from behind walls. Great is their valour among themselves; you think of them as one band, yet their hearts are divided; for they are surely lacking in judgement.

59:15 Like those who were but recently punished before them,

---

1. See p. 132, note 1.   2. Medina.

they tasted the fruit of their own deeds. And woeful punishment awaits them.

They may be compared to Satan, who, when he ordered man to disbelieve and he did his bidding, said to him: 'I do disown you. I fear God, Lord of the Universe.'

They shall both end in the Fire and therein abide for ever. Thus shall the wrongdoers be rewarded.

Believers, have fear of God. Let every soul look to what it offers for the morrow. Fear God; God is cognizant of what you do.

Do not act like those who forgot God, so that He caused them to forget themselves. Such are the ungodly.

The heirs of the Fire and the heirs of Paradise shall not be held equal. The heirs of Paradise alone shall be triumphant.

Had We brought down this Koran upon a mountain, you would have seen it humble itself and break asunder for fear of God.

In such parables We speak to people, that they may take thought.

He is God, besides whom there is no other deity. He knows the unknown and the manifest. He is the Merciful, the Compassionate.

He is God, besides whom there is no other deity. He is the Sovereign Lord, the Holy One, the Giver of Peace, the Keeper of Faith; the Preserver, the Almighty, the All-powerful, the Most High. Exalted be God above their idols.

He is God, the Creator, the Originator, the Modeller. His are the most gracious names. All that is in the heavens and the earth gives glory to Him. He is the Almighty, the Wise One.

SHE WHO IS TESTED

In the Name of God, the Merciful, the Compassionate

BELIEVERS, DO not make friends with those who are enemies of Mine and yours. Would you show them affection, when they have denied the Truth that has been revealed to you and driven out the Apostle and yourselves, because you believe in God, your Lord?

If it was indeed to fight for My cause, and out of a desire to please Me, that you left your city, how can you be friendly to them in secret? I well know all that you conceal, and all that you reveal. Whoever of you does this will stray from the right path.

60:2 If they gain ascendancy over you, they will prove themselves your enemies, and stretch out their hands and tongues to you with evil. They long to see you unbelievers.

On the Day of Resurrection, neither your kin nor your children shall avail you. He will separate you, and God is cognizant of what you do.

You have a good example in Abraham and those who followed him. They said to their people: 'We disown you and the idols which you worship besides God. We renounce you: enmity and hate shall reign between us until you believe in God alone.' But do not emulate the words of Abraham to his father: 'I shall implore forgiveness for you, although I can in no way protect you from God.'

60:5 'Lord, in You we have put our trust; to You we turn and to You we shall come at last. Lord, do not expose us to the designs of the unbelievers. Forgive us, Lord; You are the Almighty, the Wise One.'

Surely in those there is a good example for you; for everyone who puts his hopes in God and in the Last Day. As for him that pays no heed, God alone is self-sufficient and worthy of praise.

It may well be that God will put good will between you and those with whom you have hitherto been at odds. God is mighty; God is forgiving and compassionate.

God does not forbid you to be kind and equitable to those who have neither fought you on account of your Religion nor 60:9 driven you from your homes; God loves the equitable. But He forbids you to make friends with those who have fought you on account of your religion and driven you from your homes or abetted others to drive you out. Those that make friends with them are the wrongdoers.

Believers, when believing women seek refuge with you, test 60:10
them. God best knows their faith. If you find them true
believers, do not return them to the infidels; they are not lawful for the infidels, nor are the infidels lawful for them. Hand
back to them the dowries they gave; nor is it an offence for
you to marry such women, if you give them their dowries. Do
not maintain your marriages with unbelieving women: demand
the dowries you gave and let them demand the dowries they
gave. Such is the judgement which God lays down among you.
God is all-knowing and wise.

And if any of your wives go over to the infidels and you 60:11
subsequently gain victory over them, pay those whose wives
have deserted the equivalent of the dowries they gave them.
And fear God, in whom you do believe.

Prophet, if believing women come to you and pledge
themselves to serve no other deity besides God, to commit
neither theft, nor adultery, nor child-murder, to utter no monstrous falsehoods of their own invention, and to disobey you
in nothing reasonable, accept their allegiance and implore
God to forgive them. Surely God is forgiving and compassionate.

Believers, do not make friends with people who have pro- 60:13
voked the wrath of God; for they have despaired of the life to
come, just as the infidels have despaired of the buried dead.

BATTLE ARRAY

In the Name of God, the Merciful, the Compassionate

ALL THAT is in the heavens and on the earth gives glory to 61:1
God. He is the Almighty, the Wise One.

Believers, why do you profess what you never do? It is
most odious in God's sight that you should say one thing and
do another.

God loves those who fight for His cause in ranks as firm as
a mighty edifice.

Tell of Moses, who said to his people: 'Why do you seek to 61:5

harm me, my people, when you know that I am sent to you by God?' And when they went astray, God led their very hearts astray. God does not guide the ungodly.

61:6 And of Jesus son of Mary, who said to the Israelites: 'I am sent forth to you from God to confirm the Torah already revealed, and to give joyful tidings of an apostle that will come after me whose name is Aḥmad.'[1] Yet when he brought them conspicuous signs, they said: 'This is sorcery manifest.'

And who is more wicked than he that invents a falsehood about God when called to Islām? God does not guide the wrongdoers.

They seek to extinguish the light of God with their mouths; but God will perfect His light, much as the infidels may dislike it.

He it is who has sent forth His apostle with guidance and the Religion of Truth that he may exalt it above all religion, much as the idolaters may dislike it.

61:10 Believers! Shall I point out to you a profitable course that will save you from a woeful scourge? Have faith in God and His apostle, and fight for God's cause with your wealth and with your persons; that would be best for you, if you but knew it.

He will forgive you your sins and admit you into Gardens watered by running brooks; He will lodge you in goodly mansions in the Gardens of Eden. That is the supreme triumph.

And He will bestow upon you other blessings which you desire: help from God and a speedy victory. Proclaim the joyful tidings to the faithful.

61:14 Believers, be God's helpers. When Jesus son of Mary said to the disciples: 'Who will come with me to the help of God?' the disciples replied: '*We* are God's helpers.'

Some among the Israelites believed, while some did not believe. We aided the believers against their enemies, and when morning came they were triumphant.

---

1. Another name of Muḥammad's, also meaning 'The Praised One'.

FRIDAY, OR THE DAY OF CONGREGATION

In the Name of God, the Merciful, the Compassionate

ALL THAT is in the heavens and on the earth gives glory to 62:1
God, the Sovereign Lord, the Holy One, the Almighty, the
Wise One.

He it is that has sent forth among the Gentiles an apostle
of their own to recite to them His revelations, to purify them,
and to instruct them in the Book and in wisdom, though they
have hitherto been in evident error, together with others of
their own kin who have not yet followed them. He is the
Almighty, the Wise One.

Such is the grace of God: He bestows it on whom He will.
His grace is infinite.

Those to whom the burden of the Torah was entrusted 62:5
and yet refused to bear it are like a donkey laden with books.
Wretched is the example of those who deny God's revelations; and God does not guide the wrongdoers.

Say: 'You that follow the Jewish Faith, if you claim that of
all people you alone are God's friends, then you should wish
for death, if what you say be true!' But, because of what their
hands have done, they will never wish for death; God knows
the wrongdoers.

Say: 'The death from which you flee is sure to overtake you.
Then shall you be sent back to Him who knows the unknown
and the manifest, and He will declare to you what you have done.'

Believers, when you are summoned to Friday prayers hasten
to the remembrance of God and cease your trading. That
would be best for you, if you but knew it. Then, when the
prayers are ended, disperse and go your ways in quest of God's
bounty. Remember God much, that you may prosper.

Yet no sooner do they see some commerce or merriment 62:11
afoot than they flock eagerly to it, leaving you[1] standing.

1. Muḥammad.

381

Say: 'That which God has in store is far better than any merriment or any commerce. And God is the Most Munificent Giver.'

THE HYPOCRITES

In the Name of God, the Merciful, the Compassionate

63:1 WHEN THE hypocrites come to you they say: 'We bear witness that you are assuredly God's apostle.' God knows that you are indeed His apostle; and God bears witness that the hypocrites are surely lying.

They use their faith as a disguise, and debar others from the path of God. Evil is what they ever do.

They believed and then renounced the Faith: their hearts are sealed, so that they are devoid of understanding.

When you see them, their good looks please you; and when they speak, you listen to what they say. Yet they are like propped-up beams of timber. Every shout they hear they take to be against them. *They* are the enemy. Guard yourself against them. God smite them! How perverse they are!

63:5 When they are told: 'Come, God's apostle will beg forgiveness for you,' they turn their heads and you see them go away in scorn.

It is the same for them whether or not you ask forgiveness for them: God will not forgive them. God does not guide the ungodly.

It is they who say: 'Give nothing to those that follow God's apostle until they have deserted.' God's are the treasures of the heavens and the earth: but the hypocrites cannot understand.

They say: 'If we return to Madīnah,[1] the strong will soon drive out the weak.' But strength belongs to God and to His apostle and to the faithful: yet the hypocrites do not know it.

63:9 Believers, let neither your riches nor your children divert

1. To which the Prophet and his followers had fled from Mecca.

you from remembering God. Those that are so diverted will surely be the losers.

Give, then, of that which We have given you before death 63:10 befalls any of you and he should say: 'Reprieve me, Lord, for a short time, that I may give in charity and be among the righteous.'

But God reprieves no soul when its term expires. And God 63:11 is cognizant of what you do.

CHEATING

In the Name of God, the Merciful, the Compassionate

ALL THAT is in the heavens and on the earth gives glory to 64:1 God. His is the sovereignty, and His all praise. And He has power over all things.

He it was that created you: yet some among you are unbelievers, and some have faith. God observes what you do.

He created the heavens and the earth to manifest the Truth, and fashioned you into a comely shape. To Him shall all return.

He knows what the heavens and the earth contain; He knows what you conceal and what you reveal. God well knows your innermost thoughts.

Have you not heard of those who disbelieved before you? 64:5 They tasted the baleful consequences of their unbelief, and grievous punishment is yet in store for them. That is because, 64:6 when their apostles brought them veritable signs, they said: 'Shall mortals be our guides?' They disbelieved and paid no heed. But God was in no need of them: God is self-sufficient and worthy of praise.

The unbelievers say they will not be raised to life. Say: 'Yes, by the Lord, you shall assuredly be raised to life! Then you shall be told of all that you have done. That is easy enough for God.'

Believe then in God and in His apostle, and in the light We 64:8 have revealed. God is cognizant of what you do.

64:9 The day He gathers you, the day on which you shall all be gathered – that shall be a day of cheating.[1] Those that believe in God and do what is right shall be forgiven their sins and ushered into Gardens watered by running brooks, wherein shall they abide for ever. That is the supreme triumph. But those that disbelieve and deny Our revelations shall be the inmates of the Fire, wherein shall they abide for ever: a wretched fate!

No misfortune strikes except by God's leave. He guides the hearts of those who believe in Him; God has knowledge of all things.

And obey God and obey the Apostle. If you pay no heed, Our apostle's duty is only to give the veritable warning.

64:13 God – there is no god but Him; in God let the faithful put their trust.

Believers, in your spouses and in your children you have an enemy: beware of them. But if you overlook their offences and forgive and pardon them, then know that God is forgiving and compassionate.

Your wealth and your children are but a temptation. God's recompense is great: therefore fear God with all your hearts, and be attentive, obedient, and charitable. That will be best for you.

Those that preserve themselves from their own greed will surely prosper. If you give a generous loan to God, He will pay you back twofold and will forgive you. Gracious is God, and benignant.

64:18 He has knowledge of the unknown and the manifest. He is the Almighty, the Wise One.

---

1. I.e. when the blessed will 'cheat' the damned of their places in Paradise which would have been theirs had they been true believers (Al-Bayḍāwī).

DIVORCE

In the Name of God, the Merciful, the Compassionate

PROPHET (AND you believers), if you divorce your wives, 65:1
divorce them at the end of their waiting period. Compute
their waiting period and fear God, your Lord. You shall not
expel them from their homes, nor shall they go away, unless
they have committed a proven lewd act. Such are the bounds
set by God; he that transgresses God's bounds wrongs his
own soul. You never know; after that, God may bring about
some new event.

When their waiting term is ended, either keep them honourably or part with them in honour. Call to witness two
honest men among you and give your testimony before God.
Whoever believes in God and the Last Day is exhorted to do
this. He that fears God, He will give him a means of salvation
and will provide for him whence he does not reckon: God is 65:3
all-sufficient for whoever puts his trust in Him. God will
surely bring about what He decrees. God has set a measure
for all things.

If you are in doubt concerning those of your wives who
have ceased menstruating, know that their waiting period shall
be three months. The same shall apply to those who have not
yet menstruated.[1] As for pregnant women, their term shall
end with their confinement. God will ease the hardship of the
man who fears Him.

Such is the commandment God has revealed to you. He
that fears God shall be forgiven his sins and richly recompensed.

Lodge them in your own homes, according to your means, 65:6
and you shall not harass them so as to make life intolerable for
them. If they are with child, maintain them until the end of
their confinement; and if, after that, they give suck to the
infants they bore you, give them their pay and consult together

1. On account of their young age. Child marriages were common.

in all reasonableness. But if you cannot tolerate each other, let other women suckle for you.

65:7 Let the rich man spend according to his wealth, and the poor man according to what God has given him. God does not charge a soul with more than He has given it; God, after hardship, will bring ease.

How many communities have rebelled against the commandments of their Lord and His apostles! Stern was Our reckoning with them, and harrowing was Our scourge. They tasted the baleful consequence of their misdeeds: and the consequence of their 65:10 misdeeds was perdition. God has prepared for them a grievous scourge. So fear God, you that are of good sense possessed.

God has now sent down to you an Admonition; an apostle proclaiming to you God's revelations in all plainness, so that he may lead the faithful who do good works from darkness to the light. He that believes in God and does good works shall be admitted to Gardens watered by running brooks, wherein shall he abide for ever. God has made for him a rich provision.

65:12 God it was who created seven heavens, and earths as many. The commandment descends through them, that you may learn that God has power over all things, and that God encompasses all things with His knowledge.

PROHIBITION

In the Name of God, the Merciful, the Compassionate

66:1 PROPHET, WHY do you prohibit that which God has made lawful for you, in seeking to please your wives?[1] And God is forgiving and compassionate.

1. Muḥammad, according to the Muslim commentators, was once found by his wife Ḥafṣah with a Coptic slave from whom he had promised her to separate. Of this Ḥafṣah secretly informed 'Ā'ishah, another wife of his. To free Muḥammad from his promise to Ḥafṣah was the object of this *sūrah*. Some of the references are obscure.

God has given you absolution from such oaths. God is · 66:2 your Master. He is the Omniscient One, the Wise One.

When the Prophet confided a secret to one of his wives; and when she disclosed it and God informed him of this, he made known one part of it and said nothing about the other. And when he had acquainted her with it she said: 'Who told you this?' He said: 'The All-knowing, the Wise One, told me.'

If you two[1] turn to God in repentance, for your hearts have sinned, you shall be pardoned; but if you conspire against him, know that God is his protector, and Gabriel, and the righteous among the faithful. The angels too are his helpers.

It may well be that, if he divorce you, his Lord will give him in your place better wives than yourselves, submissive to God and full of faith, obedient, penitent, devout, and given to fasting; both formerly-wedded and virgins.

Believers, guard yourselves and your kin against a Fire · 66:6 fuelled with men and stones, in the charge of stern and mighty angels who never disobey God's command and promptly do whatever they are bidden. 'You that disbelieve, make no excuses for yourselves this day. You shall be rewarded but according to what you did.'

Believers, turn to God in true repentance. Your Lord may pardon you your sins and admit you into Gardens watered by running brooks, on a day when the Prophet and those who believe with him will suffer no disgrace at the hands of God. Their light will shine in front of them and on their right, and they will say: 'Lord, perfect our light for us and forgive us; You have power over all things.'

Prophet, make war on the unbelievers and the hypocrites, and deal sternly with them. Hell shall be their home, evil their fate.

God gave an example to the unbelievers in the wife of · 66:10 Noah and the wife of Lot. They were married to two of Our righteous servants and betrayed them. Their husbands could

---

1. Ḥafṣah and ʿĀʾishah.

in no way protect them from God; they were told: 'Enter the Fire with those that shall enter it.'

66:11 But to the faithful God gave an example in Pharaoh's wife, who said: 'Lord, build me a house with You in Paradise and deliver me from Pharaoh and his misdeeds. Deliver me from the wrongdoing people.'

66:12 And in Mary, 'Imrān's daughter, who preserved her chastity and into whose womb We breathed Our spirit; who put her trust in the words of her Lord and His Scriptures, and was truly devout.

SOVEREIGNTY

In the Name of God, the Merciful, the Compassionate

67:1 BLESSED BE He who in His hand holds sovereignty: He has power over all things; who created death and life that He might put you to the proof as to which of you acquitted themselves best: He is the Almighty, the Forgiving One; who created seven heavens, one above the other. You will not see a flaw in the Merciful's creation; turn up your eyes: can you detect a single crack?

Then look once more and yet again: your eyes will in the end grow dim and weary.

67:5 We have adorned the lowest heaven with lamps, missiles to pelt the demons with. For these We have prepared the torment of the Conflagration, and for those who deny their Lord the scourge of Hell: a wretched fate!

When they are flung therein, they shall hear it roaring and seething, as though bursting with rage. Every time a multitude is thrown in, its keepers will ask them: 'Did no one come to warn you?' 'Yes,' they will say, 'he did come, but we disbelieved and said: "God has revealed nothing: you are but in grievous error."' And they will say: 'If only we had listened and understood, we should not now be among the inmates of

67:11 the Conflagration.' Thus shall they confess their sin. Cursed be the inmates of the Conflagration!

But those that fear their Lord although unseen shall be
forgiven and richly recompensed.

Whether you speak in private or aloud, He surely knows
your innermost thoughts. Shall He who has created all, not
know them all? Gracious is He and all-knowing.

He it is who has made the earth subservient to you. Walk
about its regions and eat of His provisions. To Him shall all
return at the Resurrection.

Are you confident that He who is in heaven will not cause
the earth to cave in beneath you, so that it will shake to pieces?

Are you confident that He who is in heaven will not let
loose on you a sandy whirlwind? You will surely learn then
what My warning was like.

Those who have gone before them likewise disbelieved:
but how grievous was the way I rejected them!

Do they not see the birds above their heads, spreading their
wings and folding them? None save the Merciful sustains
them. He surely observes all things.

Who is it that will defend you like an army, if not the Merciful? Truly, the unbelievers are in error.

Who will provide for you if *He* withholds His sustenance?
Yet they persist in arrogance and in rebellion.

Is he that goes grovelling on his face more rightly guided
than he that walks upright upon a straight path?

Say: 'He it was who brought you into being, and gave you
ears and eyes and hearts. Yet you are seldom thankful.'

Say: 'He it was who placed you on the earth, and to Him
shall you be herded.'

And they say: 'When will this promise be fulfilled, if what
you say be true?'

Say: 'God alone has knowledge of that. I am only to give a
veritable warning.'

But when they see it drawing near, the unbelievers' faces
will be contorted with woe, and a voice will say: 'This is the
doom which you have challenged.'

Say: 'Consider: whether God destroys me and all my followers or has mercy upon us, who will protect the unbelievers
from a woeful scourge?'

67:29   Say: 'He is the Lord of Mercy: in Him we believe, and in Him we put our trust. You shall soon learn who is in evident error.'

67:30   Say: 'Consider: if all the water that you have were to sink down into the earth, who would give you running water in its place?'

THE PEN

In the Name of God, the Merciful, the Compassionate

68:1   *Nūn*. By the Pen, and what they[1] write, you[2] are not a man possessed: thanks to the favour of your Lord! A lasting recompense awaits you, for yours is a sublime nature. You shall before long see – as they will see – which of you is enchanted.

Your Lord knows best those who stray from His path, as He knows best those who are rightly guided. Yield not to the disbelievers: they desire you to overlook their doings that they

68:10   may overlook yours. Nor yield to the wretch of many oaths, the mischief-making slanderer, the opponent of good, the sinful transgressor, the bully who is of doubtful birth to boot. Though such a man be blessed with wealth and children, when Our revelations are recited to him, he says: 'Fables of the ancients.' On the nose We will brand him!

We have afflicted them[3] as We afflicted the owners of the orchard who had declared that they would pluck its fruit next morning, without adding any reservation.[4] A visitant from your Lord came down upon it while they slept, and in the morning it was as black as midnight.

68:22   In the morning they called out to one another: 'Hurry to

1. The angels.
2. Muḥammad.
3. The Meccans.
4. Without saying: 'If God wills.'

your orchard, if you would pick its fruit.' And off they went, 68:23
whispering to one another: 'No beggar shall enter it today.'

Thus they went out, fixed in their resolve. But when they saw it they said: 'We have erred indeed; we are bereft.'

The most upright among them said: 'Did I not bid you give praise?'

'Glory be to our Lord,' they said. 'We have assuredly done wrong.' And they began to blame one another.

'Woe betide us!' they said. 'We have been great transgressors. Perchance our Lord will give us a better one in its place; to our Lord we will turn.'

Such was their torment. But the torment of the life to come is more terrible, if they but knew it.

In the Gardens of Delight the righteous shall be with their Lord. Are We to treat the Muslims and the sinners alike? What has come over you[1] that you should judge so ill?

Or have you a scripture to study promising you whatever 68:37
you choose? Or have We sworn a covenant with you – a covenant binding till the Day of Resurrection – that you shall have what you yourselves ordain? Ask if any of them[1] will vouch for that!

Or have they other deities besides God? Let them produce their deities, if what they say be true!

On the day the dread event unfolds and they are told to prostrate themselves, they will not be able. Utterly humbled, they shall stand with eyes downcast; for they had long since been bidden to prostrate themselves when they were safe and sound.

Therefore leave to Me those that deny this revelation. We will lead them on step by step, in ways beyond their knowledge. I shall bear long with them: My stratagem is sure.

Are you demanding pay of them, so that they are burdened with debt?

Or have they knowledge of what is hidden? Can they write it down?

Wait, then, the judgement of your Lord and do not act like 68:48

---

1. The unbelievers.

68:49 him[1] who was swallowed by the whale when he called out in despair. Had his Lord not bestowed on him His grace, he would have been abandoned in the open to be blamed by all. But his Lord chose him for His own and made of him a righteous man.

The unbelievers well-nigh devour you with their eyes when they hear the Admonition. 'He is assuredly possessed,' they say.

68:52 Yet it is but an Admonition to mankind.

THE CATASTROPHE

In the Name of God, the Merciful, the Compassionate

69:1 THE CATASTROPHE: and what is the Catastrophe? Would that you knew what the Catastrophe is!

Thamūd and 'Ād denied the Last Judgement. By a deafening shout was Thamūd destroyed, and 'Ād by a howling, violent gale which He let loose on them for seven nights and eight successive days: you might have seen the people lying dead as though they had been hollow trunks of palm-trees. Can you see even one of them still around?

69:9 Pharaoh, and those before him, and the inhabitants of the Ruined Cities, also committed sin and disobeyed their Lord's apostle. With a terrible scourge He smote them.

When the Flood rose high We carried you[2] in the floating ark, making it a memorable event, that all attentive ears might heed it.

When the Trumpet sounds a single blast; when earth and mountains are raised high and with one mighty crash are flattened into dust – on that day the Dread Event will come to pass.

The sky will be rent asunder on that day, frail and tottering; and the angels will stand on every side with eight of them

69:18 carrying the Throne of your Lord above their heads. On that day you shall be utterly exposed, and nothing that you hid shall be hidden.

1. Jonah. 2. I.e. your forefathers.

He who is given his Book in his right hand will say: 'Here it is, 69:19 read my Book! I knew I should come face to face with my account!' His shall be a blissful state in a lofty Garden, with clusters of fruit within his reach. 'Eat and drink to your heart's content: your recompense for what you did in days gone by.'

But he who is given his Book in his left hand will say: 'Would that I were not given my Book! Would that I knew nothing of my account! Would that my death had ended all! Nothing has my wealth availed me, and bereft am I of all my power.'

'Lay hold of him and bind him. Then burn him in the fire of Hell, and then fasten him with a chain seventy cubits long. For he did not believe in God, the Most Great, nor did he care to feed the destitute. Today he shall be friendless here; only 69:35 filth shall be his food, the filth which only sinners eat.'

I swear by all that you can see, and all that is hidden from your view, that this is the utterance of a noble messenger. It is no poet's speech: scant is your faith! It is no soothsayer's divination: how little you reflect! It is a revelation from the Lord of the Universe.

Had he invented lies concerning Us, We would have seized him by the right hand and severed his heart's vein: not one of you could have protected him!

It[1] is but an Admonition to the righteous. We well know that there are some among you who will deny it.

It is the despair of the unbelievers. It is the indubitable Truth. Praise, then, the name of your Lord, the Almighty. 69:52

THE STAIRWAYS

In the Name of God, the Merciful, the Compassionate

A SCEPTIC[2] once demanded that punishment be visited forth- 70:1 with upon the unbelievers.

No power can hinder God from punishing them. He is the 70:3

---

1. The Koran.   2. Literally, a questioner.

70:4 Lord of the Stairways, whereby the angels and the Spirit shall ascend to Him in one day whose space is fifty thousand years.

Therefore conduct yourself with becoming patience. They think the Day of Judgement is far off: but We see it near at hand.

On that day the sky shall become like molten brass, and the mountains like tufts of wool scattered in the wind. No bosom friend shall ask a bosom friend when eye meets eye. To redeem himself from the torment of that day the sinner will gladly sacrifice his children, his consort, his brother, his kin who gave him shelter, and all that are on the earth, if then this might deliver him.

But no! The fire of Hell shall drag him down by the scalp, shall claim him who had turned his back and amassed riches and covetously hoarded them.

Indeed, man was created impatient. When evil befalls him he is despondent; but, blessed with good fortune, he grows niggardly.

70:22 Not so the worshippers who are steadfast in prayer; who set aside a due portion of their wealth for the beggar and for the dispossessed; who truly believe in the Day of Reckoning, and dread the punishment of their Lord (for none is secure from the punishment of their Lord); who restrain their carnal desire (save with their wives and slave-girls, for with these they are blameless: transgressors are those who lust after other than these); who keep their trusts and promises and bear true witness; and who attend to their prayers with promptitude. These shall be laden with honours in fair Gardens.

But what has befallen the unbelievers, that they scramble towards you in multitudes from right and left?

Are they each seeking to enter a Garden of Delight?

No! Of what We created them they know full well.

I swear by the Lord of the easts and of the wests that We have power to replace them by others better than they: nothing can hinder Us from so doing. So let them paddle, let them

70:43 play, until they face the day they are promised; the day when they shall rush headlong from their graves, like men rallying to

a standard, with downcast eyes and countenances distorted   70:44
and abject.

Such is the day they are promised.

NOAH

In the Name of God, the Merciful, the Compassionate

WE SENT forth Noah to his people, saying: 'Give warning to   71:1
your people before a woeful scourge overtakes them.'

He said: 'My people, I come to warn you clearly. Worship
God and fear Him, and obey me. He will forgive you some of
your sins and give you respite to an appointed time. When
God's time is come, none shall put it back. Would you but
knew!'

'Lord,' said Noah, 'night and day have I pleaded with my
people, but my pleas have only aggravated their aversion.
Each time I call on them to seek Your pardon, they thrust
their fingers into their ears and draw their cloaks over their
heads, persisting in sin and bearing themselves with insolent
pride. Then I called out loud to them, and appealed to them in
public and in private. "Seek forgiveness of your Lord," I said.   71:10
"He is ever ready to forgive. He sends down abundant water
from the sky for you and bestows upon you wealth and children. He has provided you with gardens and with running
brooks. Why do you deny the greatness of God when He created you in gradual stages? Can you not see how God created
the seven heavens one above the other, placing in them the
moon for a light and the sun for a lantern? God has brought
you forth from the earth like a plant, and to the earth He will
restore you. Then He will bring you back from it afresh. And
God has made the earth a vast expanse for you, that you may
roam its spacious paths."'

Noah said: 'Lord, they disobey me, and follow those whose
wealth and offspring will only hasten their perdition. They
have devised an outrageous plot, and said to each other: "Do   71:23
not renounce your gods. Do not forsake Wadd or Suwā' or

395

71:24 Yaghūth or Ya'ūq or Nasr."[1] They have led many astray; and You surely drive the wrongdoers to further error.'

Because of their sins they were drowned and cast into the Fire. They found none besides God to help them.

And Noah said: 'Lord, do not leave a single unbeliever on the earth. If You spare them, they will mislead Your servants 71:28 and beget none but sinners and unbelievers. Forgive me, Lord, and forgive my parents and whoever enters my house a true believer. Forgive all the faithful, men and women, and hasten the wrongdoers' destruction.'

THE JINN

In the Name of God, the Merciful, the Compassionate

72:1 SAY: 'IT is revealed to me that a band of jinn listened and said: "We have heard a wondrous Koran giving true guidance. We believed in it and shall henceforth serve none besides our Lord. He (exalted be the glory of our Lord!) has taken up neither consort, nor son. The Blaspheming One among us has uttered a wanton falsehood against God, although we had supposed no man or jinnee could tell of God what is untrue."'

Some men have sought the help of jinn, but they misled them into further error. Like you, they thought that God could never resurrect the dead.

72:8 '"We made our way to high heaven, and found it filled with mighty wardens and fiery comets. We sat eavesdropping, but eavesdroppers find comets in wait for them. We know not whether this bodes evil to those on earth or if their Lord intends to guide them.

'"Some among us are righteous, while others are not; we follow different ways. We know we cannot escape on earth 72:13 from God, nor can we elude His grasp by flight. When we heard His guidance we believed in Him: he that believes in his Lord shall fear neither dishonesty nor injustice.

---

1. Names of idols.

'"Some among us are Muslims and some of us are wrong-   72:14
doers. Those that embrace Islām pursue the right path; but
those that do wrong shall become the fuel of Hell."'

If they[1] pursue the straight path We shall vouchsafe them
abundant rain, and thereby put them to the proof. He that
pays no heed to his Lord's Admonition shall be thrust into
grievous torment.

Mosques are for God's worship; invoke in them no other
deity besides Him. When God's servant[2] rose to pray to Him,
they pressed around him in multitudes.

Say: 'I will pray to my Lord and worship none besides Him.'

Say: 'I have no control over any evil or good that befalls you.'

Say: 'None can protect me from God, nor can I find any   72:22
refuge besides Him. My mission is only to communicate
God's messages; those that disobey God and His apostle shall
for ever abide in the fire of Hell.'

When they behold the scourge they are promised, they
shall realize who had the less powerful protector, and who
were the fewer in number.

Say: 'I cannot tell whether the scourge you are promised is
imminent, or whether my Lord has set for it a far-off day. Cognizant of the Unseen, His secrets He reveals to none, except
to the apostles He has chosen. He sends down guardians who
walk before them and behind them, that He may ascertain if   72:28
they have indeed delivered their Lord's messages. He has
knowledge of all they have, and keeps strict count of all things.'

THE MANTLED ONE

In the Name of God, the Merciful, the Compassionate

You[2] THAT are wrapped up in your mantle, keep vigil all   73:1
night, save for a few hours; half the night, or even less: or a
little more – and with measured tone recite the Koran, for We
are about to address to you words of surpassing gravity. It is   73:6

1. The Meccans.   2. Muhammad.

73:7 in the watches of the night that impressions are strongest and words most eloquent; in the daytime you are hard-pressed for long.

And remember the name of your Lord and dedicate yourself to Him utterly. He is the Lord of the East and of the West: there is no god but Him. Take Him for your Protector.

Bear patiently with what they[1] say, and take leave of them courteously. Leave to Me those that deny the Truth, those that enjoy the comforts of this life; bear with them yet a little while. We have in store for them heavy fetters and a blazing fire, choking food and harrowing torment: on the day when the earth shall quiver with all the mountains, and the mountains crumble into heaps of shifting sand.

73:15 We have sent forth to you an apostle to testify against you, just as We sent forth an apostle to Pharaoh. Pharaoh disobeyed the messenger, so that with a baleful scourge We smote him.

If you persist in unbelief, how will you escape the day that will make children grey-haired, the day the sky will split asunder? God's promise shall surely be fulfilled.

This is but an Admonition. Let him who will, take the right path to his Lord.

73:20 Your Lord knows that you[2] sometimes keep vigil well-nigh two-thirds of the night, and sometimes half or one-third of it, as do others among your followers. God measures the night and the day. He knows you[3] cannot count its length, and turned to you mercifully. Recite from the Koran as many verses as you are able; He knows that among you there are sick men and others roaming the land in search of God's bounty; and yet others fighting for the cause of God. Recite from it, then, as many verses as you are able. Attend to your prayers, render the alms levy, and give God a generous loan. Whatever good you do for your own souls you shall surely find it with God, ennobled and more richly rewarded. And implore God to forgive you; surely God is forgiving and compassionate.

---

1. The unbelievers.   2. Muḥammad.   3. The believers.

THE CLOAKED ONE

In the Name of God, the Merciful, the Compassionate

You THAT are wrapped up in your cloak, arise and give warning. 74:1

Magnify your Lord, purify your garments, and keep away from uncleanness.

Bestow no favours expecting gain. Be patient for your Lord's sake.

The day the Trumpet sounds shall be a hard and joyless day for the unbelievers. Leave to Me the man whom I created helpless and endowed with vast riches and thriving children. I have made his progress smooth and easy: yet he greedily hopes that I should give him more. By no means! Because he has stubbornly denied Our revelations, I will lay on him a mounting torment.

He pondered, and he schemed. Confound him, how he schemed! Again, confound him, how he schemed!

He looked around him, frowning and scowling; then he 74:23 turned away in scornful pride and said: 'This is but sorcery counterfeited; this is but the utterance of a mortal!'

I will surely cast him into the Fire. Would that you knew what the Fire is like! It leaves nothing, it spares no one; it burns the skins of mortals. It is guarded by nineteen keepers.

We have appointed none but angels to guard the Fire, and made their number a subject for dispute among the unbelievers, so that those to whom the Book was given may be convinced and the true believers strengthened in their faith; that those to whom the Book was given, and the true believers, may have no doubts; and that those whose hearts are tainted and unbelievers may say: 'What could God mean by this as an example?' Thus God confounds whom He will and guides whom He pleases. None knows the warriors of your Lord but Himself. This is no more than an Admonition to mankind.

No, by the moon! By the departing night and the coming dawn, it is a dire scourge, a warning to mankind; alike to those 74:37

of you that would march on and those that would remain behind.

74:39 Each soul is the hostage of its own deeds. Those on the right hand will in Gardens ask the sinners: 'What has brought you into Hell?' They will say: 'We were never of those who prayed, nor did we ever feed the destitute. We engaged in vain discourse with those who engaged in it and denied the Day of Reckoning, till the Inevitable claimed us.'

No intercessor's plea shall save them. Why then do they turn away from this reminder, like frightened asses fleeing from a lion?

Indeed, each one of them demands a scripture of his own to be unrolled before him. No, they have no fear of the Hereafter.

No! This is an Admonition. Let him who will, be admon-
74:56 ished. But none is admonished except by the will of God. It is God who is the Lord of Goodness and Forgiveness.

THE RESURRECTION

In the Name of God, the Merciful, the Compassionate

75:1 I SWEAR by the Day of Resurrection, and by the self-reproaching soul!

Does man think We shall never put his bones together again? Indeed, We can remould his very fingers!

Yet man would ever deny what is to come. 'When will this be,' he asks, 'this Day of Resurrection?'

But when the sight of mortals is confounded and the moon eclipsed; when sun and moon are joined together – on that day man will ask: 'Whither shall I flee?'

No, there shall be no refuge; for to your Lord, on that day, all shall be restored.

Indeed, man shall on that day be told of all he did, from first to last. Indeed, man shall bear witness against himself,
75:15 plead as he may with his excuses.

(You[1] need not move your tongue too fast to learn this revelation. We Ourself shall see to its collection and recital. When We read it, follow its words attentively; We shall Ourself explain its meaning.)

No! But you[2] love this fleeting life, and ignore the life to come.

On that day there shall be joyous faces, looking towards their Lord. On that day there shall be mournful faces, dreading some great affliction.

No! But when a man's soul is about to leave him and those around him say: 'Will no one save him?' When he knows it is the final parting and leg and leg are twined – on that day to your Lord he shall be driven. For in this life he neither believed nor prayed; he denied the Truth and, turning his back, went to his kin elated with pride.

Well have you deserved this doom; well have you deserved it.

Well have you deserved this doom; too well have you deserved it!

Does man think he will be left alone, to no purpose? Was he not a drop of ejaculated semen? He became a clot of blood;[3] then God formed and moulded him, and gave him male and female parts. Has He no power, then, to raise the dead to life?

75:16

75:28

75:40

MAN

In the Name of God, the Merciful, the Compassionate

DOES THERE not pass over man a space of time when his life is a blank?[4]

We have created man from the union of the two sexes, that

76:1

76:2

1. Muhammad.
2. The Meccans.
3. See p. 222, note 2.
4. In the womb.

76:3 We may put him to the proof. We have endowed him with hearing and sight and, be he thankful or oblivious of Our favours, We have shown him the right path.

For the unbelievers We have prepared chains and fetters, and a Conflagration. But the righteous shall drink of a cup tempered at the Camphor Fountain, a gushing spring at which the worshippers of God refresh themselves: they who keep their vows and dread the far-flung terrors of a certain day; who, though they hold it dear, give sustenance to the destitute, the orphan, and the captive: 'We feed you for God's sake only; we seek of you no recompense nor thanks: for we fear from our Lord a day of anguish and of woe.'

God will deliver them from the evil of that day, and make their faces shine with joy. He will reward them for their steadfastness with Paradise and robes of silk. Reclining therein on soft couches, they shall feel neither the scorching heat nor the biting cold. Trees will spread their shade around them, and fruits will hang in clusters over them.

76:15 They shall be served on silver dishes, and beakers as large as goblets; silver goblets which they themselves shall measure: and cups brim-full with ginger-flavoured water from a fount called Salsabīl. They shall be attended by boys graced with eternal youth, who to the beholder's eyes will seem like sprinkled pearls. When you gaze and gaze upon that scene, you shall behold a kingdom blissful and glorious.

They shall be arrayed in garments of fine green silk and rich brocade, and adorned with bracelets of silver. Their Lord will give them pure nectar to drink.

Thus shall you be rewarded; your endeavours shall earn much thanks.

It was We who sent down to you the Koran by gradual revelation; therefore await with patience the judgement of your Lord, and yield to none of them, sinner or blasphemer. Remember the name of your Lord morning and evening; in the night-time bow to Him: and praise Him all night long.

Surely the unbelievers love this fleeting life too well, and leave behind them a heavy day of woe. *We* created them, and endowed their limbs and joints with strength; but if We please, We can replace them by others like them.

This is indeed an Admonition. Let him that will, take the 76:29 right path to his Lord. Yet you cannot will, except by the will of God. God is omniscient and wise.

He admits into His mercy whom He will: and for the 76:31 wrongdoers He has prepared a woeful punishment.

THOSE THAT ARE
SENT FORTH

In the Name of God, the Merciful, the Compassionate

BY THE gales, sent forth in swift succession; by the raging 77:1 tempests and the rain-spreading winds; by those that send down the revelations discerning good from evil and admonishing by plea and warning: that which you are promised shall be fulfilled!

When the stars are blotted out; when the sky is rent asunder and the mountains crumble into dust; when the apostles are brought together on an appointed day – when will all this be? Upon the Day of Judgement.

Would that you knew what the Day of Judgement is! On 77:15 that day woe betide the disbelievers! Did We not obliterate the early generations and cause the latter ones to follow them? Thus shall We deal with the transgressors.

On that day woe betide the disbelievers! Did We not create you from a humble fluid, which We kept in a safe receptacle[1] for an appointed term? All this We did; how excellent is Our work!

On that day woe betide the disbelievers! Have We not made the earth an abode for the living and for the dead? Have We not placed lofty mountains upon it, and given you fresh water for your drink?

On that day woe betide the disbelievers! Begone to that 77:29

---

1. The womb.

77:30 which you deny! Depart into the shadow that will rise high in three columns, giving neither shade nor shelter from the flames, and throwing up sparks as huge as towers, as bright as yellow camels!

On that day woe betide the disbelievers! On that day they shall not speak, nor shall their pleas be heeded.

On that day woe betide the disbelievers! Such is the Day of Judgement. We will herd you all, together with past genera-
77:41 tions. If then you are cunning, try your spite against Me!

On that day woe betide the disbelievers! The righteous shall dwell amidst cool shades and fountains, and feed on such fruits as they desire. 'Eat and drink, and may every joy attend you! This is the guerdon of your labours.' Thus shall We recompense the righteous.

On that day woe betide the disbelievers! Eat and enjoy yourselves awhile. Surely you are sinners all.

On that day woe betide the disbelievers! If they are bidden to kneel down, they do not kneel.
77:50 On that day woe betide the disbelievers! In what revelation, after this, will they believe?

THE TIDINGS

In the Name of God, the Merciful, the Compassionate

78:1 ABOUT WHAT are they asking?

About the fateful tidings – the theme of their disputes.

But they shall learn; then they shall surely learn.

Did We not spread the earth like a bed, and raise the mountains like supporting pillars?

We created you in pairs, and gave you rest in sleep. We made the night a mantle, and ordained the day for work. We built above you seven mighty heavens and placed in them a glowing lamp. We sent down abundant water from the clouds to bring forth grain and varied plants, and gardens thick with foliage.

78:18 Fixed is the Day of Judgement. On that day the Trumpet

shall be blown, and you shall come in multitudes. The gates of   78:19
heaven shall swing open, and the mountains shall pass away
into a mirage.

Hell will lie in ambush, a home for the transgressors.
Therein shall they abide long ages; therein they shall taste
neither refreshment nor any drink, save scalding water and
decaying filth: a fitting recompense.

They never expected a reckoning, and roundly denied Our
revelations. But We kept account of what they did and wrote
it down. 'So taste this: for We shall give you nothing but
mounting torment!'

As for the righteous, there shall surely be a triumph: gardens   78:32
and vineyards, and tender-bosomed maidens for companions:
a truly overflowing cup.

Therein shall they hear no idle talk, nor any falsehood.
Such is the recompense from your Lord – a gift that will suffice them: the Lord of the heavens and the earth and all that
lies between them; the Merciful, from whom they have no
power to speak.

On the day when the Spirit and the angels stand up in their
ranks, they shall not speak; except him who shall receive the
sanction of the Merciful and declare what is right.

That day is sure to come. Let him who will, seek a way back
to his Lord. We have forewarned you of an imminent scourge: 78:40
the day when man will look upon his works and the unbeliever
say: 'Would that I were dust!'

THE SOUL-SNATCHERS

In the Name of God, the Merciful, the Compassionate

BY THOSE who snatch away men's souls, and those who gen-   79:1
tly release them; by those who float at will, and those who
speed headlong; by those who govern the affairs of this world!
On the day the Trumpet sounds its first and second blast:
hearts shall on that day be filled with terror, and eyes shall   79:9
stare with awe.

79:10   They say: 'When we are turned to hollow bones, shall we be restored to life?' And they say: 'So it is a fruitless transformation!' But with one blast they shall return to the earth's surface.

Have you heard the story of Moses?

His Lord called out to him in the sacred valley of Ṭuwā, saying: 'Go to Pharaoh: he has transgressed all bounds; and say: "Will you reform yourself? I will guide you to your Lord, that you may fear Him."'

He showed Pharaoh the mightiest sign, but he denied it and rebelled. He quickly went away and, summoning all his men, made to them a proclamation. 'I am your supreme Lord,' he said.

So God smote him with the scourge of the life to come, and of this life. Surely in this there is a lesson for the God-fearing.

79:28   Are you harder to create or the heaven He has built? He raised it high and fashioned it, giving darkness to its night and brightness to its day.

After that He spread the earth, and, drawing water from its depth, brought forth its pastures. He set down the mountains, for you and for your cattle to delight in.

But when the supreme calamity strikes – the day when man will call to mind his labours – when Hell appears to those with eyes to see – he that transgressed and chose this present life shall have his home in Hell; and he that feared to stand before his Lord and curbed his soul's desire shall have his home in Paradise.

They question you about the Hour: 'When will it come?' But how are you to know? Only your Lord knows when the end will come. Your duty is but to warn those that fear it.

79:46   On the day they see it, it will seem as if they had lingered but one evening, or one morning.

406

HE FROWNED

In the Name of God, the Merciful, the Compassionate

HE[1] FROWNED and turned his back when the blind man came to him.   80:1

How could you[1] tell? He might have sought to purify himself. He might have remembered, and remembrance might have done him good.

But to the wealthy man you were all attention: although the fault would not be yours if he remained uncleansed. Yet to him that came to you with zeal and awe, you paid no heed.

No! This is an Admonition; let him who will, bear it in mind. It is set down on honoured pages, exalted and purified, by the hands of devout and gracious scribes.

Let man perish! How ungrateful he is!

From what did He create him? From a little germ He created him and gave him due proportion. He made his path smooth for him, then caused him to die and stowed him in a grave. He will surely bring him back to life when He pleases. Yet he declines to do His bidding.   80:19

Let man reflect on the food he eats: how We pour down the rain in torrents and cleave the earth asunder; how We bring forth the corn, the grapes, and the fresh vegetation; the olive and the palm, the thickets, the fruit-trees, and the green pasture, for you and for your cattle to delight in.

But when the dread blast is sounded, on that day each man will forsake his brother, his mother and his father, his consort and his children: for each one of them will on that day have enough sorrow of his own.

On that day there shall be beaming faces, laughing and joyful. On that day there shall be faces covered with dust, veiled with darkness. These shall be the faces of the degenerate blasphemers.   80:42

1. Muḥammad.

THE CESSATION

In the Name of God, the Merciful, the Compassionate

81:1 WHEN THE sun ceases to shine; when the stars fall and the mountains are blown away; when camels big with young are left untended, and the wild beasts are together herded; when the seas are set ablaze and souls are reunited; when the infant girl,[1] buried alive, is asked for what crime she was slain; when the records of men's deeds are laid open, and heaven is stripped bare; when Hell turns into a Conflagration and Paradise is brought near: then each soul shall learn what it has done.

I swear by the turning planets, and by the stars that rise and set; by the night, when it darkens, and the first breath of 81:19 morning: this is the Word of a messenger gracious and mighty, held in honour by the Lord of the Throne, obeyed, and faithful to his trust.

No, your countryman[2] is not possessed. He saw him[3] on the clear horizon. He does not grudge the secrets of the unseen; nor is this the utterance of an accursèd demon.

Whither then are you going?

This is but an Admonition to mankind: to those among 81:29 you that have the will to be upright. Yet you cannot will, except by the will of God, Lord of the Universe.

THE CATACLYSM

In the Name of God, the Merciful, the Compassionate

82:1 WHEN THE sky is rent asunder; when the stars scatter and the 82:5 oceans surge together; when the graves are hurled about: each soul shall know what it has done and what it has failed to do.

1. See p. 188, note 1.
2. Muḥammad.
3. Gabriel.

O man! What evil has enticed you from your gracious Lord 82:6 who created you, and gave you due proportions and an upright form? In whatever shape He willed He could have moulded you.

No! But you deny the Last Judgement. Surely there are guardians watching over you, noble recorders who know of what you do.

The righteous will surely be in bliss. And the wicked shall be in Hell, burning therein upon the Judgement-day: nor shall they ever escape from it.

Would that you knew what the Day of Judgement is! Again, would that you knew what the Day of Judgement is! It is the 82:19 day when no soul shall have power to help another soul and God will reign supreme.

THE UNJUST

In the Name of God, the Merciful, the Compassionate

WOE BETIDE the unjust who, when people measure for them, 83:1 exact in full, but when they measure or weigh for them, defraud them!

Do they not think they will be raised to life upon a fateful day, the day when mankind will stand before the Lord of the Universe?

No! The record of the sinners is in Sijjīn. Would that you knew what Sijjīn is! It is a sealed book.

On that day woe betide the disbelievers who deny the Last Judgement! None denies it except the sinful transgressor 83:12 who, when Our revelations are recited to him, says: 'Fables of the ancients!'

No! But their own deeds have drawn a veil over their hearts.

No! A screen shall on that day be set between them and their Lord. Then shall they burn in Hell, and shall be told: 'This is what you denied!'

No! But the record of the righteous shall be in 'Illiyyūn. Would that you knew what 'Illiyyūn is! It is a sealed book, seen 83:21 only by the favoured ones.

83:23   The righteous will surely be in bliss. Reclining on soft couches they will gaze around: and in their faces you shall mark the glow of joy. They shall be served with pure nectar to drink, securely sealed, whose very dregs are musk: for this let all contenders emulously strive; tempered with the waters of Tasnīm, a spring at which the favoured will refresh themselves.

Those who transgress laugh at the faithful and wink at one another as they pass by them. When they meet their own kin they speak of them with jests, and when they see them say: 'These have surely lost their way.' Yet they were not sent to be their keepers.

But on that day the faithful will at the infidels laugh as they recline upon the couches and gaze around.

83:36   Shall not the infidels be rewarded according to what they did?

THE RENDING

In the Name of God, the Merciful, the Compassionate

84:1   WHEN THE sky is rent apart, obeying her Lord in true submission; when the earth expands and casts out all that is within her and becomes empty, obeying her Lord in true submission; then, O man, who labour constantly to meet your Lord, shall you meet Him.

He that is given his Book in his right hand shall have a lenient reckoning, and shall go back rejoicing to his people. But he that is given his Book behind his back shall call down destruction on himself and burn in the Conflagration; for he lived rejoicing among his people and thought he would never turn back. Yes; but his Lord was ever watching him.

I swear by the glow of sunset; by the night, and all that it envelops; by the moon, in her full perfection: that you shall march onwards from stage to stage.

84:21   Why then do they not believe, or kneel down in prayer when the Koran is read to them?

The unbelievers indeed are in denial; but God knows best the falsehoods they believe in. 84:23

Therefore proclaim to them a woeful scourge, save those who believe and do good works; for theirs is an unfailing recompense. 84:25

THE CONSTELLATIONS

In the Name of God, the Merciful, the Compassionate

BY THE heaven with its constellations! By the Promised Day! By the Witness, and that which is witnessed! 85:1

Cursed[1] be the diggers of the trench with its consuming fire as they sat around it to witness what they did to the faithful! Nor did they avenge themselves on them for aught but that they believed in God, the Almighty, the Praised One, who has sovereignty over the heavens and the earth. And God is the Witness of all things.

Those that persecute believers, men or women, and never repent shall have the torment of Hell, the torment of the blazing fire. But those that believe and do good works shall have Gardens watered by running brooks. That is the supreme triumph. 85:11

Stern indeed is the vengeance of your Lord. He it is who brings into being and then restores to life. Forgiving and loving, He is the Lord of the Glorious Throne, the Executor of His own will.

Have you not heard the story of the warriors, of Pharaoh and of Thamūd? Yet the unbelievers are still in denial.

God surrounds them from behind. Surely this is a glorious Koran, on a Tablet preserved. 85:22

---

1. Literally, slain.

THE NIGHTLY VISITANT

In the Name of God, the Merciful, the Compassionate

86:1 BY THE heaven, and by the nightly visitant!
Would that you knew what the nightly visitant is!
It is the star of piercing brightness.

For every soul there is a guardian. Let man reflect from what he is created: he was created from an ejaculated fluid that issues from between the loins and the ribs.

Surely He has power to bring him back, on the day when consciences are searched. Helpless shall he be, with none to succour him.

By the heaven with its recurring cycles, and by the earth, ever bursting with new growth; this[1] is a discerning utterance, no flippant jest.

They scheme and scheme: and I, too, scheme and scheme.
86:17 Therefore bear with the unbelievers, and let them be awhile.

THE MOST HIGH

In the Name of God, the Merciful, the Compassionate

87:1 PRAISE THE Name of your Lord, the Most High, who created all things and gave them due proportion; who ordained their destinies and guided them; who brings forth the green pasture, then turns it to withered grass.

We shall make you read, so that you shall never forget except as God pleases. He has knowledge of the manifest and the hidden.

We shall guide you to the smoothest path. Therefore admonish, if admonishment will avail. He that fears God will pay heed, but the wretched sinner will flout it. He shall burn
87:13 in the gigantic Fire, wherein shall he then neither die nor live.

1. The Koran.

Happy shall be he that keeps himself pure, that remembers 87:14
the name of his Lord and prays.

Yet you[1] prefer the life of this world, although the life to
come is better and more lasting.

This is surely set down in the earlier Scriptures; the Scrip- 87:19
tures of Abraham and Moses.

THE OVERWHELMING EVENT

In the Name of God, the Merciful, the Compassionate

HAVE YOU heard of the Event that shall overwhelm all? 88:1

On that day there shall be downcast faces, haggard and
worn out, burnt by a scorching fire, drinking from a seething
fountain. Their only food shall be bitter thorns, which will
neither sustain them nor satisfy their hunger.

On that day there shall be radiant faces, well pleased with
their labours, in a lofty Garden. Therein shall they hear no idle
talk; therein shall be a gushing fountain; therein shall be raised 88:13
soft couches with goblets placed before them; silken cushions
ranged in order and carpets richly spread.

Do they never reflect on the camels, how they were created? On the heaven, how it was raised on high? On the
mountains, how they were set down? On the earth, how it was
flattened?

Therefore admonish; your duty is only to admonish: you
are not their keeper. As for those that turn their backs and
disbelieve, God will torment them with the supreme torment.
To Us shall they return, and then We will Ourself bring them 88:26
to account.

1. The unbelievers of Mecca.

413

THE DAWN

In the Name of God, the Merciful, the Compassionate

89:1 BY THE Dawn and the Ten Nights;[1] by that which is dual, and that which is single; by the night, as it journeys on!

Is there not in this a mighty oath for a man of sense?

Have you not considered how your Lord dealt with 'Ād? The many-columned city of Iram, whose like has never been created in the land? And Thamūd, who hewed out their dwellings among the rocks of the valley? And Pharaoh, who impaled his victims upon the stakes?

They had all led sinful lives, and made the land teem with wickedness. Therefore your Lord let loose on them the scourge of a torment; for from His eminence your Lord observes all.

89:15 As for man, when his Lord tests him by honouring him and bestowing blessings on him, he says: 'My Lord has honoured me.' But when He tests him by diminishing his provision, he says: 'My Lord despises me.'

No! But you show no kindness to the orphan, nor do you vie with each other in feeding the destitute. Greedily you lay your hands on the inheritance of the weak, and you love riches with all your hearts.

No! But when the earth is crushed to fine dust, and your Lord comes down with the angels, in their ranks, and Hell is on that day brought near – on that day man will remember. And what will remembrance avail him?

He will say: 'Would that I had been charitable in my lifetime!' But on that day none will punish as He will punish, and none will bind with chains like His.

O serene soul! Return to your Lord, well pleased, and pleas-
89:30 ing in His sight. Join My servants, and enter My Paradise.

---

1. The first ten nights of the sacred month of Dhūl-Ḥajjah.

THE CITY

In the Name of God, the Merciful, the Compassionate

I SWEAR by this city (and you[1] are a resident of this city), by the begetter[2] and all whom he begot: We created Man to try him with affliction.

Does he think that none has power over him? 'I have squandered vast riches!' he says. Does he think that none observed him?

Have We not given him two eyes, a tongue, and two lips, and shown him the two paths?[3] Yet he would not scale the Height.

Would that you knew what the Height is. It is the freeing of a slave; the feeding, in a day of famine, of an orphaned relation or a needy man in distress; to have faith and to enjoin fortitude and mercy.

Such are those that shall stand on the right hand; but those that deny Our revelations shall stand on the left, with a Fire close above them.

90:1

90:20

THE SUN

In the Name of God, the Merciful, the Compassionate

BY THE sun and his midday brightness; by the moon, when she rises after him; by the day, when it reveals his splendour; by the night, when it veils him!

By the heaven and Him that built it; by the earth and Him that spread it; by the soul and Him that moulded it and inspired it with knowledge of sin and piety: blessed shall be he that has kept it pure, and ruined he that has corrupted it!

In its presumptuous pride Thamūd denied its apostle when

91:1

91:12

---

1. Muḥammad.   2. Adam.   3. Of right and wrong.

91:13 its arch-sinner rose against him. God's apostle said: 'This is God's own she-camel. Let her drink.'

91:15 They disbelieved him, and hamstrung her. And for their sin their Lord let loose His scourge upon them and razed their city to the ground. He did not fear the consequences.

THE NIGHT

In the Name of God, the Merciful, the Compassionate

92:1 BY THE night, when she lets fall her darkness, and by the radiant day! By Him that created the male and the female, your endeavours have varied ends!

For him that gives and fears God and believes in goodness, We shall smooth the path of salvation; but for him that gives nothing and strives to enrich himself and disbelieves in goodness, We shall smooth the path of affliction. When he breathes his last, his riches will not avail him.

It is for Us to give guidance. Ours is the life to come, Ours the life of this world. I warn you, then, of a blazing Fire, in which none shall burn save the hardened sinner, who disbelieves and turns away. But the good man who keeps himself pure by almsgiving shall keep away from it: and so shall he that does good works for the sake of his Lord the Most High
92:21 only, seeking no recompense. He will surely be well pleased.

THE DAYLIGHT

In the Name of God, the Merciful, the Compassionate

93:1 BY THE light of day, and by the night when she spreads her dark-
93:3 ness, your Lord has not forsaken you,[1] nor does He abhor you.

1. Muḥammad.

The life to come holds a richer prize for you than this present life; and you shall be gratified with what your Lord will give you. 93:4

Did He not find you an orphan and give you shelter?

And did He not find you in error and guide you?

And did He not find you poor and enrich you?

Therefore do not wrong the orphan, nor chide away the beggar. But proclaim the goodness of your Lord. 93:11

COMFORT

In the Name of God, the Merciful, the Compassionate

HAVE WE not lifted up your heart and relieved you[1] of the burden which weighed down your back? 94:1

And have We not given you high renown?

With every hardship there comes ease. With every hardship there comes ease.

When your prayers are ended resume your toil, and seek your Lord with all fervour. 94:8

THE FIG

In the Name of God, the Merciful, the Compassionate

BY THE Fig, and by the Olive! 95:1

By Mount Sinai, and by this inviolate city:[2]

We created Man in a most noble image, and then We shall reduce him to the lowest of the low: except those who believe and do good works, for theirs shall be a boundless recompense.

What then after this can make you deny the Last Judgement?

Is God not the most just of judges? 95:8

1. Muḥammad.   2. Mecca.

417

CLOTS OF BLOOD[1]

In the Name of God, the Merciful, the Compassionate

96:1 READ IN the name of your Lord who created; created Man from clots of blood.

Read! Your Lord is the Most Bountiful One, who by the pen taught Man what he did not know.

No! Man transgresses in thinking himself his own master:[2] for to your Lord shall all return.

Consider the man who rebukes Our servant when he prays. Consider: does he follow the right guidance or enjoin true piety?

Do but consider: if he denies the Truth and pays no heed, does he not realize that God sees all?

No! Let him desist, or We will drag him by the forelock, his lying, sinful forelock.

Then let him call his helpmates: We will call the guards of Hell.

96:19 No, never obey him! Prostrate yourself and come nearer.

QADR

In the Name of God, the Merciful, the Compassionate

97:1 WE REVEALED it on the Night of Qadr.[3] Would that you knew what the Night of Qadr is like!

Better is the Night of Qadr than a thousand months.

On that night the angels and the Spirit by their Lord's leave come down with each command.

97:5 Peace it is, till break of dawn.

---

1. See p. 222, note 2.
2. Or: in thinking himself wealthy.
3. Literally, glory.

THE PROOF

In the Name of God, the Merciful, the Compassionate

THE UNBELIEVERS among the People of the Book[1] and the pagans did not desist from unbelief until the Proof was given them: an apostle from God reciting from purified pages infallible decrees.

98:1

Nor did those who were vouchsafed the Book divide themselves until the Proof was given them. Yet they were enjoined only to worship God and to consecrate their religion to Him, to attend to their prayers and to render the alms levy. That, surely, is the infallible faith.

The unbelievers among the People of the Book and the pagans shall in the fire of Hell abide for ever. They are the vilest of all creatures.

But of all creatures those that believe and do good works are the noblest. Their recompense, in their Lord's presence, shall be the Gardens of Eden, watered by running brooks, wherein shall they abide for ever.

98:8

God is well pleased with them, and they are well pleased with Him. Thus shall the God-fearing be rewarded.

THE EARTHQUAKE

In the Name of God, the Merciful, the Compassionate

WHEN EARTH is rocked in her last convulsion; when Earth shakes off her burdens and Man says, 'What may this mean?' – on that day she will proclaim her tidings, for your Lord will have inspired her.

99:1

On that day mankind will come out in broken bands to be shown their labours. Whoever did an atom's weight of good shall see it, and whoever did an atom's weight of evil shall also see it.

99:8

1. Jews and Christians.

THE WAR STEEDS

In the Name of God, the Merciful, the Compassionate

100:1 BY THE snorting war steeds, which strike fire with their hoofs as they gallop to the raid at morn and with a trail of dust cleave a massed army: Man is ungrateful to his Lord! To this he himself shall bear witness.

He loves riches with all his heart. But is he not aware that when the dead are thrown out from their graves and their
100:11 once-hidden thoughts are laid bare, their Lord will on that day have full knowledge of them all?

THE DISASTER

In the Name of God, the Merciful, the Compassionate

101:1 THE DISASTER! What is the Disaster?

Would that you knew what the Disaster is!

On that day people shall become like scattered moths and the mountains like tufts of carded wool.

Then he whose good deeds weigh heavy in the scales shall live in bliss; but he whose good deeds are light, the Abyss shall be his home.

Would that you knew what this is like!
101:11 It is a scorching Fire.

WORLDLY GAIN

In the Name of God, the Merciful, the Compassionate

102:1 YOUR HEARTS are taken up with worldly gain from the cradle to the grave.

No! But you shall learn. No! You then shall surely learn.
102:6 No! If you knew the Truth with certainty, you would

witness Hell: you would then witness it with the certainty of 102:7
your very eyes.

Then, on that day, you shall surely be questioned about 102:8
bliss.

THE DECLINING DAY

In the Name of God, the Merciful, the Compassionate

I SWEAR by the declining day that perdition shall be the lot of 103:1
Man, except for those who believe and do good works; who 103:3
exhort each other to justice and to fortitude.

THE SLANDERER

In the Name of God, the Merciful, the Compassionate

WOE BETIDE every backbiting slanderer who amasses riches 104:1
and sedulously hoards them, thinking his wealth will render
him immortal!

By no means! He shall be flung into the Destroying Flame.
Would that you knew what the Destroying Flame is like!

It is God's own kindled fire, which will rise up to the hearts.
It will close in upon them, in towering columns. 104:9

THE ELEPHANT

In the Name of God, the Merciful, the Compassionate

HAVE YOU not considered how your Lord dealt with the 105:1
Army of the Elephant?[1]

1. The allusion is to the expedition of Abraha, the Christian king of
   Ethiopia, against Mecca, said to have taken place in the year of
   Muḥammad's birth.

105:2 Did He not confound their stratagem and send against them flocks of birds which pelted them with clay-stones, 105:5 so that they became like the withered stalks of plants which cattle had devoured?

QURAYSH[1]

In the Name of God, the Merciful, the Compassionate

106:1 FOR THE protection of Quraysh: their protection in their winter and summer journeyings.

106:4 Therefore let them worship the Lord of this House who fed them when there was famine and shielded them from fear.

ALMS

In the Name of God, the Merciful, the Compassionate

107:1 HAVE YOU considered him that denies the Last Judgement? It is he who turns away the orphan and does not urge the feeding of the destitute.

Woe betide those who pray but are heedless of their prayer; 107:7 who make a show of piety and forbid almsgiving.

ABUNDANCE

In the Name of God, the Merciful, the Compassionate

108:1 WE HAVE given you[2] abundance. So pray to your Lord and sacrifice to Him.

108:3 He that hates you shall remain childless.

---

1. Muhammad's own clan. Some commentators connect this *sūrah* with the preceding one.
2. Muhammad.

THE UNBELIEVERS

In the Name of God, the Merciful, the Compassionate

SAY: 'YOU blasphemers! I do not worship what you worship, 109:1
nor do you worship what I worship. I shall never worship
what you worship, nor will you ever worship what I worship.
You have your religion, and I have my religion.' 109:6

HELP

In the Name of God, the Merciful, the Compassionate

WHEN GOD'S help and victory come, and you see people 110:1
embrace God's Religion in multitudes, give praise and glory to 110:3
your Lord and seek His forgiveness. He is ever disposed to
forgive.

AL-LAHAB[1]

In the Name of God, the Merciful, the Compassionate

MAY THE hands of Abu-Lahab[2] perish! And may he himself 111:1
perish! Nothing shall his wealth and gains avail him. He shall
be burnt in a flaming fire,[3] and his wife, laden with firewood,
shall have a rope of fibre round her neck! 111:5

1. This *sūrah* is also known by another title: 'Al-Masad' (Fibre).
2. The Prophet's uncle, and one of his staunchest opponents.
3. A pun on the meaning of Abu-Lahab, 'father of flame'.

ONENESS

In the Name of God, the Merciful, the Compassionate

112:1 SAY: 'GOD is One, the Eternal God. He begot none, nor was
112:4 He begotten. And none is equal to Him.'

DAYBREAK

In the Name of God, the Merciful, the Compassionate

113:1 SAY: 'I seek refuge in the Lord of Daybreak from the mischief of His creation; from the mischief of the night when
she spreads her darkness; from the mischief of conjuring
113:5 witches;[1] from the mischief of the envier, when he envies.'

MANKIND

In the Name of God, the Merciful, the Compassionate

114:1 SAY: 'I seek refuge in the Lord of mankind, the King of mankind, the God of mankind, from the mischief of the slinking
114:6 prompter who whispers in the hearts of mankind; from jinn
and mankind.'

---

1. Literally, the women who blow on knots.

INDEX

This index is designed to be of help to the general reader rather than to provide a comprehensive concordance to the text. References are to page numbers; those followed by 'n' are to footnotes. Headings and references in square brackets are mentioned by allusion, not by name. Names beginning with 'al-' are indexed under the letter immediately following.

425